THE LETTERS OF
WILLIAM AND DOROTHY
WORDSWORTH

The Later Years

1821–1850

THE LETTERS OF
WILLIAM AND DOROTHY WORDSWORTH
The Later Years

Arranged and Edited by
ERNEST DE SELINCOURT

VOLUME II
1831–40

OXFORD
AT THE CLARENDON PRESS
1939

OXFORD UNIVERSITY PRESS
AMEN HOUSE, E.C. 4
London Edinburgh Glasgow New York
Toronto Melbourne Capetown Bombay
Calcutta Madras
HUMPHREY MILFORD
PUBLISHER TO THE UNIVERSITY

PRINTED IN GREAT BRITAIN

LIST OF LETTERS

An Asterisk indicates that the letter is here printed for the first time, a dagger that a part only has been previously printed.

VOLUME II

1831

[1] v. note, p. 765.

[ix]

LIST OF LETTERS

961. D. W. to Sara Coleridge (Junr)

20th Jan^ry [1831]

... at supper time. I should not have mentioned these facts, but to prevent your good mother from building too much on the improved reports I have lately been enabled to make. For a while, at least, she must be contented if he[1] goes on as at present —making a little money perhaps—working by fits—and not wandering about in publick houses or Barns. The affection the Flemings feel for him, and their patience and kindness are admirable, and this I am convinced of—that go the world through he could not find a place where he would be likely to do so well. Harshness and excessive strictness would only drive him further from the right course, and I do believe that notwithstanding Mrs F.'s indulgence he stands in some awe of her.

Give my kindest love to your Mother. My next shall be addressed to her—after Blackwood's second payment, and I shall then be able to state the use that can be made of the money —I fear *none* will go to the liquidation of the present debt to her.

Miss H. and I are very well in [? health] and spending a quiet and comfortable winter. Now and then we long for a few chearful family faces; but are quite reconciled to their long absence, and not impatient for their return as the party have all enjoyed themselves and the improvement in Dora's health has been marvellous since she went into Sussex. Their plans are yet unsettled, and what further stay will be made at Cambridge or elsewhere I know not. Mrs Slade Smith has promised me a letter from her own Chateau. Poor Soul! She had a wretched journey, and one cannot but regret that she ever came, as no good was done. Miss H. joins with me in kindest Love to you all. Tell Grandmama *she* must kiss the Baby for us. Dora gives us charming accounts of him. Your poor Father—I fear he is very weak in Body for they speak of a great change in his appearance. Pray give him my most affectionate remembrances, and my regards to Mr and Mrs Gillman. I should have liked well to have

---

[1] i.e. Hartley C.

seen your table spread at the christening dinner. You cannot think how comfortably Miss H. has sate fixed to netting her *Doileys* (I spell the word guessing) day by day. Again my Love to your Mother. God bless you all. Yours ever

D. W.

My Love to Bertha—all well at Keswick.

The introduction to Bishop Coleridge not wanted. Capt Manning's regiment does not go to the West Indies. Thanks etc from Mr Harrison of the Green.

endorsed by Sara C. 'very kind letter of dear Miss Wordsworth— account of Hartley and family matters. I am burning old letters, but am loth to burn all hers and Miss H.'s, they are indeed most good and kind to me.'

962. *W. W. to William Rowan Hamilton*

Hamilton(—)
K(—)
Buxted Rectory, near Uckfield, Sussex,

24th January, 1831.

. . . In the *Quarterly Review* lately was an article, a very foolish one I think, upon the decay of science in England, and ascribing it to the want of patronage from the government—a poor compliment this to science! Her hill, it seems, in the opinion of the writer, cannot be ascended unless the pilgrim be 'stuck o'er with titles and hung round with strings', and have his pockets laden with cash; besides, a man of science must be a minister of state or a privy councillor, or at least a public functionary of importance. Mr Whewell, of Trinity College,[1] Cambridge, has corrected the mis-statements of the reviewer in an article printed in the *British Critic* of January last, and vindicated his scientific countrymen. . . .

You are interested about Mr Coleridge; I saw him several times lately, and had long conversations with him. It grieves me to say that his constitution seems much broken up. I have heard that he has been worse since I saw him. His mind has lost

[1] Wm. Whewell, 1794–1866, mathematician and philosopher; he married Cordelia Marshall in 1841, and in the same year succeeded C. W. as Master of Trinity.

none of its vigour, but he is certainly in that state of bodily health that no one who knows him could feel justified in holding out the hope of even an introduction to him, as an inducement for your visiting London. Much do I regret this, for you may pass your life without meeting a man of such commanding faculties. I hope that my criticisms have not deterred your sister from poetical composition. The world has indeed had enough of it lately, such as it is; but that is no reason why a sensibility like hers should not give vent to itself in verse.

Hutchins.   ## 963. W. W. to John Kenyon
K.

[Buxted, Jan.–Feb. 1831][1]

My dear Sir,

It was taking no small liberty to entangle you and Mrs Kenyon in our little economical arrangements. I am pleased, however, with having done so, as it has been the occasion of my hearing from you again. Your eloquence, as the heart has so much to do in it, has prevailed, and we will order a chaise to be here on Wednesday next in time for our reaching Brighton by five—perhaps earlier—but if the day prove fine I should like to stop an hour at Lewes to look round me.

You seem to lead a dissipated life, you and Mrs Kenyon; but I have no right to reproach you. I have left my Brother's quiet fireside for the last two days to dine with two several Magistrates at Uckfield, where, of course, I heard rather too much of obstinate juries, grand and Petty; burnings, poor rates, cash-payments, and that everlasting Incubus of universal agricultural distress.

Five times have I dined while at Buxted at the table of an Earl—and twice in the company of a Prince. Therefore let you and Mrs Kenyon prepare yourselves for something stately and august in my deportment and manners. But King, Queen, Prince, Princesses, Dukes etc are common articles at Brighton [so] that I must descend from my elevation, or pass for a downright Malvolio.

---

[1] As this letter was written from Buxted, and W. was in London before the end of Feb., its date must be Jan. or Feb.

I congratulate you upon being *un*radicalized. I wish however the change had taken place under less threatening circumstances. The idle practice of recrimination is becoming general. The Whigs upbraid the Tories as authors of the mischief which all feel, by withstanding reform so obstinately; and the Tories reproach the Whigs with having done all the harm by incessant *bawling* for it. . . .

[*cetera desunt*]

MS.   *964. D. W. to Mrs S. T. Coleridge*

March 7th [1831] Monday.

My dear Friend,

We think it very long since we heard from—or even *of* you and I am glad of the means of sending a *wee* note free of cost, especially as I have good news of Hartley. He received a second £10 from Blackwood the week before last and paid up his quarter's Board till March, leaving a small surplus in James Fleming's hands to be called for when wanted. J. Fleming wrote to tell me the above good news, and last Friday I called at the house. I was sorry not to find H. at home, and more sorry to hear that he had drawn out 5/- at two different times, but it might mainly be to pay small debts, for on the whole he has been pretty regular—even for a long time, and James Fleming assured me that he was very busy and he thought would soon have earned more money—so he hoped that in future Mr Coleridge would be able himself to pay for his lodgings etc. It is very pleasing to hear how affectionately James Fleming and his Wife speak of Hartley—indeed I never go without feeling thankful that he is in so respectable a home. My Brother in a letter received to-day tells me he has received £20 from H. N. Coleridge on Hartley's account. Now my Sister mentioned the like Sum a good while ago. Does my Brother mean the same twenty pounds or have you paid them that sum twice over? At all events it is ready to meet Hartley's wants, but if he goes on as he has lately done it will not be needed, and truly thankful shall we all be if it prove so. We were exceedingly glad to hear of the accession to Mrs Coleridge's property by the death of her Sister

(I suppose *her* Sister, but mean Henry's aunt). With a share of such a fortune in prospect Henry and Sara need not now have any care for the Future.—Poverty is never likely to stare *them* in the face, and truly do I rejoice in this both for their sakes and yours. We really long to hear from you—and pray give us one of your old-fashioned letters, tip-top full of domestic news and indeed of whatever news comes into your head. My Brother has, I find, seen H. N. C. but he says not yet S. T. C., and as he does not mention you I fear he has not seen either you or Sara since his return to London.

Last news from Keswick good—all well—Southey very busy. This is a sad scrawl to send so far; but I have not time for more or better. Going to tea with Mrs Luff, who comes home to-night having spent the winter at Graystoke. Love to S. and Henry— Pray mention all that concerns yourself in particular—health and every thing else. Good news from Joanna of sister Martha. We are all well—a comfortable winter in all respects we have had [?] for our health has been very good—only at one time S. H. suffered from weak eyes. A letter from Mrs Slade Smith but not one word of Borrowdale or debts—only she is charmed with her Lover of a Husband. God bless you all, ever your affect^e

D. Wordsworth

We sent a packet some time ago to H. N. C. by Mrs Cookson, in which I enclosed a letter for Sara.

Address: Mrs S. T. Coleridge at H. N. Coleridge's Esqre, Hampstead.

MS.   *965. W. W. to Samuel Carter Hall*[1]

My dear Sir,   [p.m. April 12, 1831]

I hope I may be able to see you again before I quit Town next Monday. If convenient, which you can let me know by the two-

---

[1] S. C. Hall (1800–89) at one time literary secretary to Ugo Foscolo, and in 1823 reporter in the House of Lords. From 1826 to 1837 editor of *The Amulet and Literary and Christian Remembrancer*. The first two volumes of *The Book of Gems; Poets and Artists of Great Britain* appeared in 1836, the third in 1846. In 1880 he was placed on the Civil List for his services to literature and art.

penny post, Mr Quillinan and I and my younger son, fresh from Germany, will breakfast with you either on Thursday or Friday as you may fix. Thursday I should prefer.

ever sincerely yours
Wm Wordsworth

Address: S. C. Hall Esqre, 59 Sloane Street.

MS.   *966. W. W. to B. R. Haydon*

Trinity Lodge Cambridge
Ap. 23^d [1831]

Dr Haydon

I had not time to answer your friendly notes. If I can command my thoughts I will write something about your Picture,[1] *in prose*, for the Muse has forsaken me—being scared away by the villainous aspect of the Times.

I regret I saw so little of you—which was in some degree my own fault. With best wishes for your success in y^r Art—and for happiness in life I remain faithfully y^{rs}

W. Wordsworth

I hope to be at home next Wed.—

Address: B. R. Haydon Esqre, 4 Burford Place, Connaught Terrace.

MS.   *967. W. W. to Henry Taylor*
K(—)[2]

Trinity Lodge Cambridge
Ap. 23^d [1831]

My dear Sir

Thus far am I on my way to the North—being suddenly called out of Town. On Sunday I visited Ch. Lamb and did not return till 4 o'c. on Monday afternoon, so that I could not breakfast with you either day, every hour of Tuesday I was engaged, and slept at Hampstead, and on Thursday arrived here. I have been thus particular to shew that it was no fault of my own that deprived me of the pleasure of giving you a farewell shake by

---

[1] i.e. of Napoleon on the island of St. Helena.   [2] K. misdates 1834.

the hand. Pray express my regrets to Mr Steven[1] that I could not see him again—being absolutely hurried far beyond my powers.

I have taken the liberty of addressing the enclosed to you for the 2ᵈ Post—they are parting notes to such friends as I had not time to see.

Of the Dissolution,[2] or *desolation* of Parᵗ as the Gyps here call it, I shall [say] nothing. You know what I must think of it—and our poor Jack Tar of a King.

God have mercy upon him, and us all! I calculate upon reaching Rydal next Wed. and to start next day for Carlisle. If anything remarkable occurs that the Papers do not notice—pray tell me.

Ever faithfully yours
Wm Wordsworth.

MS.
K.[3]

968. *W. W. to Edward Quillinan*

April 29, [1831.]

My dear Friend,

I cannot suffer this letter to go without a word from me: and first of dear Mrs Wordsworth—her complaint is lumbago and sciatica, the younger sister and scarcely distinguishable from tic-douloureux. But here my poetical reputation served us. I knew no one in Nottingham, but bethought me of the Howitts.[4] There are two brothers of them; on one I called to state my situation and found that there was a third brother, a physician. Him I sent for, and William and Mary Howitt insisted on the invalid being brought to their house, which was a great comfort on the eve of an election. We made one attempt to move her in vain; in the afternoon we succeeded, and she passed through

---

[1] Probably, as Mr McIntyre suggests, James Stephen; *v.* Letter Oct. 24, 1830.

[2] The Reform Bill was introduced on March 1 by Lord John Russell, and carried on the second reading (March 21) by 302 to 301. An amendment that the number of M.P.s for England and Wales ought not to be diminished was carried against the Government 299 to 291. On April 22 the King dissolved Parliament.   [3] K. misdates 1841.

[4] William and Mary Howitt, philanthropists, and popular writers of pious verse and prose.

the wide market-place of Nottingham, wrapped in a blanket (she could not be dressed) and in a chair, followed by a hundred boys and curious persons. So that she preceded Sir Thomas Denham and Ferguson in the honour of being chaired, and was called by us parliament woman for the loyal borough of Nottingham.

As to Rotha she is a sweet, clever child, and we were the best companions in the world. As Miss H. says, we must take care not to spoil her; she is wonderfully intelligent.

God bless you. I am called away.

Ever faithfully and gratefully yours,

W. Wordsworth.

Pearson. ### 969. *D. W. to William Pearson*

Thursday, 5th May [1831.]

My dear Mr Pearson,

You must have thought me very slow in writing, but the truth is, that I have waited for definite intelligence; and even yet am not enabled to give it. My Brother reached home this day week (Thursday) in good health, and as good spirits as an anxious mind would allow of—for he is very anxious concerning the passing of this Bill. He and his Wife and Daughter left Cambridge on Monday, and grievous to relate! Mrs Wordsworth had a wretched journey to Nottingham, where she was fast bound, by the excruciating torture of the Lumbago; and there my Brother was obliged to leave her, with his Daughter. Happily, they are under the roof of the kindest of Friends, and in the care of a most judicious physician; but you may judge of their eagerness to be at home: however, when they wrote (last Sunday) they could not venture to fix a time for their departure. Thank God! the complaint is not a dangerous one, and she is decidedly recovering, though slowly. We are now chiefly anxious lest they should venture too soon, and suffer a second detention, with the additional misfortune of being among strangers. It was very unfortunate that my Brother's Stamp Office business obliged him to leave her. He reached home in good health, as I have said, and was again compelled to leave us on Sunday afternoon. He and Mr. Carter are now at Carlisle, and are intending to go the rounds of his new district, and we cannot guess the time of their return; only I do not expect them before the end of next week. Whether he will be preceded by my Sister and Niece it is not possible to conjecture. My Nephew William (from Germany), arrived at Rydal last Monday.—He is quite well, and much improved by his travels, and very happy to find himself, once again, at his own home.

I will write to you again when my Brother returns, and then hope to be able to say when he will bo settled at home, and glad to see you. In the mean time, conclude that 'no news is good news'.

It will please you to hear, that at his first dinner, my Brother ejaculated 'What excellent potatoes!' Miss Hutchinson is well, and joins me in best regards. I need not add how glad I shall be to see you after we are settled.

I remain, dear Sir,
Yours truly,
D. Wordsworth

MS. *970. W. W. to Benjamin Robert Haydon*
Haydon.
K(—)

Rydal Mount, Kendal
11th June, 1831.

My dear Haydon,

On the other side is the Sonnet,[1] and let me have your 'Kingdom' for it.[2] What I send you is not 'warm' but piping hot from the brain, whence it came in the wood adjoining my garden not ten minutes ago, and was scarcely more than twice as long in coming.—You knew how much I admired your Picture both for the execution and the conception.—The latter is first-rate, and I could dwell upon it a long time in prose without disparagement to the former; which I admired also having to *it* no objection

---

[1] *To B. R. Haydon, on seeing his picture of Napoleon Buonaparte on the island of St. Helena*, as in Oxf. W., p. 277, except for punctuation.

[2] In answer to W.'s letter of April 23, B. R. H. had written 'I cant let you off with dull prose—though your prose is poetry—you know "High is our calling"—I must have a specimen of yours, and shall enclose you a fair proof that you may look at it occasionally, and wait for inspiration'. He concluded his letter 'Adieu my dear Friend. My Kingdom for a Sonnet'.

and therefore allowance must be made for his oddities. He feels
the poetry, and that is enough. His preface does him great credit.

ever and most truly yours,

Wm. Wordsworth.

MS.
K(—)

972. W. W. to Edward Moxon

Rydal Mount, June, Wednesday 13th [1831]

My dear Sir,

I am sorry to incur the expense of another Letter but on the
other side I have sent a more correct list of Errata for two of
which at least I know that your printer is not answerable.—But
some of these blunders destroy the sense entirely—for example
'the' for 'thy'—page 97 lawful for lawless 109.—If we are to
talk about cancelling, the passage page 51 I could wish most to
be cancelled is the last with the note about the Excursion—it
would hurt Mr Hine's feelings perhaps to tell him so—but really
the note ought not to be there. As to improving the Selection
in another Edition, I am very sceptical about that. Mr Quillinan
talks of omitting the Idiot Boy—it was precisely for his perception of the merit of this Class of Poems that I allowed Mr Hine
to make the Selection. You would find no two Persons agree
[with] you what was best; and upon the whole tell Mr H.
that I think he has succeeded full as well if not better than most
other Persons could have done.—There is another Note which
I also object to much—it is about [? Edinbro and the ? ,] but
perhaps I mentioned this before—I wish I could have sent this
letter through a Frank but I cannot without loss of one post,
probably two. Mr Leigh Hunt is a Coxcomb, was a Coxcomb,
and ever will be a Coxcomb.

ever faithfully yours

W. W.

973. W. W. and D. W. to William Rowan Hamilton
and his Sister

Hamilton(—)
K(—)

Rydal Mount, June 13, 1831.

. . . I saw little or nothing of Cambridge on my return, which
was upon the eve of the election ; but I found that the mathemati-

cians of Trinity—Peacock, Airey, Whewell—were taking what I thought the wrong side; so was that able man, the geological professor, Sedgwick. But 'what matter?' was said to me by a lady; 'these people know nothing but about stars and stones'; which is true, I own, of some of them. . . .

I have scarcely written a hundred verses during the last twelve months; a sonnet, however, composed the day before yesterday, shall be transcribed upon this sheet, by way of making my part of it better worth postage. It was written at the request of the painter, Haydon, and to benefit him, i.e. as he thought; but it is no more than my sincere opinion of his excellent picture. . . .

A selection from my poems has just been edited by Dr Hine, for the benefit chiefly of schools and young persons. . . . Fifteen hundred copies have been struck off.

D. W. writes:

As you, my dear friends, Mr and Miss Hamilton, may have discovered by the slight improvement in legibility of penmanship, other hands have been employed to finish this letter, which has been on the stocks half as long as a man-of-war! I cannot but add from myself that Miss Hutchinson and I, by our solitary winter's fire, often remembered you—talked of 'the Graces'— and all pleasant forms and faces that flitted about before our windows every sunny day of that gloomy summer.

This very moment a letter arrives—very complimentary— from the Master of St. John's College, Cambridge (the place of my brother William's education), requesting him to sit for his portrait to some eminent artist, as he expresses it, 'to be placed in the old House among their Worthies'. He writes in his own name, and that of several of the Fellows. Of course my brother consents; but the difficulty is to fix on an artist. There never yet has been a good portrait of my brother. The sketch by Haydon, as you may remember, is a fine drawing—but what a likeness! All that there is of likeness makes it to me the more disagreeable. Adieu! believe me my dear friends,

yours truly
D. Wordsworth

be tempted to come as far as the Lakes and make my house his head-quarters, taking my portrait at the same time; if you do not object to sound him upon such a subject I should thank you to do so, as a reply in the negative might be given with less of a disagreeable feeling thro' a third person than directly to myself. You must be well aware how inconvenient it would be to me after so long an absence to make a second visit to town. Considering that Parliament is likely to sit great part of the summer and that many engagements must have devolved upon Mr P. by the death of Sir T. Lawrence and Mr Jackson, I do not think it probable that anything will come of this proposal, but as one of the fellows of the Coll: told me yesterday they wish the thing to be done as soon as may be, I have thought that Mr P. will excuse the liberty I have taken. I ought to add they wish for a half-length, as a size which may range best with the Portraits of the Coll:. When you call at Moxon's pray tell him that I begged Lady Frederick Bentinck[1] w^d send for a copy of the Selections to be considered as a present from me to her son; request him to send also a copy to Colbourn's the bookseller for Wm Howitt Esqre, Nottingham—now Dora writes as you will guess from the impudence which follows. I hope you are not answerable for the sin of being the author of 'Mischief'.[2] Father says there are some lines far too pretty and pure to have been found in such company. Now comes Daddy back again. Rotha continues to gain upon us (indeed she does) and we hope that the place with all the entertaining objects and employments about it will stir her mind profitably. She is very clever like her father but with some of his flibertygibertism. Farewell. Yours affe^{ly}

Wm. Wordsworth.

See P. as soon as you can as I wish to write to the Coll:

Address: Edward Quillinan Esqre, Bryanston Street, Portman Square.

[1] Daughter of Lord Lonsdale.

[2] 'Mischief', a tale of intrigue, obviously suggested by *Beppo*, and imitative of the style introduced into English poetry by Hookham Frere in his *Monks and the Giants*, but written in the Spenserian stanza. The poem shows some metrical skill and felicities of phrasing, but as a satire it is feeble and pointless. Q. published the first section (anonymously) with Moxon in 1831, the second in 1834.

MS.
Haydon(—)

976. *W. W. to B. R. Haydon*

[p.m. 8 July 1831]

My dear Haydon,

I have to thank you for two Letters—I am glad you liked the
Sonnet. I have repeated it to one or two Judges whom it has
pleased.—You ask my opinion about your daughter learning
Music. If she had an independent fortune I should say no,
unless she have a strong inclination to the Study. I am aware
that such a natural bent is by no means necessary for the attain-
ment of excellence both in playing and singing,—I know one
striking instance to the contrary—still I am not friendly to the
practice of forcing music upon females—because I think their
time might be better employ'd; but if you look to the situation
of a Teacher or Governess for any of your Daughters Music
would serve them much in procuring such situation. I know
several persons otherwise well qualified who are unemployed
solely from their want of that accomplishment.

You ask my opinion about the Reform Bill.—I am averse
(with that wisest of the Moderns Mr Burke) to all *hot* Reforma-
tions; i.e. to every sudden change in political institutions upon
a large scale. They who are forced to part with power are of
course irritated, and they upon whom a large measure of it is
at once conferred have their heads turned and know not how
to use it. To the *principle* of this particular measure, I object
as *unjust*; and by its injustice opening a way for spoliation and
subversion to any extent which the rash and iniquitous may be
set upon.—If it could have been shewn of such or such a
Borough that it claimed the right to send Members to Parliament, upon usurpation, or that it had made a grossly corrupt
use of a legal privilege—in both these cases I would disfranchise—
and also with the consent of the owners of burgage Tenure, but
beyond this I would not have gone a step. As to transferring
the right of voting to large Towns; my conviction is that they
will be little the better for it—if at all—but een let them have
their humour in certain cases and try the result. In short the
whole of my proceedings would have been *tentative,* and in no
case would I have violated a principle of justice. This is the sum

of what I have to say. My admirers, as you call them, must have been led (perhaps by myself) to overstate what I said to Lord John Russel.[1] I did not conceal from him my utter disapprobation of the Bill; and what I said principally alluded to its effect upon the Aristocracy. I remember particularly telling him that the middle and lower classes were naturally envious haters of the Aristocracy—unless when they were *proud* of being attached to them—that there was no *neutral* ground in these sentiments—the Mass must either be your zealous supporters, said I, or they will do all in their power to pull you down—that power, all at once, are you now giving them through your ten pound renters who to effect their purpose will soon call in the aid of others below them till you have the blessing of universal suffrage; and what will become (I might have said in that case, I did hint it) of Covent Garden and Wooburn &c &c. I am called off and you must accept the wretched Scrawl poor return as it is for your [   ] letters—

[*a line or two, and the signature, torn away*]

Address: B. R. Haydon Esq e, Connaught Terrace, Edgware Road

MS.
K(—)

977. W. W. to Edward Moxon

Rydal Mount near Kendal
July 21st [1831]

My dear Sir,

Your letter of the 19th has been received—As you *know well* that I am anxious to serve you I have the less pain in saying that I cannot do it in this way. I have an aversion little less than insurmountable to having anything to do with periodicals —and nothing but a sense of duty to my family would have induced me to treat with Mr Hill. If I could bring myself out of personal kindness for any Editor or Proprietor of a Periodical to contribute, it would be to the Annual of Alaric Watts, who has a sort of claim upon me, for some literary civilities and intended services, some time ago.—I not only feel that aversion

---

[1] 'I understand at Lord Holland's you had a fierce argument with Lord John, and your admirers say "gave it him". Will you tell me what you said?' (B. R. H. to W. W., June 28.)

myself but Mrs W. has it in so strong a degree that, for the present, I put away all thoughts of looking for pecuniary emolument from that way of publication, which is tantamount to abandoning such expectation from any other.

And now may I take the liberty of expressing my regret that you should have been tempted into this experiment at all? It must be attended with risk; and *risk* I am most anxious you should avoid.—You *were sure* of succeeding if you had adhered to the Rules of Prudence we talked over together; but if you yield to these temptations, the hazard may hurt you in a thousand ways.—Allow me to say also, that I fear the possibility of author[? ship] may tempt you to write yourself, which will take your thoughts off from business, in a greater degree than you would be inclined to suspect. It strikes me also that there is something like attempting to take the public by storm in putting forth your distinguished personal friends in the way you propose to do. The Public is apt to revolt at any such step and the Contemporary Journals might be inclined to resent it, and fall upon you, in consequence—Indeed my good friend on whichever side I look at this project I dislike it.

It costs me something to write this Letter, but I do it out of sincere friendship. Be assured that I shall do all I *can* to serve you, but in this way you must excuse me.

I am glad the Selections sell—

ever faithfully yours

Wm Wordsworth

Thursday.　The sonnet on viewing Mr Haydon's picture was sent to him with permission to present it when, where, and how he liked. I wrote it to serve *him*, but I had nothing to do with its appearance in Mr Hill's Journal.

MS.　　　　*978. W. W. to Alexander Dyce*
M. G. K.
Lowther Castle, near Penrith

23^d July, [1831]
My dear Sir,

I have put off replying to your obliging Letter till I could procure a Frank; as I had little more to say than to thank you for your attention as to Lady Winchelsea, and for the Extracts you sent me.

I expected to find at this place my Friend Lady Frederick Bentinck, through whom I intended to renew my request for materials, if any exist, among the Finch family, whether MSS poems or anything else that would be interesting; but Lady F., unluckily, is not likely to be in Westnd. I shall, however, write to her. Without some additional materials, I think I should scarcely feel strong enough to venture upon any species of publication connected with this very interesting woman, notwithstanding the kind things you say of the value of my critical Remarks.

I am glad you have taken Skelton[1] in hand, and much wish I could be of any use to you. In regard to his life, I am certain of having read somewhere (I thought it was in Burns's *Hist. of Cumberland and Westnd*, but I am mistaken), that Skelton was born at Branthwaite Hall, in the County of Cumberland. Certain it is that a family of that name possessed the place for many generations; and I own it would give me some pleasure to make out that Skelton was a Brother Cumbrian. Branthwaite Hall is about 6 miles from Cockermouth, my native place. Tickell (of the Spectator, one of the best of our minor Poets, as Johnson has truly said) was born within two miles of the same Town. These are mere accidents it is true, but I am foolish enough to attach some interest to them.

If it would be more agreeable to you, I would mention your views in respect to Skelton to Mr Southey. I should have done so before, but it slipped my memory when I saw him. Mr Southey is undoubtedly much engaged, but I cannot think that he would take ill a Letter from you on any literary subject. At all events I shall in a few days mention your intention of editing Skelton, and ask if he has anything to suggest.

I meditate a little tour in Scotland this autumn, my principal object being to visit Sir Walter Scott; but as I take my Daughter along with me, we probably shall go to Edinburgh, Glasgow, and take a peep at the Western Highlands. This will not bring us near Aberdeen.[2] If it suited you to return to Town by the Lakes,

---

[1] Dyce's edition of Skelton was not published till 1843.
[2] Where A. D. then was.

I would be truly glad to see you at Rydal Mount, near Amble-side. You might, *at all events*, call on Mr Southey on your way; I would prepare an introduction for you by naming your inten-tion to Mr S. I have underlined the above Sentence,[1] because my Scotch tour would, I fear, make it little likely that I should be at home about the 10th of Sepbr. Your return however may be deferred.

Believe me, my dear Sir,

very respectfully, your obliged

W. Wordsworth.

P.S.—I hope your health continues good. I assure you there was no want of interest in your conversation on that or any other account.

MS.   *979. W. W. to Miss Carlyle*

Rydal Mount, Wednesday, July 25th. [1831]

My dear Miss Carlyle,

I have to thank you for two most obliging letters, and the great trouble you have taken on my son's account. As I knew you would give me credit for being sensible of your kindness I did not think it right to trouble you with an acknowledgement till the second letter which you promised, might reach me. I have taken a day to consider along with my son, the offer of Mrs Carrick. The lodgings seem in all respects suitable but I must own that the terms strike me as high.—Suppose the case of a young clergyman lodging at Carlisle, had he to pay £80 a year for lodging without any beverage to his meals but water found him, he would have little left to supply himself with other necessaries: if £80 be demanded on account of the additional small room that seems to me more than is reasonable. I should therefore think that £80 would be a handsome remuneration for the whole, the care of such small portion of the stamps as would devolve upon Mrs Carrick included. If Mrs C—— con-sents to this my son would be glad to take the lodgings three months hence if they should then be at liberty. I think he will

---

[1] Sentence: W. means the phrase *at all events*.

benefit by another quarter's residence here under my clerk, and his Mother is very anxious to see a little more of him, after his long absence in Germany, than her engagements have allowed, she only returned the other day from Cheltenham where she has been several weeks—not, I ought to say, on account of her own ill health but to attend a sick friend.

I am concerned to hear of Mrs Lodge's indisposition, with best wishes for her recovery and remembrances to both your Aunts I remain dear Miss Carlyle your very much obliged

Wm. Wordsworth.

Be so good as to thank Miss Grisdale for interesting herself in my concerns—I regretted much her absence from Carlisle when I was there.

Mrs Carrick will understand that my son would not be justified in taking the lodgings for *a year*, as circumstances might call him from Carlisle, or in these retrenching days, the situation be so reduced as not to be worth holding—in such case a month's notice he hopes will satisfy Mrs Carrick.

Address: Miss Carlyle, Carlisle.

MS. ### 980. *W. W. to Sir Walter Scott*

Rydal Mount, Kendal

29th August, 1831

My dear Sir Walter,

I received your kind message through Mr Taylor; it has decided me to fulfill an engagement which has long pressed upon my mind, viz to set off for Abbotsford with my Daughter in ten days, if you could receive us with comfort to you all, and Miss Scott.—As we shall travel with a young Horse our day's journeys will be short; and we mean also to stop a day on the road so that it will take us six days at least to reach you.

If it do not suit you my dear friend to receive us, pray do not let this offer embarrass you, but say frankly what you feel, or how you are circumstanced.

I hope that your health is not worse, that Miss Scott is well, and Mr and Mrs Lockhart with you.

I am in sad spirits about public affairs. The Whigs have I

fear subverted this antient and noble Government—God protect us—

Ever my dear Sir Walter
Your affectionate friend
Wm. Wordsworth

I presume we must go to Hawick—which is our best way after we leave that place?

Address: Sir Walter Scott, Bart., Abbotsford, Melrose, N.B.

MS.　　　*981. W. W. to John Marshall*

[Friday, Early Sept. 1831]

My dear Sir,

What a pity that we cannot turn this beautiful weather to better account by setting out on our journey today or tomorrow, as we had intended—but business has unexpectedly sprung up in the office, for which my presence is indispensable, and I have little hope of being at liberty in less than ten days. I thought it right to let you know of this disappointment, as you and Mrs Marshall would have been looking for us.

My Sister is on a visit to Mr and Mrs Curwen at the Island, where are also my Son and his wife. Pray mention to your young Ladies that it is regretted in this house, that we cannot have their Company to add to what is elegantly called a *cram*, which is to take place at Rydal Mount on Monday evening—*they* perhaps will not be sorry to be absent, as it is apprehended the fiddlers will not have room to move their elbows.

Say to Miss M.[1] that we were all much delighted with the verses she put into my hands—Mr S. thought highly of those addressed to his Daughter,[2] which were shewn him by Miss Hutchinson—they are *we think* eminently characteristic and tender.

I am suffering from my eyes, which obliges me to employ Mrs W.'s pen.

Ever very sincerely yours
Wm. Wordsworth

Address: John Marshall Esq[re], Hallsteads, Penrith.

[1] Julia Marshall.　　　　　　　　　　　[2] Kate Southey.

K.   *982. D. W. to Catherine Clarkson*

concluded on Friday, the 9th of September [1831]

My dear Friend,

... There is just come out a portrait of my Brother, for which he sat when last in London. It is a lithograph of a chalk drawing by Wilkins,[1] and may be had in London. I think it a strong likeness, and so does every one. Of course, to his own family something is wanting; nevertheless I value it much as a likeness of him in company, and something of that restraint with chearfulness, which is natural to him in mixed societies. There is nothing of the poet. ...

Saturday. This letter was interrupted three weeks ago, or thereabouts; and afterwards being unexpectedly called away to Belle Isle, while John and Isabella were there, I left it unfinished. I stayed there ten days. It is a splendid place for a visit such as mine; but compared with Rydal Mount dull, and to the feelings confining, though persons who live there persuade themselves there is no more trouble in being ferried over to the shore than in continuing uninterruptedly to walk on.

But what I like least in an island as a residence is the being separated from men, cattle, cottages, and the goings-on of rural life. John and Isabella are on a tour in North Wales, and my Brother, Dora, and Charles Wordsworth hope to set off next week on a few days visit to Sir W. Scott; and, if weather allow, a short tour—Edinburgh, Glasgow, Stirling, Loch Lomond, Inverary, Loch Awe, Loch Etive, and the isle of Mull. We have friends at that island. Stamp-office business prevented their setting off some days ago. ... Dora is to drive her father in a little carriage of our own, with a very steady horse. Charles will travel by coach, and on foot, or as he can. He is a fine, chearful fellow, and rejoices in the hope of this little tour, being very fond of both his uncle and cousin, and glad of the opportunity of seeing a person of so much importance as Sir Walter. Poor man! his health is shattered by a recurrence of slight paralytic strokes, but his mind is active as ever. He would write eight hours in the

---

[1] Published in a series of *Men of the Day* by William Wilkins, 20 Newman Street. W. himself spoke of it as the portrait of the Stamp-distributor.

day if allowed by the physicians, but it is the worst thing he can do; and most likely it is rather to divert him from study, than for benefits expected from the climate, that he has been advised to winter in Italy. He has fixed on leaving Abbotsford at the end of this month to proceed to Naples. The young William is still here; but on the 20th of next month is to begin residence at Carlisle as sub-distributor there—a good putting on (for it is about £180 per annum) till something better fall out, or as long as things are allowed to remain as they are. But, to tell you the truth, so many changes are going on, I consider nothing as stable; and do expect that the sovereign people to whom our rulers bow so obsequiously will not long endure the stamp office, and its distributors, or the national debt, or anything else that now is.

In October we expect Mr Jones, the companion of my Brother forty years ago over the Alps. He looks back to that journey as the golden and sunny spot in his life. It would delight you to hear the pair talk of their adventures. My Brother, active, lively, and almost as strong as ever on a mountain top; Jones, fat and roundabout and rosy, and puffing and panting while he climbs the little hill from the road to our house. Never was there a more remarkable contrast; yet time seems to have strengthened the attachment of the native of Cambrian mountains to his Cumbrian friend. We also expect Mr Quillinan in October. Whether he will leave his daughter Rotha (his youngest born) with us for the winter, or take her to school, I know not. Jemima is at school near Paris, and as Dora does not like to part with her godchild, perhaps it may be settled that she remain here till spring. She is an interesting and very clever child, the image of her father. We never saw the Tillbrooks but at church, and did not exchange a word with either of them. It is of no use to enter on a painful history; enough to say that both Tillbrook and his wife so misrepresented the truth in regard to Dora's refusal of Mr Ayling's offer of marriage, that we could have no satisfaction in holding intercourse with them, and therefore we never entered their door. For your own private ear I will just say that Mrs T. is what the world calls a fascinating woman, and that there is an appearance of simplicity and

Terrace in that field, we have lived no small part of the long bright days of the summer gone by; and in a hazel nook of this favourite piece of ground is a Stone, for which I wrote one day the following serious Inscription, you will forgive its Egotism.

> In these fair Vales, hath many a tree
> At Wordsworth's suit been spared,
> And from the builder's hand this Stone,
> For some rude beauty of its own,
> Was rescued by the Bard;
> Long may it rest in peace! and here
> Perchance the tender-hearted
> Will heave a gentle sigh for him
> As One of the Departed.

I have heard something like what you say of Campbell before, but in that case I partly suspected that the admiration might in some degree be affected to ingratiate himself with the Individual who was a friend of mine. By the bye, let you, and every other Person who has a *pet Poet* be on your guard agst that trick. How sorry I am that Mr Bailey[1] should have gone as far as Ceylon ignorant of the fact that I never have received his book, nor before the receipt of your letter was aware of the intended favour. How came your Brother to go from Manchester into Scotland without taking us by the way? but perhaps he *steamed it* from Liverpool. Tillbrook has offered his House and furniture for sale by private Treaty—the price two thousand Guineas, entre nous, 8 hundred more than its worth, except for fancy. Adieu—every one here—to wit Self and Spouse, Son and Daughter, Sister and Sister in something better than Law, join

---

[1] Benjamin Bailey (1791–1853) the friend of Keats, and from his Oxford days a great admirer of W. W. In 1831 was published *Poetical Sketches of the South of France*, by the Rev. B. Bailey, Senior Colonial Chaplain of the Island of Ceylon. It contained 40 sonnets and 15 other poems, several of which borrow from W. or are obviously written under his influence. When Mrs Fletcher (née Jewsbury) went to India in 1833 she stayed with B. B. and wrote to Dora W. that he was 'such a Wordsworthian as I have rarely if ever met: every edition of your Father is here, filled with MS. notes'. In 1835 a small anonymous book entitled *Lines addressed to William Wordsworth Esq.* was printed by the Wesleyan Mission Press at Ceylon. It contains 84 sonnets and 2 poems of 8 lines signed B., and obviously written by Bailey.

in kindest regards to you and Mrs. Kenyon, and to your brother when you write to him. Farewell again,

Very aff^{ly} yours

Wm. Wordsworth.

We shall always, not merely ' now and then', be glad to hear from you. You asked how I had ' things from London'. Pamphlets, etc., sent to J. Richardson, 91 Royal Exchange, are forwarded if directed to me under cover to Hudson & Nicholson, Booksellers, Kendal.

Address: John Kenyon Esqre, St. Leonards, near Hastings.

Pearson.
K.

984. D. W. to William Pearson

Rydal Mount, Early Sept.[1] 1831.

My dear Sir,

My Nephew, being particularly engaged with office business during Mr Carter's absence, who is keeping holiday at Liverpool, has desired me to return you his best thanks for your letter, and for all the pains you have taken to procure a horse.

As perhaps you may have heard, William and his Father set off a few days ago to look after one or more of the horses you had mentioned; and fortunately fell in with the *Grey*, and its owner. In some respects they were much pleased with it; but the man asked for it £30, which they thought too much, and besides, he was not ready to *warrant* its soundness, but only said, he 'would pass it'. These considerations induced my Brother, with his Son, to go to Crook yesterday, and there they actually made a bargain, not for the Crook Hall *Grey*, but for a bay horse, which they hope will answer their purpose.

It is an admirable walker, but unused to trotting, having only been put to carting and ploughing. We expect the horse to-day, and as soon as it has had a fair trial it is to be sent to Morosby to bring home Mrs Wordsworth; and soon after her return it may possibly have the honour of conveying the Poet and his

---

[1] P. (followed by K.) dates this letter Oct. 20, but as W. was at Abbotsford on Sept. 21, that is impossible. The date 'Oct. 20' probably belongs to the next letter to P., which is undated in P.

Daughter to Abbotsford, to visit Sir Walter Scott! This visit
has long been promised, but the late accounts of Sir Walter's
health having been very bad, we were fearful that the visit might
never be accomplished. I am happy, however, to tell you that
a friend of ours, who has just been on a visit at Abbotsford,
informs us that Sir Walter is much better at present, and quite
able to enjoy the society of friends. This information has determined my Brother to think seriously of the journey; and if Sir
Walter continues as well as he is at present, it will probably be
accomplished during the Autumn. You will be glad to hear that
the sea air has proved very beneficial to my Sister, and that Mrs
John Wordsworth's health is improved. Miss Hutchinson is at
Keswick, and will probably remain there till Mrs Wordsworth's
return.

My Brother and William would have been very glad to call
on you yesterday, but the additional three miles would have
made the ride too long for him. As it was, he was a good deal
fatigued, not being so clever on horseback as on foot. My
Brother and his Daughter unite their thanks, with William's—
It is very long since we have heard of, or seen you,—I hope you
have been in good health. My Brother begs his kind regards.

> I am, dear Sir,
> Yours sincerely,
> Dorothy Wordsworth.

_MS._
_K(—)_

985. _W. W. to Sir Walter Scott_

Carlisle, Sept. 16th 1831

My dear Sir Walter,

'There's a man wi' a veil, and a lass drivin',' exclaimed a little
urchin, as we entered merrie Carlisle a couple of hours ago, on
our way to Abbotsford. From the words you will infer, and
truly, that my eyes are in but a poor state—I was determined
however to see you and yours, and to give my daughter the
same pleasure at all hazards; accordingly I left home last Tuesday, but was detained two whole days at Halsteads on Ullswater by a serious increase of my complaint—this morning I
felt so much better that we ventured to proceed, tomorrow we

hope to stop at Langholm, on Sunday at Hawick, and on Monday, if the distance be not greater than we suppose, under your roof.

In my former letter I mentioned a nephew of mine, a student of Christch:, and I may add, a distinguished one, to whom I could not but allow the pleasure of accompanying us—he has taken the Newcastle road into Scotland, hoping to join us at Abbotsford on Tuesday, and I mention him now from an apprehension of being again retarded by my eyes, and to beg that if he should arrive before us he may be no restraint upon you whatever.—Let him loose in your library, or on the Tweed with his fishing-rod, or in the Stubble with his gun (he is but a novice of a shot, by-the-bye) and he will be no trouble to any part of your family.

With kindest regards to Miss Scott and to Mr and Mrs Lockhart if still as we hope with you, in which my Daughter unites, and with the same for yourself and a thousand good wishes,

I remain, my dear Sir Walter,

very affectionately yours

Wm Wordsworth

Address: Sir Walter Scott, Bart., Abbotsford, Melrose.

986. *W. W. to Robert Jones*[1]

Falkirk, Sept. 26, 1831

My old complaint an inflamation in my eyes and official engagements compelled me to put off my journey to Sir Walter Scott's for nearly 3 weeks in consequence of which and the uncertainty my eyes have caused me to be in I have not been able to write to you sooner. . . . Sir Walter was to leave home last Friday for London—he is to embark in a King's Ship for Malta with the intention of wintering at Naples where his younger son is attached to the Embassy. His friends say that he is much better in health than he was some months and even weeks ago, and much good is expected from breaking his sedentary habits and application to writing more than from the change of climate.

---

[1] Extract from a Bookseller's Catalogue.

K.   *987. W. W. to Lord Lonsdale*

[Sept.–Oct. 1831]¹

Perhaps the fate of the bill is already decided, or will be so, before this reaches your hands. I cannot forbear, however, writing once more upon a subject which is scarcely ever out of my thoughts. I see that a writer in the *Quarterly Review* is most decidedly against the bill going into Committee: he appears convinced, as thousands are, that no good would arise from it, and that the destruction of the Constitution must follow; adding that if the Lords resist they will at least fall with honour. In this I perfectly concur with him. . . . Residing at a distance from town, I can form no distinct notion of the mischief which might immediately arise, with an executive such as now afflicts this kingdom. But I do confidently affirm that there are materials for constructing a party which, if the bill be not passed, might save the country. I have numerous acquaintances among men who have all their lives been more or less of Reformers, but not one, unfastened by party engagements, who does not strongly condemn this bill.

Pearson.   *988. D. W. to William Pearson*

Rydal Mount

Tuesday [p.m. Oct. 20th 1831]

My dear Sir,

I have more than once said to you that we should be troubling you again for a supply of potatoes, after your last year's successful purchase of that article, and I now write, (I hope in good time) to beg that you will be so kind as to buy us. . . .

My Brother and his Daughter are not expected home before the 25th. They will meet William at Carlisle, who will be settled there as Sub. Distr. about that time. I am happy to tell you that travelling has agreed with my Brother's eyes, and that they were nearly well about ten days ago. The last tidings that have reached us were from Callendar.

¹ Misdated 1827 by K.: probably written between the passing of Reform Bill by H. of C. on Sept. 22, and its rejection by the H. of L. Oct. 8, 1831.

They were going to Bonawe,[1] Oban, and the Isle of Mull. Thence to Glasgow and to Lanark, and home by Carlisle—Sir Walter Scott was much pleased to see them; but I am sorry to say his health seems to be much broken—great hopes, however, are entertained from a change of climate and of scene.

It is very long since you were at Rydal. To this I can say no more than that you have always been a welcome guest, and that it will give my Brother pleasure to see you popping in as formerly, when he has settled himself at home; and I am sure you will be glad to inquire after his health, and to hear of their adventures.

I am, dear Sir,
Sincerely and respectfully,
your friend,
D. Wordsworth.

Sunday evening. I kept back my letter, recollecting it might be likely that our horse-proprietors would wish to have more straw, and no one being at hand to direct me. I find that they will be much obliged if you will procure them a supply, to send along with the potatoes.

Pray excuse the trouble I give you—but I know you will, having so often experienced your kindness that way. Mrs Wordsworth begs I will return her best thanks for the Partridges received whilst I was staying at Belle Isle.

K.   *989. W. W. to Basil Montagu*

[pm., Oct. 22,[2] 1831.]

On my return from an excursion in Scotland two days ago I found the fourteenth volume of Bacon, together with your note of the 9th of August, left here by Mr Romilly. On the question of the punishment by death you have written with much ability. For my own part, I am decidedly of opinion that, in the case of forgery, both humanity and policy require that an experiment should be made to ascertain whether it cannot be dispensed with.

---

[1] Bonawe] Brenane *Pearson*; but there is no such place. A letter from Dora W. to M. W. of Oct. 7 proves it to be Bonawe.

[2] So K. but probably Oct. 27. W. reached home on the 25th.

I am glad that you are proceeding with the life of Bacon. You say that he was sacrificed to Buckingham. Have you read a letter of Buckingham's to him in which he charges him with the intention of sacrificing him (Buckingham) as he had betrayed all his patrons and friends in succession? Buckingham enumerates the cases. It has always appeared to me that much of the odium attached to Lord Bacon's name on account of corrupt practices arose out of ignorance respecting the spirit of those times, and the way in which things were carried on. . . . Travelling agrees with me wonderfully. I am as much Peter Bell as ever, and since my eyelids have been so liable to inflammation, after much reading especially, I find nothing so feeding to my mind as change of scene, and rambling about; and my labours, such as they are, can be carried on better in the fields and on the roads, than anywhere else. . . .

990. W. W. to William Rowan Hamilton

Hamilton
M— G. K—   Rydal Mount, Oct. 27 [1831.]
My dear Mr Hamilton,

A day or two before my return from Scotland arrived your letter and verses; for both of which I thank you, as they exhibit your mind under those varied phases which I have great pleasure in contemplating. My reply is earlier than it would have been, but for the opportunity of a frank from one of the Members for the University of Oxford[1]—a friend of Mr Southey's and mine, who by way of recreating himself after the fatigues of the last Session, had taken a trip to see the Manchester railway, and kindly and most unexpectedly came on to give a day apiece to Southey and me. He is, like myself, in poor heart at the aspect of public affairs. In his opinion the Ministers when they brought in the Bill neither expected nor wished it to be carried. All they wanted was an opportunity of saying to the people, 'Behold what great things we would have done for you had it been in our power: we must now content ourselves with the best we can get.' But, to return to your letter. To speak frankly, you appear

---

[1] i.e. Sir Robert Inglis.

to be at least three-fourths gone in love; therefore, think about
the last quarter of the journey. The picture you give of the lady
makes one wish to see her more familiarly than I had an opportunity of doing, were it only to ascertain whether, as you astro-
nomers have in your observatories magnifying glasses for the
stars, you do not carry about with you also, when you descend
to common life, coloured glasses and Claude Loraine mirrors for
throwing upon objects that interest you enough for the purpose,
such lights and hues as may be most to the taste of the intellectual vision. In a former letter you mention Francis Edgeworth.
He is a person not to be forgotten. If you be in communication
with him pray present him my very kind respects, and say that
he was not unfrequently in my thoughts during my late poetic
rambles; and particularly when I saw the objects which called
forth a Sonnet that I shall send you. He was struck with my
mention of a sound in the eagle's notes, much and frequently
resembling the yelping and barking of a dog, and quoted a
passage in Aeschylus where the eagle is called the flying hound
of the air, and he suggested that Aeschylus might not only allude
by that term to his being a bird of chase or prey, but also to this
barking voice, which I do not recollect ever hearing noticed.
The other day I was forcibly reminded of the circumstances
under which the pair of eagles were seen that I described in the
letter to Mr Edgeworth, his brother. It was the promontory of
Fairhead, on the coast of Antrim, and no spectacle could be
grander. At Dunally Castle, a ruin seated at the tip of one of
the horns of the bay of Oban, I saw the other day one of these
noble creatures cooped up among the ruins, and was incited to
give vent to my feelings as you shall now see:

[Dishonoured Rock and Ruin! etc. *as* Oxf. W., p. 388, *but* l. 6
Now wheeling low, then with a consort paired,
l. 8 Flying *for* Flew high *and* l. 12.
In spirit, for a moment he resumes]

You will naturally wish to hear something of Sir Walter Scott,
and particularly of his health. I found him a good deal changed
within the last three or four years, in consequence of some shocks
of the apoplectic kind; but his friends say that he is very much

better, and the last accounts, up to the time of his going on board, were still more favourable. He himself thinks his age much against him, but he has only completed his 60th year. But a friend of mine was here the other day, who has rallied, and is himself again, after a much severer shock, and at an age several years more advanced. So that I trust the world and his friends may be hopeful, with good reason, that the life and faculties of this man, who has during the last six and twenty years diffused more innocent pleasure than ever fell to the lot of any human being to do in his own life-time, may be spared. Voltaire, no doubt, was full as extensively known, and filled a larger space probably in the eye of Europe; for he was a great theatrical writer, which Scott has not proved himself to be, and miscellaneous to that degree, that there was something for all classes of readers: but the pleasure afforded by his writings, with the exception of some of his Tragedies and minor Poems, was not pure, and in this Scott is greatly his superior.

As Dora has told your sister, Sir W. was our guide to Yarrow. The pleasure of that day induced me to add a third to the two poems upon Yarrow, *Yarrow Revisited*. It is in the same measure, and as much in the same spirit as matter of fact would allow. You are artist enough to know that it is next to impossible entirely to harmonise things that rest upon their poetic credibility, and are idealised by distance of time and space, with those that rest upon the evidence of the hour, and have about them the thorny points of actual life. I am interrupted by a stranger, and a gleam of fine weather reminds me also of taking advantage of it the moment I am at liberty, for we have had a week of incessant rain.

[*Signature torn away*]

Pearson. **991. D. W. to William Pearson**

Saturday Morning [29th October, 1831.]

My dear Sir,

We are exceedingly obliged for the potatoes and apples, and are, I assure you, much too selfish to desire to part with any of the latter, to our friends. . . . It is quite a treat to look at the apples, they are so beautiful.

This fine morning has tempted my brother on a walk to Grasmere with his friend Mr Jones, otherwise, I should have had a message from him—but I know he will at any time be glad to see you, though we may have other visitors;—and I hope it will not be very long before fine weather and leisure tempt you to ride over into these parts. My Brother continues quite well, and my Niece much improved by her journey, in health and strength.

As to the poor horse, I did not name him, because not able to give a good account, though *through no fault of his*. My Brother had injudiciously put him to a journey too long and too heavy for his years; and they were obliged to leave him, in comfortable quarters, to winter at Bonawe,[1] and to hire horses for their return. The horse, however, is a very good one; and judges pronounced that no harm had been done, and that a *winter's run*, and *small labour next summer*, would make him an excellent beast.—It was a great pity that he was so soon put upon a journey—however, the human creatures' tour was a delightful one.

We are daily expecting my eldest Nephew John. William is at Carlisle, and we hope very comfortable. With many thanks,

I am, dear Sir,

Yours truly,

D. Wordsworth.

K^2 *992. W. W. to John W.*[2]

[? autumn 1831][3]

My dear [John,]

. . . I have myself been moving about a good deal, twice on business; it is lucky for me that my engagements of that kind

---

[1] *v.* note, p. 577.

[2] K. gives C. W. as the addressee, and begins the letter 'My dear Brother', but Miss Elizabeth Wordsworth, in her book on W. W. (London, Percival & Co., 1891) quotes a part of the letter, and gives the addressee as John W. (son of C. W.), and she is more likely to be right. To C. W., as Master of Trinity, the last sentence of the letter would be inapplicable.

[3] Late autumn is probable; for W. visited the Duddon with M. W. in

lead me through a beautiful country. Last Friday I was called to Ulverstone. I went down the side of Coniston water; and returned by Broughton up the Duddon, and over Wrynose. The vale of Duddon I had never seen at this season, and was much charmed with it. Most of the cottages are embowered in fir trees mixed with sycamores, and in laurel, which thrives luxuriantly in the sheltered vale, and at this season is most pleasant to look upon. John was my companion; we parted five miles up the Duddon, he turning up over Birker Moor for Whitehaven.

What you tell us of Mr Rose's[1] success as a preacher is highly gratifying. He is a sincere, devout man, and, I suppose, very industrious. How honourable is it to your University that such crowds go to hear him. R is out,[2] as you are about Laodamia. No stanza is omitted.[3] The last but one is, however, substantially altered. R disliked[4] the alteration; but I cannot bring my mind to reject it. As first written the heroine was dismissed to happiness in Elysium. To what purpose then the mission of Protesilaus? He exhorts her to moderate her passion; the exhortation is fruitless, and no punishment follows. So it stood; at present[3] she is placed among unhappy ghosts for disregard of the exhortation. Virgil also places her there; but compare the two passages, and give me *your* opinion. R[5] said any punishment stopping short of the future world would have been reasonable, but not the melancholy one I have imposed, as she was not a voluntary suicide. Who shall decide, when doctors disagree? Do not let your etymological researches interfere with your fellowship studies. . . .

Ever faithfully yours,

W. W.

---

the winter of 1821, whilst most of the Duddon sonnets are spring or summer sonnets.

[1] *For* Rose, *v.* Letters 838, 839.

[2] Miss E. W. *prints* H. *for* R., *an understandable slip as she does not print the previous part of the letter.* K. *reads* He is out or you are out, about L.

[3] i.e. in ed. of 1827.

[4] R. disliked] H. disliked, Miss E. W. I have disliked, K.

[5] R. said] H. said, Miss E. W. I have said, K. (*but W. had not said it*). K.'s 'I have' may possibly be a misreading of W.'s writing of 'Rose'.

MS.
R.

993. *W. W. to Samuel Rogers*

Rydal Mount, Novr 7th [1831]

My dear Rogers,

Several weeks since I heard, through Mr Quillinan, who I believe had it from Moxon, that you were unwell, and this unpleasant communication has weighed frequently on my mind; but I did not write, trusting that either from Mr Q. or Moxon I should hear something of the particulars. These expectations have been vain, and I now venture, not without anxiety, to make enquiries of yourself. Be so good then as let me hear how you are, and as soon as you can.

If you saw Sir Walter Scott, or have met with Mr and Mrs Lockhart since their return to town, you will have learned from them that Dora and I reached Abbotsford in time to have two or three days of Sir Walter's company before he left his home. I need not dwell upon the subject of his health, as you cannot but have heard as authentic particulars as I could give you, and of more recent date.

From Abbotsford we went to Roslin, Edinburgh, Stirling, Loch Kettering, Killin, Dalmally, Oban, the Isle of Mull—too late in the season for Staffa—and returned by Inverary, Loch Lomond, Glasgow, and the falls of the Clyde. The foliage was in its most beautiful state; and the weather, though we had five or six days of heavy rain, was upon the whole very favourable; for we had most beautiful appearances of floating vapours, rainbows and fragments of rainbows, weather-gales, and sunbeams innumerable, so that I never saw Scotland under a more poetic aspect. Then there was in addition the pleasure of recollection, and the novelty of showing to my Daughter places and objects which had been so long in my remembrance.

About the middle of summer a hope was held out to us that we should see you in the North, which would indeed have given us great pleasure, as we often, very often, talk, and still oftener think, about you.

It is some months since I heard from Moxon. I learned in Scotland that the Bookselling Trade was in a deplorable state, and that nothing was saleable but Newspapers on the Revolutionary side. So that I fear, unless our poor Friend be turned patriot, he cannot be prospering at present.

We, thank God, are all well, and should be very glad to hear the same of yourself, and Brother and Sister. My Son William is gone to Carlisle as my Sub-distributor, how long to remain there, Heaven knows! He is likely to come in for a broken head, as he expects to be enrolled as a Special Constable, for the protection of the Gaols and Cathedral at Carlisle, and for Rose Castle—the Bishop's country residence which has been threatened. But no more of these disagreeables. My heart is full of kindness towards you, and I wish much to hear of you. The state of my eyes has compelled me to use Mrs W's Pen. Most affectionately yours,

Wm. Wordsworth

Notwithstanding the flourish above, I have written to my Son to stay at home and guard his Stamps.

Address: Sam¹ Rogers Esqʳᵉ, St. James' Place, London.

M. G. K. *994. W. W. to Lady Frederick Bentinck*

Rydal Mount, Nov. 9. [1831]

My dear Lady Frederick,

. . . You are quite right, dear Lady Frederick, in congratulating me on my late ramble in Scotland. I set off with a severe inflammation in one of my eyes, which was removed by being so much in the open air; and for more than a month I scarcely saw a newspaper, or heard of their contents. During this time we almost forgot, my daughter and I, the deplorable state of the country. My spirits rallied, and, with exercise—for I often walked scarcely less than twenty miles a day—and the employment of composing verses amid scenery the most beautiful, and at a season when the foliage was most rich and varied, the time fled away delightfully; and when we came back into the world again, it seemed as if I had waked from a dream that was never to return. We travelled in an open carriage with one horse, driven by Dora; and while we were in the Highlands I walked most of the way by the side of the carriage, which left us leisure to observe the beautiful appearances. The rainbows and coloured mists floating about the hills were more like enchantment than anything I ever saw, even among the Alps. There was in particular, the day we made the tour of Loch Lomond in the steamboat, a fragment of a rainbow, so broad, so splendid, so glorious with its reflection in the calm water, that it astonished every one on board, a party of foreigners especially, who could not refrain from expressing their pleasure in a more lively manner than we are accustomed to do.

My object in going to Scotland so late in the season was to see Sir Walter Scott before his departure. We stayed with him three days, and he quitted Abbotsford the day after we left it. His health has undoubtedly been much shattered, by successive shocks of apoplexy, but his friends say he is so much recovered that they entertain good hopes of his life and faculties being spared. Mr Lockhart tells me that he derived benefit by a change of treatment made by his London physicians, and that he embarked in good spirits.

As to public affairs, I have no hope but in the goodness of Almighty God. The Lords have recovered much of the credit they had lost by their conduct in the Roman Catholic question. As an Englishman I am deeply grateful for the stand which they have made, but I cannot help fearing that they may be seduced or intimidated. Our misfortune is, that those who disapprove of this monstrous bill give way to a belief that nothing can prevent its being passed; and therefore they submit.

As to the cholera, I cannot say it appals me much; it may be in the order of Providence to employ this scourge for bringing the nation to its senses; though history tells us in the case of the plague at Athens, and other like visitations, that men are never so wicked and depraved as when afflictions of that kind are upon them. So that, after all, one must come round to our only support, submission to the will of God, and faith in the ultimate goodness of His dispensations.

I am sorry you did not mention your son, in whose health and welfare and progress in his studies I am always much interested. Pray remember me kindly to Lady Caroline. All here join with

me in presenting their kindest remembrances to yourself; and
believe me, dear Lady Frederick,

Faithfully and affectionately yours,

Wm. Wordsworth.

995. *W. W. to William Rowan Hamilton*

Hamilton
$M(—) G. K(—)$ Nov. 22. 1831.

My dear Mr Hamilton,

You send me showers of verses, which I receive with much
pleasure, as do we all; yet have we fears that this employment
may seduce you from the path of Science, which you seem
destined to tread with so much honour to yourself and profit to
others. Again and again I must repeat, that the composition
of verse is infinitely more of an art than men are prepared to
believe; and absolute success in it depends upon innumerable
minutiae, which it grieves me you should stoop to acquire a
knowledge of. Milton talks of 'pouring easy his unpremeditated
verse.' It would be harsh, untrue, and odious, to say there is
anything like cant in this; but it is not true to the letter, and
tends to mislead. I could point out to you five hundred passages
in Milton upon which labour has been bestowed, and twice five
hundred more to which additional labour would have been
serviceable. Not that I regret the absence of such labour,
because no poem contains more proofs of skill acquired by practice. These observations are not called out by any defects or
imperfections in your last pieces especially: they are equal to
the former ones in effect, have many beauties, and are not inferior in execution; but again I do venture to submit to your
consideration, whether the poetical parts of your nature would
not find a field more favourable to their exercise in the regions
of prose: not because those regions are humbler, but because
they may be gracefully and profitably trod with footsteps less
careful and in measures less elaborate. And now I have done
with the subject, and have only to add, that when you write
verses you would not fail, from time to time, to let me have a
sight of them; provided you will allow me to defer criticism on
your diction and versification till we meet. My eyes are so often

[586]

useless both for reading and writing, that I cannot tax the eyes and pens of others with writing down observations which to indifferent persons must be tedious.

Upon the whole, I am not sorry that your project of going to London at present is dropped. It would have grieved me had you been unfurnished with an introduction from me to Mr Coleridge; yet I know not how I could have given you one—he is often so very unwell. A few weeks ago he had had two attacks of cholera, and appears to be so much broken down that unless I were assured he was something in his better way I could not disturb him by the introduction of any one. His most intimate friend is Mr Green, a man of science and a distinguished surgeon. If to him you could procure an introduction he would let you know the state of Coleridge's health; and to Mr Green, whom I once saw, you might use my name with a view to further your wish, if it were at all needful.

Shakespeare's sonnets (excuse this leap) are not upon the Italian model, which Milton's are; they are merely quatrains with a couplet tacked to the end; and if they depended much upon the versification they would unavoidably be heavy.

One word upon Reform in Parliament, a subject to which somewhat reluctantly you allude. You are a Reformer! Are you an approver of the bill as rejected by the Lords? or, to use Lord Grey's words, anything 'as efficient'? he means, if he means anything, efficient for producing change. Then I earnestly exhort you to devote hours and hours to the study of human nature, in books, in life, and in your own mind; and beg and pray that you will mix with society, not in Ireland and Scotland only, but in England; a Fount of Destiny, which if once poisoned, away goes all hope of quiet progress in well-doing. The Constitution of England, which seems about to be destroyed, offers to my mind the sublimest contemplation which the history of Society and Government have ever presented to it; and for this cause especially, that its principles have the character of preconceived ideas, archetypes of the pure intellect, while they are in fact the results of a humble-minded experience. Think about this. Apply it to what we are threatened with, and farewell.

Wm. Wordsworth.

MS.
M. G. K.

996. *W. W. to Mrs Hemans*

Rydal Mount, Novr 22^d, [1831.][1]

Dear Mrs Hemans,

I will not render this sheet more valueless than at best it will prove, by tedious apologies for not answering your very kind and welcome letter long and long ago. I received it in London, when my mind was in a most uneasy state, and when my eyes were useless both for writing and reading, so that an immediate reply was out of my power; and since, I have been doubtful where to address you. Accept this and something better as my excuse, that I have very often thought of you, with hundreds of good wishes for your welfare and that of your fine Boys, who must recommend themselves to all that come in their way.— Let me thank you in Dora's name for your present of The Remains of Lucretia Davidson,[2] a very extraordinary young Creature, of whom I had before read some account in Mr Southey's Review of this Volume. Surely many things, not often bestowed, must concur to make genius an enviable gift. This truth is painfully forced upon one's attention in reading the effusions and story of this Enthusiast hurried to her grave so early. You have I understand been a good deal in Dublin. The Place, I hope, has less of the fever of intellectual or rather literary ambition than Edinburgh, and is less disquieted by factions and cabals of *persons*—as to those of parties, they must be odious and dreadful enough—but since they have more to do with religion, the adherents of the different creeds perhaps mingle little together, and so the mischief to social intercourse, though great, will be somewhat less.

I am not sure but that Miss Jewsbury has judged well in her determination of going to India. Europe is at present a melancholy Spectacle, and these two Islands are likely to reap the fruit of their own folly and madness in becoming for the present generation the two most unquiet and miserable spots upon the

[1] K. misdates 1832, but Miss Jewsbury was married, and became Mrs Fletcher, in Aug. 1832.

[2] *Amir Khan*, and other poems: the remains of Lucretia Maria Davidson, with a biographical sketch by Samuel F. B. Morse, New York, 1829. The book was reviewed by Southey in the *Q.R.* of Nov. 1829.

Earth. May you, my dear Friend, find the advantage of the poetic Spirit in raising you, in thought at least, above the contentious clouds! Never before did I feel such reason to be grateful for what little inspiration Heaven has graciously bestowed upon my humble Intellect. What you kindly wrote upon the interest you took during your travels in my verses could not but be grateful to me because your own show that in a rare degree you understand and sympathise with me. We are all well, God be thanked. I am a wretched Correspondent, as this Scrawl abundantly shows. I know also that you have far too much, both of receiving and writing Letters, but I cannot conclude without expressing a wish that from time to time you would let us hear from you and yours, and how you prosper. All join with me in kindest remembrance to yourself and your Boys, especially to Charles, of whom we know most. Believe me, dear Mrs Hemans, not the less for my long silence,

faithfully and affectionately yours,

Wm. Wordsworth.

Address: Mrs Hemans, Dublin.

K.   *997. W. W. to Lord Lonsdale*

November 29, [1831.][1]

. . . The nation will now know what Lord Grey meant by his expression, 'a measure equally efficient'. If he meant efficient for a change as great, as sudden, and upon the same principles of spoliation and disfranchisement in the outset as the former bill—and the new constituency to be supplied by its coarse and clumsy contrivances, not to speak of the party injustice of their application—then it must be obvious to all honest men of sound judgment that nothing can prevent a subversion of the existing government by King, Lords, and Commons, and the violation of the present order of society in this country. Such at least is the deliberate opinion of all those friends whose judgment I am accustomed to look up to. One of the ablest things I have read

---

[1] K. misdates 1827; but *cf.* W.'s remarks on Lord Grey in his letter of Nov. 22.

upon the character and tendency of the Reform Bill is in the *North American Review* of four or five months back. The author lays it down—and I think gives irrefragable reasons for his opinion—that the numerical principle adopted, and that of property also, can find no root but in universal suffrage. Being a Republican, and a professed hater and despiser of our modified feudal institutions, he rejoices over the prospect, and his views, though in some points mistaken, for want of sufficient knowledge of English society, are entitled to universal consideration.

M. G. K.   *998. W. W. to J. K. Miller*[1]

Rydal Mount, Kendal, Dec. 17, 1831.[2]

My dear Sir,

You have imputed my silence, I trust, to some cause neither disagreeable to yourself nor unworthy of me. Your letter of the 26th of Nov. had been misdirected to Penrith, where the postmaster detained it some time, expecting probably that I would come to that place, which I have often occasion to visit. When it reached me I was engaged in assisting my wife to make out some of my mangled and almost illegible MSS, which inevitably involved me in endeavours to correct and improve them. My eyes are subject to frequent inflammations, of which I had an attack (and am still suffering from it) while that was going on. You would, nevertheless, have heard from me almost as soon as I received your letter, could I have replied to it in terms in any degree accordant to my wishes. Your exhortations troubled me in a way you cannot be in the least aware of; for I have been repeatedly urged by some of my most valued friends, and at times by my own conscience, to undertake the task you have set before me. But I will deal frankly with you. A conviction of my incompetence to do justice to the momentous subject has

[1] 'The Vicar of Walkeringham (in Nottingham), a much valued friend, who, together with some other correspondents, particularly the late revered and lamented Hugh James Rose, had urged Mr W. to exercise those powers, in writing on public affairs, which he had displayed twenty years before, in his "Essay on the Convention of Cintra".' M.

[2] For D. W. to H. C. R. Dec. 1, 1831, *v. C.R.*, p. 224.

kept me, and I fear will keep me, silent. My sixty-second year will soon be completed, and though I have been favoured thus far in health and strength beyond most men of my age, yet I feel its effects upon my spirits; they sink under a pressure of apprehension to which, at an earlier period of my life, they would probably have been superior. There is yet another obstacle: I am no ready master of prose writing, having been little practised in the art. This last consideration will not weigh with you; nor would it have done with myself a few years ago; but the bare mention of it will serve to show that years have deprived me of *courage*, in the sense the word bears when applied by Chaucer to the animation of birds in spring time.

What I have already said precludes the necessity of otherwise confirming your assumption that I am opposed to the spirit you so justly characterise.[1] To your opinions upon this subject my judgment (if I may borrow your own word) 'responds'. Providence is now trying this empire through her political institutions. Sound minds find their expediency in principles; unsound, their principles in expediency. On the proportion of these minds to each other the issue depends. From calculations of partial expediency in opposition to general principles, whether those calculations be governed by fear or presumption, nothing but mischief is to be looked for; but, in the present stage of our affairs, the class that does the most harm consists of well-intentioned men, who, being ignorant of human nature, think that they may help the thorough-paced reformers and revolutionists to a *certain* point, then stop, and that the machine will stop with them. After all, the question is, fundamentally, one of piety and morals; of piety, as disposing men who are anxious for social improvement to wait patiently for God's good time; and of morals, as guarding them from doing evil that good may come, or thinking that any ends *can* be so good as to justify wrong means for attaining them. In fact, means, in the concerns of this life, are infinitely more important than ends, which are to be valued mainly according to the qualities and virtues requisite for their attainment; and the best test of an end being good is the purity of the means, which, by the laws of God and our nature,

---

[1] As revolutionary. M.

must be employed in order to secure it. Even the interests of eternity become distorted the moment they are looked at through the medium of impure means. Scarcely had I written this, when I was told by a person in the Treasury, that it is intended to carry the Reform Bill by a new creation of peers. If this be done, the constitution of England will be destroyed, and the present Lord Chancellor,[1] after having contributed to murder it, may consistently enough pronounce, in his place, its *éloge funèbre!*

I turn with pleasure to the sonnets you have addressed to me, and if I did not read them with unqualified satisfaction, it was only from consciousness that I was unworthy of the encomiums they bestowed upon me.

Among the papers I have lately been arranging, are passages that would prove, as forcibly as anything of mine that has been published, you were not mistaken in your supposition that it is the habit of my mind inseparably to connect loftiness of imagination with that humility of mind which is best taught in Scripture.

Hoping that you will be indulgent to my silence, which has been, from various causes, protracted contrary to my wish,

Believe me to be, dear sir,

Very faithfully yours,

Wm. Wordsworth.

MS.[2]   *999. W. W. to John Forster*

Rydal Mount Decr. 19th, 1831

Sir,

I was much concerned to learn from your letter and its enclosure that Mr L. Hunt was suffering from ill health and embarrassed circumstances; to the relief of which I should be happy to contribute as far as my subscription goes, and regret that from my sequestered situation here I can do little more. The consideration of Mr Hunt being a Man of Genius and Talent, and in distress, will, I trust, prevent your proposal

---

[1] Lord Brougham.

[2] From a copy made by M. W. The 'proposal' was to relieve Hunt's financial difficulties by the publication, by subscription, of an expensive edition of his Poems. The book appeared in the following year.

being taken as a test of opinion, and that the benevolent purpose will be promoted by Men of all parties.

I am, Sir, sincerely yours

W. Wordsworth.

MS.   *1000. W. W. to J. G. Lockhart*

Storrs near Bowness, 26th Dec^{er} [1831]

My dear Sir,

The Newspapers report that your Son, who has languished
under so long an illness, is no more. Pray excuse my breaking
in upon you and Mrs Lockhart with my condolences and those of
Mrs W. and my family, upon this occasion. Of the measure of
your parental grief, or of the degree to which you may have
cause for being thankful to the Almighty for this removal, it is
impossible that I or anyone can judge; but I know that it is
some comfort under such trials to be assured of the sympathy
of friends; and I trust that mine will be acceptable.

How will this event affect Sir Walter? is a question many will
put to themselves, as I have done.

We should be glad to hear at your leisure and entire convenience how Mrs Lockhart supports herself under this loss, and
also if you have heard of Sir Walter.

Believe me my dear Sir

very faithfully yours

Wm. Wordsworth.

Address: J. G. Lockhart Esq, Sussex Place, Regents Park,
London.

MS.   *1001. W. W. to John Gardner*

Rydal Mount Kendal 27th Decb—1831

My dear Sir,

I thanked you through Mr Boxall[1] for an obliging Letter received some months ago. I now write from a hope that you may

---

[1] Sir William Boxall (1800–79), R.A. 1863, a portrait painter especially
noted for his delineation of female beauty. He had painted W. in the
previous year.

be able to assist me in a matter which *I* am able to make little progress in; I have a Nephew[1] who must now be settled in a profession—he has chosen the medical one—Surgeon and Apothecary probably; and my wish is to place him in the House and under the care of some respectable Practitioner—in a large Town, not excluding London—if that should be thought advisable by those of my Friends who are judges in the case. Do let me know what you think best—and at what rate annually he might be placed in London. I have long had this matter upon my mind—this day I have written to a Friend in Birmingham, who promised some time ago to make inquiries, and also to Dr Calvert of London.

How is Mr Boxall—and how are you yourself going on. I had a most charming Tour of 5 autumnal weeks in Scotland especially in the Highlands. My Daughter was my sole Companion, she driving a little four wheeled Phaeton, and I mainly walking by her side at the rate of 15 or 20 miles a day. The weather was a good deal broken but the appearances most exquisite of faded and fading foliage, and of mists rainbows and sunbeams. We went as far as the Isle of Mull, but the Season was too far advanced for Staffa. We stopped three days with Sir Walter Scott —but now it strikes me that I told you all this through Mr Boxall.

Lord Grey cleaves obstinately to what he calls the principle of his Bill, in other words to his presumptive rashness, which will throw the whole Country into Confusion. The preponderance in the Constitution given to the ten pound Raters or Renters, call them what you may, is irreconcileable with a representation of the property even of the several places for which they will have to [ ],[2] and if so, still more is it incompatible with a representation of the other interests of the Country. Let but short Parliaments follow, as they must, and there will be an end to all traces of a *deliberative* assembly, the nominal Representatives will become mere delegates or tools of the narrow views of the most selfish, perhaps, and ignorant class of

---

[1] i.e. John, son of R. W., known in the family as 'John of Keswick' (because he lived there with his mother) to distinguish him from John son of W. W. and John son of C. W.　　　　　[2] *word omitted.*

the community—I say ignorant because half knowledge in matters of this kind is worse than no knowledge. Remember me kindly to Mr Boxall and believe me faithfully your obliged

Wm Wordsworth.

I am sorry to send this Letter unfranked—but I am afraid of its being detained, on account of the Holiday, should I enclose it in an official one.

Address: John Gardner Esqr, 16 Foley Place, Portland Place, London.

K.   *1002. W. W. to Basil Montagu*

[1831.]

... What you Londoners may think of public affairs I know not; but I forebode the not very distant overthrow of the Institutions under which this country has so long prospered. The Liberals of our neighbourhood tell me that the mind of the nation has outgrown its Institutions; rather say, I reply, that it has shrunk and dwindled from them, as the body of a sick man does from his clothes.

We are on fire with zeal to educate the poor, which would be all very well if that zeal did not blind us to what we stand still more in need of, an improved education of the middle and upper classes; which ought to begin in our great Public Schools, thence ascend to the Universities (from which the first suggestion should come), and descend to the very nursery.

If the books from which your *Selections*[1] are made were the favourite reading of men of rank and influence, I should dread little from the discontented in any class. But what hope is there of such a rally in our debilitated intellects? The soundest hearts I meet with are, with few exceptions, Americans. They seem to have a truer sense of the benefits of our government than we ourselves have. Farewell, with many thanks.

Yours faithfully,

W. W.

[1] *Selections from the Works of Taylor, Hooker, Hall, and Lord Bacon, with an Analysis of the Advancement of Learning.*

K(—)   *1003. W. W. to Lord Lonsdale*

[Dec. 1831][1]

. . . The altered bill does little or nothing to prevent the dangers of the former. . . . The mischief already done can never be repaired. The scheme of regulating representation by arbitrary lines of property or numbers is impracticable; such distinctions will melt away before the inflamed passions of the people. No government will prove sufficiently strong to maintain them, till the novelty which excites a thirst for further change shall be worn off, and the new constituency have a chance of acquiring by experience the habits of a temperate use of their powers. A preponderance so large being given to ten-pound renters, the interest and property of the large towns where they are to vote will not be represented, much less that of the community at large; for these ten-pound renters are mainly men without substance, and live, as has been said, from hand to mouth. Then will follow frequent Parliaments—triennial perhaps at first—which will convert the representatives into mere slavish delegates, as they now are in America, under the dictation of ignorant and selfish numbers, misled by unprincipled journalists, who, as in France, will—no few of them—find their way into the House of Commons, and so the last traces of a deliberative assembly will vanish. But enough of this melancholy topic. I resided fifteen months in France, during the heat of the Revolution, and have some personal experience of the course which these movements must take, if not fearlessly resisted, before the transfer of legislative power takes place.

MS.   *1004. W. W. to John Gardner*

Rydal Mount Jan^{ry} 4th 1832 [2]

My dear Sir,

Having reason to expect other letters upon the same subject, and especially one from a valued Friend of mine, a Physician in

[1] K. misdates 1827. But the 'altered Bill' is almost certainly the third Reform Bill, brought into the H. of C. in Dec. 1831, and passed in the following Jan.   [2] Miswritten 1831.

Town—who I hope will find leisure to confer with you; I delayed to answer your friendly letter as soon as it deserved. For the attention you have paid to my wishes I feel truly obliged.

Is the *premium* a compensation in the case of an apprentice for board and lodging? I suppose it is, and if so the expence is not more than would be met without difficulty. As to the question of an open shop, I am incompetent to judge, but I agree with my Friend in thinking that *hard work* and what he calls *blind labour*, may be attended with advantages which are apt to be underrated. At the same time I should have no satisfaction in thinking my nephew should be engaged in that Profession, unless his mind were likely to be cultivated, and he were led, and taught by example, to regard the practice of medicine as an intellectual pursuit.

I should greatly prefer his being placed in the Family of a married Man for the sake of his manners, and the kindly influence of some portion of domestic female society. Nevertheless this might be waived in favour of his being placed, were that possible, with some younger unmarried Person, who as being single, might be likely to take more interest in him as a friend and companion.

My nephew[1] is 17 years of age, I think has good dispositions, fair talents and a strong desire to improve himself—and likely to take a lively interest in his profession, which is entirely his own choice—but he is shy and awkward in his manners, tho' tall and well looking. He is not a good scholar, but I cannot think justice has been done him at school. And I trust as he is fond of miscellaneous reading, that hereafter he will do justice to *himself* by proper application.

You will let me hear from you again as soon as you have leisure, and any thing further to communicate. Give my kind regards to Mr Boxall and believe me very sincerely your much obliged

Wm Wordsworth

Address: John Gardner Esq. 16 Foley Place.

---

[1] i.e. John, the son of R. W.; W. W. and C. W. were the boy's guardians, *v. M.Y.*, p. 743, and letter of June 22, 1832.

MS.   *1005. W. W. to John Gardner*

Rydal Mount, Friday Jany 19th [1832]

My dear Sir

Having the opportunity of a Frank, I merely write a line, to say, that having taken my Nephew from School I am anxious to learn whether you are likely to procure a situation for him. I have said nothing about taking him yourself, because this was placing you in a delicate situation; this business is mainly for Dr Calvert,[1] who, I am very sorry, is not likely to see you. On this point I will only state my firm belief, that you would not take him yourself if you thought he could do better elsewhere— Being therefore easy as to that consideration, I will say nothing upon the subject, nor press a matter which might be inconvenient to you

farewell

(*Unsigned*)

I am going to press with another edition of my poems to be sold for 24 shillings in 4 vols—would that answer?

MS.[2]   *1006. W. W. to John Hymers*

Rydal Mount, Jany 26th [1832]

My dear Sir,

The proposal to paint my Portrait was made to Mr Pickersgill thro' my friend Mr Quillinan, and an answer received thro' the same channel, which led me to expect Mr P. at Rydal in October last. I had deferred answering your obliging Letter a few days in the expectation of hearing that Mr Quillinan had returned from Paris to London, and would be able to tell me why I had neither seen Mr P. nor heard from him. All that I know is that about the time he was expected here, he was at Paris painting several distinguished Persons there, La Fayette and Cuvier among the number—these engagements probably detained him longer than he expected, as I am this moment told that it is only about a week since he returned to London. I have

---

[1] Dr John Calvert, son of William C. (*v. E.L.*).
[2] Printed in the *Eagle*, the St. John's Coll. Magazine.

no doubt but that as soon as Mr Quillinan returns he will see Mr P. and I shall be able to answer more satisfactorily the enquiries which yourself and other Fellows of your Col: have done me the honor to make upon the subject.

Your message has been communicated to William who is well, and not discontented with his situation at Carlisle. The obliging reference in your Letter to Henry Cookson[1] was mentioned to his Mother, who is at present at Ambleside with her Daughters. We were glad to see his name so high after the fears which had been felt by his friends lest he should break down altogether. I congratulate you upon one of your Pupils being so high upon the Tripos—and notice with regret that St John's has not made so great a figure as usual.

Would you be so kind as to let me know, at your leisure, what advantages, on the score of economy, a sizar has at St John's—and whether there are any *serious* objections to a person entering and remaining in that rank? My Brother-in-Law Mr Thos Hutchinson is about to send his Son to Sedbergh School with a view to his going to St John's and would be glad, as we all would be, to be able to form an estimate of the expense, and particularly as compared with that of a Pensioner.

The state of my eyes (tho' not bad) obliges me to use an amanuensis which I hope you will excuse. The Ladies beg their kind remembrances of you.

and I am my d^r Sir very truly yours
Wm Wordsworth

Address: John Hymers Esqr, St. John's College, Cambridge.

Hutchins.
K.

1007. W. W. to John Kenyon

Rydal Mount, 26th Jan^y, [1832.]

My dear Mr Kenyon,

You have enriched my house by a very valuable present, an entire collection of all that it is desirable to possess among Hogarth's prints—the box also contained a quarto volume,

---

[1] *v. M.Y.*, p. 529.

'Hogarth Illustrated,' and 3 Vols of a French work for Mr Southey, which shall be forwarded to him. I have been thus particular as because there was no Letter within the Box perhaps it was not made up under your own eye—and I am now at a loss where to direct to you.

We are great admirers of Hogarth, and there are perhaps few houses to which such a collection would be more welcome; and living so much in the Country, as we all do, it is both gratifying and instructive to have such scenes of London life to recur to as this great master has painted.

You are probably aware that he was of Westmorland extraction, his name is very common hereabouts, and it is amusing to speculate on what his genius might have produced if, instead of being born and bred in London, whither his Father went from West[d], he had been early impressed by the romantic scenery of this neighbourhood, and had watched the manners and employments of our rustics. It is remarkable that his pictures, differing in this from the Dutch and Flemish Masters, are almost exclusively confined to indoor scenes or city life. Is this to be regretted? I cannot but think it is, for he was a most admirable *painter*, as may be seen by his works in the British Gallery; and how pleasant would it have been to have had him occasionally show his knowledge of character, manners, and passion by groups under the shade of Trees, and by the side of Waters in appropriate rural dresses. He reminds me both of Shakespeare and Chaucer; but these great Poets seem happy in softening and diversifying their views of life, as often as they can, by metaphors and images from rural nature; or by shifting the scene of action into the quiet of groves or forests. What an exquisite piece of relief of this kind occurs in The Merchant of Venice —where, after the agitating trial of Antonio, we have Lorenzo and Jessica sitting in the open air on the bank on which the moonlight is sleeping—but enough.

Since I last heard from you I have received, and carefully read with great pleasure, the poems of your friend Baillie.[1] The scenes among which they were written are mainly unknown to me, for I never was farther south in France than St. Valier on

[1] i.e. Benjamin Bailey, *v.* Letter to Kenyon of Sept. 9, 1831.

the Rhone, where I turned off to the Grand Chartreuse, a glorious place—were you ever there? I think you told me you were.

Mr B. has, however, interested me very much in his sketches of those countries, and strengthened the desire I have had all my life to see them, particularly the Roman Antiquities there, which H. C. Robinson tells me are greatly superior to any in Italy, a few in Rome excepted. I do not know where Mr Baillie is now to be addressed, and beg, therefore, if you be in communication with him, or with any of his friends who are, you would be so kind as to have my thanks conveyed to him, both for his little volume and the accompanying letter.

It is now time to say a word or two about ourselves. We are all well, except my sister, who, you will be sorry to hear, has been five weeks confined to her room by a return of the inflammatory complaint which shattered her constitution three years ago. She is, God be thanked, convalescent, and will be able to take her place at our fireside in a day or two, if she goes on as well as lately.

We long to know something about yourself, Mrs Kenyon, and your Brother. Pray write to us soon.

We have had a most charming winter for weather—Hastings could scarcely be warmer, and as to beauty the situation of Rydal Mount at this season is matchless. I shall direct to your Brother-in-law's House, as the best chance for my letter reaching you. Mrs Wordsworth, sister, daughter and Miss Hutchinson join me in kindest remembrances to yourself and Mrs Kenyon.

Farewell, and believe me, with every good wish,

Faithfully yours,

Wm. Wordsworth.

My son Wm is at Carlisle, as my Sub-Distributor, and pretty well. John quite well, and happy with his excellent and amiable wife—a better Living would not be amiss—but where is it to come from? We conservators are out of date.

W. W.

Address: John Kenyon Esqre, John Carter's Esqre, 39 Devonshire Place, London

MS.   *1008. W. W. to John Gardner*

[p.m. Feb. 3, 1832]

My dear Sir

Your very acceptable letter I sit down to answer, as soon as I am able—not having seen my Nephew till yesterday. I am very much gratified by the prospect of his being placed under your care being assured that he will find protection and instruction in a situation most favourable to him—and were he my own Son I should send him off to you at once. But my position in regard to him is a delicate one. His Mother is living, and married to a Person with whom I have no intimacy—and she hesitates about his being sent to London, preferring his being placed for a couple of years in some country Town, naming Carlisle—to this I decidedly object, as would his other Guardian Dr Wordsworth. And as I do not find that his Mother is disposed to press the point of his not going to London—I consider *that* at present as his destiny, and am truly happy at the thought of his being placed with you, as I have said before.

Previous to this however, circumstanced as I am in respect to him—something is due to form, and I am sure that your delicacy will not be wounded when I state, that I should be obliged if you would furnish me with a reference to any Practitioner, or Person of note, who would give me such Testimony, (as might go further than my own opinion) of your merit and character, towards satisfying his Mother, and my fellow-guardian (who has not yet been consulted) that I had not taken so important a step without due precaution.

I have examined the youth this day in Latin. Justice cannot have been done to him at School, or he would have known more —I am afraid you will find him very backward. Hence I have great pleasure in the plan you propose in having a Teacher for him together with your own Nephew—to whom I hope he may recommend himself, as I believe him to be of an amiable disposition: and well inclined to improve himself.

I should be glad to write more but I am very much tired having had a series of hard work for the last two months. Of course no time must be lost—and he shall be prepared to go to London as soon [as] this point is settled.

> With great respect I remain d^r Sir
>> faithfully yours
>>> Wm Wordsworth

Give my kind regards to Mr Boxall.

Address: John Gardner Esqre, Foley Place, Portland Place, London.

1009. *W. W. to Lord Lonsdale*

M(—) *G*(—) *K*(—)

> Rydal Mount, Feb. 17th, 1832.

My Lord,

. . . As you have done me the honour of asking my opinion on Lord H.'s[1] letter, I will give it without reserve. . . . The facts upon which Lord H.'s proposal of compromise is grounded are an increased majority in the Commons in favour of the bill, and a belief that the Ministers have a *carte blanche* for creating Peers to carry it. . . . Is it not in the power of any councillors having access to the King to convince him not only of the ruinous tendency of such a step, but to make him feel, as a point of duty, that whatever power the forms of law may give him to create Peers for setting aside their deliberate resolve, the *spirit* of the Constitution allows him no right to do so? for the application of such power to particular emergencies is subversive of the principle for which the Peers mainly exist. Again, the Ministers opened the question of reform with a most solemn declaration that it was a measure indispensable for the preservation of the Constitution, and adopted in order to preserve it. Yet for the sake of carrying their bill they are prepared to destroy a vital organ of that Constitution. A virtual destruction it certainly

---

[1] i.e. Lord Harrowby, 1762–1847, President of the Council, 1812–27, a conservative with liberal opinions. He refused the premiership in 1827, and believing that the 'time for some measure of reform is come' tried to effect a compromise with Grey. In Dec. 1831 he issued a circular letter to members of the H. of Lords trying to avert the creation of new peers, but failed to get definite terms from either side, and he and those who acted with him were known as the 'waverers'.

would be; for it would convert the House of Lords into a mere slave of any succeeding Ministry, which, should it not bend to threats, would immediately create new votes to counterbalance the Opposition. Cannot, then, Lord Grey and his coadjutors be brought—by a respect for reason, or by a sense of shame from being involved in such a contradiction and absurdity—to desist from that course? . . .

As to the alternative of compromise, I agree with Mr. Southey in thinking that little is to be gained by it but time for profiting by contingencies. Would the House of Lords be sure of making such alterations in their committee as would render the bill much less mischievous? or, if they should, would the Lower House pass the bill so amended? The manner in which the committee of the Commons dealt with it is far from encouraging. . . . Suppose, however, the bill to be much improved in passing through the committee of the Lords, and accepted by the Commons, how do we then stand? We have a House of Lords, not overwhelmed indeed by new members, but in spirit broken, and brought down upon its knees. The bill is passed, and Parliament, I presume, speedily dissolved; for the agitators of the political unions would clamour for this, which neither the present Ministry, nor any likely to succeed them, would resist, even did they think it right to do so. Then comes a new House of Commons, to what degree radical, under the best possible modification of the present bill, one fears to think. It proposes measures which the House of Lords would resist as revolutionary, but dares not for fear of being served in the way that was threatened to secure the passing of the reform bill; and so we hasten step by step to the destruction of that Constitution in form, the spirit of which had been destroyed before. . . .

If a new reform bill cannot be brought forward and carried by a strong appeal to the sense, and not to the passions, of the country, I think there is no rational ground for hope. And here one is reminded of the folly and the rashness, not to touch upon the injustice, of creating such a gap in the old constituency as it is scarcely possible to fill up without endangering the existence of the State. Nevertheless, I cannot but think that the country might still be preserved from revolution by a more sane Ministry, which would undertake the question of reform with prudence and sincerity, combining with that measure wiser views in finance. . . .

If, after all, I should be asked how I would myself vote, if it had been my fortune to have a seat in the House of Lords, I must say that I should oppose the second reading, though with my eyes open to the great hazard of doing so. My support however would be found in standing by a great *principle*; for, without being unbecomingly personal, I may state to your Lordship, that it has ever been the habit of my mind to trust that expediency will come out of fidelity to principles, rather than to seek my principles of action in calculations of expediency.

With this observation I conclude, trusting your Lordship will excuse my having detained you so long.

I have the honour to be, most faithfully,
your much obliged,
Wm. Wordsworth.

MS.   *1010. W. W. to Sir Robert Inglis*

Rydal Mount Feb^ry [p.m. Feb. 20 1832]

My dear Sir,

I am not sure that I am doing right by troubling you with the enclosed, especially as I have the intention of following it up successively with two or three of its fellows, but I wish to spare the Com^tee the expense of postage, and I hope by this precaution your privilege will not be drawn too much upon—and that you will excuse me giving you the trouble of transmitting the Papers to their proper destination, when the rest shall have been received.

The Declaration has had very good success among the scattered population of our extensive Parish—we have no dissenting place of Worship among us, and had it not been that the minds of some are poisoned by a Radical Whig and Dissenting Journal printed at Kendal, the Papers would have been signed by almost every one.

I hope that your own health, and that of Lady Inglis, are

good. I have not seen Mr Southey for a long time but I understand that he is more than usually well.

Believe me d^r Sir Robt

very faithfully yours

Wm Wordsworth.

Address: Sir R. H. Inglis, Bart., M.P., Manchester Buildings, Westminster, London.

MS.
K(—)

1011. W. W. to Henry Taylor

Rydal Mount, Kendal

Feby 23^d [1832][1]

My dear Sir,

When I was over at Southeys the other day he enquired about two Vols. of Tinaboschi supposed to be left with us by you or your Father; if we received them which no doubt you will distinctly remember pray let us know. They cannot be found in our House after the most diligent search—and I conclude if they were left with us they must have been sent to S.—but none of us recollect any thing about the matter.

Will you have the kindness to two penny Post the enclosed— I hope your Father and Mother, and Miss Fenwick are well— We have had Dr Arnold and his family staying his Christmas Vacation, at the foot of our hill—they enjoyed themselves mightily—the weather having been delightful.—The Lords being threatened with destruction I say nothing of Politics

ever faithfully yours

W. Wordsworth.

K(—)

1012. W. W. to Lord Lonsdale

Rydal Mount, Feb. 24th, 1832.

My Lord,

. . . The ministers have declared over and over that they will not abate a jot of the *principle* of the bill. Through the whole of the debates in both houses, but particularly in the Commons,

---

[1] K. misdates 1831, but in Feb. of that year W. was not at Rydal, and the Lords were not threatened.

there has been a confusion between principle and the rules and measures of applying principle. The main or fundamental principle of this bill is an assumed necessity for an increase of democratic power in the legislature; accordingly, the ministers have resolved upon a sweeping destruction. This, which may be called a rule, or subsidiary principle, has been applied to the existing constituency in its three great branches,—the Burgage Tenures, the Freemen, and the Freeholders. What havoc has been made in the first we all know. The second, the Freemen, were destroyed, and are restored. Upon the third I cannot speak with the precision which I could wish, not distinctly recollecting the manner in which the votes of a portion of this body are to be affected by the franchise conferred upon them as £10 voters in towns, or retained as Freemen. None of this class of voters have been deprived of their right of voting without an equivalent, so that the change which time has effected in making—by the reduction in the value of money—the body of Freeholders so democratic, is left in its full force, and made more dangerous by new circumstances. Now, is it to be expected that the Lords in committee could succeed in a scheme for a less sweeping and less unjust destruction of the old constituency? Lord H. himself does not seem to expect it.

The only source, then, to which we can look for any improvement must be in supplying the gap in a less objectionable way. Numbers and property are the principles here. In order to foresee how the Ministry are likely to act, we must inquire how their power is composed. They know themselves that if it were not for the reform bill they must go out instantly. As constitutional Whigs, supposed to be actuated by a sincere wish to preserve the British Constitution, the leaders of them are already, as a party, annihilated. They are the tools of men bent on the destruction of Church and State. Even in their opinions many who continue to call themselves Whigs are scarcely by a shade distinguishable from the Radicals. But though such is the character of so many of their prominent leaders, there is diffused through the country a large body of Whig partisans, who, could their eyes be opened, would cease to support them, especially if they had hopes of a more moderate measure from other quarters—but they are not likely to be undeceived till too late. The Ministry, I repeat, are under Radical dictation; does not the mere act of the late appointment to the Secretaryship of War show it? Still further to propitiate the political unions, Hume[1] and Warburton will follow him into office, who can say how soon? Whatever, therefore, the Ministry in conscience think prudent and proper, they would not have the courage to act upon it, even supposing, as Lord H. suggests, that the more moderate men in the House, and those who have the fear of a Radical Parliament hanging over their heads, should support such improvement coming from the Lords. The Ministry would act, as your Lordship anticipates, by creating new peers, by seduction, and, I lament to say, by intimidation, and encouraging or conniving at agitation out of doors.

But to come to particulars. Could the £10 franchise be altered, or the delegation—for I will not call it representation—from London and its neighbourhood? As to the large towns all over the country, a worse source for a new constituency than £10 voters, they do not—in my judgment—contain. But, take smaller places, and less populous districts. Mr Senhouse thinks £10 not a bad qualification for Cumberland. Look then at Cockermouth, and read Mr Green's late advertisement. He may be a man of poor talents, and sorry discretion, but he is no stranger there. He was born, bred, and has long been a resident in the place. He may therefore reasonably be supposed to be acquainted with the present opinions and dispositions of the £10 renters in that town, to whom he would recommend himself, in the event of the bill passing. He tells them 'that he has for many years been reproached for being a Jacobin, a Radical, and a Leveller'—unjustly, he insinuates,—that a reform is wanted for making *a great change* in the present state of things. 'Do not, however, suppose,' he adds, 'that I wish to see reform run into revolution. The conduct of the King, forming as it does a glorious contrast to that of most of the Sovereigns that for half a century have appeared in Europe, *has justly entitled him to the*

---

[1] Joseph Hume, 1777–1855, for thirty years a leader of the Radicals in Parliament, famous for his attacks on financial abuses, and for his advocacy of 'retrenchment'. For Warburton *v.* p. 919.

preservation of his crown, etc. The conduct of the Ministers, too, who have aided and counselled him in his efforts for the public good, must not be forgotten; they all, or nearly all, belong to— or are connected with—the hereditary aristocracy, and by their services have at once entitled themselves to our gratitude,' etc., etc. Now what is all this but to say that the moment the king or the aristocracy do not please Mr. G. and his future constituents he will turn upon them, and, if he can, will destroy the monarchy and peerage together. Judge, my Lord, of my indignation when I read this trash—contemptible, were it not so pernicious in this emergency—addressed to the inhabitants of my native town.

Now for the delegation of London, etc., with the vast population there and in its neighbourhood, to back the agitators whenever they shall choose to call upon it. Can Lord H. expect that the Ministry would consent to any improvement in this department? Yet nothing is more clear to a sane mind than that the government by King, Lords, and Commons, and not only government, but property, in a state of society so artificial as ours, cannot long stand up against such a pressure. When I was in London last spring I mixed a good deal with the Radicals, and know from themselves what their aims are, and how they expect to accomplish them. One person at least, now high in office, is looked up to as their future head, and allowed at present to play a false part. It is not rationally to be expected that the present ministry would allow the delegation, as I have called it, of London and its neighbourhood, to be of a less obnoxious construction than the bill makes it.

Let us now look at the other side—the uncompromising resistance and its apprehended consequences in swamping the House of Lords, and passing the bill in its present state, not perhaps without popular commotions. The risk attending such resistance with this or any ministry not composed of firm-minded and truly intelligent men is, I own, so great to alarm any one; but I should have no fear of popular commotion were the Government what it might be, and ought to be. The overthrow of the government of Charles X, and the late events in Bristol, prove what mischief may be done by a mere rabble, if the executive be either faithless or foolish. Seeing the perilous crisis to which we are come, I am

3394.5

F

nevertheless persuaded that, could a conservative Ministry be established, the certain ruin that will follow on the passing of this bill might be avoided. Thousands of respectable people have supported both bills, not as approving of a measure of this character or extent, but from fear that otherwise no reform at all would take place. Such men would be ready to support more moderate plans if they found the executive in hands that could be relied upon. Too true it is, no doubt, as Lord H. has observed, that opinions as to the extent and nature of advisable reform differ so widely as to throw great difficulties in the way of a new bill. But these, in my humble opinion, might be got over, so far as to place us upon ground allowing hope for the future.

In looking at the rule for applying the principle of numbers to supply a part of the new constituency, or govern the retention of the old, I have only considered London and its neighbourhood. As far as I know, this principle is altogether an innovation, and what contradictions and anomalies does it involve? The Lords would not probably attempt an improvement here. Had such a rule come down to us from past times, had we been habituated to it, it might have been possible to improve its application. But how can any thinking man expect that with the example of America and France before us—not deterring the people, but inciting them to imitation—this innovation can ever find rest but in universal suffrage. Manchester is only to have two members, with its vast population, and Cockermouth is to retain one with its bare five thousand! Will not Manchester and Birmingham, etc., point on the one hand to the increased representation of London and its neighbourhood, and on the other to the small places which, for their paltry numbers, are allowed to retain one or two votes in the House; and to towns of the size of Kendal and Whitehaven, which for the first time are to send each a member? Will Manchester and Birmingham be content? Is it reasonable that they should be content with the principle of numbers so unjustly and absurdly applied? This anomaly, which is ably treated in the [North] American Review, brings one to the character and tendency of this reform.

As Sir J. B. Walsh observes in his pamphlet, from which I saw an extract the other day in a newspaper: 'Extensive, sudden, and experimental innovation is diametrically opposed to the principle of progressiveness, which in every art, science, and path of human intellect is gradual. . . .'

. . . Our Constitution was not preconceived and planned beforehand; it grew under the protection of Providence, as a skin grows to, with, and for the human body. Our Ministers would flay this body, and present us, instead of its natural skin, with a garment made to order, which, if it be not rejected, will prove such a shirt as, in the fable, drove Hercules to madness and self-destruction. May God forgive that part of them who, acting in this affair with their eyes open, have already gone so far towards committing a greater political crime than any recorded in history! . . .

1013. *W. W. to the Editor of the Philological Museum*
K(—)

[Rydal Mount, 1832.]

. . . Your letter reminding me of an expectation I some time since held out to you, of allowing some specimens of my translation from the *Æneid* to be printed in the *Philological Museum*, was not very acceptable; for I had abandoned the thought of ever sending into the world any part of that experiment—it was nothing more—an experiment begun for amusement, and, I now think, a less fortunate one than when I first named it to you. Having been displeased, in modern translations, with the additions of incongruous matter, I began to translate with a resolve to keep clear of that fault, by adding nothing; but I became convinced that a spirited translation can scarcely be accomplished in the English language without admitting a principle of compensation. On this point, however, I do not wish to insist; and merely send the following passage, taken at random, from a desire to comply with your request. . . .

W. W.

1014. *W. W. to John Marshall*
MS.

[Feb.–March 1832]

My dear Sir,

I have much pleasure in answering your letter, and will begin with the latter part first.

Were it not for the State of the Times, I should say without scruple that unless the price were very high with reference to the present rents the purchase of the Derwentwater Estate,[1] to sell out again in parcels, would be a promising speculation—provided the Purchaser did not care about disfiguring the Country when he came to divide it. If he should have any reserve of that kind, even in favourable times—there might be a doubt then of his making much of his bargain. One of my own neighbours, and a friend, has an eye to purchase with *that view*—and whether he or any one else should succeed, in such a plan, the beauty of that neighbourhood would be destroyed. Two or three Gentlemen's Houses might be erected under good taste with advantage, because it would lead to the preservation of the woods and other improvements. But if the most beautiful and commanding sites were broken up for paltry Cottages, rows of lodging houses, and inns with stables etc., which would be the most likely way to make money of the thing, the Lake and neighbourhood would be ruined for ever. Summarily I should say that if the Property could be bought, so as to pay a tolerable interest at present, it would be an adviseable purchase for any one who had money to command: except for the political convulsions with which we are threatened, and especially as far as the rents are dependent upon feudal claims, which is a species of private property, that the Revolutionary spirit now at work, will not long keep its hands off. The land lying so near the town will be likely to keep up its price more than other lands that have not that advantage; the future value of the woods, which is now low, one can only guess at. The Derwentwater Estate at Keswick is as to picturesque beauty above all praise—but for a Gentleman's residence its neighbourhood to the town would be a strong objection and especially for the case you mention—viz. the people and strangers having been used to range over it in all directions. A house of moderate size would stand most charmingly, even magnificently, upon a field flanked by Friar's

---

[1] The Derwentwater Estate was confiscated from the last Lord Derwentwater (beheaded in 1716) and given to Greenwich Hospital. It was bought by J. M. for his son John at two-thirds its estimated price (*v.* p. 636 and *Southey* to *John Rickman* Dec. 12, 1832) and remained in the family until a few years ago.

Crag on the right, with Cockshott hill, and Castlet, two beautifully wooded hills, behind and on the left. Upon this spot I
stood a few days ago: but there may possibly, tho' I think not
likely, be still better situations on the property.

Lady W. Gordon's property I know very well, tho' I never
went over it with a view to a choice for sites for building. But
speaking from my recollection I should say that the Greenwich
H. Estate has upon the whole finer views. The Lake never presents itself with that dignity from the Gordon Grounds, which
lie towards the middle of it, and it being only 3 miles long there
is not that stretch of view which you would have from the other
Property—but the Gordon property abounds in beauty and is
unannoyed by the Town. Your Son would observe that the
woods upon it are much inferior in character to the other,
having few trees that can be called Timber.

As to my own opinion, if my fortune were equal to erect a
House correspondent to the dignity of the situation, and sufficient to give me considerable influence over the Town, I should
prefer the G^{ch}H^1 Estate. Lyulph's Tower, on account of its noble
views with the adjoining Dell, I have always reckoned the first
situation among the Lakes, but its timber is poor compared with
the Keswick Property, and the mere ground, excepting the dell,
is in its features, greatly inferior.

I agree with your Son John that the Gordon Estate is over-
planted, and might be exceedingly improved by taste and judgment—he would observe, however, that part of it, and the part
which is nearest Keswick, looks directly over to the only weak
part of the Vale, that which opens to the Ambleside and Penrith
roads—lying between Wallacrag and Laterigg—the site he mentions probably looks on Skiddaw.

In all that I have said, having reference to profit, I reckon
my own opinion, or indeed any one else's, of little value— but
one thing is clear that if the democratic spirit be organized in
Legislation to the extent now wished for, and aimed at by many,
the pecuniary value of every thing in the world of Taste will
sink accordingly; and its intellectual estimation also will erelong
be proportionably affected. Men will neither have time, tran-
quillity, or disposition to think about any such thing. A few

years ago, tho' always apprehensive of a storm, I should have advised you or any friend of whose taste and feeling I think so highly as of yours, to purchase this Property, from a belief that it would be profitable to yourself, and a certainty that it would be a great advantage to the beauty of the neighbourhood, had you kept it in your own hands. At present no doubt it will be bought much lower than at that time, but who can form a conjecture of its value three years hence?

My poor Sister has been confined at least 10 weeks to her room in consequence of another, tho' slighter, attack of inflammation.[1] She has been for some time convalescent, and were it not from apprehension of relapse we should be full of hope that the warm weather would restore her strength which is all that she wants. Her friends might suppose that having been so fond of the country, its prospects, and exercise, she would have been in bad spirits under confinement, but it is not so—she finds compensation in reading, and her time never hangs heavy.

We are pleased to learn from Mrs M. that Ellen's health was so good during the early part of the winter—and that all your family are pretty well; faithfully yours

W. Wordsworth.

Mrs W. joins me in best regards—My Sister writes a few lines to Mrs M.

MS.   **1015. W. W. to Mrs Lawrence[2]**

Rydal Mount 2nd March [? 1832]

My dear Mrs Lawrence,

You have gratified me much by the kind Present of your two elegant Volumes,[3] which I received the day before yesterday by Mr Bolton's Servant; and as Mr B— is only to stop a day or two, and I am going to call upon him this morning I shall request him

---

[1] This statement dates the letter, *v.* my *Life of D. W.*, p. 387.

[2] Wife of Charles Lawrence, of Wavertree Hall, near Liverpool, and a friend of Mrs Hemans.

[3] *Cameos from the Antique; or, The Cabinet of Mythology.* Selections illustrative of the mythology of Greece and Italy, for the use of children, 1831 (other edns. 1833, 1834. Second ed. revised, 1849) and *Pictures, Scriptural and Historical, or, The Cabinet of History*: with poetical selections, religious and moral, for the use of children (1831, revised 1834).

to be the Bearer of this short note of thanks.—Why did you humble yourself to apologize for what I must deem an honor, your selecting a few of my Pieces for your Cabinet.—Almost the whole of yesterday I was engaged with Friends so that I have scarcely had time to glance an eye over the Contents of your little Volumes, but I promise myself much pleasure from perusing them at leisure, for your taste may be depended upon and the object is a judicious one. I am glad there [are many][1] pieces from your own pen.

Allow me to turn to another Subject. It is true that I had been furnished with your address when I was in Town last Spring, but I could neither profit by that nor any good thing, for they were all driven out of my Mind, by the Reform Bill, inflammations in my eyes and the stupid occupation of sitting to four several Artists.—I can assure you that from these and other causes I was in anything but a comfortable state of feeling; and should have proved very sorry company, so that you had a lucky escape in not seeing me.—

Mr Bolton has been so kind as to urge me several times to visit him during this Spring at Liverpool; but I fear I shall not have courage to quit home. Surely you will be tempted to visit our Lakes erelong—the Boltons often mention you with great interest, and I should be truly happy my dear Mrs Lawrence to shew you something of the beauties of our neighbourhood— But I must leave off—Mr Hamilton[2] is my Companion to Storrs, and the Carriage is getting ready

farewell most sincerely

your obliged

W. Wordsworth.

K(—)   *1016. W. W. to John Gardner*

Rydal Mount, March 12th, [1832.]

The intended edition of my poems is to be compressed into four volumes. There will be no additions beyond what appeared

---

[1] are many: MS. may.

[2] Thomas Hamilton (1789–1842), brother of Sir William Hamilton (the metaphysician) and a friend of Scott's. His novel *Cyril Thornton* (1827) had achieved a popular success. He married the widow of Sir R. T. Farquhar and settled at Elleray, John Wilson's house on Windermere.

in *The Keepsake* two or three years ago, and a sonnet or two which have already seen the light.

. . . It is to be apprehended that the French edition will still continue to injure the English sale.

I say nothing of politics. The foolish and wicked only appear to be active, and therefore it is plain that confusion and misery will follow. . . .

M.   *1017. W. W. to C. W.*

Rydal Mount, April 1. 1832.

My dear Brother,

Our dear sister makes no progress towards recovery of strength. She is very feeble, never quits her room, and passes most of the day in, or upon, the bed. She does not suffer much pain, and is very chearful, and nothing troubles her but public affairs and the sense of requiring so much attention. Whatever may be the close of this illness, it will be a profound consolation to you, my dear brother, and to us all, that it is borne with perfect resignation; and that her thoughts are such as the good and pious would wish. She reads much, both religious and miscellaneous works.

If you see Mr Watson,[1] remember me affectionately to him.

I was so distressed with the aspect of public affairs, that were it not for our dear sister's illness, I should think of nothing else. They are to be envied, I think, who, from age or infirmity, are likely to be removed from the afflictions which God is preparing for this sinful nation. God bless you, my brother. John says you are well; so am I, and every one here except our sister: but

---

[1] Joshua Watson (1771–1855), philanthropist and strenuous worker for the Church of England; in 1811 Treasurer of National Society for the Education of the Poor; in 1814 Treasurer of the Society for the Propagation of the Gospel and of the Society for Promoting Christian Knowledge; in 1817 ff. he served on Commission for Church Buildings, and a little later was Treasurer of the Clergy Orphan Schools, and in 1837 of the Additional Curates' Society. A great friend of C. W.'s, he helped in the revision of C. W. jun.'s *Theophilus Anglicanus*. For W. W.'s opinion of him *v.* Letter of June 18. In church matters he was much the most influential layman of the day.

I have witnessed one revolution in a foreign country, and I have not courage to think of facing another in my own. Farewell. God bless you again.

Your affectionate Brother,

W. W.

MS.   **1018. *W. W. to Dr John Calvert***

Rydal Mount, April 13ᵗʰ [1832]

My dear Sir,

The bearer is my nephew, John,[1] whom you have kindly interested yourself about—for which I heartily thank you, as no doubt he would do if his shyness did not prevent him.

I cannot presume, knowing how much you are engaged, to recommend him in any way to your notice—but I could not let him go to London without your being told that when this is delivered he will be with Mr Gardner upon trial, which I hope may end by his being regularly indentured with him.

I am not aware of any news from this quarter that will interest you. Your mother will be concerned to hear that my sister, though we hope convalescent, recovers slowly. Your sister Mary must have been sorry to learn from the papers that poor Mr Barber[2] is dead. His health was never good, but his end has been hastened by exasperation of mind from pecuniary dealings with a professed friend.

With the joint remembrance of all to all believe me

My dear Sir, your much obliged,

Wm. Wordsworth.

MS.   **1019. *W. W. to Edward Quillinan*[3]**

Rydal Mount, April 22, [1832]

Of Hogg's silly story[4] I have only to say that his memory is not the best in the world, as he speaks of his being called out of

---

[1] Son of R. W.   [2] A Grasmere neighbour.

[3] Written by Dora W. in the middle of a letter of her own to E. Q., and introduced with the words: 'I have got hold of Father for 5 minutes, and now he speaks.'

[4] In his *Autobiography* Hogg records 'an affront which I conceived had been put upon me. . . . One night [at Rydal] there was a resplendent arch across the zenith and we all went out to view it, and on the beautiful platform of Rydal Mt. were walking in twos and threes, W., Professor Wilson,

this room when the arch made its appearance; now in fact, Wilson and he were on their way either to or from Grasmere when they saw the arch and very obligingly came up to tell us of it, thinking, wh. was the fact, that we might not be aware of the phenomenon. As to the speech, which galled poor Hogg so much, it must in one expression at least have been misreported, the word 'fellow' I am told by my family I apply to no one. I use strong terms I own, but there is a vulgarity about that, wh. does not suit me, and had I applied it to Hogg there w^d have also been hypocrisy in the kindness, wh. he owns I invariably shewed him, wholly alien, as you must know, to my character. It is possible and not improbable that I might on that occasion have been tempted to use a contemptuous expression, for H. had disgusted me not by his vulgarity, wh. he c^d not help, but by his self-conceit in delivering confident opinions upon classical literature and other points about wh. he c^d know nothing. The reviving this business in this formal way after a lapse of nearly 18 years does little credit to Mr Hogg and it affords another proof how cautious one ought to be in admitting to one's house trading Authors of any description, Verse men or Prose men. I was at Corby and Rose Castle and much pleased with both, the horse performed well. W. and I left Carlisle at 20 m: past Six and reached home ¼ before 4. I ought to thank you for flogging Mr Mitchell[1] so openly. Who is he? I dont disapprove of Dora's

Lloyd, De Quincey, besides several other literary gentlemen, whose names I am not certain I remember. Miss W.'s arm was in mine, and she was expressing some fears that the splendid stranger was ominous, when I by ill luck blundered out, thinking I was saying a good thing "Hoot, m'em, it's neither mair nor less than joost a triumphal airch, raised in honour of the meeting of the poets". "That's very good", said the Professor, laughing. But W., who had De Q.'s arm, gave a grunt, and turned on his heel, and leading the little opium eater aside, he addressed him in these disdainful words; "Poets? poets? what does the fellow mean? Where are they?" Who could forgive this? For my part I never can and never will. The "Where are they?" was too bad. I have some hopes that De Q. was *leeing*, for I did not myself hear W. utter the words.' Doubtless De Q., if not actually *leeing*, had added a malicious sting to the story.

[1] One Nicholas Mitchell had written a 'conceited, stupid, incredibly weak, and impudent' volume entitled *Poets of the Age*, lauding L. E. L., Mrs Hemans, and Campbell, and abusing Coleridge, Southey, and W. E. Q. found the book lying on the table at 'Campbell's Club' and wrote two quatrains of satiric doggerel in it. On his next visit to the club the book had disappeared.

sending the sonnet[1] tho' the Editor may not think it worth while to insert it. The great resort to the places of Worship on that day through the whole Island as far as I can learn gave me more pleasure than anything that has occurred for a long time. What a state they are in [in] Paris—how thankful you must be for having Jemima in England. I am in poor heart about the bill—farewell. Love to Rotha,

W. W.

Address: Edward Quillinan Esqre, Ryder Street, St. James

MS.   **1020. *W. W. to H. W. Pickersgill***

Thursday [p.m. April 30. 1832]
Rydal Mount near Kendal

My dear Sir,

I learn with much and unexpected pleasure that there is a prospect of our seeing you here, and that you purpose to leave London for Manchester on Monday next. On that very day, however, I must unfortunately be at Carlisle on account of public business. I will strain every point to return on Thursday at the latest. Possibly this being Easter holidays, you may have a little leisure now, which you cannot command afterwards, otherwise I should have been startled by your coming so far when your engagements must be so pressing. When I took the liberty through Mr Quillinan of making the proposal, it was with a view of its taking effect, if acceded to, during the Summer Vacation, when a little recreation and a ramble in this fine Country during the season of its beauty might recompense you for so long a journey. At present the Spring is not so far advanced as might be wished, and your allowance of time will probably be short.

I allude to these particulars both as affecting your own gratification while here, and also a point of some delicacy to myself in relation to the College for whom and at whose expense the Portrait is to be executed. The College handsomely gave me the choice of an artist but it was at a time when it was scarcely

---

[1] *Upon the late General Fast, March 1832* (Oxf. W., p. 513). The fast was enjoined as an intercession on the outbreak of cholera in the country.

in my power, on account of official engagements, to go back to London from which I had just returned after a long absence; I therefore wrote to Mr Quillinan, submitting to him whether, if you were in the habit of giving any portion of your time to summer recreation, you might not be determined, by the consideration of obliging me in this way, to prefer the Lakes and give me the pleasure of your Company. I felt there was a good deal of delicacy in that proposal, which I was induced to make, not thinking myself justified in putting the College to any further expense than a Portrait from so distinguished an Artist must necessarily impose under ordinary circumstances. I may add that I never could have presumed to propose your coming so far at this season of the year, or any other than the summer vacation. The above particulars having been frankly and cordially stated, they may be left to our joint consideration when I have the pleasure of seeing you here, if they should make no change in your obliging purpose.

I remain my dear Sir faithfully yours Wm Wordsworth

If you reply immediately to this Letter direct to me Stamp Off: Carlisle.

Address: H. W. Pickersgill Esqr, Soho Square, London.

MS.   *1021. W. W. to H. W. Pickersgill*

Rydal Ambleside May 5th [1832]

My dear Sir,

Many thanks for your obliging Letters and your friendly Invitation, of which, during the painting of the Portrait, I should have been happy to avail myself had it been in my power to go to London. Unfortunately, for this purpose, and alas for me and my family, a most distressing circumstance.[1] My Sister, the only one I ever had, and who has lived with me for the last 35 years, is now in so weak and alarming [a] state of health that I could not quit home, except under absolute necessity. We must therefore wait for some more favorable opportunity. Let me add that I entirely release you from any engagement to come

---

[1] So MS.

hither in consequence of what has passed between us; for such a proposal would have never been made but upon a supposition, which proves not to be the fact, that you were in the habit of allotting (as almost all professional men who have leisure, do) a small portion of the Summer to recreation, and I thought that the beauty of the Country, with the opportunity of working at the Portrait without interruption, might induce you to come so far.[1] I repeat therefore that I have no claim upon you whatever in consequence of your having given me some reason to expect you. I attach, however, so much interest to the Portrait being from your pencil, that I hope many months may not pass without the College being gratified with a Production which many of its Members are so desirous of possessing.

If I should be able to come to London hereafter, I should be happy, as I have said, to be under your Roof, till your task was accomplished, and I am sure you would not take it ill if after that I removed into some Lodging; for all Persons *in the least known* are troublesome visitors in London; but till the Portrait were finished I should call upon very few of my Friends

I remain, my dear Sir,

Very faithfully yours

Wm Wordsworth

Mr Quillinan did not speak *positively* that you would be able to come.

MS.   *1022. W. W. to Rev. F. Merewether*

Moresby June 18th 1832.

My dear Sir,

Your two letters reached me duly but at times when my mind was so occupied with anxiety on private and public accounts that I could not muster courage to thank you for those marks of friendly attention.—The Reform bill being passed my *anxiety* for that cause is over but only to be succeeded by dejection to despondency—the Parliament that has past this bill was in profligacy and folly never surpassed since the parliament that overthrew the monarchy in Charles the first's time; and it is to be

---

[1] Pickersgill came to Rydal for ten days at the beginning of September.

feared that it will give birth to a Monster still more odious than itself. Of nine members to be returned by the county from which I write, seven will to a certainty be, either down right Jacobin Republicans, or of a class, in the present stage of our revolution, still more dangerous—rash or complying Whig Innovators: of the other two members one will probably be a Conservative and the ninth is in doubt, but I fear the good cause in this instance also will not prevail.

The private anxiety to which I alluded is caused by the very feeble and alarming state of my dear Sister's health which received at Whitwick a shock it never recovered from. She has been upwards of six months almost perpetually confined to her room and the greater part of the day through weakness tho' thank God not thro' pain to her bed.—We thought her something better and in consequence my daughter and I ventured a week ago upon a visit to John and his amiable Wife; and here I shall remain if we have no bad news from Rydal a week longer—John is well and no doubt would send his affect^e regards but he is gone over to his new vicarage of Brigham, the Church of w^h is 9 miles hence; the parish is of vast extent having under it several chapelries inclusive of the town of Cockermouth (5,000 inhabitants) but those under the care of the *vicar* amount only to 1500—the situation is most beautiful—rich sloping or meadowy grounds with the fine river Derwent winding thro' them, and Skiddaw with other lofty mountains in full view at the distance of 6 or 7 miles: unluckily neither in this little rectory of Moresby nor at Brigham is there a parsonage: he has some thoughts however of building at Brigham—

It is now high time to turn to your letter. I am much pleased that your residence by the sea-side proved so beneficial to your health of body and as your verses shew must have given an impulse to your mind—you were mistaken in supposing that it would be any task to me to peruse your short metrical compositions—the lines on the sea are good and you succeed best as must be the case with every one where the subject is most poetical—but as to the Reform bill and Reform the genius of Milton himself could scarcely extract poetry from a theme so inauspicious.

I was much concerned to learn from the Archbishop that Sir George Beaumont had been very poorly: pray present my kind regards to him and to Lady Beaumont and say that I shall not visit London without turning aside to Coleorton either going or returning—but for my Sister's illness I should have been in town this spring for a short time—

I am glad to learn that my dear brother's health is upon the whole better in spite of public affairs, but he tells me that that most excellent man Mr Joshua Watson is declining and that his daughter also is far from well. This if news to you will grieve you much. Mr Watson is perhaps the ablest supporter the Church has out of her own bosom—indeed he is the friend and support of all that is virtuous and rational in the country— Dora joins with me in kindest remembrances and best wishes to Mrs Merewether and yourself and believe me ever faithfully yours

Wm Wordsworth.

Address: The Revd F. Merewether, Coleorton Rectory, Ashby de la Zouche.

MS.

1023. *W. W. to John Gardner*

Moresby June 22nd '32

My dear Sir,

You will think I have been lost—I could not write sooner not having heard from Dr Wordsworth who has been dancing about between London and Cambridge. He has undertaken to advance £100 and I will advance another £100; the precise sum you named for a fee, if any were fixed upon, I do not recollect—but if it exceed £200 my brother and I will provide it, also between us.—My Nephew's situation is unfortunate as to his Father's Will; which was made before the rapid decline of land and stock prices, wh. made the sum allotted for the payments of his debts much short of what was required, and no land can be sold till he is of age without an expensive process in chancery.

You mention bills—would one payable at three months suit you for £100 and another for a like sum at *6* or *9*? by that period money would be due to my family from which without inconvenience I could advance my portion—I hope you continue to be satisfied with John, and I was pleased to find you did not think me mistaken in my estimate of his character—he writes in good spirits, seems very happy and thankful for your kindness.—May I beg of you to exhort him to frugality; not that I ever saw anything to the contrary in him:—whatever is necessary for books, dress and other expenses, will be supplied as wanted.

The printing of my new edition is finished, I promised a copy to John and beg you will accept another, which Longman shall be directed to send to Foley Place when ready—it contains nothing but what has appeared either in the last Ed: or some Miscellany since.—I return to Rydal in a few days and shall be happy to hear from you.

Remember me most kindly to Mr Boxall[1]—my brains have been racked in vain for a title to his series of paintings—wh. I am persuaded will do him much honor; the specimen he kindly sent me is very much admired and improves upon acquaintance. Mr Quillinan tells me that the engraving from his portrait of me is beautifully done and with the picture will be very acceptable at Rydal.

Believe me dear sir, ever very faithfully yours

Wm Wordsworth.

Love to John from his Uncle and his three Cousins—his dear Aunt, he will be sorry to hear, continues in a very languishing state.

Not knowing the Rev[d] Mr Judkin's[2] address I have desired my publishers to enclose three copies to you one of which Mr Boxall will be kind enough to take charge of for the said Mr J.

Address: J. Gardiner Esq. Foley Place, Portland Place.

---

[1] 'Boxall is doing a series of paintings to be engraved, an attempt to give the varieties of expression of poetical female beauty—for instance he is doing one on the expression "Quiet as a nun Breathless with adoration". He wants a title for the work. Can or will Mr W. suggest a title? It is said that B. is the *best* painter of abstract female beauty among the artists.' E. Q. to Dora W., April 4, 1832.

[2] The Rev. T. J. Judkin, author of *Church and Home Psalmody*, 1831. He was also something of an artist. *v.* Letter of Oct. 20, 1836.

1024. W. W. to William Rowan Hamilton

Hamilton.
M(—) G. K(—)   Moresby, June 25. 1832.

My dear Mr Hamilton,

Your former letter reached me in due time; your second, from Cambridge, two or three days ago. I ought to have written to you long since, but really I have for some time, from private and public causes of sorrow and apprehension, been in a great measure deprived of those genial feelings which, thro' life, have not been so much accompaniments of my character, as vital principles of my existence.

My dear sister has been languishing more than seven months in a sick-room, nor dare I or any of her friends entertain a hope that her strength will ever be restored; and the course of public affairs, as I think I told you before, threatens, in my view, destruction to the institutions of the country; an event which, whatever may rise out of it hereafter, cannot but produce distress and misery for two or three generations at least. In any times I am but at best a poor and unpunctual correspondent, yet I am pretty sure you would have heard from me but for this reason; therefore let the statement pass for an apology as far as you think fit.

The verses called forth by your love and the disappointment that followed I have read with much pleasure, tho' grieved that you should have suffered so much; as poetry they derive an interest from your philosophical pursuits, which could not but recommend the verses even to indifferent readers, and must give them in the eyes of your friends a great charm. The style appears to me good, and the general flow of the versification harmonious; but you deal somewhat more in dactylic endings and identical terminations than I am accustomed to think legitimate. Sincerely do I congratulate you upon being able to continue your philosophical pursuits under such a pressure of personal feeling.

It gives me much pleasure that you and Coleridge have met, and that you were not disappointed in the conversation of a man from whose writings you had previously drawn so much delight and improvement. He and my beloved sister are the two beings to whom my intellect is most indebted, and they are now

3394.5   [625]   G

proceeding, as it were, *pari passu*, along the path of sickness, I will not say towards the grave, but I trust towards a blessed immortality.

It was not my intention to write so seriously: my heart is full, and you must excuse it.

You do not tell me how you like Cambridge as a place, nor what you thought of its buildings and other works of art. Did you not see Oxford as well? Surely you would not lose the opportunity; it has greatly the advantage over Cambridge in its happy intermixture of streets, churches, and collegiate buildings.

I hope you found time when in London to visit the British Museum.

A fortnight ago I came hither to my son and daughter, who are living a gentle, happy, quiet, and useful life together. My daughter Dora is also with us. On this day I should have returned, but an inflammation in my eyes makes it unsafe for me to venture in an open carriage, the weather being exceedingly disturbed.

A week ago appeared here Mr W. S. Landor, the Poet, and author of the *Imaginary Conversations*, which probably have fallen in your way. We had never met before, tho' several letters had passed between us; and as I had not heard that he was in England, my gratification in seeing him was heightened by surprise. We passed a day together at the house of my friend Mr Rawson, on the banks of Wastwater. His conversation is lively and original; his learning great, tho' he will not allow it, and his laugh the heartiest I have heard for a long time. It is not much less than twenty years since he left England for France, and afterwards Italy, where he hopes to end his days, nay [he has] fixed near Florence upon the spot where he wishes to be buried. Remember me most kindly to your sisters. Dora begs her love and thanks to your sister Eliza for her last most interesting letter, which she will answer when she can command a frank.

Ever faithfully yours,

Wm. Wordsworth.

I have desired Messrs Longman to put aside for you a copy of the new edition of my poems, compressed into four vols. It contains nothing but what has before seen the light, but several poems which were not in the last. Pray direct your Dublin publisher to apply for it.

MS.   *1025. W. W. to Edward Quillinan*

July 10th [1832]

My dear Friend,

(I hold the pen for Mr W., whose eyes, I grieve to say, do not serve him for this and scarcely any other purpose at present. S.H.). From your Letter I am sorry to learn that you have been led to entertain so confident an expectation that Dora would undertake the charge of Jemima and Rotha, in case of their standing in need (which God forfend) of guardianship. The part of her letter which I dictated was meant to set you at ease upon the point that in the last necessity your Children would not be left unprotected—even by her—as far as circumstances might allow. My wish was that Miss H. and she, who were named together, should have written you a joint letter, stating their views of the proposal, but that was impossible, and when Dora wrote Miss H. had not even seen the proposal—there having been no communication between them. I therefore wished that the Letter written from Moresby should merely aim at setting you at ease upon the main point, but from the language of your last letter (in which you say 'accept my thanks') I infer that her feelings must have betrayed her into the expression of sentiments on this point very different from what would find sanction from her own understanding, uninfluenced by such feelings or rather unblinded by them. It is incumbent on me, as her Father, and as the Friend of the Children and yours, to assure you that she is utterly unfit both from her health, strength, temper, and circumstances to stand pledged for such an anxious responsibility. In the last necessity, and under no other, should I approve of her undertaking it, but you named Mr and Mrs Wake, and from what I have heard you say of her and her Family I thought that she would be likely to undertake the office and felt convinced that your Children would be infinitely better under her superintendence than any protection that my Family could afford. I will

[627]

not advert to our situation—it is enough for me to know that the ardent and anxious temper of my Daughter in conjunction with her weak frame disqualifies her from such an office—and that it ought not to be undertaken unless where it devolves upon her as an imperious duty. You say that the 'expression of your will' binds no one, but how ungracious would it be for her, the first person named, to decline the charge, and how painful, you having gone out of the world with the expectation that she would accept it. I am persuaded that such an alternative would prey upon health and do her the greatest injury.

Thanks for your amusing letter. I am truly glad that you and the dear children are enjoying yourselves so agreeably in that beautiful country.—We have had a round of visitors—Dr Arnold and his family are at Brathay for 6 weeks—and yesterday we had Mr Carr of Bolton Abbey and his two nieces—young enthusiasts, and he a handsome fresh, prosing old man of 70—with a fine feeling, a lively enjoyment, and just discrimination of nature. Mr Julius Hare—a friend of Landor—is here also, and several promising Cantabs. I could tell you much about certain Syrens of the name of Wynyard who haunt the Islands of Winandermere, and the perplexity of the young mathematicians—and are also a good deal about Rydal not perhaps without views upon the Ivy Cot that I leave you to guess at. In the Mitchell affair[1] you did well to keep your own counsel, but he is too great a booby for notice from any quarter—such trash nature intended should come into the world still born. Boxall's Picture and Prints have not yet reached us—we will do our best to procure subscribers, but we have no chance of succeeding except in summer time, therefore the delay is unlucky. Mr Hare named the picture but did not relish it, seeming to hint it was nothing of a likeness. Farewell! very faithfully yours

(Signature cut away)

Address: Edward Quillinan Esqre, Mr George Benson's, Fern Hill, Malvern, Worcestershire.

---

[1] *v.* Letter 904. E. Q. had naturally kept secret his defacing of a Club book.

MS.   **1026. W. W. to John Gardner**

Rydal Mount July 16th [1832]

My dear Sir

I have been much distressed by an inflammation in my eyes and engaged almost every hour since I rec^d your letter. Pray draw upon Dr W. at Buxted near Uckfield for a 100gs at 3 months, and upon myself for a hundred and twenty pounds at 6 mo: that will meet the expense of the Indentures etc.[1] Mr Addison of Gray's Inn, is John's Godfather, a Solicitor and an excellent Man—and it would interest him in John's welfare if *he* should be applied to to execute the Indenture.

I have a small favor to beg of you. My eyelids have sometimes suffered from exposure to sudden changes of wind, which may be guarded against by spectacles with side-glasses—I should not wish them to be green nor ordinary glass—but there are a kind that subdue the glaring light, of a cold bluish tint, would you be so kind as purchase a pair for me at Dollands.— Observe my eyes, tho' so long harassed by inflammation, are not *aged*, so that without being the least short-sighted I *can* read the smallest print without spectacles—tho' I have for some time used the first size.

The Spectacles must have a proper case, directed to me and be taken (which John can do) to Robt Hook Esqre, 18 King Street St James's, who has instructions to forward them to me.

Ever faithfully your's

Wm Wordsworth

Address: John Gardner Esqre, 16 Foley Place, Portland Place.

MS.   **1027. W. W. to Alexander Dyce**

Rydal Mount July 21st [1832]

My dear Sir,

I ought to have written to you before to say that I had not forgotten your request concerning Skelton. Mr Southey, to

---

[1] *v.* Letter of June 22, *supra.* Mr Addison was an early Penrith friend, and a partner of the late R. W.'s, *v. E. L.*, p. 337.

whom I have several times named the subject, was pleased to
hear that you had undertaken the work; but had nothing
to communicate further than that in Mr Heber's Library[1] were
certain printed poems of Skelton not to be found in any collection of his works. Mr Heber is now in England, and, as we all
know, is very liberal in giving Editors the use of anything in his
Library. I observed that Mr Southey in his extracts from
Skelton affirms that he was born at Dis in Norfolk, but I have
heard, or read, that he was born at Branthwaite Hall near
Cockermouth in Cumberland which place was undoubtedly
possessed for many generations by a family of his name—but
on the above I lay no stress as I have no means of verifying the
report.

Pray let me hear how you come on with your work and believe
me faithfully yours

Wm Wordsworth

Address: Mr Pickering, Bookseller, Chancery Lane. *For The
Revd Alex. Dyce*

MS.   **1028. W. W. to Edward Moxon**
K(—)
                                    Rydal Mount
                            Wednesday 12th Sept. [1832][2]
Dear Mr Moxon,
    Mr Pickersgill is the Bearer of this to London. He has been
painting my Portrait—We all like it exceedingly as far as it is
carried—it will be finished in London—Should you wish to see

[1] Reginald Heber (1783–1826), Bishop of Calcutta, author of *Palestine*
(1807), *Poems and Translations* (1812), *Hymns* (1827), &c. W. W. had met
him in 1808 (*v. M.Y.*, p. 458e).
    [2] For W. W. to H. C. R. July 21, *v. C.R.*, pp. 230–2. *It is there printed
from* K., *who reads* Maucker *for* Brancker *in the first paragraph, and in the
last* dissenting Tory *for* dissenting Whig. *K. also omits part of the third,
which should run:* You will grieve to hear that your Invalid friend, my dear
Sister, cannot be said to be making any progress towards recovery—She
never quits her room but for a few minutes, and we think is always
weakened by the exertion. She is however, God be praised, in a contented
and happy state of mind—and tho' subject frequently to pain bears it so
well that she seems to have little to complain of but debility. I have not
told her that I am writing to you, or she would have sent her affectionate
remembrances. The rest of the family are well—save that my eyes seem
every year more and more subject to protracted inflammation.

it in the present state you can call at his House; but not till a month hence, as it will remain here some little time.

I have to ask of you a favor; in all probability it will be engraved, but not unless we could secure beforehand 150 Purchasers. I do not say Subscribers for it would [? then be] asked as a favour. To further the object may I beg of you to receive the names of such persons as it *might* suit to write them down in your Shop?

I hope your tour in Scotland proved agreeable—my dear Sister does not recover her strength.—All send their kind regards.

ever faithfully yours
W. Wordsworth

Pray mention the Contents of this Letter to Mr Rogers with my affectionate remembrances.

I ought to have said that it is not wished to have a *Board* or Advertisement of the intention in your Shop, but merely that you should receive such Names as might offer.

K.　　　*1029. W. W. to Thomas Arnold*

Rydal Mount, Tuesday, Sept. 19th, 1832.

My dear Sir,

Yesterday Mr Greenwood of Grasmere called, with a letter he had just received from Mr Simpson—the owner of Fox How —empowering Mr G. to sign for him an agreement, either with yourself or any friend you may appoint, for the sale of that estate for £800; possession to be given, and the money paid, next Candlemas. . . . I need not say that it will give me pleasure to facilitate the purchase, as far as is in my power. . . .

Faithfully yours,
William Wordsworth.

MS.　　　*1030. W. W. to John Gibson Lockhart*

Rydal Mount September 24th [1832.]

My dear Sir,

Many thanks for your Letter. Sir Walter's death is indeed a 'Release', so that the language of condolence would be out of place here. Be assured however that every member of my family sympathizes deeply with you and Mrs Lockhart and Miss Scott—above all I cannot but feel for her upon whom her poor Father for the latter years of his life must have leaned so much. —I am very loth to be troublesome to you upon an occasion that will involve you in so many occupations and engagements, but allow me to say that we should be thankful if you let us know by and bye how Mrs Lockhart and Miss Scott support their loss, and how as to health and spirits you all are.

Believe me with kind remembrances from all here

faithfully your obliged

Wm. Wordsworth.

Mr Hamilton is in the Highlands.

Address: J. G. Lockhart Esqre, Abbotsford, Melross.

MS.   **1031. *W. W. to Robert Griffiths***

Rydal Mount Octr 6th [1832]

My dear Sir

My Sister begs that I would write you a few words, as she was obliged to close her Letter abruptly. Not knowing what it contained, and unwilling to burthen you with repetitions, I must confine myself to assuring you that we shall be glad to hear from you at all times, and happy to pay attention to any of your friends whom curiosity may lead to visit this interesting part of England. My dear Sister may not have entered into particulars of her long—but you will be happy to hear, not at all times painful illness. She is often, and for several days together, though weak, free from painfull sensations; and being fond of reading she supports confinement with chearfulness. During the summer also, and up to this time, when the air has not been damp, she has ridden out regularly in an open Carriage—but her Constitution has had a severe shock, we have however great cause to be thankful.

The health of all the rest of my family is good, and the portion of happiness which God has voutchsafed to grant us, appears to exceed the common lot of mankind. May we be duly sensible of his goodness! For my own private concerns, except my dear

Sister's illness, I have nothing to lament; on *public* accounts however I am troubled with much anxiety. A spirit of rash innovation is every where at war with our old institutions, and the habits and sentiments that have thus far supported them; and the ardor of those who are bent upon change is exactly according to the measure of their ignorance. Where men will not, or through want of knowledge, are unable to, look back they cannot be expected to look forward; and therefore, caring for the present only, they care for *that* merely as it affects their own importance. Hence a blind selfishness is at the bottom of all that is going forward—a remark which in other words was made by Mr Burke long ago—farewell believe me my dear Sir, faithfully yours

Wm. Wordsworth.

P.S. My Sister did not know that Miss Douglas was coming back this way or she would not have closed her Letter so hastily.

Address: Robt Griffiths Esqre, Philadelphia.

MS.   *1032. W. W. to [? Mr Greenwood[1]]*

[Oct. 9. 1832]

My dear Sir

Yesterday I rec^d a letter from Dr Arnold, who begs me 'to ask you, or Mr Simpson's Solicitor at Ambleside to send up an abstract of the Title and of the Terms of the Contract of the Sale to Morris Jones and Ward, No 1 S. John St Bedford Row, London'. He adds 'I have no objection to the Property continuing with Mr Simpson till Candlemas; but I suppose we might begin any Improvements which we might wish to make on the Rock when I am down there in the Winter, as so long an Interval must take place between my Visits'.

The weather and other causes prevent my calling upon you— Perhaps you will communicate direct with Dr A, if anything has to be said to him on the subject.

Very sincerely yours
W. Wordsworth.

[1] The addressee of this letter seems to have been Mr Greenwood, *v.* Letter to Arnold of Sept. 19.

MS.   *1033. D. W. to Jane Marshall*

Rydal Mount, Tuesday 20th Nov^r, 1832.

My dear Friend

Dora is writing to Mary Anne, and I cannot miss the opportunity of slipping a few lines into the frank, for though M. A. herself may be the Bearer of good news of me I know you will like still better to receive it from my own hand. I will not trouble you or myself with particulars. Enough to say that I am very much better—have now no regular or irregular maladies except the flatulence and pains in the Bowels—and I am certainly much stronger, less susceptible of changes in the atmosphere. My horrid cravings have quite left me.—It is true I have *sinkings* now and then; but any thing is better than the gnawing appetite with which I was for many days afflicted.

Dora's cough is still very troublesome; but her breathing is better; and with due care I trust she is in the road to perfect recovery. How unlucky that the pleasure of her very pleasant visit to Hallsteads should have been diminished by so troublesome a companion! Poor thing! the morning after her return she was very ill, and was right glad to apply to a blister, though it always has a very weakening effect upon her.

Every day I am anxious till the letters arrive—Mr Ferguson no doubt knows that my Friends were with you when the affecting tidings reached you, and no change having since taken place either much for the better or the worse is, I suppose, the reason of his not having written to me. My daily prayer for that best of Women[1] is now but that she may be spared from much bodily suffering. One cannot wish her life to be prolonged under the present decay of her mental powers; for there cannot be a hope remaining that *they* will be restored to her; but on the contrary her memory must daily become weaker. Do let us hear from you as soon as you have leisure, and tell us all you have heard from Halifax. Perhaps you and your Sister may yet once again see our beloved Friend. Your Sister, in a most kind letter which I received from her mentions that she had such a hope. Probably your Sisters did not tell you in what way they intended to ad-

---

[1] Mrs Rawson, *v. E.L.*, p. 1 and *passim*. She did not die till 1837.

minister to my pleasures and comforts, but *I* cannot help saying to you that so far from being ashamed of receiving such a Gift from *such* Friends I am proud of it. Already I have schemed for the supply of several small—*wants* I will not call them—but gratifications, such as I might otherwise have scrupled to indulge myself with. I will not trouble you with more on this subject, which is an affecting one to me.

We were much gratified by Mary Anne's letter, and especially her account of your delightful meeting at Headingley—the Grand-child's joy—and above all poor dear Ellen's happiness and her improved looks after such an attack of severe pain. Dear Creature! often have I thought of her when I felt the bliss of lying down upon my bed—worn out—yet free from pain. I have thought of *her* and of her grievous sufferings compared with mine. That difficulty in breathing is what I grieve for most in thinking of her. The contrast of my own easy breath makes it doubly felt by me when I lie down. Indeed I have often said that till within the last year I never knew what was the Blessing of a good bed to lie upon. Pray give my tender love to Ellen with sincerest wishes that she may be enabled to enjoy her Mother's company as long as you remain with her. When you write tell me all particulars concerning her, whether she leaves her room, if she can bear the society of the Family, and whatever occurs to you as likely to interest me in regard to her.

Lady Farquhar etc. did not leave Fox Ghyll[1] till the Friday after my Friends parted from you. I hope they will all come again; for they are very amiable Women, and they so much enjoyed the Country. My Brother's severe cold left him marvellously. The ride outside the Chaise over Kirkstone instead of giving him cold tended to his cure—indeed I always hold that the Inside of a Coach or hack-chaise is the most cold-catching place in the world. My dear Sister is quite well. She and Miss Hutchinson have been happily and busily employed in knitting garters for you and your Sisters. How I have wished that *I* also could have sent my contribution!

I must have done, for I have another letter to write, and, believe me, I am grown so careful of myself that I endeavour

---

[1] The house occupied by Mrs Luff.

always to prevent fatigue by leaving off writing while I have yet a hundred things to say. Adieu my dear Friend. With affectionate regards to Mr Marshall, and love to all the young ones, believe me ever your grateful and loving Friend

D. Wordsworth

I have never sent my thanks to Julia for her very interesting letter. The feelings and sentiments she expresses meet with my entire sympathy. Will you tell her so?

Address: Mrs Marshall, Headingley.

MS.   **1034. W. W. to John Marshall**[1]

[December 1832]

My dear Sir,

It gives me much pleasure to learn that you are the Purchaser of the Derwentwater Estate, and I sincerely congratulate you on the acquisition which you have made, I should think, upon very reasonable terms. Having never seen a plan of the Estate I do not exactly know its limits, but for beauty and grandeur of situation it has no parallel.—Great mistakes may be made in valuing the wood; so that it is of the utmost consequence that persons should be employed who can estimate fairly its value *on the Spot*. My Neighbour Mr Harrison not long ago purchased a very extensive fall of timber and other wood in Scotland. The Vendor had employed a Valuer from a distance, one of whose items was a 1,000 pounds for broom for besoms, which broom in that remote part of the Highlands was of *no value whatever*, and the Item was accordingly struck out of the Estimate.

—It will give me much pleasure to go over the Estate, with you, and together we certainly might hit upon improvements of its Beauty. I shall most likely be at Keswick before you come down, and if I can learn any thing there that will be worth naming to you I shall write. Mr Southey will be pleased to hear that you are the Purchaser, as will all men of taste, especially when they know your chief inducement for buying the property.

—Will you excuse my expressing a wish that you would procure the Conveyance Stamp through my Son William, at

---

[1] *v.* Letter to J. M. of Feb.–March 1832.

Carlisle.—Solicitors in cases of so large a purchase often interfere, to prevent, for the sake of a small benefit of their own, the Distributor of Stamps and his Sub—getting their regular profit.— If got through my Son it would throw a few pounds into his pocket, and be a little encouragement in his humble situation—

ever faithfully yours

Wm Wordsworth

K(—) **1035. W. W. to Alaric Watts**

[1832.]

My dear Sir,

I have to thank you, I presume, for a copy of *The Souvenir* for 1832, just received. . . . I have been much pleased with Mrs Watts's *Choice*, Mrs Howitt's *Infancy, Youth, and Age*, and your own *Conversazione*—a great deal too clever for the subjects which you have here and there condescended to handle. The rest of the volume I shall hope to peruse at leisure. I fear the state of the times must affect the annuals, as well as all other literature. I am told, indeed, that many of the booksellers are threatened with ruin. I enclose a sonnet[1] for your next volume, if you choose to insert it. It would have appeared with more advantage in this year's, but was not written in time. It is proper I should mention that it has been sent to Sir Walter Scott and one or two of my other friends; so that you had best not print it till towards the latter sheets of your volume, lest it should steal by chance into publication, for which I have given no permission. Should that happen I will send you some other piece.

I remain, my dear sir,

Sincerely your obliged

Wm. Wordsworth.

MS. **1036. W. W. to Alexander Dyce**
M(—) G(—) K(—)

Rydal Mount, Kendal, 7th Jan^ry, 1833.

My dear Sir,

Having an opportunity of sending this to Town free of Postage, I write to thank you for your last obliging Letter.

---

[1] *On the departure of Sir Walter Scott from Abbotsford, to Naples* (Oxf. W., p. 386). It appeared in the *Literary Souvenir* of 1833.

Sincerely do I congratulate you upon having made such progress with Skelton, a Writer deserving of far greater attention than his works have hitherto received. Your Edition will be very serviceable, and may be the occasion of calling out illustrations perhaps of particular passages from others, beyond what your own Reading, though so extensive, has supplied. I am pleased also to hear that Shirley is out.[1] You mention with commendation the last Edition of my Poems. It gives me pleasure to learn that you approve it. It was my intention to send it to you, and unless some mistake prevented it, you must have received the work: if you have not pray send to Mr Longman the Slip of Paper on the opposite Page and he will forward a copy to your Address.

I lament to hear that your health is not good; my own, God be thanked, is excellent, but I am much dejected with the aspect of public affairs, and cannot but fear that this Nation is on the brink of great troubles.

Be assured that I shall at all times be happy to hear of your studies and pursuits, being, with great respect,

sincerely yours,

Wm. Wordsworth.

MS.   *1037. W. W. to the Bishop of Limerick*[2]

Rydal Mount, Ambleside [p.m. Jan. 28 1833]

My Lord,

A short time since I received through the hands of Mr Southey, your Reprint of Burnet's Lives etc, with Preface and Notes, a

---

[1] *Dramatic Works and Poems of James Shirley*, 6 vols., 1833, the completion of Gifford's edition; A. D. edited part of Vol. VI, and wrote the Memoir.

[2] The Bishop of Limerick was John Jebb (1775–1833). The work referred to is—*Lives of Sir Matthew Hale and the Earl of Rochester: with Characters of Archbishop Leighton, The Hon. Robert Boyle, Queen Mary and other Eminent Persons, and an Address to Posterity. By Gilbert Burnett, D.D., Late Bishop of Sarum, with an Introduction and numerous Notes; to which are now added Five Hitherto Unpublished Letters by Anne, Countess Dowager of Rochester, upon her Son's Last Illness and Conversion*—edited by Bishop Jebb, 1833.

The Prefaces were written by Alexander Knox, Esq., of Dublin, M.R.I.A., a friend of Bishop Jebb.

valuable token of your regard for which I beg you to accept my sincere thanks.

The Prefaces by Mr Knox were new to me; and I have read them with greater interest because they recall to me, along with your Lordship's account of the same Individual, an interview which I had with him at Dublin three years ago. I was introduced to him by Professor Hamilton of Trinity College Dublin, and was much delighted with his eloquent, philosophical and truly christian tone of conversation.

If Bishop Burnet's Life of Bishop Bedell[1] could have been abridged without material injury, it would have given me pleasure to see it in the Collection.

Scarcely any man has done more honor to the Episcopal office, and these times require as much as any ever did to be reminded of what a Blessing to a Country a good Bishop is. I have often expressed to Dr W. my regret that Bp. Bedell's Life was not included in his ecclesiastical Biography.

Pray present my kind regards to Mr Forster, and believe me my Lord with sincere respect

most faithfully
your obliged Ser[nt]
Wm Wordsworth

MS.   ***1038. W. W. to Miss Kinnaird*[2]**

Rydal Mount 30th Jan[ry], 1833

My dear Miss Kinnaird,

It was very kind in you to avail yourself of your amiable Friends application as an occasion for writing to me with your own hand: Be assured that I take a lively interest in all that concerns you, and that I regret much we are not likely to see you in the North, during the ensuing Summer. As Dora means

---

[1] William Bedell (1571–1642). He was chaplain to Sir Henry Wootton when Ambassador to the Venetian Republic; in 1627 Provost of Trinity Coll., Dublin; in 1629 Bp. of Kilmore and Ardagh. Burnet's *Life* was published in 1685.

[2] Miss Kinnaird was the adopted daughter of Richard Sharp (*E.L.*, p. 384). Mrs Sharp was the widow of R. S.'s brother William.

to write, I need not say any thing of or about the Poem, of which we know more than you do.—

It gives me the sincerest Pleasure to learn that the Winter has dealt mildly with Mr Sharp, and that Mrs Sharp is so well.— Poor Mr Rogers and Miss Rogers! how sorry am I for their recent loss,[1] especially for hers.—And then and at the same time, (mercifully one may say if it was to be published) comes that execrable Lampoon of Lord Byron.[2]—What a monster is a Man of Genius whose heart is perverted! The weather with us has been charming through the winter, with the exception of some half a dozen foggy days. As Dora will tell you how feeble my dear Sister is I shall not dwell upon her state which weighs incessantly upon every thought of my heart. Believe me my dear Miss Kinnaird with sincere affection

most faithfully yours
Wm Wordsworth

Address: Miss Kinnaird

1039. *W. W. to William Rowan Hamilton*

Hamilton(—)
K(—)

Rydal Mount, February 8, 1833.[3]

In reply to the communication made me in your last, let me express my fervent wishes that your marriage may be attended with all the blessings you expect from it; and in this wish my family unite, not excepting my poor sister, whose life is but a struggle from day to day.

In my letter to Miss Hamilton I sent you a message of thanks for the poems, and Mr De Vere's ode.[4] Pray assure him that I am duly sensible of the honour he has done me in his animated verses, a copy of which was also sent me by Miss Rice.

---

[1] Their brother Henry had died in the previous month.

[2] It was first printed in Moore's *Works of Lord B., with Journals, Letters, and his Life*, 17 vols., 1832–3. Cf. Byron, *Letters*, ed. Prothero, ii. 210. The lampoon was 'To Lord Thurlow', who had written some feeble lines *On the Poem of Mr. Rogers entitled* 'An Epistle to a Friend'.

[3] For W. W. to H. C. R. Feb. 5, v. *C.R.*, p. 232.

[4] In 1832 Aubrey de Vere issued a madrigal, beginning 'May is the bridal of the year'.

Your lecture I have read with much pleasure. It is philosophical and eloquent, and instructive, and makes me regret—as I have had a thousand occasions of doing—that I did not apply to mathematics in my youth. It is now, and has long been, too late to make up for the deficiency.

I fear that Mr Coleridge is more than usually unwell: a letter from a London friend informs me that he is still confined to his bed. I hope, however, there is some mistake here, as not very long ago he attended at the consecration of Highgate Church, and had a long conversation with the Bishop of London, who officiated upon that occasion.

It seems a shame to tax you with postage for this letter, and I know not how to get it franked; and even still less do I feel able to make it interesting by any agreeable matter. With regard to poetry, I must say that my mind has been kept this last year and more in such a state of anxiety that all harmonies appear to have been banished from it except those that reliance upon the goodness of God furnishes:

Tota de mente fugavi
Haec studia atque omnes <i>delicias</i> animi.[1]

This must be my excuse for writing after so long an interval a letter so dull. But believe me under all circumstances, etc. . ..

<hr>

_MS._   *1040. W. W. to Edward Quillinan*[2]

Saturday, Feby 23^d
Could not get a frank before.

My dear Mr Quillinan,

I hope you will find some amusement in [? anything] during your solitude at melancholy Lee. I should like to be there a few days with you tho' my eyes would not allow me to gaze upon dazzling water; however dull the place you are surely better there than in Oporto at this time. A friend of mine in this neighbourhood occasionally sees the Athenaeum but has not the No.

<hr>

[1] Catullus, _Carm._ lxviii, _Ad Mallium_, v. 25.
[2] Written by Dora W. in red ink, crossing a letter of her own to E. Q.

which contains your contribution for which I thank you; the suppressed vow is quite characteristic of the Ed^r of the Keepsake. I dont mention my poor Sister who we hope is getting better tho' slowly. We have now in the room a beautiful bunch of Primroses, which is full of promise for her, transplanted from our green terrace. I am much mortified about Boxall's print of me, for except my sister I cannot get any one to look at it with pleasure. How kind Rogers is to Moxon, but I remember with some apprehension that when my good friend 'Joseph of Bristol, the brother of Amos'[1] went from just such a pigmy shop as Moxon's late one the change did not prove advantageous, an instance that Ambition in small matters as well as great is apt to play false with her Votaries. As you dont mention the complaint in your head I hope it is better—one is sometimes ungrateful for not thanking diseases for taking their departure. Did I tell you that your binding of my Poems was much admired by the several parties young and old who have seen the book.—Politics are too dismal to advert to. Principles are kicked out of the House of Commons and Oaths Nuts to them cracked with derision and merriment; in the meanwhile nevertheless there is a God in Heaven, as the British Empire will learn to its cost.

Be assured that in the midst of my public and private anxieties I reserve a corner of my heart for yours, and earnestly wish you were out of them. I am glad that the 4th book of the Excursion has contributed to your support. A year has elapsed since I wrote any poetry but a few lines, and I have rarely even read anything in verse till within the last week, when I have begun to accustom my ear to blank verse in other Authors with a hope they may put me in tune for my own. The Hounds are this moment making a most musical cry, which penetrates the sick room, but the silent looks of our little friend the Primrose are still more agreeable as they announce that the winter music must be near its close. Thanks for Charles Lamb's verses which are characteristic, and believe me with love to the young Ones— my dear Friend, faithfully yours

Wm. Wordsworth.

[1] i.e. Joseph Cottle, *v. E.L.*, p. 149.

MS.
M. G. K.

1041. *W. W. to Alexander Dyce*

Rydal Mount, March 20th, [1833.]

My dear Sir,

I have to thank you for the very valuable Present of Shirley's works, just received. The Preface is all that I have yet had time to read. It pleased me to find that you sympathized with me in admiration of the Passage from the Dutchess of N[ewcastle]'s poetry; and you will be gratified to be told that I share the opinion you have expressed of that cold and false-hearted Frenchified Coxcomb—Horace Walpole.

Poor Shirley! what a melancholy end was his, and then to be so treated by Dryden. One would almost suspect some private cause of dislike, such as is said to have influenced Swift in regard to Dryden himself. Shirley's Death reminded me of a sad close of the life of a literary person, Sanderson[1] by name, in the neighbouring County of Cumberland. He lived in a cottage by himself, though a man of some landed estate; his cottage, from want of care on his part, took fire in the night—the neighbours were alarmed—they ran to his rescue, he escaped, dreadfully burnt from the flames; and lay down (he was in his seventieth year) much exhausted under a tree a few yards from the Door. His friends in the meanwhile endeavoured to save what they could of his property from the flames. He inquired most anxiously after a box in which his MSS and published pieces had been deposited, with a view to a publication of a laboriously corrected edition, and upon being told that the box was consumed—he expired in a few minutes, saying or rather sighing out the words 'Then I do not wish to live'. Poor man! Though the circulation of his works had not extended beyond a circle of 50 miles diameter, perhaps, at the most, he was most anxious to survive in the memory of the few who were likely to hear of him.

The publishing trade, I understand, continues to be much depressed, and authors are driven to solicit or invite subscrip-

---

[1] Thomas Sanderson (1759–1829), schoolmaster and poet; taught at Greystoke and Blackhall near Carlisle, and spent last years of retirement at Kirklinton. His *Original Poems* were published in 1800, and *Companion to the Lakes* in 1807, *v. Life and Literary Remains of T. S.*, ed. by Rev. J. Lowthian, 1829.

tions, as being in many cases the only means for giving their works to the world.

I am always pleased to hear from you; and believe me, my dear sir,

faithfully your obliged friend,

Wm. Wordsworth.

MS.   *1042. W. W. to his Family at Rydal*

Monday Ev^g. [March 1833]

My dearest Friends,

You will be disappointed as I am grieved that you will only have this parcel instead of my body. But the urgent entreaties of Mrs Curwen and Isabella have prevailed on my stay. All was fixed for departing tomorrow, but Mrs P. has got a severe fit of the Lumbago, John is too lame to walk about, and obliged to pass so much of his time alone that I thought it common charity to give him this week. Besides I am anxious to have everything determined about the building that can be, and for this purpose Mr Peele, the Surveyor or Architect, and John and I go to Brigham tomorrow. It was our intention that this should be done, and I proceed to Keswick to be with you on Wednesday; but, as I have said, if I am [not] called home before, I shall prolong my stay here till next Monday, when I shall depart without fail, God willing. Let me express my heartfelt pleasure (after telling you that except for a slight cough Isabella is going on well—she has been downstairs in the large room all day, and the Baby well also and thriving) for the good accounts of dearest Dorothy, and let me thank you, Mary and Dora, for your interesting Letters, to dearest Dora in particular I felt especial obligation, for you know it an *imperative* duty for a wife to write to her absent Husband. For myself I have executed all commissions—ordered the stove, got the Mat as I said, for though I fear you wont like it, it is of Cocoa tree or nut material and may not perhaps be lasting, got a new tooth put in the lower ranges, a new coat and pantaloons, sent you the pattern from King, in short neglected nothing. I have walked and ridden a great deal, almost the whole day and part of the night, having

[644]

dined at Dr Angus at St Bees, and been twice in the evening at Workington, once to dine out with Mr Curwen, and yesterday at seven to hear the famous Calvinistic preacher [?] and one day with another, I have scarcely walked less than 12 miles. The sea is a delightful companion and nothing can be more charming, especially for a sequestered Mountaineer, than to cast eyes over its boundless surface, and hear as I have done almost from the brow of the steep in the Church field at Moresby, the waves chafing and murmuring in a variety of tones below, as a kind of base of harmony to the shrill yet liquid music of the larks above. I took yesterday five minutes of this [?] before going into the Church, and surely it was as good a prelude for devotion as any Psalm, though one of the Moresby female songsters has a charming voice and manages it well. But concerning my employments I have a communication for Dora especially—shall I let it out, I have composed since I came here the promised Poem upon the birth of the Baby,[1] and thrown off yesterday and today, in the course of a ride to [? Arlecdon] (Mr Wilkinson's), a sober and sorrowful sequel[2] to it which I fear none of you will like. They are neither yet fairly written out but I hope to send them for your impressions in this parcel. Mr Wilkinson we did not see, he was in bed with an inflammatory cold. I do not think Isabella will get rid of her cough till milder weather comes for a continuance. The Dr (Mr Dickinson) says the overflow of milk she has proceeds from weakness and that if she could get into the fresh air it would brace her, and the milk would be reduced in quantity and better in quality. The day we dined at W— Hall, I got Mr D. to look at John's ancle about which I was not a little uneasy, but he most confidently assured me that nothing was amiss with the bones and that time, bandages, and cold water would set all to rights. It appears from John that the Surgeon called in from Whitehaven directed his attention almost entirely to the ugly gash in the knee which was cured in a fortnight, and neglected or rather scarcely thought at all about the ancle from which real and permanent mischief was to be apprehended. Had

---

[1] *To —— upon the Birth of her first-born Child*, March 1833, Oxf. W. p. 502.

[2] *The Warning. A Sequel to the Foregoing*, Oxf. W., p. 503.

this been treated with proper care and resolution, the Dr says, it could have been healed in a month—now it will take many to make the leg useful. I dined twice with Lord Lowther and went with him to the play, he went away the next day; as there have been no franks in this neighbourhood since I received your letter for Mrs A. I sent it back—You will find some legacy Receipts for Mr Carter in the parcel.—Lord L. is very gloomy about public affairs, thinking that as this reformed Parliament cannot be altered for the better, nothing can prevent an explosion and the entire overthrow of the Institutions of the Country. He appears to have been gratified by his tour in Italy, and I believe at the bottom of his heart would return there and give up public anxieties and cares, for ever at any sacrifice. Not that he said anything of the kind to me, but from the hopeless tone of his language I draw this inference. I have now scribbled so much that I must leave off or my eyes will scarcely serve for transcribing the Poems which are rather long for such occasion. Bear in mind with respect to 2nd especially that this will be its first appearance on paper and no doubt it will require altering. One word for dearest Sister— how shall I rejoice to see her; if any mischief come to her I shall never forgive myself for staying so long beyond the intended time.—My love would be sent to Jane Pasley but no doubt they are gone. Love, kindest love to you all with blessings innumerable. I send remembrances to all the Servants and neighbours, Mrs Luff not forgotten. Tell Miss B. Harrison that I called yesterday, Sunday afternoon, upon the Browns, thinking that a favorable time, but they were gone to Hensingham. At Dr Angus's I met, with his lady, Mr Parkinson, a lively man who seemed pleased with the notice I had taken of his Poems. John who is sitting beside me—we have both been some time with the ladies—sends his kindest love. Mr Curwen has been here twice but I was gone, again farewell most tenderly yours W. W. Pray write, best perhaps by the coach as you might send any Letters beside. Remember me to Mr Archer, Mr Robinson etc.

P.S. [?] I ought to have said how much I liked Dora's elegant present, and how much cloak and hood were admired and also James' knitting shoes. When I called at the Bookkeepers that time to pay for your parcel charged one shilling he said it was the regular charge for a parcel however small, and that they charged no more for anything under a stone-weight. Tell this with my kind regards to John Carter, surely it is not correct, they never charge the Legacy parcels at this rate. I have written all the above and transcribed the Poems by candle-light this Monday evening. I was at prayers this morning at John's Church.

K.   *1043. W. W. to Benjamin Dockray*

Rydal Mount, April 25, [1833.][1]

My dear Sir,

Your *Egeria* arrived on the morning when I was setting off to visit my son, with whom I stayed nearly three weeks. This must be my apology for not thanking you for the valuable present somewhat earlier. The strain of your thoughts is, I think, excellent, and the expression everywhere suitable to the thought. I have to thank you also for a most valuable paper on Colonial Slavery. In your view of this important subject I entirely coincide. Fanaticism is the disease of these times as much or more than of any other; fanaticism is set, as it has always been, whether moral, religious, or political, upon attain-ment of its ends with disregard of the means. In this question there are *three* parties,—the slave, the slaveowner, and the British people. As to the first, it might be submitted to the consideration of the owner whether, in the present state of society, he can, as a matter of private conscience, retain his property in the slave, after he is convinced that it would be for the slave's benefit, civil, moral, and religious, that he should be emancipated. Whatever pecuniary loss might, under these cir-cumstances, attend emancipation, it seems that a slave-owner, taking a right view of the case, ought to be prepared to undergo it. It is probable, however, that one of the best assurances which could be given of the slave being likely to make a good use of his

[1] K. dates 1840, but Miss Batho (*The Later W.*, p. 219) shows that com-plete abolition of slavery in the W. Indies was carried in 1833, and that both this letter and Dockray's 'most valuable paper' would be pointless in 1840. The third part of *Egeria* appeared in 1840, but the date on the last page of the second part is June 21, 1832.

liberty would be found in his ability and disposition to make a recompense for the sacrifice should the master, from the state of his affairs, feel himself justified in accepting a recompense. But by no means does it follow, from this view of individual cases, that the *third* party, the people of England, who through their legislature have sanctioned and even encouraged slavery, have a right to interfere for its destruction by a sweeping measure, of which an equivalent to the owner makes no part. This course appears to me unfeeling and unjust. . . .

What language, in the first place, would it hold out to the slave? That the property in him had been held by unqualified usurpation and injustice on the part of his master alone. This would be as much as to say, 'We have delivered him over to you; and as no other party was to blame, deal with your late oppressors as you like.' Surely such a proceeding would also be a wanton outrage upon the feelings of the masters, and poverty, distress, and disorder could not but ensue.

They who are most active in promoting entire and immediate Abolition do not seem sufficiently to have considered that slavery is not in itself at all times and under all circumstances to be deplored. In many states of society it has been a check upon worse evils; so much inhumanity has prevailed among men that the best way of protecting the weak from the powerful has often been found in what seems at first sight a monstrous arrangement; viz., in one man having a property in many of his fellows. Some time ago many persons were anxious to have a bill brought into Parliament to protect inferior animals from the cruelty of their masters. It has always appeared to me that such a law would not have the effect intended, but would increase the evil. The best surety for an uneducated man behaving with care and kindness to his beast lies in the sense of the uncontrolled property which he possesses in him. Hence a livelier interest, and a more efficient responsibility to his own conscience, than could exist were he made accountable for his conduct to law. I mention this simply by way of illustration, for no man can deplore more than I do a state of slavery in itself. I do not only deplore but I *abhor* it, if it could be got rid of without the introduction of something worse, which I much fear would not be the case with respect to the West Indies, if the question be dealt with in the way many excellent men are so eagerly set upon. I am, dear sir,

Very sincerely, your obliged

Wm. Wordsworth.

MS. **1044. W. W. to Robert Southey**

[May 1833][1]

My dear S—

I like your Book[1] much, and have only one objection to what I have seen: viz. the notice of Mr Wilberforce[2] by name. My wish is that you should adopt it as a general Rule, not to allude (in the mention of public men),—to their *private* habits, otherwise your book will be so far degraded to the level of the magazine-writers—but probably this may be the only instance, and as it is so good natured there is little or no harm in it. A public man's public foibles are fair game!—The Popes[3] allusion is also well struck out—it is astonishing how queerly in these fantastic times the sale[4] of a Book may be checked by what might seem the arrantest trifle.—

I hope you have not forgot what I told you about the puppet-shows of Ingleton[5]—and that you will notice them in some way or other. The puppets are still to be seen there—which used to travel all England over, the great Master of the art living there.—

We are truly glad that you have had no return of your ugly attack—

ever affectionately yours

Remember Dr Green[6] the famous quack—Doctor of Doncaster, of a gentleman's family and regularly educated, he

---

[1] This undated letter must have been written after D. W.'s illness in 1829 and before Jan. 1834, when Vols. I and II of Southey's *Doctor* were published. The reference to S.'s 'ugly attack' (writing to Rickman in May 1, 1833 he refers to 'an ugly seizure some 20 days ago, and *v.* next letter), to the raw and uncertain weather, and to the 'pamphlet', point to May 1833.

[2] The reference to Wilberforce, who seems to have kept snuff loose in his pockets, is to be found in *The Doctor*, i. 23.

[3] *v. Doctor,* i. 117, where S. refers to Nepotism as 'peculiarly a Papal vice'; the MS. version of the passage may have been more severe.

[4] sale: MS. sail.   [5] *v. Doctor,* i. 213 ff.

[6] *v. Doctor,* i. 227, where S. gives an account of Dr Green based on W.'s letter.

flourished in the middle of the last century in all the Midland counties and used to prefer itinerancy with a stage and a zany to regular practice. So famous was he and so fortunate that his name was adopted for many years afterwards by many travelling Mountebanks, or rather by all of them, at least in these parts. Relatives of his own name still reside at Doncaster or near it. Old Wilsy[1] knew him well. Wilsy and all the old women used to look back with delight upon his exhibitions, and talk of them with profound reverence also for his medical skill.—

Many thanks for your Pamphlet[2]

W. W.

My Sister rather suffers from this raw and uncertain weather.

Address: Robt Southey Esqre

1045. *W. W. to Mrs. W. P. Rawson*[3]

Bulletin of
John Rylands Library,
July 1934.

[? May 1833[3]]

Dear Madam,

Your letter which I lose no time in replying to, has placed me under some embarrassment, as I happen to possess some MSS. verses of my own[4] upon the subject to which you solicit my attention. But I frankly own to you, that neither with respect to this subject nor to the kindred one, the Slavery of the Children in the Factories, which is adverted to in the same Poem, am I prepared to add to the excitement already existing in the public mind upon these, and so many other points of legislation and government. Poetry, if good for anything, must appeal forcibly to the imagination and the feelings; but what, at this period, we

[1] Mrs Wilson, the old housekeeper at Greta Hall, beloved of Hartley Coleridge, who used to call her Wilsy (*v. E.L.*, p. 279). She died in 1820.

[2] *A Letter to John Murray Esq. 'touching' Lord Nugent, in reply to a letter from his Lordship touching an article in the Quarterly Review*, 1833.

[3] Mary Ann Rawson, daughter of Joseph Read of Sheffield, an original member of the committee of the Sheffield Female Anti-Slavery Society (1825). In 1834 she published an anthology of anti-slavery prose and verse entitled *The Bow in the Cloud*, to which, among others, Bernard Barton, William and Mary Howitt, Lord Morpeth, and James Montgomery contributed. Southey, in a letter dated May 4, 1833, declined; W. W.'s letter, undated, probably belongs to the same month.

[4] 'Humanity' (composed 1829, publ. 1835): *v.* Oxf. W., p. 500.

want above everything, is patient examination and sober judgement. It can scarcely be necessary to add that my mind revolts as strongly as anyone's can, from the law that permits one human being to sell another. It is in principle monstrous, but it is not the worst thing in human nature. Let precipitate advocates for its destruction bear this in mind. But I will not enter farther into the question than to say, that there are three parties—the Slave—the Slave owner—and the Imperial Parliament, or rather the people of the British Islands, acting through that organ. Surely the course at present pursued is hasty, intemperate, and likely to lead to gross injustice. Who in fact are most to blame? The people—who, by their legislation, have sanctioned not to say encouraged, slavery. But now we are turning round at once upon the planters, and heaping upon them indignation without measure, as if we wished that the Slaves should believe that their Masters alone were culpable— and they alone fit objects of complaint and resentment.

Excuse haste and believe me, Dear Madam,
respectfully yours,
Wm Wordsworth.

P.S. Unwillingness to allude to my own writings, even though indirectly led to the subject, has prevented me from expressing the satisfaction which I felt from your Letter that they had afforded you so much pleasure.

Address: Mrs W. B. Rawson, Joseph Read's Esqre, Wincobank Hall, near Sheffield.

MS.
M. G. K.

1046. *W. W. to Alexander Dyce*

[? spring 1833.][1]

My dear Sir,

The dedication[2] which you propose I shall esteem as an honor; nor do I conceive upon what ground, but an over-scrupulous modesty, I could object to it.

Be assured that Mr Southey will not have the slightest unwillingness to your making any use you think proper of his

[1] Undated, but obviously written some time before Letter of Dec. 4.
[2] Of *Specimens of English Sonnets selected by A. Dyce*, which appeared in this year.

Memoir of Bampfylde:[1] I shall not fail to mention the subject to him upon the first opportunity.

You propose to give specimens of the best *Sonnet-writers* in our language. May I ask if by this be meant a Selection of the *best Sonnets, best* both as to *kind* and *degree*? A Sonnet may be excellent in its kind, but that kind of very inferior interest to one of a higher order, though not perhaps in every minute particular quite so well executed, and from the pen of a writer of inferior Genius. It should seem that the best rule to follow, would be, first to pitch upon the Sonnets which are best *both* in kind and perfectness of execution, and, next, those which, although of a humbler quality, are admirable for the finish and happiness of the execution, taking care to exclude all those which have not one or other of these recommendations, however striking they might be as characteristic of the age in which the author lived, or some peculiarity of his manner. The tenth sonnet of Donne, beginning 'Death, be not proud', is so eminently characteristic of his manner, and at the same time so weighty in thought, and vigorous in the expression, that I would entreat you to insert it, though to modern taste it may be repulsive, quaint, and laboured.

There are two sonnets of Russell,[2] which, in all probability, you may have noticed, 'Could, then, the Babes', and the one upon Philoctetes, the last six lines of which are first-rate. Southey's Sonnet to Winter[3] pleases me much; but, above all, among modern writers, that of Sir Egerton Brydges, upon Echo and Silence. Miss Williams's Sonnet upon Twilight is pleasing; that upon Hope of great merit.

Do you mean to have a short preface upon the Construction of the Sonnet? Though I have written so many, I have scarcely made up my own mind upon the subject. It should seem that the Sonnet, like every other legitimate composition, ought to

---

[1] John Codrington Bampfylde (1754–96) wrote sixteen sonnets (1778) which Southey called 'some of the most original in our language'.—K.

[2] Thomas Russell (1762–88), *Sonnets and Miscellaneous Poems*, 1789. Wordsworth paid him the compliment of adopting his words in the last four lines of his own sonnet on *Iona* (Oxf. W., p. 474).

[3] 'A wrinkled, crabbed man they picture thee, Old Winter' (Oxf. Southey, p. 350), written in 1799.

have a beginning, a middle, and an end—in other words, to consist of three parts, like the three propositions of a syllogism, if such an illustration may be used. But the frame of metre adopted by the Italians does not accord with this view, and, as adhered to by them, it seems to be, if not arbitrary, best fitted to a division of the sense into two parts, of eight and six lines each. Milton, however, has not submitted to this. In the better half of his sonnets the sense does not close with the rhyme at the eighth line, but overflows into the second portion of the metre. Now it has struck me, that this is not done merely to gratify the ear by variety and freedom of sound, but also to aid in giving that pervading sense of intense Unity in which the excellence of the Sonnet has always seemed to me mainly to consist. Instead of looking at this composition as a piece of architecture, making a whole out of three parts, I have been much in the habit of preferring the image of an orbicular body, —a sphere—or a dew-drop. All this will appear to you a little fanciful; and I am well aware that a Sonnet will often be found excellent, where the beginning, the middle, and the end are distinctly marked, and also where it is distinctly separated into *two* parts, to which, as I before observed, the strict Italian model, as they write it, is favorable. Of this last construction of Sonnet, Russell's upon Philoctetes is a fine specimen; the first eight lines give the hardship of the case, the six last the consolation, or the *per-contra*. Ever faithfully,

Your much obliged Friend and Ser^{nt},

W. Wordsworth.

Do not pay the postage of your letter to me.

In the case of the Cumberland poet,[1] I overlooked a most pathetic circumstance. While he was lying under the tree, and his friends were saving what they could from the flames, he desired them to bring out the box that contained his papers if possible. A person went back for it, but the bottom dropped out and the papers fell into the flames and were consumed. Immediately upon hearing this the poor old Man expired.

Address: The Revd Alex. Dyce, 9 Grey's Inn Sq^{re}, London.

[1] *v.* Letter of March 20.

1047. W. W. to William Rowan Hamilton

Hamilton.
G. M(—) K(—)

Rydal Mount May 8, 1833.[1]

My dear Sir,

My letters being of no value but as tokens of friendship, I waited for the opportunity of a frank, which I had reason to expect earlier. Sincerely do we all congratulate you upon your marriage. Accept our best wishes upon the event, and believe that we shall always be deeply interested in your welfare. Make our kind regards also to Mrs Hamilton, who of course will be included in every friendly hope and expectation formed for yourself.

We look with anxiety to your sister Eliza's success in her schemes,—but for pecuniary recompense in literature, especially poetical, nothing can be more unpromising than the present state of affairs, except what we have to fear for the future. Mrs Godwyn, who sends verses to Blackwood, is our neighbour. I have had no conversation with her myself upon the subject, but a friend of hers says she has reason to believe that she has got nothing but a present of books. This however is of no moment, as Mrs G. being a person of easy fortune she has not probably bargained for a return in money. Mrs Hemans I see continues to publish in the periodicals. If you ever see her, pray remember me affectionately to her, and tell her that I have often been, and still am, troubled in conscience for having left her obliging letter so long unanswered: but she must excuse me as there is not a motive in my mind urging me to throw any interest into my letters to friends beyond the expression of kindness and esteem; and *that* she does not require from me. Besides my friends in general know how much I am hindered in all my pursuits by the inflammation to which my eyes are so frequently subject. I have long given up all exercise of them by candle-light, and the evenings and nights are the seasons when one is most disposed to converse in that way with absent friends. News you do not care about, and I have none for you, except what concerns friends. My sister, God be thanked, has had a respite. She can now walk a few steps about her room, and has been borne twice into the open air. Southey, to whom I sent

[1] For W. W. to H. C. R. May 5, *v. C.R.*, p. 236.

your Sonnets, had, I grieve to say, a severe attack of some unknown and painful complaint about ten days ago. It weakened
him much, but he is now, I believe, perfectly recovered. Coleridge, I have reason to think, is confined to his bed; his mind
vigorous as ever. Your Sonnets, I think, are as good as anything
you have done in verse. We like the 2ᵈ best, and I single it out
the more readily, as it allows me an opportunity of reminding
you of what I have so often insisted upon, the extreme care
which is necessary in the composition of poetry.

> The ancient images *shall not* depart
> From my soul's temple, the refined gold
> Already prov'd *remain.*

Your meaning is that it shall remain, but, according to the construction of our language, you have said it shall not.

> the refined gold,
> Well proved, shall then remain,

will serve to explain my objection.

Could you not take us in your way when coming or going to
Cambridge? If Mrs H. accompanies you, we shall be glad to
see her also.

I hope that in the meeting about to take place in Cambridge
there will be less of mutual flattery among the men of Science
than appeared in that of the last year in Oxford. Men of Science
in England seem, indeed, to copy their fellows in France, by
stepping too much out of their way for titles, and baubles of that
kind, and for offices of state and political struggles which they
would do better to keep out of.

With kindest regards to yourself and Mrs H., and to your
sisters, believe me ever

My dear Mr H.,

Faithfully yours,

W. W.

MS.   **1048. W. W. to Edward Moxon**

My dear Sir,   Rydal Mount May 14ᵗʰ [1833]

My Daughter joins with me in thanks for your Sonnets[1] which
we have both read with much pleasure. There is a great deal of

---

[1] Moxon's *Sonnets* was published in 1833; a second volume appeared in
1835, dedicated to W.

sweet feeling and pleasing expression in them. In the 3ᵈ there is a mistake, the River that flows through Rydal is not the Brathay but the Rothay—This is a good Sonnet. Were I asked to name a favorite or two, perhaps I should chuse 12,—18—23—28. In the cadence and execution of your Sonnets I seem to find more of the manner of Bowles than my own, and this you must not think a disparagement as Bowles in his sonnets has been very successful. The principal fault in your style is an overfrequency of inversion. For example at the close of the first —the fall of Man is a phraze of meaning so awful, and so much in the thoughts and upon the tongue of every religious Person that the Dislocation of the words is to me a little startling—not that I have any wish that it should be altered.—As to the Selection,[1] I think you are a little too sanguine: a Collection from different Authors will always be preferred for schools, and if well done ought to be. In other times, however, I think the one from my Poems would sell, were it only for its cheapness; but as the whole of my Poems are sold at a much lower price than formerly, by means of the Pirated french Edition,[2] and my own last, the Selections are not even in respect of price so well off as before.—It is a disgrace to the age that Poetry wont sell without prints—I am a little too proud to let my Ship sail in the wake of the Engravers and the drawing-mongers. Thank you for your kind offer of your house—and also for sending Lamb's present,[3] most of the Essays I have read and with great pleasure—ever faithfully your friend W. Wordsworth.

MS.   ***1049. W. W. to Charles Lamb***
M(—) *G*(—) *K*(—)

Rydal Mount, Friday, May 17, 1833 or thereabouts.

My dear Lamb,

I have to thank you and Moxon for a delightful Vol: your last, I hope not, of *Elia*.[4] I have read it all, except some of the

---

[1] i.e. the selection of W.'s poems made by Hine, *v.* Letter 971.

[2] i.e. the edition published by Galignani in 1828.

[3] *v.* next letter.

[4] *The Last Essays of Elia, Being a Sequel to Essays Published under that Name*, 1833.

popular fallacies which I reserve not to get through my Cake all at once. The Book has much pleased the whole of my family, viz. my Wife, Daughter, Miss Hutchinson, and my poor dear Sister, on her sick bed; they all return their best thanks—I am not sure but I like the Old China and The Wedding as well as any of the Essays.—I read Love me and love my Dog to my poor Sister this morning, while I was rubbing her legs at the same time.—She was much pleased, and, what is rather remarkable, this morning, also, I fell upon an Anecdote in Madame D'Arblayes' life of her father, where the other side of the question is agreeably illustrated. The heroes of the Tale are David Garrick and a favorite little Spaniel of King Charles's Breed, which he left with the Burneys when he and Mrs Garrick went on their Travels. In your remarks upon Martin's pictures,[1] I entirely concur.—May it not be a question whether your own Imagination has not done a good deal for Titian's Bacchus and Ariadne?

With all my admiration of that great artist, I cannot but think that neither Ariadne or Theseus look so well on his Canvas as they ought to do—But you and your Sister will be anxious, if she be with you, to hear something of our poor Invalid—She has had a long and sad illness—anxious to us above measure, and she is now very weak and poorly—though she has been out of doors in a chair three times since the warm weather came. In the winter we expected her dissolution daily for some little time. She then recovered so as to quit her bed, but not her room, and to walk a few steps, but within these few days the thundery weather has brought on a bilious attack which has thrown her back a good deal and taken off the flesh which she was beginning to recover. —Her Spirits however, thank God, are good, and whenever she is able to read she beguiles her time wonderfully,—but I am sorry to say that we cannot expect that whatever may become of her health, her strength will ever be restored. I have been

---

[1] John Martin (1789–1854), landscape and historical painter. In 1821 he became widely popular by his *Belshazzar's Feast*, which was followed by many pictures on Biblical subjects and by illustrations of the Bible and *Paradise Lost*. He was ranked for grandeur among the greatest geniuses of his age, and Wilkie thought his *Belshazzar* a 'phenomenon'; but Lamb took him as an example of the *Barrenness of the Imaginative Faculty in the Productions of Modern Art*.

thus particular, knowing how much you and your dear sister value this excellent person, who in tenderness of heart I do not honestly believe [was] ever exceeded by any of God's Creatures. Her loving-kindness has no bounds. God bless her for ever and ever!—Again thanking you for your excellent Book, and wishing to know how you and your dear Sister are, with best love to you both from us all,

I remain, my dear Lamb,
Your faithful friend
W. Wordsworth.

M. G. K. *1050. W. W. to C. W. Jun[r] 1*

Rydal Mount, June 17, 1833[2]

My dear C,

You are welcome to England after your long ramble. I know not what to say in answer to your wish for my opinion upon the offer of the lectureship. . . .

I have only one observation to make, to which I should attach importance if I thought it called for in your case, which I do not. I mean the moral duty of avoiding to encumber yourself with private pupils in any number. You are at an age when the blossoms of the mind are setting, to make fruit ; and the practice of *pupil-mongering* is an absolute blight for this process. Whatever determination you come to, may God grant that it proves for your benefit: this prayer I utter with earnestness, being deeply interested, my dear C, in all that concerns you. I have said nothing of the uncertainty hanging over all the establishments, especially the religious and literary ones of the country, because if they are to be overturned, the calamity would be so widely spread, that every mode of life would be involved in it, and nothing survive for hopeful calculation. . . .

We are always delighted to hear of any or all of you. God bless you, my dear C.

Most faithfully, your affectionate,
W. Wordsworth.

[1] i.e. his nephew.
[2] For W. W. to H. C. R. of May 18 or 28, June 4, and June 5, v. C.R., pp. 238–42.

MS.   *1051. W. W. to his Family at Rydal*

Greenock Wednesday morn[g] half past ten

[July 17, 1833]

Dearest Friends one and all

Just arrived here from Ramsey, which we left yester Eve after a charming passage—no rocking of the vessel, no squeamishness. Ailsa Craig the peaks of Arran and the whole land and sea views most beautiful in sunshine with curling vapours, and an eclipse of the sun[1] between 5 and 6 this morning into the bargain. I thought of Lugano. A boat sails for Oban this afternoon which we shall take and so proceed to Staffa—which way we shall take then will depend upon weather and opportunities. I fear we shall be unable to receive Letters from Rydal till we reach Carlisle—as I am quite unable to tell you where to address me. The weather has been enchanting—but had we gone to Liverpool last Friday we should have been here by three o'clock of last Sunday morning—but then we should not ever have touched at the Isle of Man. As John wrote on Sunday evening I need only tell you that between 7 and 8 that evening Mr R[2] and I reached Bala Sala.[3] Mrs C well, Mr C with a touch of the Rheumatic gout causing lameness: Bala Sala is a little wood-embosomed Village by the side of a stream upon which stands the ruined walls of an old Abbey, a pretty sequestered place—thronged with Blackbirds and thrushes of extraordinary size and power of song—the upper part of the old Tower is over-grown with a yellow Lychen which has the appearance of a gleam of perpetual evening sunshine. In front of the Cottage where the Cooksons[4] live is a narrow sloping garden richly stocked with the choicest flowers, many of them exotics. Next morning we walked from Castleton to the new College finished all but the top of the tower and thence with the sea on our right walked to the extremity of the left Horn of the bay, where Mr C. told us we should see some *noble* rocks which did not prove quite so noble as good Mr Clarkson's Ducks, but wo were recompensed

---

[1] *v.* Oxf. W., p. 471.   [2] i.e. Crabb Robinson.
[3] *v.* Oxf. W., p. 470.
[4] Mr Cookson of Kendal, who after some financial losses had retired to the Isle of Man.

by agreeable views of Castleton bay, town, church, castle, the College, one windmill, the only one of the Island, and the grand slopes backward to the South Barsul, the Manx[1] name for mountain.—all this is chiefly for dearest Dorothy. After breakfast took a car for six miles to the summit of the mountainous slope, on the road to Peel. When we had travelled in this wretched vehicle three miles, whom should we come upon but Mrs Cookson who started up like a Hare out of her Fern—and told us that she had been waiting there an hour and a half beguiling the time with Peveril of the Peak. She put into our hands a Letter for Joanna, and we part[ed] much too soon for our mutual wish, she returning to Bala Sala something better than a mile off. From the sixth milestone where we had met a fresh bracing mountain air, we found the road descending agreeably and rapidly towards St Johns. We halted under some sycamores beside a waterfall on our left; and there took a nap, to the great delight of the neighbouring cottagers. Halted again at the Tynewald,[2] St John's, and here eleven cottage children gathered about us, and nearly on the top of Tynewald (dearest D. knows what it is) sate an old Gullion with a telescope in his hand through which he peeped occasionally having the advantage of seeing things double, for as he frankly owned he had got a drop too much. Arrived at Peel after five. Dined and went to the Castle which we sailed round to the great dismay of my Companion though the sea was calm as glass, but it broke unintelligibly with noise and foam over the sharp black rocks on which the Castle stands. At 7 next morning started and walked to Kirk Michael, 7 miles to breakfast, crossed several deep ravines and one very near Kirk Michael very beautiful. (D. will recall it). I was much pleased with Peel Bay, especially on looking back from the slope of the hill which you ascend on quitting the Town for Kirk Michael. Here about a quarter of a mile from Peel stands a Farm house, with a Summer house, that commands the Bay delightfully. From Kirk Michael walked to B[ps] Court and thence I proceeded to Ballaugh where I waited till the coach overtook me. I had left Mr R. in the grounds of B[ps] Court. Near the Deemster's very handsome house I met John going to

---

[1] MS. Manks. [2] v. Oxf. W., p. 470.

dine there—I *could not*—nor did he, but he joined me at the Inn, and we went to Joanna's. She is looking not ill. We had luncheon and tea with her. The Deemster and his Lady came down to the shore to see us embark. Margaret C. *said* to be something better. Upon the whole, Dearest D., I liked your Isle of Man better than I expected. We had charming weather, which made everything look bright. I am very anxious dearest Sister about you, and by far the worst thing about the Tour is not knowing where you should direct to me—I will call however at the Post Off. at Inverness in case we go there; also at Edinburgh and at Glasgow, for we possibly may return this way. Tell Sir Thomas Pasley that the prices of Lodging vary according to the accomodation—at Castle Mora, Table d'hote and lodging two guineas a head per week, at the principal Inn Castleton, not half that money—I could not learn that there are bathing Machines anywhere but at Douglas—but both at Peel and Castleton gentlemen may bathe conveniently on the shore—If Sir Thomas thinks of going, he had best repair to Douglas where he could be at an hotel till he found a private lodging to his mind. There is a very agreeable Hotel, as I am told, called the Crescent near Castle, here the terms are 27 shillings a head—Dearest Dorothy I thought far too much about your fatiguing walks in the Isle of Man and wished many times for you all to see the objects which pleased me so much. John has told you about shy Henry. The view of Douglas Bay is much improved lately by a new Church, by the Tower of Refuge[1] and a new Light house.—I called both on Mr Gray the Postmaster and Mrs Puttenham[2] who inquired with much interest after Dorothy. God bless you all—the Baby included—How are the Invalids? I ask but can get no answer, in the list both Dora and Julia are included—Dearest Mary, we must make a little Trip sometime to Mona—ever most affectionately and faithfully yours W. W.

John and Mr Robinson are exploring the Town.

Address: Mrs Wordsworth, Rydal Mount, near Kendal.

---

[1] *v. Sonnet* XV, Oxf. W., p. 469.
[2] Wife of the Mr Putman of D. W.'s *Tour in the Isle of Man* (ed. K. ii. 286).

MS.
K(—)

1052. *W. W. to Mrs Hemans*

Rydal Mount Aug 20th [1833][1]

My dear Mrs Hemans

It gave me much pleasure to hear from you once again, and by a letter of which your Son Charles was the Bearer; we were all glad to see how well he looks, how much he is grown, and what strength for walking and exercise he has acquired. It was agreeable to us also to make the acquaintance of Mr Graves,[2] who appears to be very amiable; and he is certainly a Man of gentlemanly manners, of talents and thoroughly well-informed. Had my eyes permitted, but they are in a state which compels me to employ an Amanuensis, I might have been tempted to write at some length, but I must be short, for our house is overwhelmed with engagements at this Season.

We are concerned to hear that your health has not been good; as far as its improvement might depend upon a change of residence, if this Country should be your choice, gratifying as it would be to see you here again, I must in sincerity say, that taking the year thro', you would not be much of a gainer by the exchange. Ireland is no doubt upon the whole a moister Climate than England—but the more level parts of Ireland are I apprehend dryer than the mountainous parts of England, Scotland and Wales. The whole of the Eastern coast of Great Britain is much less moist than the Western.

The visit which occasioned the Poem addressed to Sir Walter Scott, that you mention in terms so flattering, was a very melancholy one—My daughter was with me; we arrived at his house on Monday noon, and left it at the same time on Thursday,

---

[1] For W. W. to H. C. R. July 29, *v. C.R.*, p. 246. Mr L. McIntyre dates this letter 1834 because, he says, W. had not met Graves in 1833. But a letter from Graves to W., dated Oct. 12, 1833, proves that he and his brother, with Charles Hemans, visited the Lakes in the summer of 1833, that W. took to him, and he to W. and the Lakes. After this Mrs H. wrote asking W. to try and get him a curacy (*v.* 1834 Letters). And the allusion to D. W.'s health fits better with 1833 than with 1834.

[2] Robert Perceval Graves, son of Mrs H.'s Dublin doctor, and at this time a student at Trinity College, Dublin. Through W.'s influence he obtained in 1835 a curacy at Bowness, and became an intimate friend of the W. family.

the very day before he quitted Abbotsford for London, on his way to Naples. On the morning of our departure he composed a few lines for Dora's Album, and wrote them in it; we prize this Memorial very much, and the more so as an affecting testimony of his regard at the time, when as the verses prove, his health of body and powers of mind were much impaired and shaken. You will recollect the little green book which you were kind enough to write in on its first page.

Let me hope that your health will improve, so that you may be enabled to proceed with the Sacred Poetry with which you are engaged—Be assured that I shall duly appreciate the mark of honour you design for me in connection with so interesting a work.

My Sister is much better than she was in the winter—being able to walk about in her room unsupported, and to take an airing in the carriage when the weather is favourable. She, Mrs W. and Dora all unite with me in kind remembrances, and good wishes for yourself and your Sons.

   [ ] believe me dear Mrs Hemans to be
     ever your faithful Friend
          Wm Wordsworth.

MS.   *1053. W. W. to Edward Moxon*
M(—) G(—) K(—)
       Lowther Castle West[nd] [Aug. 1833]
My dear Mr Moxon

Accept my own hearty congratulations, and those of all my family upon the event announced by your bridal Present,[1] which along with one of the same purport for Mr Southey, reached Rydal just before I left it, to attend the Assizes at Carlisle. As I expect[ed] to procure a Frank there I deferred making my acknowledgements for your attention upon this interesting occasion, and I write from this place under cover, having been disappointed at Carlisle.—But too much of this, Be assured we all rejoice in the prospect before [? you]; as I learned from Mr Lamb sometime since, who the Lady is, and also his high

---

[1] Moxon had married Emma Isola, Lamb's adopted daughter, on July 30.

opinion of her deserts; and his favorable expectations for your then intended union. Pray present my very kind regards to your Bride, and add that we should be happy to see you both at Rydal, should it ever suit you to make so long a journey.

At Carlisle I had the pleasure of seeing in a Booksellers shop, the Illustrations of the forthcoming Edition of Mr Rogers Miscellaneous Poems.[1] As far as I could judge from a hasty inspection, without opportunity for comparison, I am inclined to think that the embellishments will be reckoned fully equal to those of the *Italy*.

There does not appear to be much genuine relish for poetical Literature in Cumberland; if I may judge from the fact of not a copy of my Poems having sold there by one of the leading Booksellers, though Cumberland is my native County.—Byron and Scott are I am persuaded the only *popular* Writers in that line, perhaps the word ought rather to be that they are *fashionable* Writers. My Poor Sister is something better in health. Pray remember me very affectionately to Charles Lamb, and to his dear Sister if she be in a state to receive such communications from her friends. I hope Mr Rogers is well. Give my kindest regards to him also

> ever, My dear Mr Moxon
> faithfully yours
> W Wordsworth

MS.　　　*1054. W. W. to John Marshall*

> [?] Lowther, Sunday Morning—[1833]

My dear Sir,

Mr Rogers and I will come to Halsteads on Thursday, if it should suit you and Mrs Marshall—I shall be on my way homewards——

> Ever faithfully yours
> Wm. Wordsworth

---

[1] *Poems, with steel engravings by Turner, J. W. M., and Stothard, J.,* 1834. *v.* Letter of Dec. 31.

1055. *W. W. to John Kenyon*

Rydal Mount, Sept. 23^d, [1833.]

My dear Mr Kenyon,

Your letter was most welcome. It is truly agreeable to be told in this unexpected way that one still lives in the memory of one's friends. We should have replied earlier, but your letter reached us when Mrs Wordsworth's mind was much depressed by the death of her eldest Brother, and as for myself, I have been and still am unable to write because of my old enemy, inflammation in my eyes.

The only remarkable events that have occurred in my family since our last intercourse by letter are the dangerous illness of my sister, and the addition to our family by the birth of a Grand-daughter, who as being the first of the 3^d. generation both by father and mother's side is highly thought of by both families. She is withal a nice little thing in herself; by name Jane Stanley Wordsworth, from her maternal grandmother. Upon the banks of the Derwent, 2 miles below Cockermouth, my native Town, her Father is now building a Parsonage house upon a living, somewhat under £200 a year, to which he was lately presented by my honored friend the Earl of Lonsdale—and I am still simple and fanciful enough to draw pleasure from the thought of his Child culling flowers and gathering pebbles upon the banks of the same stream that furnished me with the like delights 60 years ago.

> So in the passing of a day, doth pass
> Of mortal life the bud, the leaf, the flower.[1]

I congratulate you upon the noble conduct of your Br., which is quite of a piece of all we know of him. I wish he could have spared a fortnight for this country before his return to Germany —he would be welcome under this roof. Mr Southey also esteems him much, and would have been pleased to see him. May we not hope, upon some future occasion, when your sister's health is recovered, that we may welcome you and Mrs Kenyon also?

It is mortifying that so many persons, indifferent, or disagree-

---

[1] Spenser, *F.Q.* ii. xii. 75 (misquoted).

able to us, should take furnished houses in this Vale, and we never have a glimpse of you here, in that way, or any other. There is an opening preparing, and let me tell you of it, with an entreaty that you and Mrs K. would take it into serious consideration.

Within $\frac{3}{4}$ of a mile of Rydal Mount on the banks of the stream that flows between the Lakes of Rydal and Windermere, Dr Arnold, Master of Rugby School, is building a House for himself and his family to retire to, during the Summer and Winter Vacations; so that it will not be wanted by the owner more than 10 weeks in the year; and I can scarcely doubt that he would let it on very reasonable terms, to an eligible Tenant, and none could be more so than yourselves, during the time he does not want it. You would then have every accommodation, and no obligation be incurred. The pleasure this would be to us, I need not speak of.

In the way of chat I may tell you that great changes are going on in the Proprietorships of the Lake district. Mr Marshall's 2^d son, as probably you know, the Member for Leeds, has purchased the Greenwich Hospital Estate at Keswick, and is Lord of Derwentwater—and this morning has invited me to meet him at Keswick, which I cannot do, for my advice in some new Plantations which he meditates; so that we hope the beauty of the country will not suffer from this princely Estate falling into his hands. At the head of Windermere Mr Redmaine, a Silk Mercer of Bond Street, has purchased 500 acres, including the residences of Brathay Hall, and Old Brathay once occupied by Sir George Beaumont, and afterwards by Charles Lloyd—and previously, while the Lakes were an unvisited corner of the world, by two flashy Brothers, named Westren, who came hither to sculk, and were hanged for highway robbery. The silk mercer will have command of some miles of the shore of Windermere, and what he will do thereupon is perhaps better known in Bond St. than with us, but we tremble.

You speak of your own troubles, and allude to mine. It is true, as was affirmed in an offensive Paragraph in a Glasgow paper, that I have been taking a peep at the Hebrides. My tour, which was only for a fortnight, included the Isle of Man

(visited for the first time), Staffa, Iona, and a return thro'
Burns's country, Renfrewshire and Ayrshire. The weather was
mixed, but upon the whole I and my companions, Mr Robinson,
an ex-barrister, and my son John, were well repaid.

About 10 days after my return I was summoned to Carlisle
upon business, took Mrs Wordsworth with me, and we came
home up the banks of the Eden, by Corby and Nunnery, both
charming places, to Lowther, and home by Ullswater. These
two Excursions united, have since produced 22 sonnets, which
I shall be happy to read you; the more so because I cannot
muster courage to publish them, or anything else. I seem to
want a definite motive—money would be one, if I could get it,
but I cannot; I find by my Publisher's acc^t, which I rec^d the
other day, that the last Ed^n of my Poems owes us conjointly (my
share being 2 thirds) nearly £200. The Ed^n was 2000, of which
not quite 400 had been sold last June; a fact which, contrasted
with the state of my poetical reputation, is wholly inexplicable,
notwithstanding the depressed state of the book market in
England, if we do not take into consideration the injury done
by the Paris Edition, of which the sale, as we have reason to
believe, has been very large. At all events, those Paris publications, morally piratical, are extremely hurtful to those successful
writers, whose comfort, not to say their livelihood, at all depend
upon the profits of their works.

I am truly happy that you are independent of West Indian
changes and revolutions. The Stamps and Taxes, as you are
aware, are about to be consolidated, as the Boards already have
been: The result not improbably will be either the abolition of
the office of Distributor of Stamps, or such accumulation of
labour and responsibility, with diminished remuneration, as
would make the place for me no longer worth holding. This I
should regret principally because Willy, whose history you
know, and my excellent Clerk,[1] who has served me for upwards
of 20 years, would both be left suddenly without provision or
employment; but we must bear, for I fear worse things are
coming to us. My feelings at Lowther lately called forth the
following sonnet,[2] which Mrs Wordsworth will transcribe: but

[1] John Carter.   [2] v. Oxf. W., p. 477.

first you must be told that our dear sister is stronger and more comfortable than we ever expected to see her. She is now being driven out by Dora in our little Phaeton. Dora herself has suffered so much from deranged stomach, attended with long and wearying fits of tooth-ache, that we are determined to send her to Leamington for change of air, and to see some friends there, and probably not without a view to medical advice. I ought also to have told you that since we met I had a ramble of 5 or 6 weeks in Scotland with Dora, my first object having been to see Sir W. Scott at Abbotsford before his departure for Naples, which visit caused a Poem called 'Yarrow revisited' to be added to the two former ones.

Miss Hutchinson whom you kindly enquire after is with her Brother in Herefordshire and we are not likely to see her here for many months.

Now accept my parting assurances of affectionate regard to you and Mrs K. in which my wife, sister, and Dora heartily join, and with best wishes from us all for the recovery of your sister's health, believe me to remain, faithfully yours

Wm Wordsworth.

Address: John Kenyon Esqre, Twickenham, London.

MS.   **1056. *W. W. to Peter Cunningham* [1]**

[*franked* Keswick Sept. 24 1833]

Dear Sir

It is some time since I rec^d your acceptable present of Drummond's Poems,[2] which I should have thanked you for sooner, had I not waited (as I usually do on such occasions) for a frank. Your time has not been misemployed in editing so elegant a Writer as Drummond, an Author with whom I became acquainted in my Youth; it is not more than two years since I visited his charming residence at Hawthornden, with much pleasure: tho' I cannot think him utterly blameless as to the

---

[1] Peter C. (1816–69), son of Allan C. and a clerk in the Audit Office.
[2] *The Poems of William Drummond of Hawthornden*; with Life, by Peter Cunningham, 1833.

way in which he treated his friend Jonson,[1] I think his fault, such as it is, has been grossly exaggerated by certain persons, and by ably vindicating his memory on this point you have rendered a service to literature.

As your Edition, tho' copious, is still a Selection, it is possible you may have omitted something, which for some cause or other, might be worthy of preservation. I once possessed[2] an early ed: of Drummond's Poems which I should have pleasure in consulting, in order to give you my opinion whether you might have erred in this particular—but the book cannot at present be found.

I remain Sir, Your

obliged S^t.

W. Wordsworth

If you are as I conjecture the Son of my friend Mr Allan C. pray give my respects to your Father and Mother.

Address: Peter Cunningham Esqre, Dover St., London.

*London
Mercury.*   **1057. W. W. to Mrs Hemans**

Sept.–Oct. 1833

Dear Mrs Hemans,

So much was I pleased with both the Brothers Grave[s] that I should have been very happy to serve either of them in the way you point out—but at present I cannot learn that any of the few situations desired, is actually open—moreover, there is a prior claim upon me should an occasion occur where I can be useful. It must also be borne in mind that a Cure or Curacy worthy of Mr G.'s talents and attainments, is not easily found in this district they being so very few. I am aware that this is not the way in which a sincere Pastor looks, or ought to look upon

---

[1] Jonson: MS. Johnson.

[2] W. possessed, when an undergraduate, a copy of *The most Elegant and Elabourate Poems of that great Court Wit Mr William Drummond, whose labours both in verse and prose, being heretofore so precious to Prince Henry and to King Charles, shall live and flourish to all ages, while there are men to read them, or Art and Judgment to approve them,* 1659. The book can only have been mislaid, for it was in his library after his death.

his duties, still one would be sorry to see a Man like your friend buried among the lonely parts of our mountains. It is nevertheless true, that Parishes are sometimes open, where one would be truly glad to see such a man officiating. For example both Keswick and Grasmere have been recently supplied with Curates, both Irishmen: Hawkshead also has been lately supplied, and *this* we could have procured for him last winter, had he been ready to step into it at a fortnight's warning. Coniston also, I have reason to believe is about to be vacant—these particulars are mentioned merely to shew you that I take interest in the affair, both on your friend's account and your own. And I will conclude by saying should it be in my power to forward his views, I will take care to do so, only as I said before I do not think that a young man ought to be in a place where he will have very little to do—which would not happen however in any of the places I have mentioned.

Mr G. will bear in mind that the district of the Lakes lies in the dioceses of Carlisle and Chester,—principally in Chester, if he has any influence with either of those Bishops, he would be as likely to attain his end through them, as through any other channel.

I am happy to say that this family are all very well—only that my own eyes have become much worse since Mr G. left us—which compels me to employ an amanuensis—therefore you must excuse this note merely replying to the principal point in y^r letter and believe me to be, dear Mrs Hemans with the united best regards from us all to yourself and your Son

faithfully yours
W. Wordsworth.

MS.   *1058. W. W. to Mrs Hemans*

Oct 23, 1833

My dear Mrs Hemans

This note is full as much for Mr Graves as for yourself. First let me say that my pre-engagement to a friend no longer exists, so that I shall be able to avail myself of the first opportunity of

recommending Mr G. to a vacancy, may that occur—be assured
this gives me much pleasure; and now let me express my great
mortification, in having omitted, as I think I did, to acknowledge the receipt of the very elegant Sonnet which your young
friend did me the honour to address to me. The omission was
unpardonable, if Mr G. will not consider the deplorable state of
my eyes and the interest with which I entered into the affair
of the Curacy—as a sufficient apology. Let me beg you to thank
Mr G. for his interesting Letter—the tone and spirit of which
have much strengthened my desire to see him for some time
settled in this neighbourhood. He will excuse a letter directly
to himself as I am still unable to read or write, and shall I fear
for some time be so.

As my Amanuensis is unavoidably much engaged I must
conclude, with the united regards of this family to yourself your
Son and the two Mr Graves and believe me to remain my dear
Mrs H to be very faithfully yours

Wm Wordsworth

Excuse this single note sheet—having to enclose to my franking Friend, I am obliged to consider weight

Address: Mrs Hemans, 20 Dawson S^t, Dublin.

MS.
Review of Engl. Studies,
Jan. 1937.

1059. *W. W. to Robert Jones*

Rydal Mount Oc^r. 29 [18]33

My dear Jones

Your letter rec^d this morning was very acceptable, and the
more so as it gave so favourable an account of your own health
and the re-establishment of your Brothers—tho' with the drawback on the part of your two Sisters—to whom pray present
our best good wishes. I should not have replied to your letter
quite so soon, but on account of a paragraph which is going the
round of the Newspapers respecting the state of my sight—
which in all probability may fall in your way, and therefore
I wish you to know, that the account was not much exaggerated—
but thank God! the apprehended blindness of the one eye that

was so severely affected, has passed away; and I am now in as fair a way of perfect recovery as any one has a right to expect, who has been subject to such frequent attacks as I have. My safety for the future, next to God's goodness, must depend upon extreme care, both as to diet and exposure, and above all in not fatiguing my mind by intellectual labor, after the eyes become at all disordered—the severity of the last relapse was occasioned, I believe, by want of this precaution: when unable to read or write, one is naturally put upon thinking, and in my case upon Composition, which always more or less disturbs the digestion, and is accordingly injurious, even when it does not over stimulate the brain. This attack commenced the very day I last wrote to you.

Your present of Books you mention I have not received—if they have come to Mr Hodskin's hands, there will be no difficulty in their reaching me—as we can communicate with Liverpool free of expence thro' several channels. I will cause enquiry to be made of Mr H. immediately.

You alluded to a Welsh and En: Dictionary[1]—those I presume are in the Parcel—they will be truly acceptable, as I often wish to consult a book of that kind.

My Sister has been doing surprizingly well for many months, till within these three days past, when she had a bilious attack, which has reduced her a good deal, and is most unfortunate as we have now the winter to face. These last seven weeks have been very melancholy ones, as we have lost no less than 7 or 8 intimate acquaintances or friends and relatives, of all ages from 23 to 70 inclusive—the last taken was a very old friend a Mr Cookson, a manufacturer in Kendal, who having been unfortunate in business, had retired for economy's sake, to the Isle of Man, where he was living with his wife and there he died of Cholera—two months ago we lost Mrs W's eldest Brother after a painful illness. A sad case was that of my young friend Hallam[2] who was cut off at the age of 23—he was travelling with his father, the Author of the Middle Ages, and when sitting by

---

[1] W. O. Pugh's *Abridgement of the Welsh and English Dictionary*, 1826, was in W.'s library at his death.

[2] Arthur Henry Hallam (1811–33), the friend of Tennyson.

him in a public room of a Hotel in Vienna, his father turned towards him and thought he had dropped asleep—but going up to him soon after, found he was dead. He was a young Man of genius, great acquirements and high promise. Another of our young friends of Peter House Cambridge named Lionel Fraser died the other day at the age of 26—having been married and settled upon a Curacy in Shropshire—he has left a Widow and one Child. During my short summer excursion, I saw my lamented friend Mr Cookson at the Isle [of] Man, where his situation and character put into my head a little memorial of him which D. will transcribe, making one of a series of Sonnets, suggested during my ramble.[1] Heartily do I concur with you in the wish that we may meet again, before *we* go hence and be no more seen. Our friendship has been most constant—never having suffered a moment's interruption, and being now of nearly $\frac{1}{2}$ a century's standing a serious thought and deserving our gratitude in more views than one. God bless you, with united love from Wife, Daughter and Sister ever faithfully yours,

W Wordsworth

For this letter requiring haste, I cannot procure a frank.

Address: The Revd Robt Jones, Plas yn Llen, near Ruthin, N.W.

Donner.[2]   *1060. W. W. to Thos Forbes Kelsall*

[pm Oct. 31, 1833.]

Dear Sir,

As I am recovering from a severe inflammation in my eyes you will excuse my employing an Amanuensis, in reply to your

[1] *The Sonnet is headed* Rushen Abbey, near Balla Salla, Isle of Man, *and runs*:

Broken in fortune, &c., *as* Oxf. W., p. 470, *but* ll. 8, 9:
A shade but with such sparks of holy fire
As once were cherished here—*and in* l. 1, I know *for* albeit.

[2] *The Browning Box, or the Life and Works of Thomas Lovell Beddoes as reflected in Letters by his Friends*, ed. by H. W. Donner. Kelsall was the devoted friend of Beddoes. For the occasion of this letter *v.* W. W. to H. C. R. on Nov. 15 (*C.R.*, p. 252).

letter.—Agreeable to your request the Poem will be sent, not without a wish that you may not be disappointed in the perusal. The circumstances under which Yarrow was *re*visited by me, viz. in company with Sir W. Scott not more than two or three days before his departure from Abbotsford, forced my thoughts into a more Personal channel than would otherwise have happened, and this perhaps notwithstanding the illustrious character of the Individual and his poetical connection with the scene, may have interfered with the romantic idealization which would naturally have pervaded a Poem on such a subject.

And now having cordially acceded to your request, let me frankly say—that the Poem would have been withheld had it not been for the assurance you give me, as high as can be given —viz. the honour of an English Gentleman, that you will not suffer a copy to be taken, and will confine the perusal to two or three of your particular friends. The interest which you express in respect to my writings prompts me to name to you, that the reason why I withheld such minor pieces as I have written, is not what some have chosen to say—an over-weening conceit of their being above the taste of my countrymen: it is no such thing—but a humble sense of their not being of sufficient importance for a separate Publication; and a strong ground of apprehension that either my Publisher or myself might be a loser, by giving them to the world. My 4 or 5 last *separate* publications in verse, were a losing concern to the Trade; and I am not ashamed of saying that I cannot afford to give my Time, my Health and my Money, without something of a prudential reserve. Even the Sale of my collected works, tho' regular, is but trifling—this perhaps will surprize you—and, the state of my reputation considered, is altogether inexplicable, except on the supposition of the interference of the Paris Ed: of which I know the sale has been great—but too much of this into which I have been led from a wish to rid myself of a charge of being ungracious or unjust to those Persons, who like yourself, acknowledge that they have been both gratified and instructed by my endeavours. Is it worth while to add after the confiding spirit in which I have replied to your letter,—coming from a Stranger, that the thought crossed me, before I had finished the perusal of your's that it would be an act of worldly caution not to comply with your request.—Not more than ten days ago I rec^d from a Stranger a letter which was undoubtedly what is called a *hoax*, written with an intention, foolish enough heaven knows, of making me stare, and a third Person ridiculous—It would be paying y^r letter a poor compliment to suggest that it had anything of that character, but you are aware that encomiastic letters addressed to Public Men from entire Strangers are open to a like suspicion.

I am Sir respectfully yours

W Wordsworth.

Address: Thos Forbes Kelsall Esqre, Fareham, Hampshire.

MS.　　　*1061. W. W. to Sir R. H. Inglis*

[p.m. 25 Nov. 1833.[1]]

My dear Sir

　My daughter having rec^d a note from Miss Thornton franked by you, I take the liberty of enclosing the reply, and a letter to her Father from myself, hoping that without inconvenience you can forward them.—As the Frank will also contain a 3^d note, I do not scruple to ask you to send it to the Twopenny!

　When we had the pleasure to have Mr and Mrs Thornton and their family as our neighbours, neither myself nor my family were able to profit by that opportunity in any degree as we could have wished; on acc^t of a distressing complaint with which my eyes have been afflicted. You will be pleased to hear that they are now very much better, and if it pleases God that I should escape a relapse—there is good reason for believing I may soon enjoy the liberty of using them. At present I think it prudent to employ Mrs W. as my Amanuensis.

　Believe me to be my dear Sir, with kind regards to Lady Inglis in which Mrs W. begs to join, ever faithfully Yours

Wm. Wordsworth

Address: Sir R H Inglis M.P., Clapham, London.

[1] For W. W. to H. C. R. Nov. 15, *v. C.R.*, p. 250.

Pearson.   **1062. W. W. to William Pearson**

Rydal Mount, Dec. 4th [1833.][1]

My dear Sir,

Many thanks for your kind inquiries. Since I last saw you the state of my eyes, especially one, has caused me much privation, uneasiness and distress; but thank God, I am in a fair way of recovering the ordinary use of them; though I cannot but feel some degree of alarm for the future, as the vessels have been much weakened by repeated inflammations during the last twenty-five years.

The weather is so extremely stormy at present, that one can scarcely be so selfish as to invite friends from a distance, besides I have reason to look for the visit of a friend from London in a day or two, and next week we expect some of the Southey family —but as early in the week after as would suit you, (the weather being favourable) we should be glad to see you; and pray put your nightcap in your pocket, as I should really be sorry that you should have to go home at night. We have also a stall for your mule, or pony; and be so good, if you can spare the Corn-law Poet's book,[2] as to bring it along with you.

Miss Wordsworth's health is tolerable for her. I am glad the 'Excursion' improves upon acquaintance, and remain

Very faithfully yours,

W. Wordsworth.

MS.   **1063. W. W. to Basil Montagu**
K(—)

Decr 4th [1833]

Dear Montagu

I have been at a loss whether to write to you or wait for the Parcel which your Fragment of a letter announces—I say fragment for the 1st sheet or sheets are wanting.

It gives me pleasure to learn that you are disposed to resist the rash innovations which are taking place on all sides of us. Heaven grant that the efforts of those who think like you, may

---

[1] For W. W. to H. C. R. Dec. 1, *v. C.R.*, p. 254.
[2] Ebenezer Elliott (1781–1849), *Corn-Law Rhymes*, 1831.

be sufficient to stem the torrent that threatens to sweep away every thing before it. It is *principles* of Govern^t and Society that ought mainly to be looked at: if a just knowledge of these could be diffused and supported, the motives and characters of Individuals, however eminent for talent, would become of little consequence—an obvious remark which I make with special reference to the Person about whom you ask my opinion. Having never had but a very slight acquaintance with him I have had no opportunity of forming an estimate, beyond what is open to every one, of the inner workings of his mind—and therefore to give my opinion would be a mere waste of words. His ambition must be obvious to every one.

I shall here stop and wait a few days for the arrival of your parcel.—

Having an opportunity to forward this free of postage I do so without waiting longer for the parcel—as there[1] might possibly have been something in the former part of your letter, which did not reach me, that required an answer.

Believe me very faithfully
Your's

Wm Wordsworth

The Papers told a dismal story about the state of my eyes—which were truly bad enough, but which thank God are now better—but I do not think it yet prudent to use them for reading or writing—God bless you——

Address: Basil Montagu Esqre, 56 Chancery Lane.

M. G. K.   *1064. W. W. to Alexander Dyce*

Rydal Mount, Decr 4th, 33.

My dear Sir,

Your elegant volume of sonnets,[2] which you did me the honour to dedicate to me, was rec^d a few months after the date of the accompanying letter, and the Copy for Mr Southey was forwarded immediately, as you may have learned long ago by a letter from himself. Supposing you might not have returned

---

[1] there: MS. their.   [2] *v.* p. 651.

from Scotland, I deferred offering my thanks for this mark of your attention; and about the time when I should otherwise probably have written, I was seized with an inflammation in my eyes, from the *effects* of which I am not yet so far recovered as to make it prudent for me to use them in writing or reading.

The selection of Sonnets appears to me to be very judicious. If I were inclined to make an exception it would be in the single case of the Sonnet of Coleridge upon Schiller,[1] which is too much of a rant for my taste. The one by him upon Linley's music[2] is much superior in execution; indeed, as a strain of feeling, and for unity of effect, it is very happily done. I was glad to see Mr Southey's Sonnet to Winter. A Lyrical Poem of my own, upon the disasters of the French army in Russia,[3] has so striking a resemblance to it, in contemplating winter under two aspects, that, in justice to Mr S., who preceded me, I ought to have acknowledged it in a note, and I shall do so upon some future occasion.

How do you come on with Skelton? And is there any prospect of a future edition of your Specimens of British Poetesses? If I could get at the original works of the elder Poetesses, such as the Duchess of Newcastle, Mrs Behn, Orinda,[4] etc., I should be happy to assist you with my judgment in such a Publication, which, I think, might be made still more interesting than this first Ed: especially if more matter were crowded into a Page. The two volumes of Extracts of Poems by Eminent Ladies, Helen Maria Williams's Works, Mrs Smith's Sonnets, and Lady Winchelsea's Poems, form the scanty materials which I possess for assisting such a Publication. It is a remarkable thing that the two best Ballads, perhaps, of modern times, viz. Auld Robin Grey,[5] and the Lament for the Defeat of the Scots at Floddenfield,[6] are both from the Pens of Females. I shall be glad to hear

---

[1] *To the Author of 'The Robbers'* (1794).

[2] *Lines to W. Linley, Esq., while he sang a song to Purcell's music* (1800).

[3] *The French Army in Russia*, ll. 1–6 (Oxf. W., p. 321).

[4] *Poems By the most deservedly admired Mrs. Katherine Philips, The Matchless Orinda, to which is added Monsieur Corneille's Tragedies Pompey and Horace, with several other Translations ou tof French*, 1678.

[5] By Lady A. Lindsay (1750–1825), first published in Herd's *Scottish Songs*, 1776.

[6] That beginning 'I've heard them lilting, at the ewe milking,' by Jean Elliot (1727–1805), first published in Herd.

that your health is improved, and your spirits good, so that the world may continue to be benefited by your judicious and tasteful labours.

Pray let me hear from you at your leisure; and believe me, dear Sir,

Very faithfully yours,

W. Wordsworth.

How could I defer to a P.S. thanking you for the long and spirited Poem which you were so good as to transcribe from Sir E. Brydges' letter—it was duly forwarded to Mr Southey, who like myself could not but feel honored by such notice from so able and interesting an Author. It is a pity that Mr Hartley Coleridge's Sonnets had not been published before your collection was made[1]—as there are several well worthy of a place in it. Last midsummer I made a fortnight's tour in the Isle of Man, Staffa, Iona, etc., which produced between 30 and 40 sonnets, some of which, I think, would please you.

Could not you contrive to take the Lakes in your way, sometimes, to or from Scotland? I need not say how glad I should be to see you for a few days.

What a pity that Mr Heber's wonderful Collection of Books is about to be dispersed.

Address: The Revd Alexander Dyce, Gray's Inn.

K.   *1065. W. W. to John W.*[2]

Wednesday, December 5, [1833].

My dear John,

The last Cambridge paper proved to us very interesting, especially to your dear aunt, my wife, who is a keen electioneerer. Who is to be set up against Lubbock,[3] now that Peel is retired? We of this family will be mortified above measure if you do not

---

[1] They were published by F. E. Bingley, Leeds, 1833.
[2] Son of C. W.
[3] Sir John William Lubbock (1803–65), mathematician, astronomer, and banker.

triumph over any upstart. Here follows an epigram for you, allusive to the testimonials of the astronomical professor:

> For Lubbock vote—no legislative hack
> The dupe of history—that 'old almanack';
> The sage has read the stars with skill so true,
> The almanack he'll follow must be new.

... I cannot get up my spirits; everything seems going against sober sense, patience, and justice. Should the epigram give you no pleasure, the following, which I threw off this morning, may perhaps make a little amends.

> ADDRESSED TO REVOLUTIONISTS OF ALL CLASSES
> If this great world of joy and pain
> Revolve in one sure track,
> If what has set will rise again,
> And what is flown come back;
> Woe to the purblind crew that fill
> The heart with each day's care,
> Nor learn from past and future, skill
> To bear and to forbear.

Pray find a moment to tell us how you all are. Love to yourself and Charles, and to your dear father. God bless him. He's a good man and true. If you think it worth while to print the epigram don't tell that I wrote it. Your most affectionate friend and uncle,

W. Wordsworth.

MS.
K(—)

1066. W. W. to Edward Moxon

[p.m. Dec. 9, 1833.]

My dear Sir,

Having an opportunity to send a note to London free Postage I wish to enquire after Mrs Moxon and yourself, and to let you know that we are all doing well, in which account I include my Sister, tho' she had, after making progress all the Summer, a rather severe relapse about six weeks ago.

You would see a notice which might well have been spared

about my eyes in the Newspapers, and it is true that since the 12th of Aug. they have been suffering from more inflammation in the first instance which has left a disability to bear exposure and fatigue. Some want of care in these points occasioned two relapses, which have annoyed me so much. Had the weather been more favorable I believe that before this time I could have been capable of using them as much as I have been able to do for the last 15 or 20 years.

Some time ago I rec^d from you the Maid of Elvar by A. Cunningham. If you happen to see him let him know that we have lately read it aloud in my family, and that we were all exceedingly pleased with it. The beauties are innumerable, and it is much to be praised both for the general spirit of the narrative and a faithful description of rural scenes and manners. The faults are, an over luxuriance of style and something of a sameness, and occasional impossibility in the incidents.

I have also to acknowledge Mr Kenyon's Plea for Tolerance.[1] It is ably done and full of animation, but I shall write to the Author myself ere long.

We indulge a persuasion in this house that Mr Rogers will not forget us when his beautiful book which I see announced, makes its appearance. We are all impatience to see it, which he will be happy to hear the present state of my eyes will allow me to do with little or no inconvenience.

During the earlier part of last summer I made a fortnight's Tour in the Isle of Man and the Hebrides which produced from 30 to 40 sonnets some of which will, I think, be read with pleasure. These are bad times for publishing Poetry, in short nothing but low prices and utilitarian works seem to go down, with the exception of a few expensively illustrated works. Those of Mr R. have the advantage of being [? managed] under the direction of his own very fine taste.

Give our affectionate regards to the Lambs whom we should be very glad to hear from and pray tell them how we are going on, adding that H. Coleridge, in whom we know they are much interested, has returned from Leeds to Grasmere, where on the

---

[1] Kenyon's *Rhymed Plea for Tolerance* was published in 1833, and second ed. appeared in 1839.

whole he seems to conduct himself creditably but alas! we have only seen him once here, which is owing to his habitual want of resolution. He flies off occasionally to Pothouse wanderings, and these [?] he is probably so far ashamed of as to make him shy in coming to us lest we should reproach him *inwardly*, for he knows very well that we should not teize him with *continual comments* upon a custom which has become a sort of second nature to him.

Remember me kindly to young Mr Cunningham[1] who favoured me with a letter and believe me with kindest regards to Mrs M. and yourself, in which all my family unite, to remain faithfully yours

Wm Wordsworth

Pray send for me c/o Whitaker's (to be sent by Hudson & Nicholson's Parcel to Kendal) a Copy of Selections from my Poems neatly bound in calf, and enclose your little Bill for these matters.

Address: Mr Moxon, Bookseller, Dover Street, London.

1067. W. W. to Mrs Hemans

London Mercury(—)

Dec. 27th 1833.

My dear Mrs Hemans,—

Archⁿ Wrangham is in error as to part of his statement. The present incumbent of Ambleside[2] is indeed old, but so far from being infirm, that there is not one man . . . of half his age to be found among a hundred with his share of bodily strength and activity. His teeth however are gone which makes him inaudible and very inefficient in the reading-desk and pulpit—and I am persuaded that a successor in Ambleside, who in point of doctrine, manners and character might prove unobjectionable would be in a high degree acceptable to all his Parishioners. It is my intention to call upon him, to sound him upon the subject of Mr Graves' views, and if I had not the opportunity of enclosing

---

[1] i.e. Peter Cunningham, v. Letter of Sept. 24.

[2] Mr Dawes, who had formerly kept a school at Ambleside where Hartley Coleridge was a pupil, and later a teacher.

this letter for a frank, I would have deferred writing till I had seen Mr Dawes. I have already named the subject to an Inhabitant of Ambleside, who is willing to subscribe £10 towards the salary of a Curate—there is only one other person in the Chapelry, who I think is in the least likely to be as liberal— but others I am persuaded would do something—and probably Mr D. himself a trifle. From him much could not be expected as his income from the Chapel is only at present between £50 and £60, as he told me himself some time ago. So that Mr G. would have a very small allowance to look to, and if he be not already ordained, and is in want of a title there would be a great obstacle to his being placed at A:, as Mr D. has an almost insuperable objection to have any dealings with his Diocesan that he can avoid, and the sanction of the Bp would be necessary in case a title were wanted—besides he could not feel himself at liberty to ordain but to a sufficient Stipend.

There are two or three particulars that I should wish to know from Mr G. at his earliest convenience—the one is, what is the amount of Stipend he would be content with, and next (which is a matter of importance and far more delicacy, before I could stir farther in the business) I should like to know from himself what his notions are of that Party in the Church who are somewhat vulgarly known by the name of Saints or Evangelicals. The present Bp. of C. has been the means of bringing into this neighbourhood several ministers, and is known to countenance others, who partly from the doctrine they preach and still more from the injudicious zeal with which they prosecute their views—are exceedingly obnoxious to the leading and most respectable People in A., and to Mr D. not less than to others. Indeed the proceedings of these men have been very irregular, to my knowledge—and I learn from their hearers that their tenets, as to the main point of faith and works are such as I, without pretending to be a great Divine, should deem unscriptural. Will Mr G. as frankly as he well can, write to me on these subjects . . . Observe one thing that the Bp. of C. must not interfere at the present stage of the affair and the less he has to do with it, the more likely will it be to prove satisfactory to the Incumbent. . . .

MS.   *1068. W. W. to Edward Moxon*

Rydal Mount Decr 31st —33.

My dear Sir,

The Bearer of this (to London at least, but I hope he will be able to present it himself) is my neighbour Mr Hamilton,[1] author of Cyril Thornton, Men and Manners in America etc. Thinking it would be agreeable to you to hear something viva voce about me and mine, I have requested him, tho' his stay in Town will be short, to call upon you. He tells me also he shall be happy to charge himself with anything that you might have to communicate or to send. My nephew Chris. Wordsworth tells me that his fellow traveller in Greece, Mr Milnes,[2] designed for me his Memorials in Greece of which, as he says, you are the Publisher; it might be sent by Mr H. if not already forwarded thro' some other channel.

Remember us all affectionately to the Lambs when you see them. A letter from C. would be a great treat in this house. The other day I met with a few pleasing lines addressed by him to the veteran Stoddart[3] the artist upon his illustrations of Rogers' Poems. The *Book* we have not seen but I learn from my son Wm this morning, that it is very much admired at Carlisle where he lives, not less but even more so than the Italy. Pray do not forget to present all the good wishes of the season from this House to Mr Rogers and his Sister when you see either of them.

I have written this day, by the same channel, to Mr Kenyon. I do not mention my eyes further than by saying that they are doing well, but from the severe inflammation one of them has undergone I feel it necessary to spare them.

---

[1] *v.* Letter of March 2, 1832, *note*.

[2] Richard Monckton Milnes (later Lord Houghton) (1809–85), the friend, at Trinity, Cambridge, of Tennyson, Hallam, &c. On returning from a tour in Greece with C. W. (jun.) he published *Memorials of a Tour in some parts of Greece, chiefly Poetical*, 1834. In 1838 he published two more vols. of verse, and in 1844 *Palm Leaves*; in 1848 appeared his *Life and Letters of John Keats*. He was for many years a prominent figure in London literary society. His last speech was made to the Wordsworth Society in July 1885.

[3] To T. Stothard, Esq., on his Illustrations of the Poems of Mr. Rogers. The lines first appeared in the *Athenaeum* of Dec. 21. Stothard (1755–1834) was then 78 years old, *v. Poems* of Lamb, ed. E. V. Lucas, pp. 75, 371.

With our united good wishes to Mrs Moxon and yourself
I remain my dear Sir,
Very faithfully yours
W. Wordsworth

Pray send a neatly bound copy of the Selections[1] and an acc^t
of what I am indebted to you.

MS.   *1069. D. W. to W. W. Junr*

Thursday 2nd Jan^y, 1834

My dearest William,

Your Cousin Chris. arrived last Sunday—to our great surprize, and, as you may guess, joy. He is anxious to see you, and
we should all much regret it if business will not allow of your
coming for a few days while he is here. I do not think his stay
can be prolonged beyond Friday, Saturday or Sunday (17th, 18th,
19th) therefore I cannot help writing to you, though one of my
short dull letters would not otherwise be worth the postage. It
would be grievous should I wait for a parcel till too late.

Do not let the low state of your purse prevent your coming—
I will admit of no excuse or reason except that of business—as
to the money I will help you out with all you may want, and take
it without scruple as I have a little Fund of my own which
enables me with great satisfaction to myself to give pleasure to
the rich, or comfort to the poor.

John wrote that he would be with us last Monday or Tuesday;
but we did not expect him on the former day as Isabella and the
Babe were going to spend the time of his absence at Workington,
and we thought John would stay there all night—Then came
the tempest of Tuesday—and this is Thursday and he is not
arrived!—We are much puzzled for a reason for their not
writing if he actually should not come at all this week, which
seems probable, as it will cut his parson's week very short—for
most likely he can only have his pulpit filled on one Sunday.
This morning brought a letter from Bertha to tell Dora that E's
marriage is fixed for Wednesday the 15th.[2] Perhaps you have

---

[1] i.e. of W.'s own poems.
[2] Edith Mary Southey, to the Rev. J. W. Warter.

already heard that the Archbp. of C. gives him a Living in
Sussex, and of course they will speed away to their future home
as soon as the ceremony is over—What a melancholy house
Greta Hall will be when she is gone—and soon to be followed by
Cuthbert who is to be prepared for College by Mr Warter. Dear
Wm—the Collectorship is not, I believe, yet disposed of and
what should hinder your own application for it through Mr
Curwen or any other Friend? If your own conscience and feelings allow you to accept any thing from the party there can be
no reason why you should not apply. There is no need for you
to take any part in politics, and indeed did you feel yourself
obliged to do so I think you could not ask any favour from them.
As to your Father's asking Mr Curwen or any one else among
the Whig supporters it must, if you *think* for a moment, be plain
to you that he *could* not do it. Mr Thornton holds place on the
terms I have held out to you—takes no part in opinions and does
Government Duty. Poor Betty will I doubt not receive pleasure
from your Xmas remembrancer—Though she will never more
set foot on the house floor, your thought for her will draw a tear
of grateful joy from her languid eyes. Than[k ? God] for me
that I begin this year m[uch] better than the last—I only fear
[   ] the cold—God bless you dear William and with wishes
for many happy years for you and all whom you love believe me
ever your affec^te Aunt

D. Wordsworth

Dora goes in a day or two to Keswick.

Address: Mr Wordsworth, Stamp Office, Carlisle.

C.   **1070. D. W. to Lady Beaumont**
K(—)

Monday, January 13th, [1834.]

My dear Lady Beaumont,

I will not tire you with explanations of the causes of my long
silence, and still less would I burthen you with excuse and
apology; but in justice to Rydal Mount I must take upon myself
the blame of the long silence kept up by the whole household, for
it belongs to me alone; but so far from its being a proof that I
was indifferent to the kindness expressed in your letter, it was

the fulness of my gratitude which impelled me to assure my sister that I would myself write when she offered, as she has too often been obliged to do, to write for me. I did, however, then think (as I have double reasons now for thinking) that you would be no gainer by my choice; yet it was not an unpleasing fancy to me to believe that the pleasure of seeing my handwriting (as a proof of increased strength and better health) might more than compensate for your loss. You may believe that during the long time passed since you so kindly wrote to me, there have been many days in which, as an invalid, I have not been able to use my pen; but latterly I have delayed writing in hopes I should be able to tell you that my niece was really soon to have the satisfaction of meeting with you at Leamington. Nothing, however, could be fixed till after Miss Southey's marriage; an event which, as to time, remained all uncertain till the Archbishop, your venerable father, in his goodness, thought fit to present Mr Warter, the intended husband, to a living which will enable them to live in all the comfort they could wish for.

The pair are to be married on Wednesday, and Dora is gone to Keswick to act as bridesmaid to this, the last of her unmarried friends of an age agreeing with her own. Of course Dora is happy in anticipation of her friend's happiness; but she so dreads the loss of her, and knows so well what a chasm will be left in her parents' house, that she would have gone off with a sad heart under any circumstances; but at present the weight is twofold. To spend a few 'last days' with Edith Southey she was obliged abruptly to part from her eldest brother and her cousin Christopher, who had both come unlooked for to see us, and the former is already gone, and the cousin must depart to-morrow, to prepare for a commencement of College duties as Greek Lecturer to *Undergraduates* (I add the last words to explain, not knowing exactly the title of his office). Mr and Mrs Merewether (Christ[r] W. has not the happiness of being personally acquainted with *you*) will be sorry to hear that we think he has drawn too largely upon his strength during a nine months' residence in Greece, and long pedestrian travels in Switzerland. He is thin and pale, and his lively spirits are often oppressed by the scholar's malady, headaches, attended, as I think, by something of a bilious disorder.

He is, however, so much better than, as it seems, he was some weeks ago, that I hope nothing is wanted but a little more time for perfect restoration.

Wednesday, January 15th.

I began my letter upon too large a scale, by which, my dear Lady Beaumont, you are no gainer, for in this case, as in most others, the longer the letter the more tiresome or dull. This, however, I trust you will kindly excuse, and this is not my reason for making this complaint against myself. It is, that I happened to be a little unwell, and therefore I was obliged to put aside my paper and have been unable to go on from various causes until this day, the very day of the wedding. My brother and sister are preparing to go down the Rydal Mount Hill to the turnpike road, where they will pace backward and forward to shake hands with and give their blessing to the bride and bridegroom on their way southward. Though the air is as mild as in the month of May, and the sun, after many days of gloom and darkness, shines sweetly upon them, and though there is every cause for thankfulness and hope, I fear neither sunshine nor genial breezes will dispel the sadness of Greta Hall; yet Mr Southey himself, who will perhaps most constantly and most deeply feel the loss, will, I am sure, make such efforts to hide or to stifle his feelings that the saddest heart among them cannot but be cheared. Mr Warter is much beloved by the whole family into which he has entered, and *we* have formed a very favourable opinion of him. He and Miss Southey, and her sister and brother, spent a few days with us as soon as my brother's eyes would allow him to enjoy *any* company. For a very long time his wife and daughter were in constant watchful attendance,—either reading to or writing for him,—and I was beginning to hope that Dora might summon the resolution to go to Leamington after the marriage, but this she now declares she cannot do, she should be so very wretched at a distance from her father, till his eyesight is more strengthened and secure; so we must now look forward to the time when the two may venture on their travels together, which I hope, whenever it is, may take them within reach of you. My sister cannot make a third, as, Miss Hutchinson not being at Rydal, she could not leave me. I somewhat boldly did once hope

that *I* might next spring be able to visit Cambridge and Coleorton, but I now feel that home is likely to be the place for me—
and no hardship! for my prison (if we may so call it) is one of the
prettiest and most chearful in England, including what is to be
seen from the windows; and I have no bodily oppression but
from weakness, with occasional fits of uneasy pain that is not
violent. I was grateful to you for all your communications,
domestic and parish, for as long as I live I must retain affectionate and tender recollections of Whitwick and Coleorton, and
shall be thankful if the day ever comes when I again set foot in
the Hall and the two parsonage-houses; and need I add that it
would delight me to see your little boys playing on the lawn?
How distinctly do I recollect the nursery, and you, with your
baby on your knee, and the delighted *grandmother*, I began to
write (and let it stand), looking on.

Great and melancholy the changes since that day,—and your
own families have been severely tried,—yet happy are you in
having such a comforter and such support at the head of them.
I do not speak of public anxieties and public cares, the subject
is too weighty and perplexing for my poor mind; and I hope that
the Archbishop's lessons are not so thrown away upon me as
that I am not enabled to trust with calmness that God's good
providence will order all things for the best. It is time that I
should lay down the pen, for again I am getting into my old
fault—seeking brevity, and never finding it. You must forgive
me, for it is in confidence of your friendship that I go on. My
brother promises to add a few words, therefore I conclude with
begging you to present my respectful and affectionate regards
to Sir George, with sincerest wishes that the next year may be
a happy one—not like the last, a year of much sorrow and care.

Pray remember me affectionately, and with best wishes, to the
Merewethers, and believe me ever, my dear Lady Beaumont,
your affectionate and much obliged friend

Dorothy Wordsworth.

You will excuse my irregular handwriting, and my many blots
and erasures, especially when told that I always write with the
paper outspread on my knee.

Thursday morning. Mr Merewether will be interested in knowing that my nephew John was summoned from us by the death of his wife's valuable uncle Mr Stanley, Rector of Workington, a great loss to the whole family, and it has been a heavy affliction to John and his wife. Mrs J. W. Warter left us marriage tokens at the foot of the hill, but was so much affected as to be unable to speak to the person who took them in charge. We have not heard that you are actually gone to Leamington, but I conclude you are there; yet the winter has been warm enough even for Coleorton. I hope you are stronger.

MS.
C(—)
K(—)

1071. *W. W. to Lady Beaumont*

[1834][1]

My dear Lady Beaumont,

You will excuse my employing Mrs W's pen to express my regret that the health, neither of Sir Geo. nor yourself, is fitted to bear the climate of Coleorton during the winter season. Sincerely do I wish the air of Leamington may agree better with you. My dear Sister was timid and scrupulous about sending so long a letter [[2]] but in her confinement and the [[2]] [she d]welt upon the events of the day and the hour as [   ] upon her, in her now comparatively narrow sphere of earthly hopes and interests.

Believe me, dear Lady B[t], my wish is very strong to see your rising family, and especially if I could have that pleasure in my old haunts at Coleorton. Our thoughts in this house turn very much upon the impending fate of the Church, and also, as is natural, they are directed often to y[r] Father,[3] whose high office had never more anxious duties attached to it since the overthrow of the Church in Charles the First's time.

Were you ever told that my Son is building a parsonage house upon a small Living, to which he was lately presented by the Earl of Lonsdale? The situation is beautiful, commanding the windings of the Derwent both above and below the site of the

---

[1] This undated letter, attributed by K. to 1833, must have been written either to accompany D. W.'s letter of Jan. 13–15, or soon after.

[2] Partly cut away, doubtless for the sake of the signature on the reverse.

[3] William Howley, Archbishop of Canterbury.

House; the mountain Skiddaw terminating the view one way, at a distance of 6 miles—and the ruins of Cockermouth Castle appearing nearly in the centre of the same view. In consequence of some discouraging thoughts—expressed by my Son when he had entered upon this undertaking, I addressed to him the following Sonnet,[1] which you may perhaps read with some interest at the present crisis.

Pray accept Mrs Wordsworth's affectionate remembrance (and in her own name, let her add her apologies for such an ill-penned note) to yourself and Sir George, and at the rectory [? please make] our united regards, and believe me, my dear Lady B., to be, [faithfully yours,

Wm. Wordsworth].[2]

MS.
R.
K(—)

1072. W. W. to Samuel Rogers

Jan. 14th [1834]

My dear Friend,

Yesterday I received your most valuable present of 3 copies of y^r beautiful Book,[3] which I assure you will be nowhere more prized than in this house. My Sister was affected even to the shedding of tears by this token of your remembrance. When a Person has been shut up for upwards of 12 months in a sick room it is a touching thing to receive proofs, from time to time, of not being forgotten. Dora is at Keswick to attend as Bridesmaid upon Miss Southey, who loses her family name to-morrow. Your book has been forwarded, and we hope it will be rec^d at Greta Hall to-day.

Of the execution of the Plates, as compared with the former Vol., and the merit of the designs, we have not yet had time to judge. But I cannot forbear adding that as several of the Poems are among my oldest and dearest acquaintance in the Literature of our day, such an elegant edition of them, with their illustrations, must to me be peculiarly acceptable. As Mr Moxon does not mention your health, I hope it is good, and

---

[1] *At bottom of page is written the Sonnet*—'Pastor and Patriot', &c., *as* Oxf. W., p. 465, *but in* l. 9: To Him who dwells in Heaven will be the smoke.

[2] Cut away from MS., but possibly *after* K. had seen the letter.

[3] *v.* next letter.

your Sister's also, who, we are happy to hear, has drawn nearer
to you. Pray remember us all most kindly to her, and accept
yourself our united thanks and best wishes.

> I remain, my dear R., faithfully yours,
> Wm. Wordsworth.

We were grieved to notice the death of the veteran Sotheby.[1]
Not less than 14 of our relatives, friends, or valued acquaintance
have been removed by death within the last 3 or 4 months.

MS.
K(—)

1073. *W. W. to Edward Moxon*

[January 14th, 1834][2]

My dear Sir,

The valuable Parcel is arrived; we are charmed with the
design and execution of the illustrations and with the taste of
the whole work[3] which and its companion the Italy will shine
as Brother stars, tho' not twin-born, in the hemisphere of literature for many centuries. I have read also some part of Mr
Milnes's Book, the Dedication[4] of which is for its length one of
the most admirable specimens of that class of composition to be
found in the whole compass of English Literature. Of the
Poems also I can say, tho' I have yet read but a few of them,
that they add another to the proofs that much poetical genius
is stirring among the youth of this Country. In the work of
Alan Cunningham[5] to which you refer he has trifled with his own
good name in Authorship. He is a man of distinguished talents,
both as a Poet and a Biographer and ought to be more careful
than he has been in the work you criticize, were it only for considerations of pecuniary gain. I do not know who would take
the liberty to tell him this, but I am sure it would be a friendly
act. Many thanks for the truly friendly invitation which Mrs M.

---

[1] William Sotheby, 1757–1833, *v. E.L.*, p. 371.
[2] Added in another hand.   [3] The *Poems* of Rogers (*v.* last letter).
[4] *Memorials of a Tour in some parts of Greece*, by R. Monckton Milnes,
1834. The volume is dedicated to Henry Hallam in memory of Arthur H.
'whom I loved with the truth of early friendship ... we the contemporaries of
your dear son ... are deprived not only of a beloved friend, and of a delightful
companion, but of a most wise and influential counsellor in all the serious
concerns of our existence, of an incomparable critic in all our literary efforts,
and of the example of one who was as much before us in everything else, as
he is now in the way of life'.   [5] *written* Alingham.

and you have sent us: it would delight me to renew my acquaintance with her, a desire which I feel still more strongly, both since she became your Wife, and since I read Mr Lamb's discriminating verses[1] which I had not seen till the copy of the Athenaeum you kindly sent, reached me. C. Lamb's verses are always delightful, as is everything he writes, for he both feels and thinks. Will he excuse me for observing that the couplet,

> like a signet signed
> By a strong hand seemed burnt

appears to me incorrect in the expression, as a signet [is] a seal and not the impress of a seal; we do not burn by a seal, but by a branding iron.

It grieved us all to the heart to hear of dear Miss Lamb's illness. Miss Southey is to be married to-morrow. Our daughter is with her, or she would have sent her thanks for the plates you have been so good as to add to the little collection she formerly received from you. But I may say that she is very sensible of your kindness.

I feel so many difficulties in the way of publishing the Poems you allude to, as I do of profiting by your hospitable invitation, that I know not what to say upon either subject more than that it would please me and mine *much* to meet your wishes in both cases.

My eyes continue to improve, but I cannot say that they can yet stand all seasons and [? all Winter][2] My Sister continues better and we all unite in sincere regards and best wishes to you and your wife.

I remain my dear Sir
sincerely your friend
Wm. Wordsworth

K.   *1074. W. W. to Allan Cunningham*

My dear Sir,   [p.m., January 17, 1834.]

. . . Mr Moxon, from whom I heard yesterday, tells me that you were gratified by my commendation of your *Maid of Elvar*.

---

[1] *To a Friend on his Marriage* (*Poems*, ed. E. V. Lucas, p. 75) appeared in the *Athenaeum* of Dec. 7, 1833.   [2] *This may be* ill weather.

. . . The little audience of my family were as much pleased as myself; and indeed I can sincerely say that the poem is full of spirit and poetic movement. We have also read with pleasure the volume of your *Lives of the Painters*, containing that of my lamented friend, Sir George Beaumont. I wish I had seen the MS. before the book was printed, as I could have corrected some errors in matter of fact, and supplied some deficiencies. If this life should be reprinted shortly, I shall with pleasure do this for you. I have also a copy of verses inspired by his memory,[1] which, if not too long—I think they amount to between fifty and sixty lines—I would place at your disposal for the same purpose.

I was gratified by learning from his handsome edition of Drummond,[2] which your son sent me, that he had taken a turn for letters. . . .

I remain, my dear sir,

Faithfully your obliged friend,

Wm. Wordsworth.

1075. *W. W. to R. P. Graves*

London Mercury.   Rydal Mount Jan. 30th [1834]

My dear Sir,

My first words must thank you for your admirable letter, which is in every point satisfactory; my next, to express my belief that you will have imputed my silence to anything rather than remissness. I have made several fruitless attempts at an interview with Mr Dawes. He promised some time ago to call upon me, but he has not kept his engagement—yesterday I went again to his house, but did not find him at home, so that I have resolved to defer writing to you no longer. I do not know whether it was before or since my last letter, that I accidentally met him in the road, when he told me 'that if you were not in orders, there was an end of the business, as he would not give any one a title'. This objection I should have considered insurmountable, but that he has since offered to give a title to the son of a friend of his, as I know from a gentleman who was

---

[1] *Elegiac Musings*, &c., Oxf. W., p. 583.   [2] *v.* p. 668.

present when he made the offer. During that short accidental conversation Mr D. said to me that as long as his health was as good as at present he did not think it right that he should receive any portion of income from the Chapelry without doing its duties. This feeling I met with observing that as there was much to do, an assistant Curate might be desirable and with that view I was disposed to recommend you. He concluded by saying that you had best come over in summer and then perhaps the matter might be arranged. So that tho' I cannot reckon the affair promising in its present state it is not altogether hopeless. But far the most discouraging thing about it is Mr D's unsteadiness of mind. Tho' a person of wonderful strength for his years, and in many respects a very amiable and excellent Man, he has been, during his whole life remarkable for extreme irritability of nerve; in fact some of his nearest relatives have been insane— and this restless temperament has produced in Mr D. contradictions and changes of purpose which have both disappointed and harassed his neighbours and friends upon many occasions. It is no doubt the cause of his not having called upon me, as he promised to do. I assure you, I attach so much importance to your being employed as a Minister of the Gospel at Ambleside, and feel confident that by the good you do there, you would entitle yourself to the gratitude of the Parish, that I will exert myself to the utmost to effect what we both desire. This is all that I can say at present—but you shall hear from me as soon as anything decisive or important occurs—in the meanwhile believe me very faithfully

Yours

Wm Wordsworth

Pray give my kind regards to Mrs Hemans and your Brother.

MS.   **1076. D. W. to Mrs Pollard**
K(—)
Begun Saturday 12th April, ended Thursday. [1834].[1]
My dear Friend,

I ought long ago to have thanked *you* for your kind and welcome letter; but ought *now* to be writing to *Mrs Marshall*; and

[1] For W. W. to H. C. R., April 3, v. C.R., p. 258.

indeed if I knew exactly where a letter would find her you would not perhaps have had this, even yet; but as you, no doubt, are in constant correspondence with her, I flatter myself that, as you will report to her that you have had good tidings from me, it will answer the same purpose as if, by chance, I had rightly directed to her. She intended visiting Julia at Easter and is probably still with her; and, if all parties be in good health, it would not be easy for us to find a happier mother than our dear Jane, during this first visit to her Daughter and excellent Son-in-law.[1] Of his *merits* I always hear whenever his name is mentioned; and I cannot but believe that the Pair are far more than *contented* with each other, they having entire sympathy in matters of most importance in this world. It must be a never-failing delight to Julia to witness the good done by her Husband, both as a preacher, and comforter and assistant to the sick and afflicted; while in these latter named duties her good sense and charitable and amiable disposition will enable her to be a most effectual helper. I will not say I envy my Friend the happiness she enjoys in her numerous and flourishing Family; but often do I think how large a portion of good has been dealt out to her, and I join in that feeling of gratitude to God which we well know is habitual to her noble mind. Never surely was there a Mother who had had so little sorrow in the bringing up of eleven Children, notwithstanding the affliction of poor Ellen's life-long sickness; for in that sorrow the alleviations are many and powerful, and of these the foremost is the heavenly disposition and temper of the sufferer—her piety, resignation, and even chearfulness when not bowed down by pain—and surely the most active life of virtue and usefulness could not have afforded so precious an example to her Brothers and Sisters. Everyone must have been bettered by intercourse with Ellen.

But I go on prosing, unconscious that these sentiments must be so familiar to your own mind that the task of reading them is at least useless—you will, however, forgive me; for a solitary bedchamber does not furnish a variety of incidents—solitary I call it; but my Friends are very kind and sit with me as much and as often as leisure will allow, except when the apprehension

[1] Julia Marshall was married to Mr Elliott, a Brighton clergyman.

of fatiguing me keeps them away. I sometimes of late have chid myself for impatience; for the sun shines so bright and the birds sing so sweetly that I have almost a painful longing to go out of doors, and am half tempted to break my bonds and sally forth into the garden; but I must be contented to wait till the wind changes its quarters; and before that happens rain will surely come, which may still keep me confined, for damp is almost as dangerous a foe as the East wind. There has been little change with me since I last wrote, yet as I have had no bilious attack and no violent attack of *pain* (though seldom entirely free from gentle visitations) I *must* be actually much better; but the change is so very slow that I am forced to check myself and think of the past when I (perhaps somewhat peevishly) have exclaimed 'I gather no strength'.

I laid down my pen half an hour ago to receive a visit from a Sister of our old Friend, Peggy Taylor, whom you will remember at Mrs Threlkeld's. I am glad to be enabled to tell you that she is now, after much affliction and anxiety, in good health and spirits. Mr Lewthwaite, her Husband, about a year ago had an alarming illness, but is now perfectly recovered. Mr Briggs of Halifax was, I find, an invaluable Friend to the Lewthwaites when in distress; but the bitterest part of it no friendship could heal, for it proceeded from the unfeeling misconduct of a Son. Speaking of Halifax I must say that I have nothing to tell you; for it is long since I heard from E. Ferguson, and the correspondence with our aged Friend is for ever snapped off. No doubt, all things continue as when he wrote, in a state of melancholy decay, yet comforted by peaceful resignation. I always rely upon hearing from Edward whenever any important change either for the better or the worse happens among the three Beings to him the most interesting upon earth, but I am anxious for all fresh particulars, and my next letter shall be to Edward and indeed I ought sooner to have written, to tell him about myself and Rydal Mount. My dear Brother's eyes are comparatively well, though very weakly; and at present he is unluckily confined by a trifling malady, a sore upon the great Toe. I trust Dora is better than she has lately been, for her cough and shortness of breath have yielded to Mr Carr's prescriptions; but she still looks wretchedly and is very thin, and has no appetite for any kind of food, while from some kinds the stomach instantly revolts.

Thursday. Strange to say it! this poor scrawl has been the work of four days, and it is *five* since I began with it. The truth is, that a small matter stops me, and if a visitor, or two or three in succession, come in, my time and strength do not serve to fill up the rest of the day with other labour. Yesterday with a thankful heart I revisited the garden and green-terrace in my little carriage. I cannot express the joy I felt, and though much fatigued I did not suffer in any other way. No one but an invalid, after long confinement, can imagine the pleasure of being surrounded again by sunshine and fresh air, budding trees, flowers and birds. I looked about for young Lambs but discovered not one. Do not think, however, my dear Friend that my confinement has been irksome to me. Quite the contrary, for within this little square I have a collection of treasures and on the outside of my window I have had a garden of ever-blooming flowers, and you know what a beautiful prospect. Never have my flower-pots been seen unadorned with flowers in addition to the bright berries of winter, the holly etc. I have plenty of good old Books and most of the news are supplied by Friends or neighbours, and I cannot help adding (for my heart prompts me to it and you will forgive) I cannot help adding that within the last two years I have had a source of enjoyme[nt] that but for your and your dear Sisters' delicate kindness my consci[ence] would not hav[e] allowed me. I have had the power of doing many [a] charitable deed, that I should otherwise have felt it my duty not to ind[ulge] in, besides exercising a liberality towards those who on me bestow willing and affectionate service. As to personal comforts I need not say that I never want any thing that I can desire or wish for.

I give you now the same promise I have already given to Mrs Marshall, never again to mention to you the good you have done, and are doing, so let me be assured by your sending no reply to what I have said, that you take it kindly as the overflowing of a grateful mind.

The month of April gets on rapidly and you are to return to

Old Church in May, when I shall be anxious to hear of your being seated in your accustomed quiet Hold, in perfect resignation to your loss and in chearful enjoyment of the many blessings around you. I hope that before summer days are much shortened both you and Ellen will find your way to Rydal Mount. You must by no means venture over Kirkstone; but coming round by Keswick only adds a few miles to the journey, of which we should think nothing, if there were not a shorter way. It is longer than usual since I heard from Mrs Marshall, and I am beginning to crave tidings concerning *her* and the Many who are bound to her in love and duty, yet I have had no right to expect a letter, for I have not written to her since her last reached me. This is again a mild and lovely day, and I must prepare for my Baby Ride in the garden. Pray excuse bad penmanship, a wretched pen, and this shabby sheet of paper. The worst part of the business is, that I fear you will find my writing not always legible and at best difficult. I hope however that two pair of eyes will make out the whole, and you have leisure enough not to grudge the requisite time. My Brother, Sister and Dora send their united regards and best wishes. Believe me ever, my dear Friend yours most affectionately

D. Wordsworth

I hope you have comfortable accounts of your Friend Mrs Whitaker and her Family.

Address: Mrs Pollard, at Mr Oddy's Lodgings, Harrowgate, Yorkshire.

M.
G.   *1077. W. W. to Sir William M. Gomm*[1]
K.

Rydal Mount, April 16, 1834.

My dear Sir,

Your verses, for which I sincerely thank you, are an additional proof of the truth which forced from me, many years ago, the

---

[1] Sir William Maynard Gomm (1784–1875), Field-Marshal. He served in the Peninsula under Wellington and was with Moore at Corunna, distinguished himself at Salamanca (1812), and fought at Waterloo. His leisure was devoted to travel and literature. In 1839 he was appointed to Jamaica,

exclamation—Oh! many are the poets that are sown—By Nature.[1]

The rest of that paragraph also has some bearing upon your position in the poetical world. The thoughts and images through both the poems, and the feelings also, are eminently such as become their several subjects; but it would be insincerity were I to omit adding that there is here and there a want of that skill in *workmanship*, which I believe nothing but continued practice in the art can bestow. I have used the word *art*, from a conviction, which I am called upon almost daily to express, that poetry is infinitely more of an art than the world is disposed to believe. Nor is this any dishonour to it; both for the reason that the poetic faculty is not rarely bestowed, and for this cause, also, that men would not be disposed to ascribe so much to inspiration, if they did not feel how near and dear to them poetry is.

With sincere regards and best wishes to yourself and Lady Gomm

Believe me to be very sincerely yours,

W. Wordsworth.

MS.   *1078. W. W. to Mrs Hemans*
M(—)
K(—)

[p.m. 30 April 1834.]

My dear Mrs Hemans

My first duty is to thank you for your National Lyrics and the accompanying Letter—the little Volume for my daughter-in-law was delivered by myself, as I happened to be upon a visit to her and her husband, when your Parcel arrived. Mrs Harrison's was sent to her, and she begs you to accept her thanks for its own sake, and as a token of your remembrance. How did it happen that all this was not written some time ago? You will be sorry to hear the reason. My eyes tho' not actually inflamed, are in that state that I am prohibited from reading and writing,

in 1842 he was Governor of Mauritius, in 1850 Commander-in-Chief in India. For a short time before going to Mauritius he was in charge of the forces in the N. district of England, and became intimate with W.

[1] *The Excursion*, Book I, l. 77.

by my medical attendants; and in consequence, there are upon my Table, three Volumes besides yours that I have rec^d from their Authors some time ago—and are as yet unacknowledged— as I do not like to write on these occasions without saying something more than that the Books have been received.

With respect to your own last work I was not precisely in the same difficulty, as many of the Pieces had fallen in my way before they were collected; and had given me more or less pleasure—as all your productions do. Nevertheless I deferred my acknowledgements with a hope that open air with fine weather, might soon so far strengthen my eyes, as to enable me to report of the whole as a Volume, but the sharp east winds which I am sorry to hear have inflicted you with the influenza, have been against me, and the pleasure is yet to come of perusing your Pieces in succession. I can only say that whenever I have peeped into the volume—I have been well recompensed. This morning I glanced my eye over the Pilgrim Song to the evening Star with great pleasure.

And now my dear Friend to a subject which I feel to be of much delicacy—You have submitted what you had intended as a Dedication[1] for your Poems to me. I need scarcely say that

---

[1] The Dedication to which W. objected ran as follows:

My dear Sir,

I earnestly wish that the little volume here inscribed to you, in token of affectionate veneration, were pervaded by more numerous traces of those strengthening and elevating influences which breathe from all your poetry —'a power to virtue friendly'. I wish, too, that such a token could more adequately convey my deep sense of gratitude for moral and intellectual benefit long derived from the study of that poetry—for the perpetual fountains of 'serious faith and inward glee' which I have never failed to discover amidst its pure and lofty regions—for the fresh green places of refuge which it has offered me in many an hour when
> The fretful stir
> Unprofitable, and the fever of the world
> Have hung upon the beatings of my heart;
and when I have found in your thoughts and images such relief as your 'sylvan Wye' may, at similar times, have afforded to yourself.

May I be permitted, on the present occasion, to record my unfading recollections of enjoyment from your society—of delight in having heard from your own lips, and amidst your own lovely mountain-land, many of those compositions, the remembrance of which will ever spread over its hills and waters a softer colouring of spiritual beauty? Let me also express to you, as to a dear and most honoured friend, my fervent wishes

as a *private letter* such expressions from such a quarter could not have been rec^d by me but with pleasure of *no ordinary kind*, unchecked by any consideration but the fear that my writings were overrated by you, and my character thought better of than it deserved. But I must say that a *public* testimony in so high a strain of admiration is what I cannot but shrink from—be this modesty true or false, it is in me—you must bear with it, and make allowance for it. And therefore as you have submitted the whole to my judgement, I am emboldened to express a wish that you would instead of this Dedication in which your warm and kind heart has overpowered you, simply inscribe them to me, with such expression of respect or gratitude as would come within the limits of the rule which after what has been said above, will naturally suggest itself. Of course, if the sheet has been struck off, I must hope that my shoulders may become a little more Atlantean than I now feel them to be.

My Sister is not quite so well. She, Mrs Wordsworth, and Dora all unite with me in best wishes and kindest remembrances to yourself and yours ; and

believe me, Mrs Hemans, to remain faithfully yours,

Wm Wordsworth

Pray thank Mr Graves for his last letter, and say that I am very anxious to find an opening by which his wishes might be gratified—but with respect to Mr Dawes he has lately given such additional proofs of his temper, tho' not on this subject, so discouraging that I cannot look forward with pleasure to any arrangement with him—We see Mr Archer frequently who speaks of you and your Poetry with much interest. Your message has been delivered to Mr Hamilton. I regret that

for your long enjoyment of a widely-extended influence, which cannot but be blessed—of a domestic life, encircling you with yet nearer and deeper sources of happiness ; and of those eternal hopes, on whose foundation you have built, as a Christian poet, the noble structure of your works.

I rely upon your kindness, my dear Sir, for an indulgent reception of my offering, however lowly, since you will feel assured of the sincerity with which it is presented by your ever grateful and affectionate Felicia Hemans.

The published dedication ran: To William Wordsworth, Esq. In token of deep respect for his character, and fervent gratitude for moral and intellectual benefit derived from reverential communion with the spirit of his Poetry this Volume is affectionately inscribed by Felicia Hemans.

there is not time for sending this letter to London to be franked.

Address: Mrs Hemans, 20 Dawson Street, Dublin.

K(—) **1079. W. W. to C. W. Junr**

My dear C.   May 15, 1834.

You will wonder what is become of us, and I am afraid you will think me very unworthy the trouble you took in writing to us and sending your pamphlet.[1] A thousand little things have occurred to prevent my calling upon Mrs Wordsworth, who is ever ready to write for me, in respect to the question that you have so ably handled. Since the night when the Reform Bill was first introduced, I have been convinced that the institutions of the country cannot be preserved. . . . It is a mere question *of time*. A great majority of the present Parliament, I believe, are in the main favourable to the preservation of the Church, but among these many are ignorant how that is to be done. Add to the portion of those who with good intentions are in the dark, the number who will be driven or tempted to vote against their consciences by the clamour of their sectarian and infidel constituents under the Reform Bill, and you will have a daily augmenting power even in this Parliament, which will be more and more hostile to the Church every week and every day. You will see from the course which my letter thus far has taken that I regard the prayer of the Petitioners to whom you are opposed as formidable still more from the effect which, if granted, it will ultimately have upon the Church, and through that medium upon the Monarchy and upon social order, than for its immediate tendency to introduce discord in the universities, and all those deplorable consequences which you have so feelingly painted as preparatory to their destruction.

I am not yet able to use my eyes for reading or writing, but your pamphlet has been twice read to me. . . .

God bless you. . . .

                                    Affectionately yours,
                                        Wm. Wordsworth.

[1] C. W. wrote a letter to Lord Althorp 'On the admission of Dissenters to graduate in the Univ. of Cambridge' in which he opposed a Bill to admit them, which had been brought before the H. of C.

MS.
K(—)[1]

1080. *W. W. to Henry Taylor*

Rydal Mount, June 10th [1834].

My dear Sir,

I have just received your two volumes,[2] and send my thanks before I have read them; not from the fear that I might not be able to report favorably of their impression upon my mind, but from apprehension that some time may elapse before the state of my eyes will allow me to read them. My eyes, I am glad to say, are not actually inflamed, nor have they been for some time, but I am under medical restrictions as to the use of them; on my table are no less than six books, lately received from the kindness of different authors, that I have not acknowledged, having deferred doing so from a hope that I might without injury peruse them; and I have really been so harassed in mind by this procrastination that I am determined your case shall not be added to them. When we meet again we will talk over your dramatic labours.

You are young, and therefore will naturally have more hope of public affairs than I can have: principles which after all are the only things worth contending about, are sacrificed every day, in a manner which I have foreseen since the passing of the Reform Bill, and indeed long before, but does not on that account the less disturb me. The predominance given in Parliament to the dissenting interest and to Towns which have grown up recently without a possibility of their being trained in habits of attachment either to the Constitution in Ch: and State, or to what remained of the feudal frame of society in this Country, will inevitably bring on a political and social revolution. What may be suffered by the existing generation no man can foresee, but the loss of liberty for a time will be the inevitable consequence. Despotism will be established, and the whole battle will be to be fought over by subsequent generations.

I remain very faithfully your much obliged

Wm Wordsworth.

---

[1] K. prints this as two letters, giving to the second half the date 1832.
[2] *Philip von Artevelde* was published in 2 vols. in 1834.

MS.   *1081. W. W. to Edward Quillinan*

Rydal Mount, June 11th, [1834][1]
(for W. W., M. W. holds the pen)

Dear Mr Quillinan

Having an opportunity to send a letter to Town, I cannot let it pass without condoling with you upon the death of poor Barrett.[2] Whether on his own account his decease is to be regretted we are ignorant—one cannot however but feel sorrow that a Man who made so many sacrifices for others should be taken out of this selfish world. Upon one thing his surviving friends—his *true* ones I mean, may congratulate themselves, viz. that by his removal from Earth a temptation is removed from them who abused his goodness to the dishonor of their names and in disregard of some of the nearest charities of life. Requiescat in pace—he was in many respects a more deplorable wreck than the unhappiest of those near whom, as you tell us, he lies buried. After the warnings you have had I hope you will be able to defeat every attempt of the Plunderers, and to establish justice and reason among concerns, with which for a long time they have had little to do.[2]

You are silent on the cause which made you think of going to Portugal[3]—You must remain in England as a duty to your Children and those who have a common interest in the remains of what will probably be their inheritance. I should like to hear some good news of Lee itself; it is a place in which I feel much interest and should be glad to learn that it were occupied by some family that could enjoy and take care of it.

Miss H.[4] whom we had expected to be now with us, but whom we are not to see till Saturday next—as she announces in a letter rec^d this morning, will bring us news of your Children, whom she is about to see—we shall be glad to hear of their looks and every thing relating to them—we are vexed that the Aunt takes

---

[1] For W. W. to H. C. R. June 10, *v. C.R.*, p. 263.

[2] Colonel Brydges Barrett, E. Q.'s brother-in-law, had died at Boulogne early in the month. In the financial difficulties of the Brydges family E. Q. was already seriously involved.

[3] E. Q. sailed for Oporto at the end of August; he returned to England in Jan. 1836.   [4] i.e. Sara Hutchinson.

Mima for the holidays, and could not find room for my Godchild Rotha—if however she does not feel it a slight, there is no harm in Sisters being separated for a short time, they learn to value each other the more—*thinking* about friends especially before the character is formed, often does as much good as being with them.

Poor Mrs Fletcher (Miss Jewsbury that was[1]) has found a grave in India—from the first we had a fore-feeling that it would be so. She was a bright Spirit, and her sparkling, of which she had at times too much, was settling gradually into a steady light. Her journal is to her friends very interesting, and I cannot but think that if she had survived, we should have had from her pen some account of Indian appearances and doings with which the public would have been both amused and instructed. She died of Cholera, but the particulars of her death have not reached her friends.

Dora told you that I had been much pleased with the second part of Mischief;[2] it is written with great spirit and a variety of talent which does the Author no small credit. I cannot guess why this performance has not made more impression than I am aware it has done, but the political agitations of the times leave no leisure for any thing but 1d Mags and 5/- books with cuts which may be looked at but are seldom read. (William has done and I (M. W.) might have gone on but the last bell rings for Chapel and I must take up his last words) Ever aff^ly yours

Wm Wordsworth.

If you have no objection to Rotha running wild at Rydal for a couple of months, if you or we could meet with an opportunity to send her down we should like to see her here though we cannot receive her for 6 weeks, as our Nephews will be here at their vacation, and other summer visitors—But you must understand what I mean by 'running wild'—it is going without tuition. Dora's health and thoughts are too much deranged and occupied to allow of her making the least exertion in this way and indeed she is unequal to it but on this condition it will give

---

[1] She had died at Poona on Oct. 4, 1833.
[2] *v.* Letter of July 4, 1831.

us all great pleasure to see the Child, and we hope that you will consent, and we will be upon the lookout for some proper escort for her, and some opportunity before the end of autumn may occur for her to get safely back to school. W. W.

MS.
K. *1082. W. W. to Allan Cunningham*

Rydal Mount, June 14th, [1834.]

My dear Sir,

I have just heard from my Son, who now lives at Workington,[1] that the Bust[2] you kindly forwarded to him has been received; and, as I learned some little time ago, that those intended for my two Nephews at Cambridge have also reached their destination—I now write with pleasure to thank you for your obliging attention to my request, and have to beg that you will let me know the amount of my debt to you—so that I may give directions for its being discharged.

It is a long time since I was in London, nor can I foresee when I am likely to be there again; which I regret principally on account of my losing, in consequence, an opportunity of keeping up my acquaintance with works of art, ancient and modern—and of seeing my friends, who reside there, without occasionally coming into this Country. One of the last times, if not the last, I had the pleasure of seeing you was at dinner at Sir R[t] Inglis's—Mr Sotheby was of the Party. He was an old Man, and is no more—Scarcely a Month passes without taking away some of my literary friends. Mr Chantrey and yourself I hope continue to enjoy good health—Pray make my kind regards to him, and to Mrs Chantrey, and also to Mrs Cunningham—not forgetting to present my remembrances to your Son, who I am glad to see from his elegant and judicious selection from Drummond, which he kindly sent me, has a turn for literature.

Last summer I visited Staffa, Iona, and part of the Western Highlands, and returned through your town of Dumfries, having

---

[1] The living of Workington had just been presented to J. W. by his father-in-law, Mr Curwen.

[2] A. C. was clerk to Chantrey, who had executed a bust of W. in 1820.

for the first time passed through Burns's Country, both in Renfrewshire and Ayrshire (if I am correct). It gave me much pleasure to see Kilmarnock, Mauchlin, Mossgeil Farm, the Air, which we crossed where he winds his way most romantickly thro' rocks and woods—and to have a sight of Irwin and Lugar, which naebody sung till he named them in immortal verse. The banks of the Nith I *had* seen before, and was glad to renew my acquaintance with them, for Burns's sake; and, let me add without flattery, for yours. By the bye, what a sorry piece of sculpture is Burns's monument in Dumfries churchy^d—monstrous in conception and clumsy in its execution. It is a disgrace to the Memory of the Poet. In my native county of Cumberland I saw a piece of art which made ample amends—it is at Wetheral Church, upon the banks of the Eden—a monument to the Memory of the first Mrs Howard of Corby—You no doubt have either seen or heard of it—I first saw it many years ago in the Studio of Nollekens,[1] in London. How a man of such a physiognomy and figure could execute a work with so much feeling and grace, I am at a loss to conceive! Believe me, with kind regards from my Wife and all my family who know you,

Very faithfully, your obliged friend,

Wm. Wordsworth.

Address: Allan Cunningham Esq., Lower Belgrave Place, London.

MS.
(K—)

1083. W. W. to Edward Moxon

Rydal Mount July 17th [1834]

My dear Sir,

Reluctant as I am, I have at last given way—and am about to send a Vol: of Poems to the Press. Wishing to connect your name and mine by publication, I mentioned to Longman's that

---

[1] Joseph Nollekens (1737–1823), R.A. 1772, a distinguished sculptor of monuments; his two finest works are generally held to be the Captains in Westminster Abbey and Mrs Howard at Corby. In personal appearance he was 'grotesquely ill-proportioned', with an immense head, short neck, narrow shoulders, large body, and a nose that '"resembled the rudder of an Antwerp packet-boat"' (*D.N.B.*), v. Oxf. W., p. 476.

it would be pleasant to me to offer the publⁿ to you, especially as we had had some conversation together on the subject—but I left it to their decision—as I felt myself bound to do, from very long connection with them—and from their answer I transcribe.

'It would be very detrimental to the sale of your books to have part of them published by another House'—'We think you have done right to abandon the Illustrations; to have them executed as those in Rogers' Works would be so very expensive, that we should doubt their ever answering' He then adds that the sale of the last Ed. has been good.

Hoping that you and Mrs Moxon are well—and with best regards in which my family joins, I remain my dear Sir

very sincerely yours

W. Wordsworth

K.   *1084. W. W. to Henry Nelson Coleridge*

July 29, 1834.[1]

My dear Sir,

Though the account which Miss Hutchinson had given of the state of our friend's[2] health had prepared us for the sad tidings of your letter, the announcement of his dissolution was not the less a great shock to myself and all this family. We are much obliged to you for entering so far into the particulars of our ever-to-be-lamented friend's decease, and we sincerely congratulate you and his dear daughter upon the calmness of mind, and the firm faith in his Redeemer, which supported him through his painful bodily and mental trials, and which we hope and trust have enrolled his spirit among those of the blessed.

Your letter was received on Sunday morning, and would have been answered by return of post, but I wished to see poor Hartley first, thinking it would be comfortable to yourself and his sister to learn from a third person how he appeared to bear his loss. Mrs Wordsworth called on him yesterday morning; he

---

[1] For D. W. to H. C. R. July 24, *v. C.R.*, p. 267.
[2] S. T. Coleridge died on July 25.

promised to go over to Rydal, but did not appear till after post-time. He was calm, but much dejected; expressed strongly his regret that he had not seen his father before his departure from this world, and also seemed to lament that he had been so little with him during the course of their lives. . . .

I cannot give way to the expression of my feelings upon this mournful occasion. I have not strength of mind to do so. The last year has thinned off so many of my friends, young and old, and brought with it so much anxiety, private and public, that it would be no kindness to you were I to yield to the solemn and sad thoughts and remembrances which press upon me. It is nearly forty years since I first became acquainted with him whom we have just lost; and though with the exception of six weeks when we were on the Continent together, along with my daughter, I have seen little of him for the last twenty years, his mind has been habitually present with me, with an accompanying feeling that he was still in the flesh. That frail tie is broken, and I, and most of those who are nearest and dearest to me, must prepare and endeavour to follow him. Give my affectionate love to Sara, and remember me tenderly to Mrs Coleridge; in these requests Mrs Wordsworth, my poor sister, Miss Hutchinson, and Dora unite, and also in very kind regards to yourself; and believe me, my dear sir,

Gratefully yours,
W. Wordsworth.

Pray remember us kindly to Mr and Mrs Gillman[1] when you see them.

MS.   *1085. W. W. to Edward Moxon*

Aug. 25th 1834

My dear Sir,

Your last very friendly and judicious letter would have received an immediate answer, but I deferred writing till I should have occasion to communicate with Mr Longman etc. Be assured that I shall be most happy and proud to have your

---

[1] Coleridge had lived with the Gillmans at Highgate since 1817.

name on the title page of my new volumes and that I shall state my feeling on the point in such a way that my old Publisher I have no doubt, will readily comply with my proposal—I am of your opinion that the sale of my Works would be promoted by being published monthly as you propose, and if I live to see another Edition it shall be done.

Yesterday arrived, to the great joy of this House, our excellent Friend Mr Rogers, but also he made his appearance lame, having had an attack of the Gout in his foot. He talks of returning to London almost instantly in consequence, but we anxiously hope that the symptoms will abate, and allow him to stay. This moment has brought me a note from him (he is at Low Wood) in which he tells me he will leave almost immediately, he seems now assured that it is only a spasm.

Pray do you know Mr Heraud,[1] author of the judgment of the flood etc. He has sent me a beautiful Copy of his Poems the receipt of which I have acknowledged, telling him that the state of my eyes did not allow me to read it. This is true. My eyes are not indeed at present inflamed, but reading makes them so irritable that I am obliged to leave off almost as soon as I begin. Mr H. not satisfied with this acknowledgment has written most urgently for a criticism from me upon his work, and this distressed me greatly, for I cannot read his work without injury, nor have I yet been able to read Mr Taylor's[2] for if I become interested in what I read, I am tempted on till I feel the bad effect. Pray assure Mr Heraud if you know him that I much admire what I have been able to peruse of his work, and think very highly of his genius.

Ever most faithfully yours
Wm. Wordsworth

I sent you this to London having a Frank handy, but pray don't pay the Postage of your letter to me. I must congratulate you on your success as a Publisher of which our common friend Mr R. gives me most favourable accounts.

W. W.

Address: Mr Moxon, Dover Street. By favour of Mr Rogers.

---

[1] *v.* Letter, Nov. 23, 1830.   [2] *v.* Letter of June 10, *supra.*

MS.   *1086. D. W. to Elizabeth Hutchinson*[1]

My dear Godchild   Tuesday—about the 14th Sept. [? 1834]

This is not one of my vigorous days, therefore you must take it kindly though I send you a short, unentertaining, and ill-penned letter. For the last mentioned failure my excuse is, that I lie upon my back in bed and with uplifted knees form a desk for my paper. Do not suppose, however, that I spend all my time in bed—It is only that I rise late and go to bed before sunset, because it tires, and in other respects disagrees with me to sit up more than from 4 to 6 hours in the day.

I hope you will find the green gown useful: but wish I had also been able to send you some *book* to help you to adorn the mind, while the Body is gaily dressed in its 'gown of green'. My dear Elizabeth, I hope your good Father and Mother will consent to allow you to visit your Friends at Rydal very soon—*I* say the sooner the better—but am afraid we must not look for you till George's return at Christmas—and indeed it would be unreasonable to expect you to leave home before the end of the holidays, when so large a troop of your companions will be assembled there; but we all (your Uncle and Aunt W. Aunt Sarah, Dora and myself) join in the wish and the request that your Parents will spare you to us when George returns. Probably Cousin Dora will not be at home during the first part of your visit, and you will in that case, be a lively companion and useful help to us, the old, and for myself I must add the *infirm*.

I trust you may gather much improvement among us with your own painstaking; but cannot promise you any regular instruction, and indeed if Dora should be at home (which I trust she will *not* be) when you arrive, she has not health or strength sufficient for a Teacher. You may however, learn much, indirectly, while contributing both to my amusement and instruction by reading to me, which will be to me of great use and comfort. I can promise to do nothing more for you in the way of instruction than drawing out your comments and remarks and making my own: and further; it will be a pleasure to me to point

---

[1] Daughter of Thomas H. and Mary H. (*née* Monkhouse).

out whatever may appear to me amiss in your manner of reading. It would fatigue me to instruct you in French—and indeed perhaps you *need* little instruction except in the pronunciation —and *that* I could not give: but a French-master has been fixed for some time at Ambleside, and we hope, and even expect, that he will *stay*, as he has a number of scholars, and there will be no difficulty in having him here to attend on you, if we cannot get you introduced into some friend's house where he may have other pupils. I feel as if I had much to say both to you and Mary, and to your dear Mother: but as I took too much exercise yesterday (tempted by the fine weather) I must spare myself and conclude with this one assurance that I have it much at heart to have some intercourse with you, my dear God-daughter before I quit this world—Do not suppose however, that I have any feelings which make me expect the speedy approach of death. Far from it—I suffer comparatively little, and have a full enjoyment of all the blessings with which I am surrounded: but life is uncertain even with the strongest—and still more so with the old and feeble, therefore I hope the time for your coming (if all be well at home) may be fixed for next January— I send you a God-mother's Blessing, with sincerest wishes that you may not waste the happy days of Youth. Make the most of them. They will never return, and if you do not profit by present advantages you will bitterly repent when it is too late, but however happy you may be in the enjoyment of youth, health and strength, never, my good child, forget that our *home* is not here and prepare yourself for what will come, sooner or later to every one of us—Give my love to all the Inmates of Brinsop-Court—not forgetting the unseen little Sarah—I have had many anxious thoughts concerning your Uncle Monkhouse: and it is with a thankful heart that I congratulate him on the hopes of a complete restoration of his eyesight. Pray give my affectionate regards to him with earnest wishes that all may end as it has begun.

Again God bless you! Believe me
ever your faithful and affectionate Friend
Dorothy Wordsworth.

Remember dear Elizabeth, that my penmanship affords no

example for you. How I wish I could ever again climb the
Credenhall hill with all of you—young and old!—or visit that
old Tree on the top of the Hill opposite to dear Brinsop! Tell
Mary I hope she will not fail to send me a sketch of your little
Church—and mark Aunt M.'s grave.

M.
G.
K.

1087. W. W. to Mrs Hemans

Rydal Mount, Sept., 1834.

My dear Mrs Hemans,

I avail myself gladly of the opportunity of Mr Graves's return
to acknowledge the honour you have done me in prefixing my
name to your volume[1] of beautiful poems, and to thank you for
the copy you have sent me with your own autograph. Where
there is so much to admire, it is difficult to select; and therefore
I shall content myself with naming only two or three pieces.
And, first, let me particularise the piece that stands second in
the volume, *Flowers and Music in a Room of Sickness*. This was
especially touching to me, on my poor sister's account, who has
long been an invalid, confined almost to her chamber. The
feelings are sweetly touched throughout this poem, and the
imagery very beautiful; above all, in the passage where you
describe the colour of the petals of the wild rose. This morning
I have read the stanzas upon *Elysium* with great pleasure. You
have admirably expanded the thought of Chateaubriand. If
we had not been disappointed in our expected pleasure of seeing
you here, I should have been tempted to speak of many other
passages and poems with which I have been delighted.

Your health, I hope, is by this time re-established. Your son
Charles looks uncommonly well, and we have had the pleasure
of seeing him and his friends several times; but as you are aware,
we are much engaged with visitors at this season of the year, so
as not always to be able to follow our inclinations as to whom
we would wish to see. I cannot conclude without thanking you
for your sonnet upon a place so dear to me as Grasmere;[2] it is

---

[1] *Scenes and Hymns of Life* (1834), dedicated to W.
[2] *A Remembrance of Grasmere*, included in 'Records of the Spring of
1834'.

worthy of the subject. With kindest remembrances, in which
unite Mrs Wordsworth, my sister, and Dora,

I remain, dear Mrs Hemans,

Your much obliged friend,

Wm. Wordsworth.

MS.   *1088. W. W. to M. W.*

Whitehaven Monday Morn. [1834 or 35]

My dearest Mary

Thanks for the good news of your Letter.—John was at St
Bees when I arrived; did not see him till next morning. Found
Isabella suffering from a cough and cramp, and both the Children
pulled down somewhat by teething.—We had a nice chat all the
evening. Next day John brought me here, and dined one of a
very large party—I shall follow the direction about bathing,
meaning to go in at noon to day. The family here all wonderfully well; my arm is something better; my eyes are pretty well,
but there is more [?] and aching occasionally in the ball of the
right eye than I used to have, and I am not sure that the pain
in the jaw on that side of the face may have something to do
with it, as it makes all that side of the face so sensible of cold.
Isabella told me that her mother's face was very nervously
affected in the same way when having got her new teeth, and
they not fitting, she was obliged to masticate, as I have had for
a long time, on one side of her jaw. She was very ill with it, the
cold always flying to that side of the face.—I shall not write
much from here; Lord L. being the only franker, and having so
few covers to dispose of.

I send you without comment Miss Peabody's Letter, which I
found in the Parcel. I did not look at the book, so far even as to
ascertain that it was hers.—John continues to look very well.—
This morning I put the watch into Edgar's hands, and called at
tho [?]—the man not at home—was not [ ]¹ to pay a
bill.—I have nothing more to say except pray write. The family
here stay till friday at least, perhaps saturday, but write me by

¹ Word omitted?

[715]

tomorrow's post. Be particular about Dora also—remember me kindly to Mrs Ellwood, if she depart before my return, which will not perhaps be before the middle of next week.

Ever most affectionately yours, with kindest love to Dora and Sister

W. Wordsworth.

MS.   *1089. W. W. to Basil Montagu*

Rectory, Workington, Sep. 30th [1834]

My dear Montagu,

Your parcel for which you will accept my cordial thanks reached Rydal just before I set off for this place, so that I have not had time to read a word of your Life of Bacon,[1] from which I promise myself much pleasure, knowing with what industry it has been executed. This last edition of the Selections[2] which you have kindly sent me, enables me to place the former one, your present also, in the hands of my younger Son, who is at present settled as my agent at Carlisle, where he has a good deal of leisure for reading; and I trust will profit by so valuable a book.

My journey to Leamington, of which I spoke to you in my last, has been deferred from week to week on account of the deranged state of my daughter's health—I still hope that she may have courage to move after my return to Rydal at the end of this week.

Since I came here where I am on a visit to my Son who is pro tempore Incumbent of this place, (the patronage of which is in his Father-in-Law, Mr Curwen) I have learnt that there is at home a letter for me, from our old and excellent friend Wrangham[3]—written in a hand scarcely legible—from which I infer he must have suffered from a paralytic attack—of which I had heard a vague report. This grieves me much—he is a very kind-hearted Man; and tho' fonder of new acquaintance than many

[1] In Montagu's edition of Bacon's *Works*, 16 vols., 1825–37.
[2] *Selections from the Works of Taylor, Hooker, Hall, and Lord Bacon, with an analysis of the Advancement of Learning*, 1805, 3rd ed. 1829.
[3] For Wrangham *v. E.L.*, p. 143.

are—that propensity never seemed to me to weaken his attachment to his old friends.

The weather here is delightful—and I am this moment returned from bathing in the [sea] which I have done for several days past—between 7 and 8 in the morning, with a hope principally of strengthning my eyes—against the winter—which in consequence of repeated inflammations during the last 30 years are become so weak as to make reading and writing, unless for a very little at a time, injurious to them.

Farewell believe me over aff^{ly} yours
Wm. Wordsworth.

Address: Basil Montagu Esqre, Lincolns Inn, London.

MS.   **1090. D. W. to Edward Moxon**
K(—)

Rydal Mount, October 2nd, 1834.

My dear Sir,

In the absence of my Brother (on a visit to his Son at Workington) I have ventured to offer to furnish Mr Godwin, a neighbour of ours, with an introduction to you. He is much respected in our Family; but that is not the cause of this introduction. He is the Bearer of a manuscript volume of Poems by his Wife,[1] who is very anxious to entrust her work to your inspection and, if you approve and do not think the speculation would be altogether unprofitable, Mrs Godwin would be happy and thankful if you would undertake to be her publisher. I cannot give either advice or opinion, not knowing whether my Friend's writings are likely at all to hit the taste of the publick—only this I *can* say that her style, language, and versification *appear to me* very much superior to those of most of the popular female writers of the present day. I may add also that my Brother thinks highly of Mrs Godwin's powers and attainments. Further I will say, for the satisfaction of my own friendly feelings, that Mrs G. is a very amiable woman, and that both the Husband and Wife are excellent and agreeable neighbours to the Inhabitants of Rydal Mount.

[1] Catherine Grace Godwin, *v.* p. 438.

You will, I am sure, be glad to hear that my health and strength improve, though slowly. My Brother's eyes are better, yet unfit for much service.

Though I have not the pleasure of a personal acquaintance with Mrs Moxon, I feel as if she were not unknown to me, and will therefore beg you to offer to her my kind regards.

I am, dear Sir,

Yours faithfully,

D. Wordsworth—Senr.

P.S. Pray do not let any thing I have said through friendly regard to Mrs Godwin have the least influence on your determination respecting the publication of her poems or, in the smallest degree, influence your prudential arrangements or views.

MS.   *1091. W. W. to W. W. Jun*^r

Saturday [1834 or '35]

My dear Wm

Here I have been just a week, and shall stay till Monday or Tuesday. I have bathed in the warm sea-baths three times, with some benefit to my arm and shall take another bath on Monday. I shall stay 3 or 4 days with John, and a day with Sir Francis Vane (who is here) and then home.—The accounts I have from Rydal of our Invalids are good.—

What a frightful accident your's was; I hope you will soon be clear of the necessity of poulticing.

Lord and Lady L. are wonderfully well; so is Lady Frederick who is here.—This note goes through a frank of Miss Grisdale's.

Your ever affectionate Father

W. Wordsworth

I had a Letter from Isabella yesterday, the Children pretty well; John had had a bad cold. She does not mention her own health; but I was sorry to see when I was at Workington Hall that her cough had come back. My [?] leaves me little command of my finger, so you must excuse this bad writing.

K(—)   *1092. D. W. to Catherine Clarkson*

My dear Friend,   Begun Monday, 18th Oct. [? 1834]

. . . If autumnal cold and dampness had not come on, I think
I should now be able to walk far enough to have a look at the
prospect from the old terrace, but cold is my horror, so I must
not execute this large scheme till we have spring breezes and
sunshine. Whenever the weather allows it I continue to go out
daily either in the family phaeton, which is dragged by one of
the steadiest and best of horses, guided by a very skilful driver
(my dear niece), or the man-servant who takes me round and
round the garden and upon the lower new-made green terrace
in a Bath chair. . . .

C.   *1093. W. W. to Sir George Beaumont*
K.
Dear Sir George,   Rydal Mount, Nov. 27th [1834][1]

The letter with which I now trouble you will not seem to
require an apology, when I have mentioned the circumstance
which occasions it.

In the private sitting-room of my deceased friend Lady Beaumont a small picture was hung, painted by Sir George, which he
presented to me, and which at Lady Beaumont's request I gave
up to her for her lifetime. The subject is a scene in Switzerland,
and on the back of it will be found a memorandum in Lady
Beaumont's handwriting, certifying, if I am not mistaken, to
whom it belongs. Sir George in his kindness intended to paint
for me a companion to this little piece, as characteristic of Italy
as this is of Switzerland, but the intention was not fulfilled.
Having mentioned these particulars, I need scarcely add that
I should be obliged by your forwarding this memorial of Sir
George's friendship for me to Rydal at your convenience.

My sister is much better in health, though still obliged to
manage herself as an invalid. She and Mrs W. unite with me in
kind remembrances to yourself and Lady Beaumont, and believe
me, dear Sir George, faithfully yours,

Wm. Wordsworth.

[1] For W. W., M. W., and D. W. to H. C. R., Nov. 24, *v. C.R.*, p. 268.

MS.   *1094. W. W. to Basil Montagu*

Rydal Mount, Jan^{ry} 1st 1835

My dear Montagu,

Your sheets have been read with much pleasure—they begin at the first chapter and end at page 336—inclusive—the Title page etc. and the remaining sheets being wanting. If you forward what you kindly design for me to Longman's it will reach me free of expense either to yourself or me—as I shall have two parcels coming down in succession—but send it as soon as you can, and I may perhaps have it by the former. I congratulate you sincerely on bringing to a close this important and laborious work.[1]

The baser part and it is to be feared much the larger of the Whigs having made common cause with the Enemies of the British Constitution, I concur with you that the prospect of the Gover^{nt}[2] and the Nation is indeed a sad one.—All this was distinctly foreseen by the Internal part of the Community from the first broaching of the Reform bill. Good and discreet men must act cleaving to the Roman virtue of never despairing of the Country —this they must do for Conscience sake, whatever come of it.

Ever faithfully yours,

W. Wordsworth.

Address: Basil Montagu Esqre, Lincoln's Inn, London.

K(—)[3]   *1095. W. W. to Thomas Noon Talfourd*

Rydal Mount, Jan^{ry} 1st, 1835.

My dear Sir,

Your letter brought a great shock to us all. I had not heard from yourself when you were here that any thing was threatening Lamb's health, and Miss Hutchinson who saw him late in the spring reported that he was looking wonderfully well and appeared in excellent spirits. He has followed poor Coleridge

---

[1] i.e. the last volume of M.'s edition of Bacon.

[2] In the previous July Lord Melbourne had succeeded Lord Grey as Prime Minister. In November he was summarily and unaccountably dismissed, and in December Sir Robert Peel formed a Tory administration. On April 8, 1835, Peel resigned and Lord Melbourne succeeded him.

[3] K.'s text has here been corrected and supplemented by a facsimile of p. 1 of the Letter. I have not been able to trace the original.

within six months.[1] It seems to us upon reflection, that his Sister will bear the loss of him better than he could have borne that of her; and we are bound to believe so, as it has pleased God to take him first. There seems to be, with respect to his dear Sister, from your account, enough to provide her with all comforts which her melancholy situation will admit of—Should it however not be so, there can be no doubt that Lamb's surviving friends will be too happy to contribute whatever might be desired. I need scarcely have mentioned this, because L., tho' exceedingly generous, and charitable above measure—was also prudent and thoughtful. Do let us hear from you again on the subject by and bye; for our minds and hearts are full of the sad Event, and one cannot but be very anxious to know the state of poor Miss Lamb's mind—after she has been more tried. . . .

MS.
K(—)

1096. W. W. to Henry Taylor

Rydal Mount, Jan. 6th, [1835.]

My dear Sir,

Thank you for the King's speech, which I have not yet read, having been employed all the morning in writing letters. Political knowledge is at a low ebb in the village of Rydal, nor will you think much of its political sagacity when I tell you that a leading man among our humbler yeomanry refused to sign the laity's declaration of attachment to the Church 'because the list of signatures would be sent up to London there to be kept in a safe place, till the Dissenters and Papists had got the uppermost, which they would soon do, and then, with the list in their hands, they would come and cut off the heads of all who had signed it'! And, would you believe it, that this Person, in the concerns of daily life, is one of the shrewdest of our little yeomen. This caution reminds me of the prospective prudence of a Gentleman of rank and large Property, who resided in our neighbourhood some years, and would never attend the parish Church, lest he should become the unwilling eye-witness of some misconduct of the Clergyman, and be consequently called upon to give evidence

[1] Lamb died on Dec. 27, 1834.

against him in some of the Courts. The Clergyman was in fact a graceless [   ] and the discretion came from Scotland. What other country could have given birth to it?

The Doctor[1] seems to take well. I am heartily glad of it.

One of the enclosed letters I have [not] directed. It is merely an acknowledgement for a couple of volumes received yesterday —and the like for Mr Southey—which ought to have come to hand some months ago. I cannot defer my thanks till I have an opportunity of getting a frank here. Will you therefore *at your convenience* procure one for me, and forward the note? I shall not trouble you in this way again.

We had pleasant accounts from Keswick yesterday—including good tidings of the Bride and Bridegroom,[2] who are at present at their Father's house in Shropshire. My sister, you will be glad to hear, has been in a comfortable state since we had the pleasure of seeing you here. And my eyes are well and would be useful to me for reading and writing if I could keep my mind quiet; but the worst part of my case is that mental labour, *if persisted in*, is always injurious to them; and, unfortunately for me, if I am not *possessed* by my employment, I cannot work at all.

I hope that Mrs Taylor, as also our good friend Miss Fenwick,[3] have enjoyed health throughout the late boisterous and rainy, though mild season. With the united good wishes of this household, believe me to be, my dear sir, very sincerely yours,

                                                  Wm. Wordsworth.

MS.   *1097. W. W. to Edward Moxon*
K(—)
                                                  Lowther Castle
                                          [p.m. January twelfth 1835]
My dear Sir,
    Your letter of the 7th followed me to this place, and I warmly thank you for it. The distressing intelligence of our lamented

----

[1] i.e. Southey's book published in the previous year.
[2] Edith Southey and her husband, the Rev. J. W. Warter.
[3] Isabella Fenwick, the cousin and intimate friend of H. T.'s stepmother: she had a great influence over H. T. in his youth, and became the dearest friend of W. W. and M. W. in their later years. She died in Dec. 1856.

Friend's death had been communicated by Mr Talfourd; and the disposal of his property had been mentioned also though less in detail than by you—As far as our fallible judgments are entitled to decide upon such an event there appears to be cause for congratulation that it should have pleased God to remove the Brother before the Sister—We can all under my roof sympathize with your heavy loss and Mrs Moxon's. The shock to us was great, for we were not in the least prepared for it. It is a great consolation that Miss Lamb has so judicious a Friend to take care of her.—You allude to his Letters. I agree with you they must be valuable. Unfortunately we possess very few; much the most interesting we ever received, unaccountably disappeared within a day after its arrival, and we never could make out what became of it; which, I assure you, is a subject of mortification to which we have not infrequently recurred.—

The proof of the Title page of my Poems[1] has just reached me here, and [it] gives me great pleasure to see your name there. Owing to the state of the times I have been very slack and indifferent about pushing it through the Press; and I care as little about its Publication, my mind being wholly engrossed by the wretched state of public affairs.—I have been in the midst of one Revolution in France, and recoil with horror from the thought of a second, at home. The Radicals and foolish Whigs are driving the nation rapidly to that point, [that] soon, alas! it is likely to be found that power will pass from the audacious and wicked to the more audacious and wicked, and so to the still more and more, till military despotism comes in as a quietus; and then after a time the struggle for liberty will re-commence, and you, young as you are, should your life be prolonged to the seventy years of the psalmist, will not live to see her cause crowned with success. Farewell—give my kindest regards to Mrs Moxon and believe me ever faithfully your much obliged friend,

W. Wordsworth.

Mrs Moxon will be so kind as to paste the under written in a copy of my Poems which I shall order to be sent to her—

[1] *Yarrow Revisited and Other Poems*, 1835, was published by both Longman's and Moxon.

Should you ever have a parcel of any kind to send me, pray enclose a Copy of Southey, Selections. The Second Edition of my Selections[1] is very neatly got up—Thank you for the Copy sent and also for the Trial of Wm Shakespear[2]—very clever.

Address: Edward Moxon Esq., 44 Dover Street, London.

MS.　　　*1098. W. W. to John Thornton*[3]

Jany 13th [1835] Lowther Castle near Penrith.
My dear Sir,

Bearing in mind your very kind attention to me and my interests, I venture to write to you upon a point in which I am at present much concerned. You will probably remember that when I had the pleasure of seeing you in Westmorland I more than once mentioned the parental anxiety which I felt for my younger Son, having been, through an error of judgement, the cause of his losing his health, and greatly impairing his constitution, by sending him while yet too young for so great a change, to the Charterhouse.—He was consequently turned out of the course of life, viz, the university, for which I designed him. He is now 25 years of age and has been acting more than three years as my Subdistributor, a situation that leads to nothing and is dependent on many contingencies. In the present Government I have more than one Friend who is desirous to serve him, but an opening might not occur till a change takes place; and I have therefore written to my honored Friend the Earl of Lonsdale expressing a wish to give up my office of Distributor of Stamps which I have held nearly 22 years, in case his Lordship through the present prime minister could procure a transfer of it to my son. And now my dear Sir you will guess why I have troubled you with this Letter; which is to request that you would, upon this occasion, if the matter should come before you or the Board,

---

[1] The *Selections* published in 1831 (*v.* p. 555) went into a second edition in 1834.

[2] *Citation and Examination of William Shakespeare touching Deer-stealing*, by Walter Savage Landor, 1834.

[3] John Thornton (1783–1861), Commissioner of Boards of Audit, Stamps, and Inland Revenue.

do what you can consistently with your public Duty, to forward my views, which I am sure you as a Father will deem laudable. Should I be cut off, my Wife and Daughter would have little, though enough to support them in their humble way; but my Son would suffer exceedingly in mind were he to become in the least burthensome to them; indeed he would not endure it. I am myself nearly sixty five, and my Contemporaries are dropping fast around me—I need say no more—as I am sure you will enter into my feelings.

I sincerely hope that yourself Mrs Thornton and all your family have enjoyed good health since we had the pleasure of seeing you. My Sister still languishes, and alas! my only Daughter is confined to the couch, and has long been so, going through a course of bleeding and blistering on account of a spinal complaint.—My eyes, though tender, are very much better.

With kindest regards to yourself Mrs Thornton and my young friends of your family I remain my dear Sir

very faithfully your much obliged

Wm Wordsworth

I return to Rydal tomorrow.

1099. *W. W. to Francis Wrangham*

Rydal Mount, February 2^d, [1835.]

My dear Wrangham,

Sincere thanks are due from me for the attention you paid to Mrs W.'s letter, written during my absence. You know the favourable opinion I entertain of Mr Graves, and I was under a promise to let him know if any vacancy occurred in this neighbourhood, and to do all I could, without infringing upon prior or stronger claims, to promote the attainment of his wishes. Mrs W. judiciously and properly stated in her letter that it was not her desire, and she trusted it was no one's else, to interfere with any claims which in the judgment of the Bi[sho]p the sons of our late friend might have. Had she not made this proviso, I should have regretted she mixed at all in a business of so delicate a nature; but I will not conceal from you that out of these well-intended and right endeavours of hers has arisen much uneasiness to herself—from the circumstance that Mr Thos. Fleming, who was his Father's Curate at Bootle, is now likely to be without employment. Of him *personally* we have but slight knowledge, but it redounds much to his honour that he had set aside, before his Father's death, the proceeds of his Fellowship to maintain a younger Brother at College, his Father not being able to do it; he himself living upon his stipend as his Father's Curate. This fact was mentioned some little time ago to Mrs W. by a friend and benefactress of the family. It grieves me to add, that the eldest Son, our Minister,—a most excellent Person and a zealous Pastor,—has taken offence at what we have done in this business, the whole particulars of which were laid openly before him. This gives *me* no concern but on his own account, because all that has been done by us was done with deliberation, and from motives pure, and entirely disinterested. We were governed only by joint considerations of what was due to Mr G., to the Family of Fleming, and, above all, of what promised to be beneficial to the Parishioners; for without this last thought I should not have stirred in the affair for the sake of any Friend whatsoever.

And now my dear friend to a point which I have a good deal at heart. Could the situation of Mr T. F. be suggested to the Bp in such a way as might tend to reconcile him to this disappointment, by placing him in some *other* eligible Curacy for which he might be fit?

The mind of every thinking man who is attached to the Ch: of England must at this time be especially turned to reflections upon all points of Ecclesiastical polity, government, and management, which may tend to strengthen the Establishment in the affections of the People, and enlarge the sphere of its efficiency. It cannot then I feel be impertinent in me, though a Layman, to express upon this occasion my satisfaction, qualified as it is by what has been said above, in finding from this instance that our Diocesan is unwilling to station Clergymen in Cures with which they are locally connected. Some years ago, when

the present Bp of London,[1] then of Chester, was residing in this
neighbourhood, I took the liberty of strenuously recommending
to him not to ordain young men to Curacies in places where they
had been brought up, or in the midst of their own relatives. I
had seen too much of the mischief of this, especially as affecting
the functions and characters of ministers born and bred up in the
lower classes of society. It has been painful to me to observe
the false position, as the French would call it, in which men so
placed, are. Their habits, their manners, and their talk, their
acquaintanceships, their friendships—and, let me say, their
domestic affections, naturally, and properly draw them one way,
while their professional obligations point out another; and
accordingly, if they are sensible of both, they live in a perpetual
conflict; and are liable to be taxed with pride and ingratitude,
as seeming to neglect their old friends, when they only associate
with them with that reserve and under those restraints which
their sacred profession enjoins. If, on the other hand, they fall
into unrestrained familiarity with the Associates of their earlier
life and boyish days, how injurious to their Ministry such intercourse would be, must flash upon every Man's mind whose
thoughts have turned for a moment to the subject. Allow me to
add a word upon the all-important matter of Testimonials,—
the case of the Rector of Bowness and of Grasmere[2] presses it
closely upon my mind. Had the Individuals who signed his
been fitly impressed with the awfulness of the act they were
about to engage in, they could not have undertaken it. His
character was at that time too notorious. Would it not be a good
rule for Bishops to exclude Testimonials from Relatives and near
Connections? It is painful to notice what a tendency there is in
men's minds to allow even a slight call of private regard to out-
weigh a very strong claim of Duty to the Public, and not less in
sacred concerns than in civil.

Your hands,[3] my dear friend, have failed, as well as my eyes,
so that we are neither of us in very flourishing trim for active
correspondence—be assured, however, I participate in the feelings you express. Last year has robbed me of Coleridge, of

[1] Blomfield.   [2] Sir Richard le Fleming, Bart.
[3] v. Letter to Montagu, Sept. 20, 1834, supra.

Charles Lamb—James Losh—Rudd of Trinity, Fleming just gone—and other Schoolfellows and Cotemporaries. I cannot forget that Shakespear, who scarcely survived 50—(I am now near the close of my 65th year) wrote

> In me that time of life thou dost behold
> When yellow leaves, or few, or none, do hang
> Upon the bough.

How much more reason have we to break out into such a strain? Let me hear from you from time to time. I shall feel a lively interest in all that concerns you.

I remain, faithfully yours

(*Signature cut off*)

MS.   **1100. W. W. to Henry Taylor**

Saturday morning.[1]

Your kind Letter has just been received—I wish you were stronger in body. Among my friends the yellow leaf has been falling and the green leaf swept off lately in an appalling way—So it appears to have been among yours.

Your view of the Case is quite correct and I repeat that I am sorry I mentioned it to you. Farewell. I have nothing to add to-day.

Affectionately yours,

W. Wordsworth.

Address: H. Taylor Esqre, Colonial Office.

MS.   **1101. W. W. to Viscount Lowther[2]**

Feb. 14th [1835]

My dear Lord Lowther,

It is my present intention to set off in a day or two for London as you recommend—but, this season being trying to the eyes, I

---

[1] Undated, but probably written about the time of the previous letter to Wrangham.

[2] This letter is an answer to one from Lord Lowther, dated Feb. 12, 1835, stating that he had seen Sir Robert Peel who was anxious to do something for W. and his family, but that a recommendation of the late Government to unite Cumberland and Westmorland to the little Lancaster district made it difficult to allow W.'s son to succeed him in his office of stamp dis-

may be prevented, and therefore trespass upon your kindness by answering some of your questions by Letter, as briefly as I can—first thanking you sincerely for your zealous exertions.

My first object of anxiety is my younger son, who is now in a dependant situation, which leads to nothing. He would be fit for such an Office as I hold, or any other connected with the revenue, or other department where the confinement is not excessive, or the labour *severe*. In which case his health, tho' now good, might break down—as he suffered so much from ill-health during 3 or 4 years of his boyhood. He is prudent, methodical, observant, ingenious and in action very persevering —his book attainments are not as extensive as I could wish, owing to that long sickness—but he has read a good deal, and knows and speaks the German Language. Seeing how difficult it is to find an opening, I should have been pleased to resign in his favour—but to this there was one great objection, the emolument of the place would not have allowed him to insure his Life for my benefit in case he died before me—and *our common* income would have been reduced by giving up the Sub-distributorship of Carlisle—so that if anything respectable could be found for him in another quarter I should be well content to continue as I am—tho', as I told you, I have an ardent desire to be at liberty (now that the state of my eyes interferes so much with reading) to travel a little on the Continent—in Italy especially.

As to the civil pension list—under no circumstances would Mrs Wordsworth, myself, or any of the family desire such a thing—rather let me say accept it. In fact it would not be necessary—my Wife and Daughter, in case of my death would be left in circumstances equal to their *very* moderate wishes. I have not laid up anything—my literary distinction, such as it is, having involved me in unavoidable expenses, without bringing in a pecuniary equivalent. I have however insured my life for £2,000 and have not spent my own little patrimony, nor my

tributor. He and Peel suggested, as possible alternatives, placing Mrs W. on the Civil List and appointing W. W. Jun. to some other office if a suitable one could be found. He urged W. to come to town at once 'when *we* with other of your friends might decide the specific mode of serving yourself or family'.

Wife's—but during the life of Mrs W. and my Daughter nothing could be spared for my Sons, which makes me so anxious on account of the younger *especially*.

I think the Lord Chancellor[1] would be disposed to serve me should anything under his patronage fall vacant that there might be no professional obstacle to my younger Son's holding—but perhaps there is no such thing.

Odd things are done in party arrangements—and not the least odd is the scheme of the late Gov^t for attaching the very large District to the very small one—the Breast of Veal (excuse the allusion) to the Sweet-bread[2]—and not the Sweet-bread to the Breast of Veal! I am an old man—Mr G.[3] a young one—that might put it into their heads—but I fear it was a stroke unfairly aimed at your Family.

I wish I could be in better heart than your Letter upon the returns[4] allows.—I certainly concur with you, in the way in which the present Gov^t ought to behave. The Ship of the Constitution is in a storm and must sink if the men now at the helm are obliged to abandon her—therefore let them stick to their post to the last.

Again and again I thank you for the proof of cordial friend-ship which you have given me on this and all other occasions—

and believe me, dear Lord Lowther

ever faithfully—your most obliged

Wm Wordsworth

Address: *Private*—Viscount Lowther, M.P. etc., etc.

M. **1102. W. W. to the Rev. Robert Montgomery**[5]
K(—)

Feb. 1835.

My dear Sir,

On my return home, after an absence of some length, I have had the pleasure of receiving your two volumes. . . .

----

[1] Lord Lyndhurst (J. Singleton Copley).   [2] *written* Sweat-bread.
[3] Probably the Distributor for 'the little Lancaster district'.
[4] In the elections then proceeding the Tories were gaining seats. After repeated defeats Peel resigned on April 8, and Lord Melbourne became Prime Minister.
[5] Robert Montgomery (1807–55), *The Omnipresence of the Deity*, of which

With your 'Omnipresence of the Deity' I was acquainted long ago, having read it and other parts of your writings with much pleasure, though with some abatement, such as you yourself seem sufficiently aware of, and which, in the works of so young a writer, were by me gently judged, and in many instances regarded, though in themselves faults, as indications of future excellence. In your letter, for which also I thank you, you allude to your Preface, and desire to know if my opinion concurs with yours on the subject of sacred poetry. That Preface has been read to me, and I can answer in the affirmative; but at the same time allow me frankly to tell you that what *most* pleased me in that able composition is to be found in the few concluding paragraphs, beginning 'It is now seven years since', etc. . . .

I cannot conclude without one word of literary advice, which I hope you will deem my advanced age entitles me to give. Do not, my dear Sir, be anxious about any individual's opinion concerning your writings, however highly you may think of his genius or rate his judgment. Be a severe critic to yourself; and depend upon it no person's decision upon the merit of your works will bear comparison in point of value with your own. You must be conscious from what feeling they have flowed, and how far they may or may not be allowed to claim, on that account, permanent respect; and, above all, I would remind you, with a view to tranquillise and steady your mind, that no man takes the trouble of surveying and pondering another's writings with a hundredth part of the care which an author of sense and genius will have bestowed upon his own. Add to this reflection another, which I press upon you, as it has supported me through life, viz., that Posterity will settle all accounts justly, and that works which deserve to last will last; and if undeserving this fate, the sooner they perish the better.

Believe me to be faithfully,

Your much obliged,

W. Wordsworth.

the 11th ed., together with *Satan, a Poem*, 1830, were so severely handled by Macaulay in the *Ed. Rev.* of April 1830, was first published in 1828.

MS.　　　*1103. W. W. to Alexander Dyce*

Monday morn^g March 2 [1835]

56 Jermyn Street

My dear Sir,

Many sincere thanks for your elegant and valuable editions of *Akenside*,[1] *Beattie*,[1] and *Shakespear*,[1] from the perusal of which I promise myself much pleasure.

On Wednesday at half past six I shall be happy to take dinner with you.

Mr Southey's Book shall be conveyed to him—he leaves Town, perhaps has already left it, this morning, but I will take care of the Book for him.

I remain my dear Sir

ever faithfully yours,

Wm Wordsworth

Address: Revd Alexander Dyce, 9 Gray's Inn.

MS.　　　*1104. W. W. to Alexander Dyce*

19 South Parade

Floodyer Street Gate

[p.m. March 11, 1835]

My dear Sir,

Here we are.

I lent Mr Rogers your Akenside, on returning it he writes me: Akenside's life is very entertaining and I could not leave it till I had done it. Many thanks for it. Tell Mr Mitford[2] that the passage in King John is at the close of the 4th Act[3]—the words these, or something like it—

Vast Confusion waits as doth a Raven *on*, etc.

The imminent decay—

near the commencement of the fifth act you meet the word *Amazement*[4]—all shewing that Gray when he wrote his Ode was

---

[1] Contributed to Pickering's *Aldine series*.

[2] John Mitford (1781–1859) had edited the *Poetical Works of Gray* in 1814 and 1830: he brought out an ed. of the *Works* in 4 vols. in 1836.

[3] *King John*, IV. iii. 152–4.

[4] *ib.* v. i. 35. 'And wild amazement hurries up and down'.

fresh from the perusal of these scenes. The parallel passages in the Ode are—

> Confusion on thy banners wait
> Amazement in his Van

And the acknowledged passage threatening the Air with colours idly spread.[1] I hope we shall meet again before I leave London. I shall be here about 10 days.—

ever very sincerely yours
Wm Wordsworth

On the 18th I dine at the Rev^d Mr Johnson's,[2] 107 Regent Street—to meet Mr Southey. Mr Johnson is a particular Friend of mine and it would give me great pleasure to introduce you to Mr Southey at his house if you would call in the evening.

Address: The Revd A. Dyce, Gray's Inn.

K.   ## 1105. W. W. to Allan Cunningham

Wednesday Morning,
[p.m. March 19, 1835.]

My dear Friend,

In extreme hurry I sit down to thank you for your life and edition of Burns,[3] received last night, and for your obliging letter.

It would give me much pleasure to be of any use to you in your meditated edition of the poets, but I am not aware how I can, except by my opinion as to the authors which it might be expedient to add to your selection, or to exclude. This, after conference with Mr Southey, I should do with great pleasure. . . .

Ever faithfully yours,
Wm. Wordsworth.

---

[1] *ib.* v. i. 72. For W.'s other criticisms of Gray *v.* Oxf. W., p. 936, and my Index.

[2] The Rev. William Johnson, *v. M.Y.*, p. 445.

[3] *The Works of Robert Burns, with a New Life and Notes*, 8 vols., 1834.

1106. *W. W. to Robert Jones*

Review of Engl. Studies, Jan. 1937.

Trinity Lodge Mar 30 [1835.]

My dear Friend

Your letter dated Feb 7th has remained far too long unanswered, a short time after the receipt of it, Mrs W. and I started
for London and took the letter along with us, meaning to reply
to it, from that place, where we knew we could procure franks
with great ease,—but during a residence of 5 weeks in Town
whither we had gone on business—we were so much hurried and
fatigued, that we had neither time nor spirits to sit down and
write, in the way we wished to write to you. We have been now
3 days here, where we are like ships in harbour after a storm.
My Br tho' much harassed by business, and having survived a
dangerous attack of cholera last Autumn, is very active—and
looking well for him. Two of his Sons, who are fellows of this
College, are also well, and we have the pleasure of seeing them
at all hours when they are not elsewhere engaged. You remember Greenwood,[1] my old Schoolfellow—he is still here residing
as Senior fellow—he looks pretty well, but complains of many
infirmities. I called upon the Master of St John's[2] yesterday,
but did not see him, he is said to wear well—I had a friend with
me who took me thro' the Lodge and in the Combination room
I saw my own Picture—which the Master and Fellows did me
the honour of subscribing for—it looks well, but is of too large
a size for the room and would be seen to much more advantage
in the Hall. But had there been room for it there, there is an
objection to that place—the charcoal smoke I am told, is ruinous
to Pictures, and this which is really well done cost much money.

We were glad to hear of your good health, and it was kind in
you, giving a particular account of my old Friends of your
family—I hope your brother will continue to be as careful of
himself as the state of his constitution seems to require—pray
give my kind remembrances to him, and best wishes to your
Sisters. My own Sister continues to languish—as she may do

[1] R. H. Greenwood (1770–1840), Fellow of Trinity, 1792–1840.
[2] James Wood, Dean of Ely, Master of St. John's, 1815–39.

perhaps for a long time—during 8 months of the year she can scarcely be said to quit the House—and is not for a much less time confined to her room—and during the severity of the winter, in a great measure to her bed. But her sufferings are upon the whole less than they used to be, and she endures her privations with resignation—and unless when she has a recurrence of a bilious attack, she reads a good deal, and is in mind active and cheerful.

We have another cause of sorrow in our house, which is the state of my poor Daughter's health—her appetite has gradually failed for several years—and a consequent weakness has superinduced a spinal complaint, which has subjected her to severe courses of bleeding and blistering, which, you will be grieved to hear, have not yet produced for us steady hopes of her recovery. During our stay in London, we have been in frequent consultation about her cure, with a kind medical friend Dr Holland—and we [hope] she will have as much benefit from the best advice as can be had without her being actually seen by the Persons consulted. If it should be in our power to have her brought to London, that will be done, but at present she cannot bear such a journey.—You will be much concerned to hear that our excellent friend Mr Southey and his family have been suffering from a severe domestic affliction. Symptoms of mental derangement appeared in Mrs S. last autumn.—She was removed to the Retreat at York—but there appears to be little hopes of her final recovery—and her husband is about to take her back to Keswick.

The business which brought me to London arose out of a hope of procuring some respectable situation for my Son Wm. from Sir R^t Peel's Government—and in this I should have had no doubt of succeeding, if the present administration could have kept their ground. But the Whigs have behaved more dishonorably than any great Party ever did. The consequence will be, the displacing of the only Men who are able to have deferred, at least for some time, a general convulsion. The Whig Lords will and must take the alarm, but it will be too late to save either themselves or their constitutional opponents.

A Copy of the MSS. of Coleridge which you possess, would be

welcome to his Executor Mr Green, I have no doubt; and with a view of having it conveyed to him, I request you would be so kind as to enclose it as follows—First a cover to—Green Esq, Surgeon, Lincolns Inn fields—to whom you will please to signify how it was given to you—and that I had requested you to forward it to him. This packet enclose to 'Henry Taylor Esqre and again enclose 'to The Under Secretary of State, Colonial Office, London'. The Book upon Mona[1] which you kindly offer I should be glad to receive. When you should have an opportunity to send it to Liverpool, if you direct it to John Bolton Esqre for Mr Wordsworth Rydal—it will not be long before it will reach me by some parcel of his to his residence on Windermere. I have ordered my forthcoming little volume to be sent to you through the Bookseller at Ruthen—it will be out in about a fortnight.

You will recollect Mr Fleming[2] of Rayrigg, formerly of St John's, he died suddenly about 3 months since, and not in good circumstances.

My Son John is still at Workington, where he holds the Living for his Brother in Law—but he will soon have to fall back upon his Vicarage at Brigham—he is building a house which will cost not much less than £1,000—£400 of which is contributed by the Patron and the Building Society. In the volume about to appear you will find a Sonnet beginning 'Pastor and Patriot' upon the building of his house—I think he has had a Son born since you heard from us last—who, tho' an uncommonly fine Child when we saw him, at about a month or six weeks old, has since been a great sufferer, together with his Mother—from Influenza and Low fever—and the Child has been reduced to a state of weakness which has caused much anxiety to the Parents—he is however beginning, we hear, to gather strength. John seems to think that the situation of the Rectory at Workington is not favorable to health—being low and contiguous to marshy ground—so that we shall be glad of the change, when his family retire to the banks of the Derwent.

---

[1] *A History of the Island of Mona, or Anglesey*, by A. Llwyd, 1833: it was in W.'s library at his death.

[2] Rev. John Fleming, rector of Bootle, 1814–35, *v.* Letter 1099.

My wife joins me in every good wish to yourself and Sisters— Had I not now been so long absent, we had some of us meditated paying you a visit this summer—as it is, we must hope to be spared to meet at some more distant time—unless you can muster courage—should you have leisure—to come to see us at Rydal.

Believe me my dear Friend to remain
faithfully and affectionately yours
Wm Wordsworth

I regret not having a frank—but I shall not wait for one thinking you would rather pay postage than that I sh^d do so.

Address: The Revd Robt Jones, Plas yn Llan, near Ruthin, N.W.

MS.   **1107. W. W. to Mr Liddell**[1]

Trinity Lodge, March 30th [1835]
My dear Sir,

I hope you have not thought me insensible to your kindness for having deferred so long my acknowledgements for your very kindly letter written upon a subject so interesting to me. Your letter followed me to London, but I was then in a course of frequent interviews with Dr Holland[2] relative to my Daughter's case—and her mother, who was with me was in correspondence with her on the subject: in order to Dr Holland's being put into possession of particulars with a view to lay them before Sir B. Brodie,[3] whose skill had restored your suffering Brother to health. I did hope that the result would have been, that I might have accompanied my thanks for your suggestions with an account that my daughter had been much relieved, and was

[1] Probably Henry Thomas Liddell (1797–1878), like W., educated at St John's, Cambridge; from 1837–47 the popular Tory M.P. for N. Durham, and like W. a strong opponent of the Reform Bill and the disestablishment of the Irish Church. In 1833 he published *The Wizard of the North and other Poems*. On the death of his father he became Lord Ravensworth.

[2] Probably Sir Henry Holland (1788–1873), the popular London doctor and famous traveller.

[3] Sir Benjamin Collins Brodie (1783–1862), one of the most famous surgeons and doctors of his day. Made a baronet in 1834. P.R.S. 1858, Pres. Royal College of Surgeons 1844, first Pres. of the General Medical Council.

in a fair way of recovery—on which account I deferred writing. It grieves me to say that for various causes with the statement of which you need not be troubled, Dr H. in the end did not think that any good would arise from consulting Sir B. B——; and accordingly it has not been done—and the same treatment which my daughter was under when we left home 6 weeks ago, continues to be used,—with some change in the mediums recommended by Dr H. to strengthen the digestive organs. I ought to have begun with mentioning that your letter was shown to Dr Holland, and taken by him into serious consideration. The sum of her case is, that she is relieved for a time by bleeding and blistering but after a week or so, the pains, and the disorder in the stomach recur—and the same course is repeated so that our anxiety cannot be said to be much less diminished on her account, and we long for the day when it shall be possible to bring her to Town in order that she may be seen both by Dr Holland and Sir Ben Brodie.

With persons who come to London so seldom as Mrs Wordsworth and I, and only for a short time—they are unavoidably much hurried, and glad to return to any quiet harbour, so is it with us—we are now guests with my Brother, the Master of Trin: Coll., Cambridge. This day, we are told, is to decide the fate of the Ministers, and with them that of the Nation. Never having been hopeful, I am much less disturbed than is natural to one, who has so deep a feeling of the miseries that will be produced by those convulsions towards which we are rapidly advancing. Nevertheless the scenes that I witnessed during the earlier years of the French Revolution, when I was resident in France, come back on me with appalling violence—we are told that the King will send for Lord Grey, does he hope that hoary-headed Magician, whose wand with Royal concurrence excited the storm, will be able to appease it. Alas, alas, for the short-sightedness of our nautical Sovereign!

Pray be so kind as to tell me how my little vol: of Poems[1] must be sent to you? It is printed, but my Publisher does not chuse to send it forth till the middle of April. You will find in it some political verses, which highflying critics will not allow

[1] *Yarrow Revisited*, 1835.

to be poetry—enough for me, if they be admitted to be good rhetoric and enlightened patriotism, which the Whigs will, of course, be slow to consent to.

Pray present my kind respects to Mrs Liddell and best wishes for her recovery, and believe me, with sincere thanks, my dear Sir,

Y^r much obliged
Wm Wordsworth.

P.S. We shall remain here at least a fortnight.

MS.
R.
K(—)*1108. W. W. to Samuel Rogers*

Trinity Lodge,
April 5th [1835]

My dear Rogers,

The papers record the death of your, and let me add *my*, long-known and long-valued Friend, R^d Sharp;[1] sincerely do I condole with you and with his nearest connections upon this loss. How a thought of the presence of living friends brightens particular spots! and what a shade falls over them when those friends have passed away! This I have felt strongly in the course of the last twelve months in respect to London, vast as the place is. And even in regard to the Lakes, it makes me melancholy to think that Sharp will visit them no more. If you be in communication with Mrs Sharp and Miss Kinnaird, pray assure them that Mrs W. and I sympathise sincerely with them in their bereavement.

The Papers also tell us that you have suffered a serious loss of Property by a robbery[2] committed in your house—the offender one of your own Servants. Was it the footman? I remember being a good deal startled by your telling me that that Servant took the liberty of being absent as much as 4 hours

---

[1] *v. E.L.*, p. 384, &c.

[2] *The Times* of April 2 records that, on March 31, Rogers's footman, ordered to get out some plate which had not been in use for some time, absconded. It was then found that much valuable silver (including four dishes worth over £1,000) was missing, and it was conjectured that his thefts had extended over a considerable period.

at a time. I made some observation upon what you said, but
not in such strong terms as would have been used had I not been
in the habit of placing reliance upon your discretion. You expressed dissatisfaction and talked of dismissing him. After all,
this may not be the man. Have any valuable pieces of virtu
been taken? if not I shall be glad, and also to hear both that the
value of the Property, viz., £2,000, has been exaggerated, and
part of it, at least, recovered.

Pray write to us at your early convenience. The great public
unsettling with which we are threatened unsettles my little
plans also, causing me to doubt whether I shall return to London
or not. Whatever may be shaken or altered, be you assured of
my unchangeable attachment, and that I am, and ever shall be,
firmly yours,

Wm. Wordsworth

Kindest regards from Mrs W. and myself to your Sister.

MS.   *1109. W. W. to Samuel Rogers*
R.
                                    4ᵗʰ May, 1835: Rydal Mount.

My dear Rogers,

I enclose a line barely to say that after a journey of three
days, having slept at Birmingham and Manchester, we reached
this place in good health.

My poor Sister is rather better; but every day and hour add
to our anxiety for the removal of my Daughter to London for
medical advice.

I hope when we return we shall find you in London. It grieved
me to come away without seeing you again. My Son Wm is now
with us, and looking better than I have seen him do for some
years. He bears his disappointment in being still without a
better provision as well as could be expected. You would be
pleased to see how sensible he is of your affectionate kindness
towards him, and happy am I to see he is not unworthy of it.
He is a great comfort to us all in our distress. Poor Mrs Southey
appears to be but little, if at all, improved. Your Portrait is

much liked in this house—I own, elegant as it is, I could have wished for something with more strength. Love from everyone here to yourself and sister,

And believe [me], my dear Friend,

most faithfully yours,

Wm. Wordsworth

Address: Sam¹ Rogers Esqʳᵉ, St. James' Place.

MS.   *1110. W. W. to Edward Moxon*[1]

My dear Sir,   [p.m. May 15, 1835]

Thank you for the sonnets.[2] I am not at all disappointed in them. They are very pleasing; and we all like them much.— You need not apologize for dedicating them to me—for they aim at no rivalship with mine, being so different both in the unity of the subject, and in the metre and style of versification. Yours are of Elizabeth's and James's and the 1ˢᵗ Charles' time; mine rather after the model of Milton.

We reached home without mischance—but found little in either of our invalids to rejoice over—I am most anxious for my daughter's moving southward as soon as her Doctor shall give her leave. With kindest remembrances to yourself and Mrs M. and your Br and sister, in which Mrs W. and my family unite,

I remain my dear Sir

Your sincere Friend

Wm Wordsworth.

Address: Ed. Moxon Esqʳᵉ, Dover Street.

MS.   *1111. W. W. to J. Macrone*

Rydal Mount Ambleside

Sir,   June 2ⁿᵈ [1835]

Accept my thanks for the life of Milton[3] which you have sent me, and my sincere acknowledgements of the honor done me by

---

[1] For two letters, W. W. to H. C. R., May 1835, *v. C.R.*, pp. 271 and 275.

[2] Moxon's *Sonnets*, dedicated to W. W., were published in 1835.

[3] *Poetical Works of John Milton*, ed. by Sir Egerton Brydges, with

the Dedication which is more acceptable as uniting my name with Mr Southey's. This mark of respect to us both will I trust meet with the approbation of our common Friend, the Author, who is well fitted to do justice to the arduous task which he has undertaken.

I remain

Sir

respectfully

your obliged Servant

Wm Wordsworth

This Letter would have been posted earlier but it was detained for the opportunity of a Frank.

Address: J. Macrone Esqre, 3 St James Square, London.

MS.   **1112. *W. W. to Robert Southey***

(*with postscript by M.W.*)

Sunday Morning, June 7 [1835]

My dear Southey,

We have been and are, in sad distress in this House. My Beloved Sister's days are drawing steadily to a close; She grows obviously weaker and weaker every day; And dear Miss Hutchinson too is still suffering under her severe attack; lumbago, at first, then rheumatic fever, with frequent delirium, which is not yet quite gone. We hope however and trust that she is recovering; Mr Carr, who has been very anxious about her, tells us that it is chiefly weakness that causes the symptoms, which continue to make us uneasy. The changeable weather during the last month was very injurious to both these Invalids, and to Dora also; they were all attacked with severe Influenza; Dora's stomach is certainly improved but in other respects I fear she is but little better. The blistering that was suspended by the severity of her Influenza has been resumed, but the benefit has been greatly frustrated by her anxiety and restlessness on account of her two Aunts.—

imaginative illustrations by J. M. W. Turner, Esq., R.A., 6 vols., London. John Macrone, St. James's Square. The volumes are 'appropriately dedicated' to W. W. and R. S.

I hope, my dear Friend, you have better accounts to give of your own family. God bless you, and may he in his goodness give us both strength to support our trials, and the same to all who suffer along with us. ever affectionately yours

W. Wordsworth

M. W. adds:

My dear Girls,

I cannot put up this scrawl to y^r good father, without telling you that my beloved Sister in all her wanderings by night and by day, which have continued for at least a week, often turned her thoughts to you, with anxiety that you should be told *why* she was seeming to neglect you—'They never forget me, in their and my anxiety' has she often exclaimed—Sainted Miss W's pleasant and beneficent days on Earth will soon be closed—as far as human foresight may so say. God love and support us all—Aff^{ly} yours   M. Wordsworth

Pray send the enclosed to J. W.

MS.   *1113. W. W. to John W.*[1]

Sunday morning, June 7th [1835]

My dear John,

You will grieve to hear of the state of this House, which makes it quite impossible that we can see you here. Your poor Aunt is growing weaker and weaker every day and hour; and Miss Hutchinson lies suffering under a severe and still somewhat dangerous attack of Rheumatic fever, it began with lumbago, upon which was accumulated the Influenza, under which Dora suffered very much and which did not spare your Aunt Dorothy, so that we have a sad House of it. Mr Carr trusts that the worst is over with Miss Hutchinson, but she is light headed at this moment I am now writing, as she has been frequently, and for a length of time together. As soon as a decided change takes place in any of our patients I shall write again. Your poor Aunt Wordsworth is much harassed.

[1] i.e. the son of R. W.

During the attack of Influenza Dora's blistering was stopped, it has been resumed but with less benefit on account of her anxiety and restlessness about her poor Aunt.

Pray give my kind regards to your Mother and comp^{ts} to Mr Lightfoot; and believe me my dear John, with love from all, which I know they would send you, could I tell them that I was writing,

ever your affectionate Uncle
Wm Wordsworth

Address: Mr Wordsworth, Keswick.

MS.   **1114. W. W. to Joshua Watson**

Rydal Mount Ambleside
16th June, 1835

My dear Sir

Pray excuse my breaking in upon you with the old concern; viz—the interests of my younger Son into which you entered in so friendly a manner. The Papers announce that a new Church Commission is formed; among the members are several of the present administration, who, I have no doubt, are well disposed to me *personally*, in particular the Marquis of Lansdown[1] and Spring Rice.[2]—Should the new appointments rest wholly with Lord Melbourne, Wm's prospect would I fear be unfavorable enough; as of him I know nothing. If the Archbishop of C—[3] could be satisfied as to my Son's fitness, I should be pretty sure of his support. Pray my dear Sir, could you do any thing for us in this emergency, or put me in the way of exerting myself with men now in power, without compromising my own independence

---

[1] Henry Petty-Fitzmaurice (1780–1863), third Marquis of Lansdowne (1809), educated at Edinburgh where he was the friend of Brougham, Jeffrey, and Horner, and at Trin. Coll., Camb. At 25 years old he was Chancellor of the Exchequer in the Grenville Ministry—and later a strong supporter of R.C. Emancipation and of the Reform Bill. In 1830 he was President of the Council, and held the same post in Melbourne's ministry. He was a moderate Whig much respected on both sides of the House; he was much interested in national education, on which he held views similar to W.'s.

[2] Spring-Rice, Chancellor of the Exchequer.

[3] William Howley, Lady Beaumont's father.

as a Writer or in conversation. The Bp of London[1] also I think is one of my well wishers.

You will grieve to hear that our House has been greatly afflicted with sickness since Mrs W— and I reached home. My poor Sister has been gradually growing weaker if her state be measured by weeks, and now she cannot stand. My daughter continues to be confined to the Couch: My Wife's Sister who has passed three parts of the last 30 years under our roof, has been, and still is, suffering from a rheumatic fever, by which she is reduced to deplorable weakness, and lastly one of our two Maid Servants had been ten days confined to her bed by the same complaint. Through all these trials Mrs W bears up in an admirable manner, though attendant day and night upon one sickbed or another. Her Sister-in-Law[2] has come from Hereford to help us, and we wait patiently God's pleasure.

My Publisher tells me that upwards of nine hundred Copies of my late Vol. are disposed of, so that your little Paragraph upon the *right* of the poor to public support, has had a chance of being pretty extensively read. Pray give my affectionate remembrances to Miss Watson in which, as well as in the like to yourself, Mrs W. unites—

ever faithfully your obliged friend
W. Wordsworth

MS.   *1115. W. W. to ?*[3]

Rydal Mount, Ambleside.
June 17th 1835.

Sir,

Accept my thanks for your valuable Pamphlet. The subject is of high importance, and you have treated it in a convincing and masterly manner.

You have proved that the argument drawn from the supposed

---

[1] Blomfield, *v. M.Y.*, p. 513.

[2] Mrs. Thomas Hutchinson (*née* Mary Monkhouse).

[3] Mr L. A. McIntyre suggests that this letter was written to Sir Robt Inglis, but the formality of the bare 'Sir' with which it opens makes this improbable.

practice of antiquity is without foundation. As to the question of expediency one is surprised that men above the lowest vulgar should be unable to see that selection of Spiritual Teachers, as a general measure for the Mass of the people, is strictly *preposterous*: in as much as it presumes the preexistence of that state of judgement in religious matters, and those acquisitions of knowledge, which it is the office of a fit Minister to labour all he can to produce, and to communicate. Moreover, what cabals and factions and heart-burnings, and antichristian feelings and practices of all kinds does the popular mode of election excite and prolong!

I remain, Sir,

With thanks and sincere respect

your obliged Servnt

Wm Wordsworth.

MS.   *1116. W. W. to W. W. Junr*

Wednesday morn. half-past nine

[June 24, 1835.]

My dear Wm.,

From the black seal of this letter you will have concluded that your poor Aunt Wordsworth was no more. It is not so. Dear Aunt Sara has gone before her. She never gained strength after the severe fever was subdued. On Monday she sank alarmingly, at noon yesterday we had not the slightest hope of her recovery, and it pleased God that she should depart this life before the day was closed.

She was an excellent woman, and we trust that she is among the blessed. Your Mother and Aunt Hutchinson support themselves, as I have said in my letter to John, in a way becoming their characters and their faith in God's goodness. How this awful event will ultimately affect Aunt Wordsworth and Dora it is impossible to foretell. I have not seen either of them this morning, but shall see them before this letter is closed, and if nothing be added you will conclude they are doing well at present.

Pray come to the funeral unless the Inspector's visit makes it impossible. God bless you my dear Son. I give the love of all, or rather you must take it, for no one is in the room where I am writing. Farewell. Let us all be good to each other.

Your affectionate father

W. W.

If your Uncle Henry should have [? passed] pray forward to him this letter.

K.   *1117. W. W. to Robert Southey*

June 24,[1] 1835.

My dear Southey,

My letter of yesterday must have prepared you. All was over before seven in the afternoon. She had no acute suffering whatever, and within a very short time of her departure—when Dora asked Mr Carr if something could not be done to make her easier—she opened her eyes in strength, and with a strong and sweet voice, said, 'I am quite, I am perfectly comfortable'. Mr Carr supposed that her debility produced a suffusion on the brain, which was the immediate cause of her death. O, my dear Southey, we have lost a precious friend; of the strength of her attachment to you and yours, you can but imperfectly judge. It was deep in her heart. I saw her within an hour after her decease, in the silence and peace of death, with as heavenly an expression on her countenance as ever human creature had.[2] Surely there is food for faith in these appearances; for myself, I can say that I have passed a wakeful night, more in joy than sorrow, with that blessed face before my eyes perpetually, as I lay in bed. We are all much better than our friends could think possible. God Almighty bless you and yours! Your dear girls have had a loss to which time will never make them insensible; but God is good, as they will feel in all their sorrow. Farewell.

Ever most faithfully yours,

W. W.

[1] K. dates June 25, but S. H. died on June 23.
[2] *Cf*. Sonnet: Even so for me a Vision sanctified, Oxf. W., p. 258.

MS.   *1118. W. W. to William Marshall*

My dear Sir,   Rydal Mount, Thursday [June 25, 1835][1]

Read the enclosed, and send or take it to your Mother. Mrs W. Marshall I know will feel for us, as must all our friends. God bless you,
                    faithfully your friend
                              Wm Wordsworth

Be so good as send the enclosed for Mr Rogers to the two-penny Post.

Address: Wm Marshall Esq., M.P., London.

MS.   *1119. W. W. to Jane Marshall*

My dear Mrs Marshall,   Rydal Mount, Thursday

We have been greatly afflicted for some time past in this House. Miss Hutchinson five weeks ago was seized with rheumatic fever, and I grieve to say, as you will grieve to hear, that she has departed this life. She expired on Tuesday, having never been able to recover strength after the fever was subdued. Mrs Hutchinson, Mrs W.'s Sister in Law has been with us during the last fortnight, otherwise I think my poor Wife must have sunk under watchings and unremitting anxieties; for in addition to what you know so well, our valuable servant Anne who has lived with us twelve years has been confined to her bed for some time by severe and alarming sickness. She is recovering.

Your beloved Friend, my poor Sister, survives. How this event will ultimately affect her and Dora cannot be foreseen.

We trust in God's Goodness. Farewell.

May the Almighty bless you and yours.

Be so kind as to write to your Sisters.

I have written many Letters, for the poor departed had many and dear Friends. She suffered no acute pain after the fever was subdued by medicine and passed away with gentleness as perfect as could be wished
                    again farewell.
                                        W. W.

Address: Mrs Marshall.

[1] For W. W. to H. C. R., June 24, *v. C.R.*, p. 277.

MS.
R.

1120. W. W. to Samuel Rogers

Rydal Mount

Thursday—[25th June, 1835]

My dear Rogers,

I write merely to announce that one of the many anxieties with which this house has been afflicted is over. Miss Hutchinson, after an illness of five weeks, expired on Tuesday Evening. After the fever was subdued she suffered no acute pain, and passed away as gently as her dearest Friends could wish. She will be deeply lamented by many out of her own family.

According to your request I did not write after the melancholy tidings of your last; nor need you write now. We have in this house more before us, which *must* be passed through shortly, and much that may. Pray for us—my poor Wife bears up wonderfully.

Be assured, my dear Friend, that in pleasure and pain, in joy and sorrow, you are often and often in my thoughts. Present our united love to your Sister

affectionately yours,

Wm Wordsworth

Address: Samuel Rogers, Esq., St. James's Place.

MS.

1121. W. W. to Robert Percival Graves

Friday morning

[June 26, 1835]

My dear Mr Graves,

We are grateful for your sympathizing Note; and take very kindly your proposal of testifying your respect by attendance on the funeral. According to her own wishes it will be quite private, no one *invited* but the Clergyman and Medical Attendant;[1] but of course our Friends are at liberty to yield to their feelings, and do as they think right—all will be taken well—

As you are so near a Neighbour I will not enter into particulars, further than to let you know that my family are supported

---

[1] Mr Fleming and Mr Carr.

under this affliction by God's goodness, and have not yet suffered much, (apparently at least) in their bodily health. The rest I will speak of when we meet.

farewell most affectionately yours

W. Wordsworth

P.S. the funeral will take place at 12 o'clock on Tuesday.

Address: Rev. R. P. Graves, Bowness.

MS.   *1122. W. W. to Henry Taylor*

[*last week in June*, 1835]

My dear Mr Taylor,

Little did we think when we hastened home upon the summons of Miss Hutchinson, who was then so anxious about my sister's and daughter's state, that she herself would be the first member of our household whose loss we should have to deplore. This inestimable Person, as I know you will grieve to hear, expired after an illness of five weeks' continuance. She suffered little or no acute pain after the rheumatic fever that had seized her gave way to medicine, but she did not recover strength. Nevertheless we were not alarmed till within two days of her departure, as her weakness did not seem to increase.

Knowing that Mr Robinson had more leisure than any other of our most esteemed friends in London I wrote to him the day after her decease, which took place on Tuesday, and expressed a wish that he would make it known among those who valued her or were likely to feel for us. Perhaps you would hear the tidings from him. I hope you did, and may I beg that you would mention the event to your Father. Miss H. when she lived at Middleham Hall used to see much of your uncle and aunt, and had no common esteem for both them and your Father. As this letter could gain nothing by being put into the Post to-day, I hope to enclose one for dear Miss Fenwick.

Pray do not trouble about the business I mentioned in my[1] last. The commission, I now understand, is of a character and composition that would not allow you to serve us, in connection

---

[1] *written* your.

with it. I am sorry I mentioned the matter at all. I need only add a hope that your health is re-established, and an assurance that my poor sister and daughter bear this severe shock far better than could have been thought possible. My dear wife supports herself as it becomes her to do under all our trials.

I remain with a world of good wishes

affectionately yours

W. Wordsworth

I have heard from Mr Southey this morning. He loved Miss H. deeply, as did all his daughters. Her fortune in this particular was remarkable that so many Persons influential for their genius and talents were so strongly and firmly attached to her. I may name Charles Lamb and Coleridge above all. Poor Mrs Southey[1] will not, I think, remain long in this world. Farewell.

MS.
M.

1123. *W. W. to Isabella Fenwick*

[last week of June, 1835]

My dear Miss Fenwick,

Mrs W. would have written in a way more agreeable to my wish than I am able; but at present she has not courage to touch the Pen. Dear Miss Hutchinson, her beloved Sister, and let me say, mine also, was seized with Rheumatic fever five weeks ago —the fever was subdued by medicine, but she did not recover her strength—nevertheless (she had been in such fine health before the attack) we had little fear about her, but an alarming change took place on Monday, and she departed this life on Tuesday evening. This has been a grievous shock, little did we apprehend when her anxiety for my sister and daughter hastened us home, that she herself would be the first called away. Upon the beauty of her character I will not dwell—she is we humbly trust among the blessed. We are comforted by this faith, and bear up as well as human infirmity allow. My poor Sister *must* soon follow her, she is calm and said to me only yesterday 'my tears are all to shed', and to another of the family she said, 'I do not feel that I have lost her, I am brought nearer to her'.

---

[1] Mrs Southey died on Nov. 16, 1837.

[751]

Dora does not yet seem to have suffered in her health to the degree that we feared—and my Wife is wonderfully supported. She had her sister-in-law with her, from Herefordshire, nearly three weeks; otherwise she must have sunk with anxiety and care and watching, for in addition to what you know, I must mention, that one of our two maid-servants who has lived with us twelve years has also been severely ill with something of the same complaint that carried off the one of our small household that we have lost.

It would have seemed unjust to our friendship for you, dear Miss Fenwick, if I had withheld these melancholy details—they will distress you, but the distress may do your spirit good. Pray for us, and do not forget how feelingly we love you. Farewell, May the Almighty bless you—

ever faithfully yours,

Wm Wordsworth.

MS.   *1124. W. W. to Edward Quillinan*

[late June 1835]

My dear Mr Quillinan,

Poor Miss H.—It is my sad duty to let you know that one of our anxieties, that for her, is over. How different an account am I to give from that you would receive from Dora. When the fever was subdued, we continued full of hope, though she did not recover strength, but we did not doubt, as she was so well and strong when first seized, that strength would return. Weeks passed and she did not seem to lose ground, so we were still without fear. But last Monday she sunk alarmingly and before seven the following day she expired.

I know not how she has escaped from us, but it was God's will that this excellent creature should quit the earth. My poor dear sister and Dora seem to bear up wonderfully—so does Mrs W. We have had Mrs Hutchinson with us for a fortnight— a great blessing. I know how you valued the dear departed, her loss [is] irreparable to us all.—It is astounding to me that she should have gone before my beloved sister who is very feeble and suffers much at times—Her departed friend had little or no acute pain after the fever left—O—What a heavenly expression was on her face after the breath had left her body; it would have done your Soul good to see it.

I write through tears, but scarcely tears of sorrow—so has it been often and often since she left us—farewell—I know not where you are; perhaps on your way to England, perhaps landed. We have not yet written to your children.

Dora is not I think quite so well as when she wrote to you, the distress of the family with so many sick—Anne has been perilously ill—has made her quit her couch oftener that she ought to have done.

[*Remainder of letter and signature cut away.*]

Address: Ed. Quillinan Esq., Oporto.

M.
G.
K.
 1125. W. W. to Lady Frederick Bentinck

[1835][1]

. . . You were not mistaken in supposing that the state of public affairs has troubled me much. I cannot see how the government is to be carried on, but by such sacrifices to the democracy as will, sooner or later, upset everything. Whoever governs, it will be by out-bidding for popular favour those who went before them. Sir Robert Peel was obliged to give way in his government to the spirit of reform, as it is falsely called; these men are going beyond him; and if ever he shall come back, it will only, I fear, be to carry on the movement in a shape somewhat less objectionable than it will take from the Whigs. In the meanwhile the Radicals, or Republicans, are cunningly content to have this work done ostensibly by the Whigs, while in fact they themselves are the Whigs' masters, as the Whigs well know; but they hope to be preserved from destruction by throwing themselves back upon the Tories when measures shall be

---

[1] K. dates 1832, but the reference to Peel's administration in the past tense and to the proposed corporation reform proves the letter to have been written between April and September 1835. Moreover, the 'new volume' can only be *Yarrow Revisited*, published 1835.

For W. W. to H. C. R. July 6, *v. C.R.*, p. 278.

urged upon them by their masters which they may think too desperate. What I am most afraid of is alterations in the constituency and in the duration of Parliament, which will bring it more and more under the dominion of the lower and lowest classes. On this account I fear the proposed corporation reform, as a step towards household suffrage, vote by ballot, etc. As to a union of the Tories and Whigs in Parliament, I see no prospect of it whatever. To the great Whig lords may be truly applied the expression in *Macbeth*,

> They have eaten of the insane root
> That takes the reason prisoner.

I ordered two copies of my new volume to be sent to Cottesmere. And now farewell; and believe me,

Dear Lady Frederick, ever faithfully yours,

W. Wordsworth.

MS. **1126. *W. W. to Edward Moxon***

Rydal Mount August 2nd [1835]

Dear Mr Moxon,

I have been from home eight days or I should have written sooner, the Frank also was delayed by being sent round through Dublin.

If I had given way to my feelings I should have observed upon the beauty of many of the sonnets.[1]—

I have made a few verbal alterations which I hope you will think improvements.

Many thanks for your kind invitation. It will be borne gratefully in mind, but I know not when I shall move southwards, as I cannot venture to go more than a few days' journey from home, while my poor Sister is in this [?].

My Daughter, thank God, is a little better.—I have had reprinted and republished at Kendal my little Book on the Lakes,[2]

---

[1] i.e. Moxon's, which had just been published with a dedication to W. W.

[2] *A Guide through the District of the Lakes in the North of England, with A Description of the Scenery, etc. For the Use of Tourists and Residents,* by W. W. Kendal: Published by Hudson & Nicholson, and in London by Longman & Co., Moxon, and Whittaker & Co., 1835.

with some additions. I took the liberty of adding your name to Longman's on the Title page; the Publishers, on their part, added their own London publisher, Whitaker.—I hope some Copies have been forwarded to you, as I requested they might. Pray remember the English Dictionary, and keep Copies for me which I shall direct my Nephew to call for.— My Yarrow appears to have sold well and to be generally liked. Do not fail to remember me to Mrs Moxon and your Sister and Brother, ever very sincerely and faithfully your friend

W. Wordsworth.

MS.   *1127. W. W. to Catherine Clarkson*

Rydal Mount August 6th 1835
My dear Mrs Clarkson,

Mrs W— has just come with her eyes full of tears begging I would write to you, for she, much as it has been upon her mind cannot, nor ever has been able to undertake the task, since our days have lately darkened so much upon us. Mr R. as we requested would let you know how we were deprived of our beloved Sister Sarah—She is we trust among the blessed, but to us the loss is upon earth irreparable. My poor Sister languishes in her sick room and mostly upon her sick bed, how long she may yet have to struggle we cannot foresee—her weakness is deplorable, but of acute pain we hope she has not much to endure; I say hope for her mind since Sarah's departure has been so confused as to passing events, that we have no distinct knowledge of what she may actually have to support in the way of bodily pain. She remembers and recollects all but recent things perfectly, and her understanding is, as far as her strength will allow her to think, clear as ever it was.

The Complaint in Dora's spine has been a good deal subdued by bleeding and blistering, but her digestive organs seem as weak and as liable to derangement as ever; but had we been less afflicted there is reason to think she might have been better by this time.—Our Cook, Anne, is also recovering steadily—Out of our small family, eight persons servants included, four were incapable of serving each other; and in a house small as ours it was a great addition to our distress, that the Invalids unavoidably disturbed each other, so that Dora who stood so much in need of the refreshment of sleep often was kept all night, and unable to remain in bed from a hope of being useful in some degree to the others. This is a sad tale, but God tempers the wind to the shorn Lamb, blessed be his holy Name! Mrs Hutchinson came to us from Brinsop, otherwise my poor wife must have been quite worn out—She looks harassed and aged, but makes no Complaint.

It is now time that I should inquire after you and dear Mr Clarkson—pray let us know how you both are. I do not like to conclude without filling up this page; but what to touch upon I know not—Perhaps a particular or two concerning your departed Friend's illness may be acceptable. Her bodily sufferings were not we think very great after the violence of the first attack of fever was subdued. It left her legs much swollen, and though she made no progress towards recovery of strength, if she grew weaker at all it was slowly and to us insensibly, till within two or three days of her decease. Upon the morning of that event she told me that she was doing well, quite well, and only required time to bring back her strength, but between twelve and one at noon a change took place that left not a shadow of hope:—she died a little after six in the afternoon, with a heavenly expression left by death upon her beloved face.

God bless you my dear Friend—Remember us affectionately to Mr Clarkson—I could not write any more if my paper were not filled—

Ever faithfully yours

W. Wordsworth—

P.S. by M. W.—O yes, Wm is mistaken—I have written two or three letters—but to *you*, dearest Mrs Clarkson, who loved her so well, and knew so well what you loved—I could not trust my own feelings—God bless you and good dear Mr C—

M. W.

Address: Mrs Clarkson, Playford Hall, Ipswich.

MS.   *1128. W. W. to Robert Southey*

Lowther Castle Monday 26th

My dear S.   [Sept. 1835]

Many thanks for two notes. I am glad you liked the Medallion; I was anxious for your opinion of it, and more particularly as it was not to be seen by my Friends and Family at Rydal.

Mr Wyon[1] seemed a person of agreeable and gentlemanly manners: In common with all here, I thought his likeness of you a very successful one, and I shall be glad *to hang* in such good company.

It gives me much pleasure to hear that your Cowper[2] is in such a state of forwardness. I see it advertised in the London papers, which announce the first Vol: will be out in October.

Your improved Wesley[3] will prove a most interesting Work, and will be well timed as through the force of factious passions, and presumptuous opinions, a great secession from the Society as established by its Founder, appears to be taking place.

My accounts from home respecting my Sister are pretty much such as you give of Mrs Southey. Her bodily health is decidedly improved, but the state of the mind, I fear, not at all. The change shewed itself soon after the death of dearest Miss H—, but must have been preparing before. For my own part, her age being not sixty four, I cannot but ascribe the failure of recollection of passing events, and her impaired judgement as to her bodily powers and in regard to time and space, these I cannot

[1] William Wyon (1795–1851), R.A. 1838, chief engraver at the Mint, a fine medallist and famed for his skill in portraiture. On Sept. 29, 1835, Southey wrote to Grosvenor Bedford: 'Mr. Wyon has killed two birds with one shot. Seeing how perfectly satisfied everybody here was with his medallion of me, he asked for an introduction to W., which I was about to have offered him. Off he set in good spirits to Rydal, and not finding W. there, was advised to follow him to Lowther. To Lowther he went, and came back from thence delighted with his own success, and with the civilities of Lord and Lady Lonsdale, who desired that they might have both medallions. Nothing, I think, can be better than W.'s, and he is equally pleased with mine.'

[2] *Life and Works of Cowper*, 15 vols., 1835–7.

[3] *Life of Wesley*, 1820: the 'improved edition' did not appear till 1846, edited by S.'s son Cuthbert.

but ascribe to the great quantity of opium which it has been thought proper to give her. At present it is reduced considerably more than one half and we are going on reducing it, with the approbation of Mr Carr.—Dora is upon the whole better.

With affectionate wishes for an improvement in dear Mrs Southey, I remain

Most faithfully yours

W. W.

I quit this place to-day for Mr Marshall's and I shall be home on Thursday *at the latest.*

Address: Robert Southey Esqre, Keswick.

MS.
R.

1129. *W. W. to Samuel Rogers*

Lowther Castle Septr 28th [1835]

I have long owed you an acknowledgment, my dear Friend, for an affectionate Letter, which was very welcome, distressed as we were, had been, and alas! still are.

It is a week since I came to this hospitable mansion, which I leave today. The Country is most beautiful, the leaves in many places changed to the exact point of autumnal splendor and variety. During my walks I missed you much, and also our Friend Sir George. Lady Frederick is not here, she comes at the end of the week. Lord Lonsdale had a sharp attack of indisposition when he first came, but he threw it off in two or three days, and, to the great joy of his Friends, is as active and well as ever. Lady Lonsdale also, one of the best of Women, is quite well. Lady Anne and Miss Thompson are both here; so is Mrs O'Callaghan.

You will be desirous, I am sure, to learn how our invalids are. My dear Sister, in bodily health, is decidedly better, though quite unable to stand. Her mind, however, is, I grieve to say, much shattered. The change showed itself upon the death of dear Miss Hutchinson, but probably was preparing before. Her case at present is very strange; her judgement, her memory, and all her faculties are perfect as ever, with exception of what relates to her own illness, and passing occurrences. If I ask her opinion upon any point of Literature, she answers with all her former acuteness; if I read Milton, or any favourite Author, and pause, she goes on with the passage from memory; but she forgets instantly the circumstances of the day. Considering that she is not 64 years of age, I cannot but hope that her mind may be restored, if her bodily health should go on improving.

My daughter is a good deal better, but very far from being strong and well.

Lady Lonsdale is in the room and begs to be remembered to you.

When shall wo meet again? You know well how much I delight in your conversation and what a value I set upon your friendship. I am not likely to be soon in London, but when will you come again Northwards?

Miss Kinnaird, I am told, is about to be married to Mr Drummond,[1] of calculating celebrity. Is he an amiable Man? I should like to know, for she is a great favourite with me and mine.

Miss Rogers, I hope, is well. My poor Body is always getting into some scrape or other. Last year it was my foot, now it is my right arm which I have sprained so violently that I can scarcely guide my pen; and I much fear you will not think my letter worth the trouble of decyphering.

Southey, from whom I heard this morning, is upon the point of finishing his first Vol: of Cowper. His edition will have 101 original Letters of the poet. Pray write, at your early convenience, as I wish to know how you are and where spending the summer.

most affectionately yours,
W. Wordsworth.

[1] Thomas Drummond (1797–1840) entered the Royal Engineers in 1815 and soon distinguished himself as a mathematician and chemist, inventing the use of limelight (known as the 'Drummond light') and an improved heliostat. In 1831 he met Brougham and was drawn by him into the public service; in 1835 was made Under-Secretary at Dublin Castle. Lord Mulgrave was Lord-Lieutenant and Lord Morpeth Chief Secretary, but Drummond was in fact the Governor; he won over O'Connell and for five years administered Irish affairs with wisdom and justice, winning a widespread popularity. His unremitting devotion to his work overtaxed his strength, and in 1840 he died from the effects of over-work.

MS.　　　　　*1130. W. W. to Edward Moxon*

Lowther Castle near Penrith

[Nov. 12–17 1835][1]

Dear Mr Moxon,

I thank you for the present of valuable Books which arrived
at Rydal since I left it.

You may depend upon having Lamb's Letters, which I am
glad you mean to publish.

Don't give yourself the least trouble about pushing my Lake
Book—it is a mere trifle, and I had your name put into the title
page solely out of regard to you.

I am in great difficulty about a new edition of my Poems, as
I know not how to contrive so that the last Vol. (Yarrow Revisited) and the four others shall be out of print at or near the
same time. Longmans are going to press with another edition
of the Yarrow——

If it were not for those vile French Piracies we should do well;
I am informed that an edition of my entire works, no doubt
including the Yarrow is just advertized in Paris, not by
G(alig)nani who pirated the other vols, but by another publisher.
This will prove very injurious.

—Be so good as to pay the foreign postage of this Letter,[1] I
enclose a shilling which I believe is the amount for that purpose,
from London, it costs two from this place.—

Kind regards to Mrs M. your Sister and Brother and believe
me my dear Mr Moxon faithfully your much obliged

W. Wordsworth.

MS.　　　　　*1131. W. W. to Edward Moxon*
K(—)

Rydal Mount Nov. 20ᵗʰ 1835

My dear Sir,

In a few days I hope to have an opportunity of sending
through a private channel such a selection of Lamb's letters, to

---

[1] Mr L. A. McIntyre so dates this letter. He points out that Moxon had
written on Nov. 9 asking for such portion of Lamb's letters as W. chose to
part with (*v. C.R.*, p. 281), and this seems to be an answer to that request;

myself and this family, as appear to us not unfit for immediate
publication. There are, however, in these some parts which had
better be kept back, but being very fearful of using the pencil
rather too freely we have left the decision to your discretion and
that of our common friends—especially Mr Talfourd[1] and Mr
Robinson,—I need scarcely add, Mrs M. and poor dear Miss L.,
if she be in a state of mind that allows of her attending to such
a matter. I have kept back several letters—some because they
relate merely to personal and domestic concerns, others, because
they touch upon the character and manners of individuals who
are now living, or too recently deceased to be brought under the
public eye, without indelicacy.—I have also thought proper to
suppress every word of criticism upon my own Poems—though
the strictures [?] are merely such, as might prove generally
interesting—and occasionally lead to the pleasing strain of sentiment and descriptions which he has himself felt or observed.
The suppressed letters shall not be destroyed.—Those relating
to my works are withheld, partly because I shrink from the
thought of assisting in any way to spread my own praises and
still more as being convinced that the opinions or judgements of
friends given in this way are mostly of little value. On this
point I have no more to say, than that I trust to your care for
preventing the possibility of any suppressed portion of the
letters sent, being copied by anyone, from any motive whatever
—and that the originals may be returned to me through safe
hands after you have done with them.

On the other page you have the requested Epitaph.[2] It was
composed yesterday—and, by sending it immediately, I have
prepared the way, I believe, for a speedy repentance—as I do
not know that I ever wrote so many lines without some retouching being afterwards necessary. If these verses should be
wholly unsuitable to the end Miss Lamb had in view, I shall

but that it must be before his letter of Nov. 20 (q.v.) in which he says he 'only
returned home last Wednesday'. He suggests that the letter to France was
written to W.'s daughter, now Madame Baudouin, who had been paid a sum
of £400 in the previous April, in lieu of her annuity of thirty pounds which
she had received from him since her marriage in 1816.

[1] Talfourd was to be the editor of Lamb's *Letters, with Life*, &c. The book
appeared in 1837.
[2] *Written after the death of Charles Lamb*, Oxf. W., p. 584.

find no difficulty in reconciling myself to the thought of their not being made use of, though it would have given me great, *very* great pleasure to fulfil, in all points, her wishes.

The first objection that will strike you, and every one, is its extreme length, especially compared with epitaphs as they are now written—but this objection might in part be obviated by engraving the lines in double column, and not in capitals.

Chiabrera[1] has been here my model—though I am aware that Italian Churches, both on account of their size and the climate of Italy, are more favourable to long inscriptions than ours— His Epitaphs are characteristic and circumstantial—so have I endeavoured to make this of mine—but I have not ventured to touch upon the most striking feature of our departed friend's character and the most affecting circumstance of his life, viz. his faithful and intense love of his Sister. Had I been pouring out an Elegy or Monody, this would and must have been done; but for seeing and feeling the sanctity of that relation as it ought to be seen and felt, lights are required which could scarcely be furnished by an Epitaph, unless it were to touch on little or nothing else.—The omission, therefore, in my view of the case was unavoidable: and I regret it the less, you yourself having already treated in verse the subject with genuine tenderness and beauty.

Now for a few words of business. What is doing with the engraving of my Portrait?[2] of which I hear nothing. If I told you that my Yarrow was out of print, I said more than was true. Messrs L. only told me that it was so nearly out that it would be well to go to press with another Ed: which accordingly they set about—but what progress has been made I do not know, never hearing from them. If you see Mr Talfourd tell him that we are all delighted with his Drama[3]—and which may seem odd—*that* is the very reason why I have put off writing to him—as I wished to do more than merely let him know, with thanks, how much he has pleased us. If you should be in communication with Mr

---

[1] Gabriello Chiabrera (1552–1638). W. had a great admiration for his epitaphs, and translated nine of them, *v.* Oxf. W., pp. 572–6, and W.'s Essays on Epitaphs (G. ii. 27–75).

[2] i.e. the Pickersgill portrait, but *v.* Letter of Feb. 8, 1836.

[3] *Ion*; W. witnessed its first performance in the following May.

Trench[1]—say I beg, a few words for me to him which may be done with the utmost sincerity to the same effect. I had a sprain in my right arm three months ago and I am yet unable to write with my own hand. You know how much the only pen I can command must be occupied—but I will express my gratitude and admiration to both the gentlemen as soon as I shall be able.

I cannot conclude without adding that the Ep:, if used at all, can only be placed *in* the church. It is much too long for an out-door stone, among our rains, damps, etc. Dora is much better and my poor Sister easier in body though her mind has of late faded sadly.

Kindest regards to yourself and everyone about you—My [?] friend

I remain faithfully yours

W. Wordsworth.

After an absence of thirteen weeks I only returned home last Wednesday as you should have heard from my Letter. Kindest remembrances to Mr Rogers if he is returned from Ramsgate.

Address: Edward Moxon Esq., 44 Dover Street, London.

MS.   *1132. W. W. to Edward Moxon*

Rydal Mount Nov[r] 23rd 1835

My dear Mr Moxon

I have already written this morning rather more than agrees either with my hand or eyes, so you must excuse this short note from the pen of another and I have little scruple in sending it as it will reach London in a frank. It has been in respect to the Epitaph as I foretold; I have been tempted to retouch it, and beg that after the word 'overflowing heart' you would read thus:

So Genius triumphed over seeming wrong,
And poured out truth in works by thoughtful love
Inspired—works potent over smiles and tears.

---

[1] Richard Chenevix Trench, 1807–86, at Trinity, Cambridge, with Tennyson, Hallam, Milnes, &c., and one of the 'Apostles', in 1831 he was curate to Rose at Hadleigh, in Suffolk; in 1863 he became Archbishop of Dublin: a prolific writer in prose and verse—his best-known book is the *Study of Words* (1851). In 1835 he produced his first volume of verse—*The Story of Justin Martyr and other Poems.*

The composition is by this alteration a little inspirited, but at the cost of an add[1] line—for which room may be made by striking out the two that follow, some lines below—viz

    'Or suddenly dislodged by strong rebound
    Of animal spirits that had sunk too low'—

and indeed these two lines may easily be spared. Again I cannot help expressing a wish that Miss L.'s purpose had been better carried into effect. Suppose Mr Talfourd or yourself were to try? I cannot *put* aside my regret in not having touched upon the affection of the Brother and sister for each other

Ever faithfully yours
Wm Wordsworth

Address: Edwd. Moxon Esqre, 44 Dover St., London.

MS.
K(—)
1133. W. W. to Edward Moxon

Tuesday [November 24, 1835]

I have sent you the Epitaph again revised. Yesterday I went through [it] to make a few alterations, those which the present sheet contains being added, I send the whole [?] I hope the changes will be approved of. At all events, they better answer my purpose. The lines, as they now stand, preserve better the balance of delicate delineation, the weaknesses are not so prominent, and the virtues placed in a stronger light; and I hope nothing is said that is not characteristic. Of this you and Mrs Moxon will be more competent judges than myself, as I never saw my poor dear Friend when his affliction was lying most heavily upon him—written in extreme haste to [catch] the post

Affectionately yours,
W. W.

If the length makes the above utterly unsuitable, it may be printed with his Works as an effusion by the side of his grave; in this case, in some favorable moment, I might be enabled to add a few lines upon the friendship of brother and sister.

Address: Edward Moxon Esqre, 44 Dover Street, London.

MS.   *1134. D. W. to Mary Anne Marshall*[1]

Wednesday Nov. 25th [1829][2]

Many thanks, my dear Mary Anne, to yourself and your kind
Father for your bountiful presents, all of which, in their several
ways, will be very useful, and the more prized as coming from
you. Dora is much pleased with the green-house plants, and
with James's[3] assistance, hopes to nurse them well during the
winter. I was delighted to see your Mama's hand-writing on
opening the cover of your letter; and though the first page of its
contents was distressing, as reporting of poor Ellen's severe
sufferings after her Comforters arrived, the conclusion was con-
solatory—the worst for the present having passed away—and
even the worst, as my dear Friend says, less distressing actually
to behold than to image to oneself at a distance, the calmness
and patience of the Sufferer being such, as it appears, as almost
to amount to happiness—nay happiness it is—and what at one
period or other of our lives each one of us may, and probably
will, have cause to envy if such a word may be used in connection
with our needs and our desires for what is heavenly.

But dear Mary Anne, I did not intend to moralise, and hardly
know how my feelings have led me into this strain. You will
forgive, and now let us turn to the *business* of my present letter.

In the first place Mrs Luff returns her best thanks for your
kind remembrance of your promise to her Green-house; and in
the second I must tell you that she is the Friend who wishes to
dispose of some of her treasures, and that by this day's Mail she
will send the Chess-men and chess-board—directed for you *to
the care of Mrs Jackson at the King's Arms*, Kendal. The price
of them is ten guineas. Now Mrs Luff desires me to entreat that
you will consider yourself, in this matter, as treating with a
perfect stranger, and in deciding whether you shall keep them
or not she earnestly entreats you will entirely set aside her wish

---

[1] Daughter of Jane M.

[2] The late Mr Gordon Wordsworth attributed this letter to 1835, on the
ground that in that year Nov. 25 was on a Wednesday, and in preparing
this volume for press I followed his dating. It has since been pointed out
to me, but too late to alter its position, that the letter was really written
in 1829, and should follow No. 895, *q.v.*

[3] James Dixon was the gardener and handyman at Rydal Mount.

to sell them—and if the purchase does not please you (and there may be many reasons why it should not—the Chess-men may not be handsome enough—or their shapes may not take your fancy) she begs that you will leave the parcel to Mrs Jackson's care, to be returned to her; and be assured that, so far from being hurt at your rejection of her offer, it would grieve her very much that you should accept it unless more agreeable to yourself than not. Mrs Luff adds to the parcel a black mantle inwoven with silver, which was worn by a Madagascar Princess, and was very costly in that country. The only use that can be made of it, as we think, is for a Table cover—and, *for that,* it is remarkably handsome. The price fixed upon for it by Mrs Luff is ten guineas (as for the Chess-men and board). Should you entirely reject this latter article, leave it to Mrs Jackson's care—but unless *that* be the case, as the carriage of it will be no inconvenience you might take it to Headingley for your Mama's inspection; and if she does not chuse to have it keep it to be sent by the first arrival from Headingley next spring or summer. With regard to the Chess-men it would be better *not* to take them to Leeds, *unless* you determine to keep them.

Mr and Mrs Elliott, whom we are about to lose as neighbours; are just come to spend the day with us, through driving snow-showers. They had engaged to come if weather favoured and it is truly so bad that we had no hope of seeing them. This being the case you must excuse a hasty conclusion. I fancied I had much more to say to you, but this arrival has driven it out of my head, and indeed I have no right to go on scribbling while our good friends are chattering around us. I believe *you* know something of the Elliotts (your Mama and Aunts I know do). They are excellent people and we are heartily sorry to lose them. Their House, the Wood, was rented by Mrs John Barlow, who let it to *them,* and is now coming to live there herself.

My Brother's very kind regards to Mr Marshall, whom he begs to assure that he shall rejoice to see again next summer, and to talk with him and your Brother James over their adventures in the Sister Isle.

I shall shortly write to Mrs Marshall. In the meantime I thank her, through you, for her welcome letter.

God bless you all! and grant you a happy meeting—and pray let me hear of it ere long. My Sister and Dora beg their kind Love. Remember my message to Julia. Ever your affectionate Friend

D. Wordsworth.

James was delighted with his visit. He was never so well treated in his life before; and it was so kind in Mr Marshall to send for him to speak to him in his own room; and he was 'such a nice quiet spoken Gentleman. I never saw such a pleasing nice Gentleman'; and you were a very 'kind Lady'. I did not desire you to mark James's Bow. I wish I *had*, for you might not notice it. James's Bow is the most exquisite sample of respectful Simplicity I ever saw.

Sad penmanship!—I hope you are a good Reader and have not weak eyes.

MS.   *1135. W. W. to Edward Moxon*
K.

Rydal Mount
Friday [? Dec. 4, 1835][1]

My dear Mr Moxon,

Thanks for the verses, they will be quite correct when you have replaced the line

  Otherwise wrought the will of the Most High
  Yet etc.

I do not forget your friendly invitation. Take care in respect to the Selections that your liberality does not injure yourself. I think it probable that I shall be in Town in the Spring, and if it be after the earlier part of April, if you can make room for me for a little while I should be glad.

I have never heard of Hartley's intention to write his Father's Life, nor do I think it probable, but your message shall be conveyed to him. He is preparing for the Press another Vol. of Poems, as I understand, and I shall recommend to him to publish with you if you will undertake the work. Since the above

---

[1] For W. W. to H. C. R. Nov. 25, v. *C.R.*, p. 283.

was written Mrs W. has seen H. C. He has no intention of writing his Father's life, but he has Poems[1] and other works which he would be glad to publish with you.

ever faithfully yours

W. W.

MS.   ***1136. W. W. to Edward Moxon***

[Dec. 1835]

My dear Moxon,

Thanks for the printed Copy, which, tho' a line longer than I supposed, *looks* at least a good deal shorter than in MS.—The *italics* at the close must all be struck out except in the word *her* —Mrs W accounts for the *if air* being in italics by the supposition of her having made a stroke to signify the lines were finished —The rest she marked designedly. The only thing I am *anxious* about is, that the lines should be approved of by Miss L. as a not unworthy tribute, as far as they go, to her dear Brother's memory.

Ever faithfully yours

W. Wordsworth

MS.   ***1137. W. W. to Edward Moxon***
K(—)

Dec. 6th [1835]

Dear Mr Moxon,

I send you an epitaph volunteered for Ch. Lamb by the son of his old friend Charles Lloyd, to whom I had shewn my Verses, observing that they were unfit on acc^t of their length. I did the same to Mr Hartley Coleridge, and *asked* him to try his powers. Now as he is very ready, and has *great* powers, and retains a grateful affection for our deceased friend, we expect something good and appropriate. Not that it is our wish that anything from this quarter should take [the] place of what may be produced by Mr Talfourd, yourself, or any other friend. Mr Owen Ll.'s verses are not without merit, and would be read with

---

[1] The Poems did not appear till 1851, two years after his death; they were then collected and edited by his brother Derwent, and published by Moxon.

pleasure in many a church, or ch^{yd}, but they are scarcely good
or characteristic of the Subject.

I forwarded by the Post to-day a Newcastle Journal, in which
you would find some verses of mine, suggested by the death of
the Ettrick Shepherd.[1] They were sent to you on account of the
mention of our departed friend, and of Mr Coleridge.

There are two or three mistakes for which the printer is not
answerable—the adjectives mortal and godlike are both correct;
and for For ripe fruit should be O'er ripe fruit. It also might
be a question for criticism whether the stanza beginning 'Our
haughty life' should not be separated from the foregoing either
by asterisks or a break, as if it were the beginning of a second
part of the same lyric effusion.

Should you see Mr Robinson [tell him] that we think our
Sister going on so favorably that we should be glad to see him
at his convenience, and if he will *drop us* a line to say when his
rooms are wanted, they shall be prepared for him.

We enclose a parcel which if Mr Q does not call and receive at
your house *soon* (he is shortly expected in London) we shall
thank you to send to the address in Wyndham Place when perfectly convenient. Dear Love to Miss Lamb, is she well enough
to receive it [?] and with affec. remembrances to yourself and
Mrs M. ever faithfully

Yours in haste
W. Wordsworth

MS.   *1138. W. W. to Mrs Drummond*

Rydal Mount 7th Decr 1835

My dear Miss Kinnaird, that *was*,

My dear Mrs Drummond, (as I learn from the Westmorland
Gazette) that *is*,

In the name of all this family, and on my own part, I offer you
most hearty congratulations upon the event which has just
taken place. May it prove as happy a union as you deserve!—
ever faithfully yours

Wm Wordsworth

---

[1] *Extempore Effusion upon the Death of James Hogg*, Oxf. W., p. 586.

Dora offers her *condolences* to Mrs Sharp—I wish I could say that D— had got rid of her Complaint. I have not the honor of knowing Mr Drummond, it cannot however be taking an unwarrantable liberty if I beg you to present to him my respects; my best wishes are of course included in what has been already said to you—farewell—

Address: Mrs Drummond, Park Lane, Corner of Grosvenor St. To be forwarded.

K(—)   *1139. W. W. to Basil Montagu*

Rydal Mount, December 10, 1835.

My dear Montagu,

. . . Under this roof we have indeed had our share of affliction, a great part of which continues to this hour; but it must be borne, and we trust for the ultimate benefit of all concerned. In answer to your very friendly offer, I can only say, with most sincere thanks, that it is quite out of our power to profit by it. If my daughter were well enough to go to London, she would be well enough to go anywhere, the seat of her complaint being in the spine; and as to my poor sister, there is no prospect of her being other than a prisoner in her bed or room for the remainder of her days.

I congratulate you heartily on your release from the labour of your profession, not doubting that your mind has resources which will prevent leisure from being a burden.

With kindest remembrances, believe me, my dear Montagu,

Faithfully yours,

Wm. Wordsworth.

MS.   *1140. W. W. to Robert Percival Graves*

[Dec. 1835]

My dear Sir,

To save you the trouble of hunting for the verses,[1] I have had them transcribed, with the stanza given to the memory of our

---

[1] The verses are the *Extempore Effusion*, on reading in a Newspaper the notice of the death of the poet James Hogg.

[770]

lamented Friend.[1] We should be glad to hear that your sisters
have not been detained by the snow.

ever faithfully yours
Wm. Wordsworth.

Address: Revd R. P. Graves, Bowness.

MS.   *1141. D. W. to Jane Marshall*

[late Dec. 1835][2]

My dearest friend, risen from the bed of death I write to you
with a thousand thousand blessings on y^r dear head and on all
your family. May we meet again in this world.

Dorothy Wordsworth[3]

Many many thanks for the Turkey etc—and love and thanks
to dear Mr Marshall for using his own hand to direct them. Come
to see me when you return to Hallsteads. Love to all and every
one, Mr M. at

Ever your aff^{ate} Friend D. W.

Address: Mrs Marshall, Headingley, near Leeds.

MS.   *1142. W. W. to Edward Moxon*
K(—)

Jan. 9th 1836

My dear Sir,

Thanks for Lamb's Poems, and the Verses—they are now
quite correct and I have no wish to alter them further: the only
thing which I find amiss in them is the position of the words By
God in the beginning of the line which gives them the appearance
of an oath, but I cannot alter it without weakening the passage.
Pray send a Copy to Mrs Marshall 81 Upper Grosvenor Street,
another for Miss Fenwick 2 Lower Seymour Street, Portman

---

[1] i.e. Mrs Hemans: the stanza referring to her is different from the
printed version, reading:

She too, a Muse whose holy spirit
Was sweet as Spring as Ocean deep
She, ere her Summer yet was faded,
Has sank into a breathless sleep.

For W. W. to H. C. R. Dec. 16, *v. C.R.*, p. 287.
The letter is enclosed in one by M. W. The signature is barely legible.

Square, and let Mr Robinson have one for Mr Cookson, a friend of mine. And pray send 3 copies enclosed to Joshua Watson Esq No 6 Park Street Westminster.

I have been much pleased with several things in Lamb's Poems that I had not sufficiently noticed before, particularly with the latter part of Lines upon the death of a newborn infant. At Mr Southey's two days ago I had a peep at the two vols: about Coleridge.[1] The Editor is a man without judgement, and therefore appears to be without feeling. His rule is to publish *all the truth* that he can scrape together about his departed Friend, not perceiving the difference between the real truth, and what *appears to him* to be true. The maxim nil de mortuis nisi *verum* was never meant to imply that *all* truth was to be told, only nothing but what *is* true. This distinction also has escaped his sagacity and ever will escape those of far superior talents to Mr A. who care not what offence or pain they give to living persons provided they have come to a conclusion however inconsiderately that they are doing justice to the dead.

My prospect of getting to London this Spring is rather darkened. Messrs. Longman have proposed, if the Excursion is out of print, to have it stereotyped as the Yarrow has been, and to do the same with the other 3 Volumes. But I cannot give them an answer, as they have furnished me with no facts as to the Expense, or other particulars.—do favor me with your guidance for my judgement. There are left of the 4 volumes 180 and they wish to begin printing. I wish much to correct [?] substantially with this Publication, but how is it to be done? and what would you advise, as to any ornaments such as prefaced to Murray's Edit. of Crabbe and Boswell's Johnson. This was strongly recommended to me by a spirited Bookseller of Carlisle. The third Volume also if they are to be uniform with the Yarrow in the inside ought to be spread over 4, one Sonnet only being on [a] page with correspondent resemblance in other respects. Do you think that Poems which have been so long before the Public would bear this? The whole would then consist of 6 Volumes, and certainly would have a much better

---

[1] *Letters, Conversations, and Recollections of S. T. Coleridge*, ed. by T. Allsop, 2 vols., 1836.

appearance. If you see Mr Robinson ask him about this; he complains of the present Edition having a shabby appearance from the crowded page.

With kind regards from all to yourself and Mrs M. very sincerely

Yours

Wm Wordsworth

1143. *W. W. to William Rowan Hamilton*

Hamilton(—)
G(—) K(—)

Rydal Mount, Jan. 11, 1836.

. . . With much pleasure I have received two letters from you through the hands of my son, for both of which accept my cordial thanks. We took it very kindly that you were so particular in entering into the state of your family and your relatives. We often think with much interest of your sister Eliza, and with a thousand good wishes that her bold adventure may turn out well. If she finds herself at liberty to move about, her sensitive imagination and thoughtful mind cannot but be profitably excited and substantially enriched by what she will see in that most interesting part of the world—Smyrna and the coast of Asia Minor. How should I like, old as I am, to visit those classic shores, and the Holy Land, with all its remembrances, so sweet and solemn!

. . . Mrs Wordsworth and my daughter have just read the Bishop of Limerick's[1] and Mr Knox's correspondence with great interest. So should I have done, but the allowance of daylight is now so short; and I do not venture to read or write at all by candlelight. This is the cause why Mrs Wordsworth now holds the pen for me. I never shall forget Mr Knox, to whom you introduced me, nor his eloquent and dignified conversation. I remember we differed upon one point, viz., the inward unchangeableness of Romanism; the opinions which I find expressed by him about the year 1824 are much more in accordance with what mine have always been than those which he expressed during the interview I have alluded to. I wish I had seen more of him. His friend and correspondent, the Bishop of Limerick, as also

---

[1] Bishop Jebb, *v.* Letter of Jan. 28, 1833.

the editor of the letters, Mr Forster, I saw more than once at Clapham. The good bishop was so obliging as to send his carriage to London for me, and I passed a night at his house.

Surely I ought to have said before this a word upon the honour thrust upon you by the Lord Lieutenant, in his Majesty's name; and so I should, but the great Bully O'Connell[1] stood in my way, and the Protestant Established Church of Ireland, which I hold precious as my life, seemed to cry out to me, 'What honour can come from men who are the slaves of bigots and traitors bent upon my destruction!' But whether Sir William, or plain Mr Hamilton, be you assured of my affectionate admiration. I *must* congratulate you, however, upon your growing family and your happiness as a married man. Pray present our united regards to Lady Hamilton, and give each of your young philosophers, perhaps they may prove poets, a kiss for my sake. You are growing rich as a father, while I am keeping pace with you as a grandfather. Do let us hear of you, from time to time.

Ever affectionately yours, . . .

W. W.

MS.　　　　**1144. W. W. to Isabella Fenwick**

Rydal Mount, Jan^{ry} 18th, [1836]

My dear Miss Fenwick,

I am about to ask a favor of you, let me rather say another testimony of that friendship which Mrs W. and I value so highly. My eldest Son has just had a Son born, his 2nd, the Boy is to bear my name. His Father, in consequence, looking beyond his Relations, is desirous of having a Sponsor among my Friends, and has just referred the matter to me. I have therefore turned my thoughts to you as in the first rank of those whom we love and esteem, and request you would do us the honor to undertake the office for the newborn. I am sorry that I cannot at present name the other Sponsors, but they will, I understand, be applied to upon the same principle.

---

[1] David O'Connell (1775–1847), the great Irish orator and patriot, founder of the 'Catholic Association'. At this time he was agitating for the repeal of the Union, and in Jan. 1836 addressed huge crowds in Liverpool and Birmingham.

Mr Henry Taylor probably told you that we had a glimpse of each other at Keswick—he parted with some hope held out that he might call at Rydal on his return from Edin:. We were much disappointed in not seeing him. Pray tell us how far you were satisfied with Mr Pickersgill's Portrait of him.

A friend of mine was lately visiting in the same house with the Duke of Wellington—he was in excellent health and high spirits, and is of opinion that *we are looking up in the world.*

I cannot guess how far the municipal elections will affect the future Parliamentary returns; not however I am sure to the degree that the Whig Radicals believe or pretend, nor on the other hand will they prove so insignificant as the Times or Conservatives represent. It is affirmed that in those Corporations where the Whigs were before exclusively predominant, the elections of Councilmen are in favor of the Tories, and vice versa. If this is so, they are not so undeniable a proof as they would be otherwise, that the lower in the scale of society you go, the surer are you to find Radicals and revolutionists set upon the work of destruction without being capable of being turned aside by other considerations or passions.

My poor Sister's health especially as affecting her mind is to us a constant source of anxiety, and my Daughter though much better is far from well. We are going to Church, Mrs W. will add a few lines on her return. Farewell my dear Miss Fenwick, believe me with the highest esteem, most faithfully yours

Wm Wordsworth.

MS.   **1145. W. W. to Mrs Hook**

Rydal Mount Jan. 21. [1836]

Dear Mrs Hook,

The Papers have just informed us of the loss which you have suffered in the decease of your Brother Sir Thomas.[1] Be assured we sincerely condole with you upon the melancholy event, for which Lady Farquhar had prepared us; the case, we learned from her, admitting of no hope. Knowing the power of religious

---

[1] Sir Thomas Farquhar, Bart., banker, and Treasurer of the Institute of British Architects. He died on Jan. 12.

faith on your own mind and that of Georgina, we do not presume to offer you any consolation, beyond that of the expression of our cordial sympathy, which perhaps will have still more value in your estimation as proceeding from friends afflicted as we are, and have been. May God support you through this and all your future trials.

With respect to our family I need not enter into particulars. In my poor Sister there is upon the whole no improvement and Dora's progress towards recovery under these sad circumstances cannot be expected to be other than subject to interruption. She was again bled last Saturday.

My daughter-in-law has got well through her confinement. Her new-born is a fine child, and is to bear my name.

I should not have adverted to public affairs but that I have just heard through a friend from one who is much among official persons in London, that if the King will consent, ministers will dissolve Parl^t before Easter; if not, they will resign; after making allowance for loss in the Counties, they calculate upon an acquisition of 30 members upon the whole, which will enable them to keep their places. What a wretched condition is this country brought to!

The weather has with us been much less severe than you have had it in the South. Not a day has it prevented my taking my usual exercise.

We have staying with us a Mr Robinson, a friend whom we highly value who came down from London about a month ago. His society has helped us through the winter, by the interposition of many and chearful hours.

Believe me dear Mrs Hook with affectionate regards to Georgina in which we all unite   most faithfully yours

Wm Wordsworth.

1146. W. W. to William Rowan Hamilton

Hamilton(—)
K(—)

Rydal Mount, January 26, 1836.

You being a father and a good churchman, I have no scruple in making the proposal I am about to do. You must know then that my son's new-born is to bear my name; and his father being desirous that he should provide the babe with sponsors from among my particular friends, you—as one whom I especially reckon upon as such, and furthermore, as also bearing the name of William—I hope will not object to stand in that interesting relation to my family. If I am not mistaken, it would give me great pleasure if you will write to my son, who does not feel himself sufficiently acquainted to make this request himself, and propose doing him this honour. I know how much it would gratify both him and his wife. Should you have any conscientious or delicate scruples upon this subject, have no more hesitation in giving me a refusal than I have had in making the proposal. . . .

W. W.

MS.   *1147. W. W. to Mr Lightfoot*

Rydal Mount Friday 29th Jan. 1836.

Dear Sir,

It gives me pleasure to learn that you purpose to accompany John[1] to Penrith. Your advice and assistance cannot but be of great use to him—He tells me that you will undertake such processes as may be necessary for the recovery of arrears due from Jackson, which as far as my Powers of acting Trustee extend, I authorize you to do.

I hope also you will advise with John and Mr Blamise and Mr Nicholson, as to the eligible distribution of the property in lots for sale. Lying scattered, as it does, much must depend, I should think, upon the judgement with which it is divided for sale into parcels.

John is become of age this day, and I cannot conclude without expressing my trust that his affairs will be wound up in such a way as will prove satisfactory to himself and to all parties interested and concerned.

I remain dear Sir
sincerely yours
Wm Wordsworth

[1] i.e. the son of R. W. On Mr Lightfoot, and the projected sale, v. *C.R.*, pp. 291, 292, 294.

MS.
K.
1148. *W. W. to Edward Moxon*

Jany 30, [1836]

My dear Sir,

I am glad you like the verses.[1] I wrote them (how could it be otherwise?) with feeling for the subject. Do with them what you like as to the number of Copies you will strike off—I wish for 25—Only I submit that it would not be desirable they should get into the Athenaeum, or any other periodical, before they come out with this book. I should not like it, nor would it be so respectful to dear Lamb's memory.

May I beg that you would send me down a Revise, through Mr Robinson who can promise me a Frank; should I think any alterations necessary I will return it immediately, if I do not, then take it for granted it is right, and the copies may be struck off.

We feel ourselves greatly indebted to Mr Robinson, in giving us his Company at this time, and coming so far to see us.

No material changes in our Invalids.

Ever faithfully yours
Wm Wordsworth

MS.
1149. *W. W. to Joshua Watson*

[Jan. 1836]

Extract of a Letter from the Earl of Lonsdale

'On this subject (Cockermouth Ch:) I know not what to add to what I have already said upon it—I am ready to provide an Endowment to the amount of one Hundred and Fifty Pounds per ann: and I presume, as in all such cases the Clergyman derives some Benefit from Pews'

My dear Sir,

The above noble offer I have this morning received from Lord Lonsdale, with authority to mention his name, so with what may be fairly expected from the Pews in addition, the Minister, as times go, would have a respectable Endowment. By tomorrow's

---

[1] i.e. those on Charles Lamb.

post I shall write to Mr Wood—and if necessary will go over to Cockermouth. Could Lord Egremont be prevailed upon to contribute somewhat generously towards the Building, the way would be pretty smooth before us; tho' I am certain that the most zealous part of the People of C. are not favorable to the Patronage being vested in our Friend, not from personal objections to his L^{dsp}, but preferring popular, or *other* Patronage, and therefore I do not expect any considerable Contributions from the Place—and for my own ability to raise money among my Friends etc, I fear must not be rated at more than 7 or 8 hundred pounds, but I cannot say, till it is fairly tried—as it *now shall* be—it is proper for me to *restate* this, because in a former letter from you, I observed you had misread or I had miswritten, the amount—as you understood me to have said *17* or *18* hundred—which must be very *very* far beyond what I can raise.

In answer to your question of 'how we are to proceed as to the return made by Mr F.'[1] I should say, that such are his dispositions as to allow no hope of more favorable returns being extorted from him, either thro the Bp: or otherwise. But if Mr F's return could be by you laid before the Board, with liberty on your part to accompany it with such information as has been given by Mr Wood—and the rules of the Boards would permit them to act upon such colateral representation, then I think it would be best, to proceed in this manner. It is of great importance that we should know as soon as possible what extent of aid we may look for from the Societies—the fact respecting the Endowment being settled.

As to the Vicar of B—,[2] he is so circumstanced in respect to Cockermouth, and has so much to do among the Dissenters in his own district—and thro' the whole Parish, in which they swarm—that he cannot afford to place himself in hostility with his Br. Minister at Cockermouth, as would be the case, if he should take the part you allude to in this business—Furthermore, *his* active interference would place me in an invidious situation among the Inhabitants.

[1] Mr. Fawcett—Vicar of Cockermouth.
[2] Brigham, i.e. W.'s son John.

I shall trouble you again when I have communicated with Mr Wood meanwhile, believe [me] ever my dear Sir faithfully and very aff^{ly} yours

Wm Wordsworth

Our kindest remembrances to Miss W.

Address: Joshua Watson Esqre, 6 Park St., Westminster.

1150. *W. W. to C. W. (Junior)*

$M(—)$ $G(—)$ $K(—)$

Rydal Mount Jan. 1836.

My dear Christopher,

... Now let me tell you, but more for your father's sake than yours, that in a letter which I received from Lord Lonsdale yesterday he generously proposes to endow a new church at Cockermouth with £150 per annum. From a conversation with him in the autumn, I expected he would do as much, though he did not then permit me, as he has done now, to mention it publicly.

W. W.

1151. *W. W. to Edward Moxon*

MS.
K(—)

Monday 8th Feb^y [1836]

My dear Sir,

I am quite ashamed of being so troublesome. Upon reconsidering the Verses, I think the sense in one altered passage is not sufficiently clear if the line

'Otherwise wrought the Will of the most High',

be omitted; therefore let it stand as before, and the line that follows thus—

Yet in all visitations, through all trials,

Still etc

through instead of *and*, as I think it stood before.

Mr Pickersgill states and has found so many objections from the engraver, that being altogether indifferent on my *own account*, respecting the Engraving of the Portrait, I have abandoned the Project—

Ever faithfully yours

[*not signed*]

I am glad you have seen Mr Robinson he would tell you about us.—

P.S.

Dear Mr Moxon,

I am truly sorry to have caused you so much trouble about these unlucky Verses, but all Poetry upon a domestic or personal subject especially if not helped by rhyme requires to be written with extreme care in all that concerns style or it offends without the reader knowing why.—I have not yet seen H. Coleridge, he has been off on one of his drinking bouts.—

My dear Sir,

Dont send more than 12 Copies of the Verses here, keep the rest for London distribution, and if not too late alter the line Haply received etc thus

Received, *there* may it stand, I trust, unblamed and print for 'Still were they faithful' 'Still they were faithful'. You will notice the reason in the previous *inversion* of 'were they'.

W. W.

MS.

1152. *W. W. to Joshua Watson*

Rydal Mount 9th Feb^{ry} [18]36

Private

My dear Sir,

The Vicar of Brigham and Mr Hodgeson his Curate are both now in my house; and the subject of a 2nd Church at Cockermouth has of course been conversed upon in my presence.

The obstacles are as follows.

1st the character and dispositions of the Incumbent of Cockermouth, who is indifferent or even averse to the Project:— which will prevent neighbouring Clergymen interfering for the purpose—

2nd a deadness in the body of the people which appears to be in no small degree consequent upon the character and disposition of their Clergyman.—The present Church is far from being filled; and therefore it is naturally enough said, 'that another is not wanted'.—

On the favorable side—

1st a strong sense in the minds of many persons, of the desire-ableness of the thing.—

2nd—an all but certainty that Lord Lonsdale would assist in it, as he has just offered to do in the case of Keswick, with which he is not by property connected; whereas he is Patron and Lay-impropriator of the parish of Brigham.—

3d—Lord Egremont has recently given [£]100 to Keswick, where he has *no* property, whereas as you know he is owner of Cockermouth Castle, and has a large estate immediately above the Town, and is furthermore known to be a munificent Person—

Now I take the liberty of asking two questions—1st I under-stand from Dr Wordsworth that 200 was lately offered to Kendal from a small surplus of the Church building society.—Could any portion of that surplus not less than 200, be conditionally offered by the society as a nucleus for subscriptions to gather round.

2nd Does your experience enable you to suggest a plan by which the difficulty arising from the *covert* dispositions of the Incumbent could be got over; so that an attempt might be made?—

With regard to the former of these questions, I am aware that your Boards expect that the advance should be made, in the first instance, by the parishes themselves coming forward with a certain sum; but could not the general rule be dispensed with in a case like the present, particularly where you are so near the end of your fund?—

My Son having previously furnished you with the particulars of the case, I beg to refer you to his Letter, and have only [to] add that we should be much gratified if the scheme could be realized—

I remain my dear Sir

with the highest respect

faithfully yours

Wm Wordsworth

Address: Joshua Watson Esqre, Park St., Westminster.

MS.
R.

1153. *W. W. to Samuel Rogers*

Rydal Mount [18th Feb., 1836]

Many and sincere thanks, my dear Friend, for your Grand
Present of Matthias's Gray,[1] which reached me a few days ago.
I have already skimmed the 2nd Vol. which was new to me; and
I hope for much pleasure and profit from the perusal of most of
it, at *leisure*. This last word, by the bye, reminds me of a refer-
ence I found to Oldham, for the words—

I have not yet leisure to be good.[2]

You recollect that long ago I said to you I was sure the line
would be found somewhere, and if I am not mistaken you told
me, some time after, you had met with it in Owen Feltham's
prose.[3] Was this so?

I shall greatly value these two superb Volumes, and more for
your sake than for their own, and I hope that they of my family
into whose hands they may pass will also prize them as a
memorial of our Friendship.

I have not forgotten that I am in your debt for a Letter
received many months ago; and for which you would have been
thanked long since, if I could have added any thing respecting
myself or family which it would have gratified you to learn. We
struggle on, bearing up under our trials and afflictions as well
as with God's help we can. My daughter is some thing better,
though not able to exert herself; but for my poor Sister, though
her bodily health is upon the whole better, this blessing is more

---

[1] *The Works of Thomas Gray, with Memoirs of his Life and Writings, etc.*,
by William Mason, *Extracts from the Author's original MSS.*, by J. T.
Matthias, 2 vols., elegant 4to, 1814—with Autograph Presentation 'To
William Wordsworth from Samuel Rogers,—January 27, 1836' (Catalogue
of Sale of W.'s Library).

[2] From Oldham's *Satyr against Value—Pindarique Ode*, stanza v.

Let Gambling Age be grave and wise
And Vertue's poor contemn'd idea prize
Who never knew, or now are past the sweets of Vice

.   .   .   .

While my plump veins are fill'd with lust and blood
Let not one thought of her intrude
Or dare approach my Breast,
But know 'tis all possesst
By a more welcome guest
And know I have not yet the leisure to be good.

[3] Owen Feltham (1602 ?–68); his *Resolves* were published in 1623.

than counterbalanced by a disorder of the mind, obviously proceeding from some inflammatory action upon the brain. Mrs. W. continues pretty well.

Last summer I saw a good deal of our excellent Friends both at Lowther and Whitehaven. Lady Frederick was there, and you were often talked about. At Whitehaven I had frequent walks upon the cliffs, which were not unproductive of poetic *suggestions*, I do not presume to say inspirations.

Possibly, and even probably, I may visit London before the spring is over; if so, how happy shall I be to renew my conversations and walks with you. These are (truly may I say it) among the principal attractions London has for me. With kindest remembrances to yourself and Sister, in which my own poor dear Sister is still able to join with us all, I remain, my dear Friend, faithfully yours,

W. Wordsworth

Pray enclose this slip to Moxon[1]

P.S. Be so good as to say to Moxon that I wish him to present you, as from me, a couple of copies of my verses upon Lamb, one for your Sister. I should have expressed this wish to himself upon the slip on the other side had there been room.

Address: Sam¹ Rogers Esqre, St. James's Place, London.

MS.   1154. *W. W. to Joshua Watson*

Rydal Mount Feb. 19ᵗʰ [1836]
Private

My dear Sir,

I was much gratified in learning from your Letter that you do not think Cockermouth is to be despaired of.—Your proposal of naming the project to the Diocesan, is I think the best thing that can, at present, be done. It was upon the application of the Bp of Carlisle that Lord Egremont gave 100£ to Keswick, and when upon being applied to for the same place Lord Lonsdale offered to assist, it was with the Proviso that the Bp approved.—I am persuaded that if these two Noblemen were applied to through the Bp, they would both countenance and aid the Building of the Church, in a place where, to all but the

---

¹ The bottom of the page, containing the note to Moxon, is cut off.

indifferent or the prejudiced in religious concerns, it must appear to be so much needed. At present the main obstacle, is the slackness, and I fear aversion of the Incumbent; but I feel confident that if these Noblemen would support the undertaking, we need not dread much from the covert indisposition of the Incumbent, which as things now are, would stand greatly in our way; though he would not openly oppose the attempt.

This is a matter of delicacy; and it is only to you that by Letter I would venture to speak as openly as I have done. If Lord Lonsdale had been in the North I would have seen him upon the subject, and treated this part of it with some thing of less reserve, than I feel necessary in communications by Letter. A copy of your last has been forwarded to my Son, and no doubt he will have the papers filled up as desired, and sent.

There are in the manufacturing Districts many, many places far more destitute than Cockermouth; but surely for an encreasing population of nearly six thousand, more than 100 free seats are required for the poor, and I question when the Sunday schools are supplied if there be that number in Cockermouth Church. But what makes the main difference between this place and the manufacturing towns and villages is, that there is ground for hope of success here notwithstanding the deadness of most of the Inhabitants; whereas in many parts of Lancashire and Yorkshire people spring up so fast, and float about so irregularly that the demand for religious instruction and consolation *cannot* be adequately supplied. Believe [me] my dear Sir

ever faithfully yours

W. Wordsworth

Address: Joshua Watson Esqre, 6 Park Street, Westminster.

MS.   *1155. W. W. to Lincoln Fairchild*[1]

Rydal Mount Feb^ry 23rd [? 1836][2]

Sir,

Your letter with an enclosure from Mr Griscom has been received. It will give me pleasure to pay to a Friend of that

[1] An American traveller.

[2] In 1836 W. W. changed his publisher from Longman to Moxon; hence the dating of this letter.

gentleman such attention as my opportunities and engagements will allow.

At present I am not connected with any London Bookseller, and my acquaintance with that Body of Men is so confined, that not more than two of them are known to me even by sight, except those of the Firm of Messrs Longman who were till lately my Publishers. I am sorry therefore that I cannot be of use to you in the way of introductions among them nor am I upon those Terms of intimacy with any literary Men to allow me to take the liberty, at this distance, to introduce any one with whom I have not the honor to be personally acquainted.

Should you write to your friend Mr Griscom I will thank you to convey my respectful remembrance to him—I need scarcely add, that if you come into this Country in search of a Residence, I should be happy to give you all the assistance, as to that point, which I am able.

And am Sir your
obd^t S^t
Wm Wordsworth

MS.   1156. W. W. to Joshua Watson

Rydal Mount 28 Feb^{ry}—1836

My dear Sir,

I trouble you with this note on account of the Extract from an *intended* Tithe Commission Bill, contained in a Letter of my Son Wm, which you will find on the other page. For myself I can give no opinion upon the matter, but if it have any promise about it, perhaps you would not object upon a fit occasion to mention it to the Archbishop. You know how anxious I am that my Son should obtain some office or situation in which his time might be turned to better account both for himself and for the publick than at present.

I avail myself of this opportunity to condole with you on the death of the excellent Bp. of Durham.[1] It is an event which every rational Friend of the Church must have long looked for-

---

[1] William van Mildert (1765–1836), the last Count Palatine of Durham, and founder of Durham University.

ward to, with mournful apprehensions. Then there are Salisbury, Ely, Peterborough all opening to receive any unworthy Person whom it may suit the purposes of unscrupulous men to appoint. The Bp of Norwich also cannot be expected to last long. Of Dr Hampden's opinions[1] I know no more than any one may have learned from the extracts from his Lectures in the newspapers—But surely it is astounding that he and others can remain in the Church at all. The notions of Dr H— (if correctly given in the Extracts) respecting Creeds declarations and articles appear to me irreconcilable with *any Church* however latitudinarian its character.

I do not recollect whether I have written to you since Chris^t became public orator. As a personal question it seems every where admitted that he was the better man. His success gave us in this House much pleasure. With affectionate regards to Miss Watson, I remain dear Sir

most respectfully yours
Wm Wordsworth

Extract

'The only point remaining is the constitution of the B^d of Commiss^{rs}

'They are to be three, two appointed by the Secretary of State, one by the Archbp of Canterbury, and all removable only on the joint pleasure of the Secretary and Archbp: They are to be a body corporate, but to be appointed for 5 years only.

'They may appoint any number of *Assistant* Commiss^{rs} not exceeding *nine*, without the consent of the Treasury, and may delegate any of their powers to their Assistants, except the Acts required to be under their seal, such as confirming and authenticating agreements and awards.'

---

[1] Dean Dickson Hampden (1793–1868), Bishop of Hereford, 1847, a liberal evangelical churchman. In 1827 he wrote *Essays of the Philosophical Evidences of Christianity*. In 1836 Lord Melbourne appointed him Regius Professor of Divinity at Oxford. The appointment was opposed by the Tories and High Church party and he offered to withdraw, but Melbourne, 'for the sake of the principles of toleration, felt bound to persevere in the appointment'.

It is the *Assistant* Commiss^rs that my Son wished me to ask your opinion about—if the app^t could be held by any but a Barrister?

W. W.

Address: Joshua Watson Esqre, Park Street, Westminster.

M.
K.
1157. W. W. to James Stanger[1]

[? Feb–March 1836]

My dear Sir,

The obstacle arising out of conflicting opinions in regard to the patronage, one must be prepared for in every project of this kind. Mutual giving way is indispensable, and I hope it will not ultimately be wanting in this case.

The point immediately to be attended to is the raising a sufficient sum to insure from the Church Building Societies a portion of the surplus fund which they have at command, and which I know, on account of claims from many places, they are anxious to apply as speedily as possible. If time be lost, that sum will be lost to Cockermouth.

In the question of the patronage as between the bishop and the people, I entirely concur with you in preference of the former. Such is now the force of public opinion, that bishops are not likely to present upon merely selfish considerations; and if the judgment of one be not good, that of his successor may make amends, and probably will. But elections of this sort, when vested in the inhabitants, have, as far as my experience goes, given rise to so many cabals and manœuvres, and caused such enmities and heart-burnings, that Christian charity has been driven out of sight by them: and how often, and how soon, have the successful party been seen to repent of their own choice!

The course of public affairs being what it is in respect to the Church, I cannot reconcile myself to delay from a hope of succeeding at another time. If we can get a new church erected at Cockermouth, great will be the benefit, with the blessing of God,

1 Son-in-law of W.'s old friend William Calvert.

to that place; and our success cannot, I trust, but excite some neighbouring places to follow the example.

The little that I can do in my own sphere shall be attempted immediately, with especial view to insure the coöperation of the societies. Happy should I be if you and other gentlemen would immediately concur in this endeavour.

I remain, etc.,

Wm. Wordsworth.

MS.   *1158. W. W. to Joshua Watson*

My dear Sir   [March 1836][1]

I am sorry that a wish to save postage caused so long a delay for my unlucky letter.

The Papers relating to Cockermouth Church could not, as my Son and Mr Hodgeson his Curate thought, be filled up on account of the unwillingness of the Cockermouth Incumbent to stir in the business, without a request from the Bp. Accordingly my Son wrote to his Lordship, stating particulars, and begging that he himself would write to Mr Fawcett. I left Workington last Tuesday, but the Bp's answer had not been received. I am not very sanguine, but still think the project ought not to be abandoned. Could we induce Mr Stanger of Keswick to take it up and subscribe, as he was prepared to do at Keswick, there would be no difficulty, though the religious tenets of Mr Stanger are not what the judicious, I think, would approve. Lord Lonsdale has just given a 100£ towards the enlargement of Bootle Church. That of Distington near Whitehaven wants it full as much and Maryport far more. The enclosed Paper gives an account of what is to be done at Keswick; with which Mr Stanger and his Party who were prepared with no less than 4000£, have nothing to do. And it is said he talks of building a third Church at Keswick, where the *Gospel* may be preached. This would be a nuisance in so small [a] place. Mr Hodgson and Mr Hoskins of the High near Bassenthwaite Lake have both a good deal of influence over Mr S— and may perhaps prevail upon him to favor Cockermouth.

[1] For W. W. to H. C. R. March 16 and 26, *v. C.R.*, pp. 294–8.

A thousand thanks for your kindness. I am *very* anxious on my Son's account, and not the less so, as my own Income from the Stamp off: has already been much reduced by various causes; and if the Registrary is to be removed from Carlisle to London, as proposed in the new Bill, it will be reduced still further by 70£ per ann: This is rather hard after 23 years service, in which I have had from the first a Clerk, whose salary I cannot curtail, but would much rather encrease, so great are his deservings.

The Chancellor of the Exchequer[1] is of my acquaintance, and I have reason to believe well-disposed to me, though not ignorant of my Politics. So no doubt is Lord Lansdown,[1] but as you will easily conceive it goes against the grain with me to ask any thing of these gentlemen that even looks like a government favor, I do so deeply deplore, and so strongly disapprove of their public conduct, especially in respect to the Protestant Church in Ireland, and their municipal Bill for that wretched country. As to the latter measure and the arguments by which it is supported what should we say of an order for two men's shoes being made off the same Last though their feet differed some inches in size! We have as yet little reason to applaud the new-casting of the Corporations for England; but for Ireland and the Empire at large, the application of the same plan must in its tendency, be ruinous. But to return—I will consider seriously about writing to the Chancellor of the Ex: and Lord L: but I do not think I shall be able to prevail upon myself to take the step as I cannot ask any thing as a *favor*; if I thought they would admit that supposing my Son's qualifications sufficient for an office, I have a claim, from my writings and general character, in his behalf upon my Country, upon those terms but upon no other could I ask for an appointment. [As] to the good Archbishop I should feel no difficulty. It is time to bring this tedious Letter to a close. Believe me my dear Sir, under all circumstances,

most gratefully and respectfully yours

Wm Wordsworth

Mr Moxon of Dover Street will send you three Copies of some printed, but not published Verses upon my deceased Friend

---

[1] *v.* Letter of June 16, 1835, *supra.*

Charles Lamb—one for Cambridge as soon as you may have an opportunity of giving it to the Doctor, or either of [his] Sons, and one for Charles if they could convey it to him without expense—

My Sister is very much better in bodily health and so also in mind, though still feeble in certain points, from the effect of the late violent inflammatory actions upon the brain.—

Pray excuse this shabby paper which has been taken up inadvertently.

MS.   *1159. W. W. to Miss Peabody*[1]

Dear Madam,   Rydal Mount 7ᵗʰ April '36.

It is some time since I had the honour of receiving a Letter from you accompanying the Present of a Volume of your writing, The Records of a School. For both these marks of your attention I beg to return you my sincere thanks, which ought to have been done sooner, and would have been so, but that I rarely write to any one. You may have perhaps heard that my eyes are subject to inflammations, which so curtail the little time I have for reading, that I have none almost for writing except what I am under the necessity of making. I cannot however omit thanking you both for the interesting Contents of your Volume, and for the account you are so obliging as to give me of the effects which some of my poems have produced upon the minds of young persons in your presence. Beyond these acknowledgements I have nothing to add which would make my Letter more worthy of being wafted over the Atlantic, except the expression of my good wishes that your efforts for the benefit of the rising generation may be crowned with the success they so amply deserve.

Believe me to remain dear Madam with sincere admiration and respect

faithfully yours

Wm. Wordsworth

[1] Elizabeth Palmer Peabody (b. 1804), a teacher and prolific writer on Education. Apart from *The Record of a School* her chief books were *Spiritual Culture* and *First Steps to History*.

P.S. Dr. Channing[1] lives, I believe, at Boston. Some time since I had a note from him announcing his intention of sending me, or his having sent me a Copy of a sermon of his recently published. If you be in communication with him will you be so kind as to express my thanks, adding that unfortunately I have not received his discourse.

Address: Miss Peabody, Boston, America.

MS.   *1160. W. W. to Joshua Watson*

Rydal Mount 10th April 1836

My dear Sir,

I enclose two Letters from Mr Wood of Cockermouth. The 2nd is much more encouraging than the former had led me to expect—I am particularly pleased with the subscription of the Indivi[d]ual of Papcastle, as it was in no small degree with a view to the benefit of that place that I first pointed out Cockermouth as deserving your consideration and that of the society.—

I should be much obliged if you could furnish me with any Instructions towards answering the Queries in Mr Wood's first Letter, which I am almost ashamed to send you, it was so soiled in the pocket of a chaise-driver to whose care, for expeditions sake, it had been entrusted.

I shall be further obliged if you would circulate Mr Wood's Letter in any way which may seem likely to further the end we have in view. You will probably see the new Master of Harrow[2] very soon, pray shew it to him, or tell him of the Contents. I shall exert myself to the utmost among my Friends in all quarters.

Believe [me], my dear Sir

faithfully yours

Wm Wordsworth.

Address: Joshua Watson Esqe, Park St.

[1] William Ellery Channing (1780–1842), educ. at Harvard; a distinguished American divine, and author of *Discourses on the Evidences of Revealed Religion*.   [2] C. W. (Jun.).

MS.   *1161. W. W. to William Wood*

Rydal Mount April 11th —36

Dear Sir,

   I am much obliged by your Letter reporting the proceedings
of the Vestry-meeting for taking into consideration the desire-
ableness of building a new Church or Chapel at Cockermouth.
The result of that meeting is exceedingly promising, and the
mode of opening the business appears to me to have been very
judicious. Till after next Wednesday I shall be a good deal
engaged, but be assured that I will do all in my power to forward
an affair in which as you know I feel a strong interest, and that
as speedily as possible.

                        I remain, dear Sir,
                            sincerely your obliged serv^{nt}
                                        Wm Wordsworth.

Address: Wm Wood Esqre, Cockermouth.

MS.   *1162. W. W. to Thomas Noon Talfourd*[1]

16th April [1836]

My dear Sir,

   I wrote twice to Mr Moxon not long ago, through a sort of
private channel and am not sure as I have not heard from him
since that my last Letter has reached him. One of them contained
corrections of the Verses upon Lamb, which I wished to be
looked to when the Lines were printed in your Work. They are
as written down on the other leaf.[2]

   Have you any Friends, who out of joint attachment to the
Church of England, to poetry, and to my attempts in that way,
would assist in a Project of Building a Church, in my *native
place* Cockermouth. This Undertaking I was the means of
originating, the good people who are any thing but rich depend
upon my doing more towards it than my influence is equal to;
but I will do my utmost having the thing much at heart. To

---

[1] The name of the addressee is missing, but the lines on Lamb were to
be included in Talfourd's *Life and Letters*.
[2] The other leaf has been detached.

you I need not say more. No one needs to give his or her name (unless it be agreeable to do so), for publication of names of persons not locally connected might subject them to impertinent applications from other quarters.

Messrs. Longman have proposed to me to stereotype my poems, and I think it will be done.

ever my dear Sir

affectionately yours

Wm Wordsworth.

MS.   *1163. W. W. to Thomas Poole*

Rydal Mount April 19th [1836]

My dear Mr Poole,

If I had been a money-maker instead of a verse-maker, though I often think of you as I trust you do of me, I should not have come a begging to you upon the occasion which has now tempted me, to take up the pen. I will be brief.

As far as concerns the Church of England, Cockermouth, my native place, is in a state of much spiritual destitution; nearly six thousand souls, with only 300 sittings for the Poor, of which two thirds are taken-up by the children of two Sunday Schools. The place is poor, but increasing. I have been the means of setting on a foot the Project of erecting a new Church there; and the Inhabitants looked towards me for more, much more assistance than I can possibly afford them, through any influence which I possess. Nevertheless, I would gladly do my utmost, and therefore I have not scrupled to apply in many quarters, where I thought that I had friends, and even *Admirers* excuse the Word, who out of joint love for the Church and gratitude to me, for such pleasure as my verses might have given them, might be determined to give their beneficence a direction favorable to my wishes in this particular case.

Now, if there were any probability that any one of your wealthier acquaintances who had a trifle to spare would help me in this good work I should be truly thankful, having the thing much at heart. The time is not far distant, when unless great exertions are made, the same arguments of disproportion between church-men and non-church men which have been so ruinously applied to the Protestant Establishment in Ireland, will be brought to bear against the National Church of England. —Heaven forbid they should be successful. A 2nd Church is now building at Keswick, one is just built at Kendal, another near Ambleside, and if we can succeed at Cockermouth, where there is a promising opening, we shall excite other Towns to follow our example.—I will leave the matter in your hands, knowing well how many claims so public spirited a man as yourself must have upon both your time and your purse. A sum howover small will be acceptable, name given or not, as agreeable.

You were very kind in writing to me after your return to Somersetshire from the North. My family has been much afflicted since that time. We have lost dear Miss Hutchinson, my Wife's sister. At the time when she was taken from us, out of a family of eight, Servants included, four were confined to the Bed or the Sofa, and my poor Sister, one of them, expected to be called away every hour. She has survived almost miraculously, but she cannot walk, and scarcely can stand; my Daughter is a good deal better, but still a feeble Invalid. Mrs Southey's recovery is hopeless—Southey and his Daughters bear up wonderfully. When are we likely to see you again among us? Your neighbourhood is very dear to me, the more so since poor Coleridge is gone. If my daughter were strong enough to travel I certainly would visit you before the summer is flown. Farewell, Mrs Wordsworth, my Daughter and poor Sister unite in kindest remembrances. Ever yours,

W. Wordsworth

Address: Thos. Poole Esqre, Nether Stowey, Somersetshire.

MS.   *1164. W. W. to J. G. Lockhart*

Rydal Mount April 27th —36.

My dear Sir

Your Letter was duly received but I have hesitated about answering it on account of my intention to be in London in the course of a fortnight or so, when I could communicate in conversation all that I remember of your lamented Friend at the period of our first acquaintance. In this I should be aided by a journal which my dear Sister kept of that interesting tour, and which I would take with me. The notices there of Sir Walter are certainly not so copious as they would have been, had she anticipated what he was to become in the eyes of the world, but brief as they are they would, I am sure, interest you and Mrs. Lockhart.

If anything should prevent my going to London, I will write again; I had totally forgotten that I wrote the Letter you allude to. His kindness to us claimed every sort of acknowledgment of looks, words, pen, and *actions* in grateful return, had they been in our power. Mrs W. my Sister and daughter, unite with me in cordial remembrances to yourself and Mrs Lockhart. Believe me, my dear Sir,

faithfully yours,
Wm Wordsworth

Address: J. G. Lockhart Esq., Sussex Place, Regents Park.

1165. *W. W. to James Spedding*[1]

Rydal Mount 28th April [1836][2]

. . . The Monody upon C. Lamb was given to my friend Serjeaunt Talfourd, Lamb's Ex[r], to be published with his Life, Letters, etc. Moxon, with my permission, struck off a few copies for private circulation, one of which for yourself and another for Mr Taylor, if he wishes for it, it would give me great pleasure you should have.

[1] Extract quoted in T. J. Wise's Two Lake Poets: a Catalogue of Books, &c., by. W.W. and S.T.C., 1927. James Spedding (1808–81), intimate friend of Henry Taylor and James Stephen, and their colleague at the Colonial Office (1835–47)—at Cambridge with Tennyson, Hallam, &c.—also a great friend of Hartley Coleridge. His life was devoted to editing the Works of Bacon (7 vols., 1837–59, followed by the *Life and Letters*, 1861–74). In 1847, when Stephen retired from the Under-Secretaryship of the Colonies, Spedding was offered the post, but declined it.

[2] For W. W. to H. C. R. April 27, *v. C.R.*, p. 301.

MS.   *1166. W. W. to Edward Moxon*

Rydal Mount 28th April.[1] [1836]

My dear Sir:

The bearer is Mr Spedding a particular friend of mine, and a man of first rate talents. (He is of the Colonial Off^e). Let him have two copies of my verses on Lamb, one for himself and one for Mr Taylor.

I hope to be in Town in the course of three weeks at the latest. My first place of abode will be Park Street West^r, but I have not forgotten your most friendly invitation. I shall call on you the day after my arrival, wishing very much to talk with you about the intended stereotype of my Poems.

farewell

in great haste

affectionately yours

Wm Wordsworth

Address: Edward Moxon Esq., 44 Dover Street.

MS.   *1167. W. W. to Joshua Watson*

Rydal Mt. May 5th [1836]

My dear Sir

My present intention is to profit by your hospitality on Tuesday night next, if I can find a place *in* or *out* of the Coach which quits Manchester at 5 oc in the morning and reaches London at 11 in the night—this will allow me to knock at your door before twelve. I have therefore to beg you to be so good as to direct one of your Servants to sit up for me till that hour, as I have a particular objection to sleep at a London Coach Inn.

I much regret, along with you and Miss Watson, that neither my Wife, Daughter nor my poor Sister can accompany me— the Invalids not being in travelling condition, and Mrs W. of course unable to leave them. The Vicar of Brigham is here at present, and will deliver a letter from me to Mr Wood tomorrow,

---

[1] April: *W. writes* May, *but the letter of May 5 to Watson proves that he ought to have written* April. It was probably enclosed in the letter to Spedding.

in which I shall state your apprehensions.—and beg of him to forward under cover to you at the Society, every particular which may tend to enable us to get over that obstacle. This I know that Mr Fawcett the Minister of Cockermouth, admitted, that inclusive of the villages of Papcastle and the Goat, the population was now little less than 6000—and Mr Wood told my Son that there was a probability of a considerable increase in a short time. Land close to the Town which I myself sold as Exr: to my eldest Br. 20 years ago, at less than a £100 an acre, has been resold—(a £1000 worth of it) at the rate of £1200 to build upon.

If I am disappointed of a place in *that* Coach at Manchester—you will see me I trust, in the course of the next day. But pray do not let either you or Miss W. derange any of your plans on my account, because, to use your own words, I shall regard your house as an Hotel till I have the pleasure of seeing the Host and Hostess.

You will be surprized when I tell you that the Chancellor of the Ex^r:[1]—out of compliment to the Poet, and love of the Est^t: has subscribed £10 to our embryo Church. 'What will they say of this at Cockermouth?'

With our united kindest regards from all here, I remain my d^r Sir

very faithfully yours

Wm Wordsworth

Address: Joshua Watson Esqre, 6 Park Street, Westminster, London.

MS.   *1168. W. W. to John W.*[2]

[May 1836]

My dear John,

Business of different kinds makes it very advisable that I should go to London, before a fortnight is over. Could not you

---

[1] Spring-Rice.

[2] This and the following four undated letters are proved to have been written in May 1836 by the following data: (1) W. was in town at that time and stayed some days with Moxon, and also some with the Marshalls; (2) cf. the reference to Mr Courtenay with the letter to H. C. R. (*C.R.*, p. 301); (3) E. Q. was living at Woolwich in May 1836. John W. (son of R. W.) was reading medicine under the charge of Mr Gardner, *v.* Letter of Jan. 1832.

contrive to despatch your business so that we might be Fellow
travellers? I see Lectures are going to begin at King's Coll. At
all events come over here, either at or before the end of the week;
for I am anxious to bring our affairs to a settlement. Mr
Courtenay is going soon on the Continent for 4 months, and he
is my fac-totum in money matters, and I wish to have what is
owing to your Aunt and me placed under his management,
which has hitherto proved so advantageous.

We expect your cousin John in a day or two. Pray forward
the enclosed to Mr Wood

ever faithfully your affectionate Uncle
Wm Wordsworth

Invalids pretty much as usual.

Address: John Wordsworth Esq, Keswick.

MS.   *1169. W. W. to John Wordsworth*

My dear John,   [May 1836]

I leave Mr Marshall's Monday next for Mr Moxon's. I am
now going to call at Gray's Inn with a chance of finding Mr
Addison[1] at home. If I do not I shall leave a note for him,
begging an account of your affairs as far as he had to do with
them.

You have not written me your wish about the army,[2] and the
particulars; for as I told you I cannot bear them in mind.

The accounts from Rydal are much as usual.

Your affectionate Uncle
W. Wordsworth.

I breakfast at home tomorrow, if it should suit you to call.

MS.   *1170. W. W. to John Wordsworth*

Lincoln's Inn.

My dear John,   Wednesday afternoon [May 1836].

Pray breakfast with me at Mr S. Cookson's, 45 Torrington
Square at 9 on Saturday next, and bring with you any state-

---

[1] Partner of the late R. W. (died 1816) and one of his executors.
[2] The Army Medical Service into which J. W. entered.

ments of accounts you have relative to your father's affairs. I have been at Mr Addison's and seen him.

If you cant come be so good as to let me know.

Ever yours
W. W.

Address: John Wordsworth Esq., 28 Great Ormond Street.

MS.   *1171. W. W. to John Wordsworth*

[May 1836]

My dear John

I have unfortunately mislaid your letter, with Mrs Smith's address, and know not where to call on her.

You will do right to call on Miss Rogers, or upon any person at whose house you have been received.

I hope to call on you in a day or two.

Your affectionate Uncle
W. Wordsworth

I am sadly hurried

Address: John Wordsworth Esq., 28 Great Ormond Street.

MS.   *1172. W. W. to John Wordsworth*

Wednesday Morning
41 Upper Grosvenor Street [May 1836]

My dear John,

Could you get ¼ lb. of Blue Pills and leave it at Mr Moxon's, directed for me. Mr Jackson[1] of Waterhead wants it for his daughter.

Yesterday I left a note for you requesting you would go down with me by Steamboat to Woolwich to Mr Q.'s.

Will you come also and breakfast here at half past nine that day, and then we can go down together. ever your affectionate Uncle W. Wordsworth

Address: John Wordsworth Esq., 28 Great Ormond Street.

[1] Son of Rev. Thomas Jackson, rector of Grasmere and Estate Agent to Rydal Hall: he had succeeded his father in the latter capacity.

MS. *1173. W. W. to Lady Theodosia Spring Rice*[1]

44 Dover Street 5th June[2] 36

Dear Lady Theodosia

I cannot promise myself the pleasure of being one of your Party on Thursday Evening, as by that time I hope to be at Rydal Mount. I leave London this afternoon at three o'clock, for St Albans. I need not repeat how happy I should be to see you and the young Ladies at my beautiful place of Abode.

With kindest regards to all around you, I have the honor to be

dear Lady Theodosia

faithfully yours

Wm Wordsworth.

MS. *1174. W. W. to Edward Quillinan*

Tuesday noon [July 5th 1836][3]

My dear Mr Quillinan

I am ashamed of myself, in having forgotten a commission of my Friend and Neighbour the Revd Robert Graves of Bowness. He has two Sisters, *young* Ladies, who want to go to Bowness but are unable to accompany him at present, and are anxious for the benefit of an Escort within the next fortnight or three weeks; in other words as soon as convenient to you after a week is over. I am able to say that they are young Ladies who will give you little trouble, and Mr Graves would meet them at Kendal. I may add that you would find them very interesting Companions, and it would give me great pleasure to know that this request is one which you are able to comply with. If so, or rather in any case, be so kind as to let their Mother Mrs Graves know. Her address is 28/B/ Devonshire Street, Portland Place, Corner of High Street.

Ever faithfully yours

Wm Wordsworth.

---

[1] Daughter of the first Earl of Limerick.
[2] MS. *July*, but W. left London early in June.
[3] For W. W. to H. C. R. June 24, *v. C.R.*, p. 304.

MS.   *1175. W. W. to Thomas Poole*

Rydal Mount Aug. 20th 1836[1]

My dear Friend

Your Letter gave me great pleasure. I was fully assured that you would do your best to promote the good object I have in view, and therefore relied upon hearing from you in due course of Time. Thanks for your exertions; and for your contribution. By this day's post I shall write to Sir P. Ackland as you suggest. His liberal contribution was grateful to me, both upon public and personal considerations.—As to the draft, I am sorry to be obliged to request you would keep it as well as your own contribution till the Project takes a more substantial Shape. My own little influence has not been exerted in vain, but a great disappointment has occurred in a high quarter. The Earl of Egremont is Lord of the Castle of Cockermouth and has a large property in the neighbourhood. Knowing his munificence I had over confidently relied upon his support. He thought it better, in which view he is quite mistaken, to enlarge the old Church and encrease the Endowment. But even to this I fear he is not likely to contribute; as he has just made an offer of two thousand pounds to the Inhabitants, to be disposed of for the benefit of the place in any way which they may approve. Preferring temporal things to spiritual they have chosen to have a new Market place with Buildings etc. This was wanted, and therefore one cannot complain. The other and still higher want will and must be supplied in course of time. I shall shortly go over to Cockermouth and learn the state of things upon the spot. In the meanwhile let me beg of you either to take charge of Sir Peregrin's subscription till you hear further from me, or if you prefer it return the draft to him, taking for granted it may be called for if the project be not dropped.

You express yourself as becomes an old and most valued Friend upon the affliction of my family. Of dear Miss Hutchinson I shall say no more than that her memory is consecrated in our hearts. My poor Sister cannot stand unsupported, and she

---

[1] For W. W. to H. C. R. July 11, and August 1836, *v. C.R.*, pp. 308 and 313.

suffers daily in body, but we trust by no means to the degree
that a Stranger might suppose. If her *mind* had not been impaired by the disease its pressure would have been very much
lighter upon the body. And this thought, Melancholy as it is,
affords us some consolation.—My Daughter is certainly better
as far as concerns pain: but the inflammation in the spine
returns with carriage motion so therefore she cannot benefit by
change of air; so that her strength comes back slowly if at all.
Had she been able to travel the hope I had encouraged of seeing
you and Stowey and Alfoxden would certainly have been fulfilled. As it is, we must submit to God's will.—My Wife and
your old Friend my dear Sister, unite with me in the kindest
remembrances, as does my daughter also.—With what you say
upon our dear departed Friend Coleridge I entirely concur.

Ever faithfully yours

W. Wordsworth

Dora would be hurt to see a letter from her Father to you, in
which her name was omitted among those of the Family who
bear a delightful recollection of your friendly, tho' short visit at
Rydal Mount—Most respectfully d^r Friend

Yours W. Wordsworth

Address: Thos. Poole Esqre, R. King's Esqre, Redcliff Parade,
Bristol.

MS.   **1176. W. W. to Joshua Watson**

Rydal Mount August 22 [1836].

My dear Sir,

   I have just received the enclosed from Mr Stanger; my
answer, which I hope you will approve, was that I could not
concur in his proposal.

   I should be glad if Mr S—'s Letter should suggest any observations to you, to have the benefit of them.

Ever faithfully yours

Wm Wordsworth

Address: J. Watson Esqre, Park St, Westminster.

MS.   *1177. W. W. to Joshua Watson*

Rydal Mount Sepr 26th [—]36

My dear Sir

In regard to Cockermouth Church my prospects brighten. But first let me tell you that in passing thro that Town the other day, I had a meeting with 4 Gentlemen who had taken an interest in the Subject: one, the Mr Wilson who had proposed to subscribe a £100—but I am sorry to say with the exception of Mr Wood, who is Lord Lonsdale's Law Agent, I found them all most unfavourably disposed to the old mode of Patronage, and strongly tinctured with what you will allow me to call Saintship and Simeonism. But to come to the point. I am sure it will not have escaped your memory, that you said to me ' Get the Church endowed by — — and we will build it'. Now I am prepared to say that a friend of mine, in every respect unobjectionable as a Patron will endow the Church if we will engage to build it. I told the Person, whose name in the present stage of the business I am not at liberty to mention, that less than £150 pr ann—proceeding from the endowment, and the letting of the Pews *in the Gallery*, the amount of which was an uncertainty would not suffice: he agreed with me in this, so that I have no doubt that he will act liberally. I told him that the Body of the Church, as the New Ch: at Workington, must be free sittings.

Now my dear Sir, can the Church be built by us, if the Radicals and Ultras of C— refuse their aid, which I fear many of them may ? If it can it will be a great and good work, and all will be well. It would have grieved you to hear the account of the emptiness of the old Church, as I had it, and it was painful also to hear the present Incumbent spoken of in respect to his Ministry as I did.

In a few days I shall have an interview with Mr [St]anger, but I do not expect that we can come to any terms. Pray let me have an answer at your earliest convenience that I may know whether the hope you held out can be fulfilled, in order that I may communicate with the Individual who is so well disposed towards the Place.

With our united affectionate remembrances to yourself and Miss Watson; I remain my d^r Sir

faithfully yours

Wm Wordsworth

Address: Joshua Watson Esqre, Park Street, Westminster.

Our Invalids are better—

MS.   *1178. W. W. to Joshua Watson*

Rydal Mount Oct^{br} 5th [1836]

My dear Sir

Your letter has rather discouraged my hope of succeeding in the way I mentioned to you, so that I was glad to avail myself of an opportunity for a second interview, which I had with Mr Stanger yesterday. The result is, that if my Friend who offered to endow the Church provided it could be built, does not disapprove, or feel hurt, I am disposed to co-operate with Mr Stanger, if sanctioned in such a measure by your judgment. As I found that so large a sum, as will appear by the enclosed was likely to be at Mr S—'s disposal I thought it expedient that I should give way to him, and the more so, because I am persuaded, that in so doing those Inhabitants of Cockermouth who have shewed the most favorable dispositions, would be best pleased; I wish I were at liberty to treat this part of the subject more openly.

Finding that I could not induce Mr S. to join in my plan beyond a small contribution towards erecting the Church, and feeling very loth to let so large a sum as he offers be lost towards the Place, I proposed—first stipulating for time to consult my friends—to aid him to the utmost with such subscriptions as I could raise—but upon these conditions. 1st that the Trustees of Mr Simeon[1] should have nothing to do with the concern, and

---

[1] Charles Simeon, 1759–1836, was the acknowledged leader of Evangelical Churchmen—in 1797 he had been one of the founders of the Church Missionary Society, and he was a staunch supporter of the British and Foreign Bible Society. He founded a body of Trustees for acquiring Church patronage and administering it according to his own views. Stanger was a Simeonite; W. W. and Watson were of the High Church party.

2d^{ly} that in preference to Elective trustees of any kind, the Patronage sh^d be lodged in one Individual and that I had no objection to that Individual being himself on account of the large sum he was prepared to advance. He replied, that tho' very unwilling to undertake the responsibility of Presenting, yet rather than lose my cooperation he would do so—consenting further, for, for this I stipulated, that in case of his death the Patronage as far as was in his power, should be preserved in one hand. He then said, if he survived his Brother, it should pass to him—or otherwise, he should leave it to some one who, to the best of his judgment—would act towards the trust conscientiously.

Now my dear Sir, I am well aware that this plan cannot be carried into effect without the sacrifice of the first presentation at least—being under the *influence* not to say dictation, of the Simeonites. But is not this better much, than that the Church should not be built at all, where it is so deplorably needed? Will you then assist cordially in this project? And give me the benefit of your directions how to proceed?

I remain dear Sir

faithfully y^{rs}

Wm Wordsworth

N.B. I ought to say that Mr S. is a Conservative in politics—so there is no fear of a Radical being appointed.

MS.   **1179. W. W. to Edward Moxon**

Octr 10th [1836]

My dear Sir

The Box has just arrived, and I have only time to thank you cordially and say a very few words.

The Print as far as we can judge seems excellently engraved[1]—but for my own part I cannot but think, (wishing it may be liked by others) that in following the plan of giving the head and part of the Person, independent of the reclining attitude, an air

[1] A steel engraving by Watt of a portrait by Pickersgill, designed for the frontispiece of the 1836–7 ed. of the *Poems.*

of feebleness is spread thro' the whole; which is the more felt
from a fault in the original Picture, of a weakness of expression
about the upper lip.

I shall write to Mr Judkin as soon as I can command a
moment's time—but I have been sadly hampered by some
corrections of minor import which have taken up my time in a
way which I cannot excuse myself for. I am at this moment far
from well in consequence.

You say you have sent the *remainder* of the Sheets—but are
you aware that what you before sent only commence at the
145th Page—so that you must kindly forward those which pre-
cede in order to hunt out errors—Mrs W. says why did Mr
Moxon tear the heads from the worthies whose autographs are
sent me for a sample?

Messrs Masterman's Bank is the one in connection with Wake-
fields, of Kendal and who will receive on my account with that
Bank, what you have to transmit to me.

Ever dear Sir with our united best regard to you and yours

Wm Wordsworth

We will be much obliged by your having a doz. more prints
struck off for us.

Address: Edward Moxon Esqre, Dover St.

MS.   **1180. W. W. to Joshua Watson**

Rydal Mt Octr 17th [1836]

My dear Friend

I will plague you no further, than merely to ask you, If I can
get a Church at Cockermouth endowed—and by my own efforts
raise perhaps £6 or 700 towards its erection—can you aid me
from the Societies etc—to complete the Building?—When I
have an answer to this, I must either determine to give up the
scheme altogether to Mr S—, who is prepared to build in union
with the People of C – who generally entertain his views, or,
we must proceed independant of him; in which case he will apply
his money to the building a Chapel, having as he told me,

another neighbouring Place in view. So that you see the £3 or 4000, which he has at command, *is* to go forth to propagate Simeonism, and in a worse shape than I had brought him to consent to. Therefore, you will perceive, that there was policy in my attempt to draw him from investing Patronage in the Trustees of Mr S.

It grieves me to ask for an early reply knowing how valuable your time is, but I am anxious to give my final answer to Mr S.

ever faithfully
your obliged
Wm Wordsworth

Pray be so good as to tell how your health is, and Miss Watson's.—This is sent through the twopenny post—to save time.—

MS.   *1181. W. W. to Edward Moxon*

Octr 20th 1836

My dear Sir,

I have looked over the 1ˢᵗ Vol, and with the exception of the one erratum in the table of Contents—and one Stanza in which there are two gross errors, which by the bye arose out of a correction without a revise, I have no blunders to lay to the charge of the Printers—though there is one serious one for which I am myself accountable. I have enclosed by this Post a list of Errata and emendations for Mr Evans.[1]

The book I think executed in a way which will do the Printers and yourself credit—As to the Portrait I am still of opinion, in which others concur, that the attitude has an air of decrepitude in consequence of the whole Person not being given—it appears to me to be beautifully engraved; and pray tell the Artist with my compliments that I think so.

I have had such strong opinions given respecting the disadvantages the Ed. will labour under in not having one illustration at least for each Vol. that I regret much for your sake that

---

[1] Printer, of the firm Bradbury and Evans.

an arrangement was not made between us, with a proper sacrifice on my part, to include this. It is now I fear too late. I hope however that the apprehensions which have led me to speak in this way may prove groundless.

I wish Copies to be sent in my name *before* publication, as the vols come out to

Mr Stephen, Colonial Office
Sir Ben Brodie Bart, or rather to Lady B.
Mr Quillinan
Mr Judkin and to my nephew J. W. who will call for it, likewise to Sir Charles Bell, Edinburgh and to Mr Montgomery, Sheffield.

_____

We hope Mrs Moxon and your baby are well—and dear Miss Lamb, to whom always remember us with love. Thanks for the parcels you have sent us.

Before you pay any money for me into the Bank, let me beg you to make out my account which has been of long standing, and settle it.

With our united regards to you and yours,

> I remain sincerely yours
> Wm Wordsworth

Wise[1]   ## 1182. *W. W. to T. J. Judkin*

Oct. 20. 1836.

. . . I am truly sensible of your kind offer to assist in illustrating my Poems, I regret that this was not thought of when we met in Town, and something might have been contrived for our Mutual satisfaction—It is now too late for the present edition. . . . I have desired Mr Moxon to send you my volumes as they come out. If you think it worth while to compare the pieces entitled 'Evening Walk', 'Descriptive Sketches', and 'The Waggoner', you will find I have made very considerable alterations, which I trust will be found to be improvements—at all events they ought to be so, for they cost me much labour.

[1] Quoted in *Two Lake Poets, a Catalogue*, &c., by T. J. Wise, 1927.

MS.
K(—)[1]

1183. W. W. to James Stephen

My dear Sir   Rydal Mount October 24th 1836.

I am sorry for the Printers carelessness by which you were left in doubt as to the destination of the Pacquet. I reckon it one of the happinesses of my life to have had few secrets either of my own or of others to take care of—and should such another instance of neglect occur, you need not scruple to be as bold as you have been. And now let me thank you gravely and cordially for the service you have done me in press-reading the proofs of this Publication. We have already got through 2 Volumes and part of a third. I have directed Mr Moxon to send them to you in succession, as they come out. I am sorry to say that the first Volume has several Mistakes, for which I am answerable mainly, having trusted to the Printer, in several cases where alterations were made in the proofs, without having a revise sent down. The Excursion (the last of the six volumes) is one of those already printed, and will be sent shortly for your kind acceptance; in this I hope few errors will be found, but I have not seen it yet.

May I beg that some one about you would take the trouble of correcting in your Copy the Errata with a Pen, at least the most important of them.

Repeating my thanks for this kind service, I remain
My dear Sir
faithfully
Your much obliged
Wm. Wordsworth

MS.
K(—)

1184. W. W. to Edward Moxon

My dear Sir,   [late Oct. 1836][2]

I was looking somewhat anxiously for your letter which I rec^d this morning. I entirely concur with you in all you say ;

¹ K. heads this letter 'To Correspondent Unknown'. James Stephen (1789–1859), a friend of Sir Henry Taylor, and his colleague at the Colonial Office. In 1834 he became Colonial Under-Secretary, and was said by Taylor to rule the Colonial Empire. He took a great interest in the Slavery question and prepared the measure passed in 1833. He contributed to the *Ed. Rev.* and was greatly interested in literature. In 1849 he became Regius Professor of History at Cambridge.

² Undated, but clearly written soon after letter of Oct. 20.

and if you can get the 3000 disposed of in a reasonable time, we can try our fortune with illustrations. Both Mr Hone and Mr Judkin have [?]¹ drawings gratis—an artist whom I met with the other day promised to send me a finished drawing from a sketch which he had made of the Valley in which I have placed the Solitary and which would be an appropriate ornament for the Excursion. I have no doubt but that I could procure drawings from various artists, so that the expense would be confined to engraving and striking off—Many years ago I mentioned to Messrs Longman a scheme of printing in one Volume, for the purpose you advert to, but they thought it would leave so little profit to me, that it would be negligible. I did not press the matter upon them, tho' I was unconvinced.

We have not yet seen the Excursion, but when it reaches us—which it may do along with the other Volumes, 12 copies, (and the sooner the better) it shall be carefully looked over—and the errata made out.

I am convinced that if any alterations be made in the proofs, which one is tempted often to make, it is impossible to have a book correctly printed without a revise. There are now and then blunders, in rhyme and verse and metre which are inexcusable—some of which however, are not always to be ascribed to the Printer, but arise from neglect on our part (when a change has been made) to erase the old text.

Let the copy of the Excursion, which you send down to have the errata made out, be bound up in cloth before it comes, and pray send also a print to bind up with the sheets of the first Volume, which was sent for the same purpose.

I am contented that my small account should remain unsettled as you wish, rather than disturb the generous arrangement you have made—and I sincerely wish that the bargain may be as advantageous to you as it is to myself, compared to any of my previous ones ; and independent of this consideration, it is a great pleasure to be thus connected with you. With best regards to Mrs M. in which Mrs W. and my Daughter join believe me

sincerely yours

Wm Wordsworth

¹ Word quite illegible. K. reads 'offered' which gives a possible sense, but is certainly *not* what is written.

Hutchins.
K. **1185. W. W. to John Kenyon**

[late Autumn 1836.]

My dear Mr Kenyon,

I won't waste time in thanks, having told you heretofore thro' Mr Moxon how much I was obliged by your letter.

You ask how the Muses came to say, 'weep in the public roads *alone.*'[1] Did you ever attend an execution? Funerals, alas! we have all attended, and most of us must have seen then weeping in the public roads on one or both of these occasions.

I was a witness to a sight of this kind the other day in the Streets of Kendal, where male mourners were following a Body to the grave in tears. But for my own part, notwithstanding what has here been said in verse, I never in my whole life saw a man weep *alone* in the roads; but a friend of mine *did* see this poor man weeping *alone*, with the Lamb, the last of his flock, in his arms. I hope you are satisfied, and willing that the verse should stand as I have written it.

Dear Mrs Kenyon was right as to the *bare*—the contradiction is in the *words* only—bare, as not being covered with smoke or vapour;—clothed, as being attired in the beams of the morning. Tell me if you approve of the following alteration, which is the best I can do for the amendment of the fault.

> The city now doth on her forehead wear
> The glorious crown of morning; silent, bare,
> Ships, towers, etc.[2]

It was in the English tongue[3]—you say 'is not this, in an English poem, superfluous?' Surely here is an oversight on your part; whether the poem were in English, or French, or Greek is a matter wholly indifferent as to the expression I have used. She came from afar. The Emigrant Mother came from France, as is told in that other Poem, but I do not think it necessary to say, in this latter case, that her griefs found utterance in French —only that I have put them into verse. But in the instance to which you object it was expedient to specify, that—though she

---

[1] *The Last of the Flock*, Oxf. W., p. 114.
[2] Oxf. W., p. 269. The alteration was, fortunately, not adopted.
[3] 'Her eyes are wild', l. 10, Oxf. W., p. 144.

came from far, English was her native tongue—which shows her either to be of these Islands, or a North American. On the latter supposition, while the distance removes her from us, the fact of her speaking our language brings us at once into close sympathy with her.

As to the *Old forest of civility*,[1] you are, I fear, right; I say *fear*, because I may have much trouble in correcting the passage. I had no particular allusion in my mind; the line before spoke of the *citadels of truth*, and the Forest was intended, in like manner, as a metaphor to express those usages and habits of civilization, which from their antiquity may be compared to a forest whose origin is unknown.

I *do* rejoice at my change of plan: two or three days ago I heard at Lowther that Lady Westmorland had just been stopped at Pavia, on her way to Rome, in consequence of the Cholera. I have had a great deal of dry and wearisome labour, of which I do not repent, however, in preparing my Poems for the new Edition, especially those which were among my first attempts.

I hear from many quarters of the impression which my writings are making, both at home and abroad, and to an old man it would be discreditable not to be gratified with such intelligence; because it is not the language of praise for pleasure bestowed, but of gratitude for moral and intellectual improvement received. Do not suppose, however, that I am not prepared for the language of censure and discouragement from many quarters. I hear of that also occasionally, and should be sorry were it otherwise; for I should then be sure that the igneus vigor and cælestis origo did not belong to me, but that I was of the world, worldly, and of the earth, earthy—but too much of this. I trust that, if I am to go to the Continent, I shall see you in passing thro' London.

My Church is, after all, likely to be built and endowed, notwithstanding you, one of the most valued of my friends, will not assist me. But I know that half a finger's breadth, if it be near

---

[1] *Thanksgiving*, Ode, ll. 108, 109 (Oxf. W., p. 330). The 'old forest' was altered to 'fair gardens'. J. K.'s objection had been that 'the two words "forest" and "civility"—both in derivation and in their actual usage—contradict each other.'

enough to the eye, will blind. Mrs Wordsworth says O the impudent man! To-morrow we are to have a Chapel conse-crated within less than 3 miles of this place; there is no situation out of the Alps, nor among them, more beautiful than that where this building is placed. Mrs Wordsworth and I walked thither this afternoon. You know the River Brathay—the Chapel stands upon a rocky knoll above it, and commands a view of the stream to Langdale Pikes, which this afternoon were white with snow, as was also nearly half the mountainside below them. The meadows were as green as the after-grass could make them, and the woods in the full foliage of many-coloured Autumn. I wish you had been with us, and I am sure you would have subscribed for a peal of bells, that their harmony might be wafted up and down the river. How glad we were that we were not dissenters—likewise that we were true Conservatives.

We are something better at home—at least we hope so. Why did you not mention your Brother—we are always glad to hear of him.

Affectionately yours,

Wm. Wordsworth.

MS.   *1186. W. W. to Henry Taylor*

Rydal Mount Nov. 4th [1836]

My dear Mr Taylor

I have been roving about or your letter would have been earlier noticed. The enclosed which I hope it will be convenient to you to get franked if you do not happen to learn that Sir G. Beaumont is at Lambeth Palace, is upon the subject. For your sake and other friends I wish Sir G. B. would entrust the Bust to Chauntry[1]—and in some degree I wish it for my own—since I have seen the print designed for the new edition of my poems. It is well engraved but partly owing to a fault about the upper lip, and still more to its having preserved the inclination of the body (natural in a recumbent attitude) without an arm to

---

[1] Presumably for engraving: the bust of W., which was executed by Chantrey for Sir G. B. (sen.) was generally considered the most impressive likeness of the poet.

explain it or account for it, the whole has an air of feebleness and decrepitude which I hope is not yet authorized by the subject. It was an unfortunate suggestion from Mr Rogers that the portrait should be given in this half sort of way.

I am glad that you are about to see Miss Fenwick again in London, and rejoice in that re-establishment of her health which allows her to quit her country home. She will be glad that we think Dora a good deal better. She moves about pretty freely in the house, and walks out, or rides a little almost every day. My poor sister is no worse. I have thought a hundred times of writing to Miss Fenwick. But it seemed I had so much to say that it ended in a feeling that I could say nothing.

Ever faithfully yours
W. Wordsworth

The pleasure of being with Miss Fenwick and you during my short stay in London will be one of my great inducements to leave home. My intention is to set out from Rydal Mount towards the end of February. W. W.

MS.   *1187. W. W. to C. W.*

Novr 16, 1836

My dear Brother,

My Friend Lady Frederic Bentinck, when I saw her lately, mentioned an engraved Portrait, in the possession of Mr Roper, who inherited through Lady Sunderland, Mr Malone's property. Mr R— is desirous to have some explanation of this portrait, and I observed to Lord S— that from your minute acquaintance with those times, I thought it not unlikely that you would be able to throw some light upon it. If you can do so, I shall be glad to hear from you upon the subject at your perfect leisure, but that I fear never comes,—at all events at your convenience.

I have just received a Letter from Mr John Ellis, upon the subject of his political projects in connection with the Borough of Cambridge, and requesting my interest in his behalf, upon the ground of our coincident opinions. I wrote to him in answer, that having received some time since a circular Letter from the

Board of Stamps forbidding the Distributors to interfere in Elections, upon pain of their severest displeasure, and informing us that certain functionaries had been superseded on account of interference, I must decline meddling and could only wish him well which I heartily did.

Now as Mr Ellis has his fortune to make in the world, I have to beg that, as he tells me he has called upon you, you would not be a jot the less guarded with him on account of any knowledge which you may suppose I have had of him. He came down into this country with Henry Curwen on a visit to the Island, he then called upon me; he also called upon me in London, and I dined at his House; he has been a week in my Son John's house at Brigham, and passed an evening in mine, a few weeks ago. Upon all these occasions he invariably maintained conservative opinions, and at his own house in particular in opposition to some of his Guests who held the contrary. But my knowledge of him extends no further; he is of a gentleman's family of the West, his Brother an Ultra Radical and Candidate, as he told me in his Letter, for one of the divisions of Cornwall. Mr Ellis is of gentlemanly manners as you would see, and I believe ready and ingenious both with tongue and pen.—

You would hear of Wm's disappointment,[1] nothing could be more kind than Mr Frank Lloyd and all his connections were to Wm. and I am not sorry that he made the attempt, though it was of course attended with expense—He made two journeys to Birmg.

I am sadly hampered about Cockermouth Church. Lord Lonsdale is in the best disposition, and would write to Lord Egremont, but I cannot go forward, Mr Fawcett, the Minister of Cockermouth, having declined as Mr Wood informed me, to make the official Returns, indispensible for Mr Watson, before he can give an assurance of what may be expected from the Societies. How would you advise me to proceed, in order to procure these returns. The Bp of Chester wrote sometime since to the Secretary and he to Mr F, but the returns have not been made.

---

[1] He was a candidate for the post of Secretary to the Birmingham and Derby Railway.

Unless something considerable can be had from the societies, I am afraid the thing will fall into the hands of Mr Stanger and the Simeonites and my Friends and I will be obliged to withdraw altogether except for my own Individual trifling sub^n—which I must give to Mr Stanger he having promised me a small contribution if he were to have no further interest in the Concern.

Love to all. Dora is better though still suffering much from her side—Sister no worse—

ever most affectionately yours

Wm Wordsworth

We want to hear of our Nephews'—as well as of your own health.

Address: The Rev Dr Wordsworth, Trinity College, Cambridge.

K.   *1188. W. W. to Thomas Noon Talfourd*

Rydal Mount, November 28, [1836.]

My dear Mr Talfourd,

Yesterday brought me the second edition of your drama,[1] together with your very friendly note. Part of the play was read aloud last evening and I finished it this morning. . . . You have most ably fulfilled your own purpose, and your poem is a distinguished contribution to English literature. I reserve the sonnets as a *bonne bouche* for to-morrow. But I must tell you that Mrs Wordsworth read me the second preface, which is written with much elegance of style and a graceful modesty. I cannot help catching at the hope that, in the evening of life, you may realize those anticipations which you throw out. Chaucer's and Milton's great works were composed when they were far advanced in life. So, in times nearer our own, were Dryden's and Cowper's; and mankind has ever been fond of cherishing the belief that Homer's thunder and lightning were kept up when he was an old man and blind. Nor is it unworthy of notice that the leading interest attached to the name of Ossian is connected with gray hairs, infirmity, and privation.

---

[1] *Ion*, first published in 1836, but privately printed in two previous editions, those of 1835 and 1836.

God bless you! I have not mentioned Lamb's epitaph, having said all I have to say on that subject to Mr Moxon and Mr Robinson. Let me, however, be excused for adding that I was sorry to see the italics at the close of the printed copy sent me down to-day. Mrs Wordsworth takes to them all,[1] except those in the last line. That upon the word 'her' is the only one I approve of, or wish to have retained.

Ever faithfully and affectionately yours,

Wm. Wordsworth.

K. **1189. W. W. to James Montgomery**

[Rydal Mount, Nov. 30, 1836.]

My dear Friend,

Through the kindness of Mr Younge your volumes, and the little book belonging to my daughter,[2] which you have been so good as to enrich with a most valuable contribution, were received yesterday at Rydal Mount. For these tokens of your regard, and for the accompanying letter, accept our joint thanks. I can assure you with truth that from the time I first read your *Wanderer of Switzerland,* with the little pieces annexed, I have felt a lively interest in your destiny as a poet; and though much out of the way of new books, I have become acquainted with your works, and with increasing pleasure, as they successively appeared. It might be presumptuous in me were I to attempt to define what I hope belongs to us in common; but I cannot deny myself the satisfaction of expressing a firm belief that neither morality nor religion can have suffered from our writings; and with respect to *yours* I know that both have been greatly benefited by them. Without convictions of this kind all the rest must, in the latter days of an author's life, appear to him worse than vanity. My publisher has been directed to forward to you (I suppose it will be done through Messrs Longmans) the first volume of my new edition, and the others as they successively

---

[1] So K, but a word, such as 'exception', has probably dropped out after 'takes'.

[2] An album, which contained lines by Wordsworth, Coleridge, Southey, Scott, Wilson, De Quincey, Campbell, &c. See *Memoirs of James Montgomery* by John Holland and James Everett (1854).—K.

appear. As the book could not be conveniently sent to you through my hands, I have ventured to write a few lines upon a slip of paper to be attached to it,[1] which I trust will give you a pleasure akin to what I received from the lines written by your own hand on the fly-leaf of your first volume. With earnest wishes that time may deal gently with you as life declines, and that hopes may brighten and faith grow firmer as you draw nearer the end of your earthly course, I remain, my dear sir,

Faithfully yours,
W. Wordsworth.

MS.　　　*1190. W. W. to Joshua Watson*

Dec. 2 [1836]

My dear Friend

I have had a great deal of mortification about Cockermouth Ch: When I passed thro' the place some little time ago, I learned from Mr Wood that Mr Fawcett had declined to send the official returns, as requested by the Bp thro' his Secretary—I was so much hurt at this, that I did not like to trust myself with a conversation with Mr F.—nor did chuse to take upon myself to write to the Bp. I simply applied to Mr Stanger, with a request that if he were personally acquainted with Mr F. and had no objection to speak to him upon the subject—that he would try to induce him to make the returns. You may think this was injudicious—but indirectly I had heard from Mr Stanger and having occasion to write to him—I thought it might be as well to use that mode of coming at our object. I have however heard no more of him.

I also mentioned the subject, being unwilling so often to trouble you, to Dr Wordsworth, and he tells me that I must apply to you. I hope that in so doing I do not press too much upon your health, which was in so delicate a state, when I last had the pleasure of being with you.

---

[1] The following were the lines: 'In admiration of genius, and as a grateful token of profound respect for the pure and sacred uses to which that genius has been devoted, these volumes are offered to James Montgomery by his sincere friend, William Wordsworth. Rydal Mount, Nov. 30, 1836.'—K.

I am happy to say that Lord Lonsdale is in the best possible disposition for having the thing done, and for keeping it out of the hands of the Party.

I think it may not be superfluous to send you the accompanying papers rec^d from Mr Wood.

Hoping that yourself and Miss Watson bear this unfavourable season without injury to your health. My Sister remains in her usual uncomfortable state—but you will both be glad to hear that my daughter is gradually improving—Mrs W. and myself well and we all unite in affectionate regards

ever faithfully yours
Wm Wordsworth

Address: Joshua Watson Esqre

MS.   **1191. W. W. to Henry Taylor**

Rydal Mount Dec. 19 [1836]

My dear Sir,

I have received your interesting communication,[1] and cannot apply to the Marshalls as you suggest—because I have, more than once, heard Mr Marshall express his disapprobation of attempts to raise people from their station in this way. The whole family are, according to their own views, charitable and generous—and even munificent. But Mr Marshall, as I know, having once contributed to like patronage, discontinued his subscription, from a belief that he was not acting judiciously, tho' the young man fully justified the expectations of those who took him up from a very low condition.

Mr Bolton, my neighbour, is one of the most generous of men—but as he is upwards of 80 years of age and his powers of duly

---

[1] On Dec. 12 H. T. had sent to W. 'an account of a poetical vagabond for whom Mr Gladstone and I are raising a subscription to send him to college', and asked him to put the case before Mr Marshall and Lord Lonsdale. A penniless youth of 18, Henry Thompson of Oakham, had stopped Gladstone on Constitution Hill, and asked for money wherewith to publish his poems. Both Gladstone and H. T. thought well of his verse, but felt that he would be better served by giving him the chance of some further education. G. found him a temporary post as usher at a school in Liverpool, and with H. T. raised money to send him to Magdalen Hall, Oxford, G. undertaking to be responsible for any deficiency in the sum subscribed.

considering any point that may be laid before him somewhat impaired, I feel some little reluctance in applying to him as I have hitherto done, on the subject of Cockermouth Church, never having mentioned it to him. But fortunately I know he has a very high opinion of Mr Gladstone, which will encourage me to send the papers to him, as I shall do by this day's post. Had your letter reached me a few days ago while I was visiting at Lowther, Levens and elsewhere in this neighbourhood, I might have done something by conversation which I do not like to introduce by letter.

There is a class, I hope I do not deceive myself in thinking I am worthy of being reckoned one of them, whose outgoings in this line fully keep pace with their incomings, be they what they may; and on this account I must confine myself to so small an anonymous contribution as £3—fearing that if my name were attached it might prevent others out of delicacy from giving as much as they would else have done. The particulars of this case upon the whole seem promising—but weak eyes and ill health are spoken of—and Mr G. and you must be aware that one of the evils to be apprehended in projects of this sort is that the student may destroy his health by over-application from an anxious desire to prove himself worthy of what has been done for him. One sees the result in far less urgent cases. Travellers sent out at the expense of Societies, or of Governments, perish in far greater numbers than those whose expenses are met by their own means. From my connection with the University I have seen a good deal of these experiments, but though several to my knowledge have failed, the balance has been upon the whole decidedly in favor of such as have come under my notice.

The Cholera frightens me, but say to Miss Fenwick, with our joint love (and thanks from Mrs W. for her last kind letter) that under any circumstances I trust I shall see her, either in London or at her own home, in the course of the spring. Dora, thank God, is so much better that she talks confidently of being able to go to Leamington in February—and after conducting her thither, if I do not go to Italy, I am under engagement to pay a few visits in Warwickshire and Leicestershire and shall extend my journey either to London or Somersetshire as may best suit

Miss F.'s arrangements. Should I find her in Town, would it be possible to tempt her back with me into the North? but this is castle-building.

Farewell—remember me kindly to Spedding and Mr Gladstone and other friends and believe me faithfully yours,

W. Wordsworth

I have heard nothing more of the bust. Chauntry would be your best informant. I have no doubt Sir G. Beaumont would apply to him, as stated in his letters, which I forwarded to you. I regret much that Miss Fenwick is not quite pleased with your portrait. The expression she complains of was certainly there when I saw it.

MS. **1192. W. W. to Henry Taylor**

[late Dec. 1836][1]

My dear Sir,

I enclose the reply which I have just received from Sir G. Beaumont upon the application for the Bust. I am afraid it will not be practicable upon the plan proposed—but I hope Sir F. Chantrey will be able to remove Sir George's apprehensions of injury to the Bust.

We have not heard from Keswick for a week—before that time our accounts of poor Mrs Southey were not more unfavorable than when her husband was at home.

We should be glad to hear good tidings of dear Miss Fenwick, who we surmise is in London by this time—and that you are enjoying the society of each other. With love to her from Mrs Wordsworth, very sincerely but in haste, Wm. Wordsworth.

MS. **1193. D. W. and M. W. to Jane Marshall**

Christmas Eve [1836]

(D. W. writes)

My dear good Friend,

My heart is too full for many words. May God comfort you

---

[1] The date of this letter is fixed as late in December by that one written to Taylor on Dec. 19 (q.v.). Southey was away from Keswick in the West country from Oct. 1836 to Feb. 1837.

under your heavy loss! and he *will* comfort you—all things here
below will speak to you of your dear Son's[1] goodness. I have had
a tremendous struggle. This morning, I trust, has brought the
last of it.

A thousand thanks for your kind presents. The Turkey will
be our Xmas day dinner—thank you for all, and may God bless
you and all yours.

Dorothy Wordsworth

How my heart yet beats at the sound of Christmas Day

(*M. W. writes*)

Your precious letter addressed to Dorothy—was felt by us all
—and to myself so touchingly, as a Mother, that it would be
unjust to you and to my own feelings to dwell upon the several
situations you placed before me, at the close of a letter—but
thoughts were raised, that, if it please God we should meet, will
revive in my mind; as does the animated countenance of your
now blessed Son, when I think of *your own* as first presented to
me—at the door of my Brother's farm-house in Yorkshire when
you called to inquire for your beloved friend.[2] The change that
took place, when I told you 'she was gone' will never be forgotten—the look is always like a visitation that I can call up.

Your letter dear friend with its enclosures I took to Dorothy
—she gave me *her* portion, to take care of, till she considered
what to do with it—The other £5 you have so kindly entrusted
to me, is most acceptable, and has anticipated a petition I meant
to make to you for a little assistance to a poor family whose
worthy head is now in the asylum at Lancaster—his wife and
5 children living in our village, meanwhile, have 4 shillings a
week allowed by the Parish, and she makes a couple of shillings
more by going out to wash—but the children are young—and
this, without aid, is a poor pittance. She is however well taken
care of, but as the family are not within the pale of the Rydal
Hall charity, I thought I might be authorized to ask for your
help—which you have supplied me with *unasked*—and so

---

[1] i.e. her second son John M., M.P. for Leeds.
[2] In September, 1802; *v. E.L.*, p. 310.

liberally as will be felt beyond this individual family. God bless you for it, and for all your kindness.

I take a greater liberty with you than common by forwarding *such* an untidy and I fear *illegible* letter, and must pray your forgiveness—writing with a Poet beside me ought not to be an excuse—tho'—as at this moment, he takes the pen, bad as it is, literally out of my hand. This reminds me of what *you* say of his *alterations*, or corrections. I must say that he never makes one that he does not *seem* to convince my understanding and judgment—but like you, not always my *feelings*—however we must give him credit for being right—and *we* can always cherish where we like, what we have loved and cling to—and hope that those to whom the Poems are new, may find a higher—I am sure not a *deeper*, pleasure from them than we have done.

Best love to Mr M. and every one from all. I feel deeply for dear Dora and her household—of Ellen we have not heard any late news—hope for good. Of the afflicted ones at Scarboro'—we shall be glad to hear when they are returned home. Alas! my first introduction will be to the widow—not to the happy wife of your beloved son!

Most aff^ly yours

M. Wordsworth

Does not this little uncouth letter remind you of one of D.'s youthful epistles? I mean in appearance.

Address: Mrs Marshall, Headingley, near Leeds.

MS.   **1194. *W. W. to Henry Taylor***

Rydal Mount Dec. 31 [1836]

My dear Mr Taylor,

My application to Mr Bolton in behalf of our young Poet has I am sorry to say proved unsuccessful. Mr B.'s answer being that owing to the innumerable distressed persons with whom he is in various ways connected—and to other calls for his money, he cannot feel himself justified in making advances for a stranger. Knowing how munificent and charitable he was, I ventured to ask him, but only on account of the respect which

I knew he entertained for Mr Gladstone. Circumstanced as I am amongst my other neighbours I have no hope of being useful on this occasion, which I assure you I regret much. Be so good as to advance the £3 for me which shall be repaid, either through Moxon, or when we next meet.

I hope that Miss Fenwick and you stand the severities of the season—with every good wish in the old-fashioned way to you both—in which my wife and daughter unite,

I remain, dear Mr Taylor, Faithfully yours

W. Wordsworth

Would it not be well that I should return the papers, to be used in some other quarter?

I hope you have good news of Mr and Mrs Taylor—Pray remember us respectfully to them.

_MS._ *1195. W. W. to Joshua Watson*

Rydal Mount Decr 31st, 1836

My dear Sir

Many thanks for your letter and for the kind interest and all the trouble you have taken and are prepared to take about Cockermouth Church.

Your communications have furnished me with an occasion to address Lord Lonsdale again on the subject, and as soon as I have his answer I shall know how to proceed—and then I shall write to you—meanwhile accept my best thanks.

It delights us, to learn that your valuable health is amended, and as you do not mention Miss Watson, we trust she is well.

We have had a long letter from Chris: to-day with the comfortable news that the Master of Trinity is particularly well— and that Charles takes kindly to his Profession—finding the labour easier and the pleasure more, than at first. My Daughter I am thankful to say is much better—my poor Sister struggling on as before—but without loss of strength. Perhaps you heard of the pains my Son Wm. took about a situation at Birmingham —they proved unsuccessful, further than that I believe he recommended himself in his Canvass—to many Persons—some of whom possibly may hereafter befriend him. You will be glad to hear that neither he nor I suffered by the great failure of the Forster's Bank at Carlisle—we had however a narrow escape.

The Ed: of my Poems now going thro' the Press, I hear is selling very well.

With our united kindest remembrances, and every good wish of the Season, which you feelingly call holy and happy, to you and Miss W. I remain my dear Sir your faithful and affectionate friend,

Wm Wordsworth

MS.
K(—) *1196. W. W. to Edward Moxon*

[late Dec. 1836]

Dear Mr Moxon,

Thanks for your letter. Notwithstanding my double responsibility at Carlisle (for my Son is my Subdistributor there) we have not suffered from the failures, tho' we had a narrow escape: and I assure you the state of the commercial world does not leave me free from anxiety—both with respect to my Office, and some other concerns. I hope you will be able to take care of yourself, for I apprehend the storm is coming.

Your account of the sale of the book is as favorable as I ventured to expect: being myself quite at ease in regard to the reception which writings, that have cost me so much labour, will in the end meet with, I can truly say that I have not the least anxiety concerning the fate of this Edition, further than that *you* may speedily be repaid what you have generously advanced to me. The labour I have bestowed in correcting the style of these poems now revised for the last time according to my best judgment no one can ever thank me for, as no one can estimate it. The annoyance of this sort of work is, that progress bears no proportion to pains, and that hours of labour are often entirely thrown away—ending in the passage being left, as I found it.

I hope that Mr Evans will comply with my request, to send clean sheets *as they are struck off*—along with the succeeding proofs—and if it were possible to do this so that an opportunity may be given to us to return readings perfectly correct before the stereotype plates are taken.—At all events, if the plan be adopted the errata may be sent *in time*—and perfectly correct.

You will remember I mentioned to you, by note, that I had been applied to by the Editor or Publisher of the Ch: of Eng. Mag: for permission to introduce the Ecclesiastical Sonnets into his Publication. In my hasty reply to this Gentleman I neglected to notice his obliging offer to send me his Mag., an omission for which I am sorry. Will you if you pass that way be kind enough to mention this, and add that I should be glad to receive it from him.

With our united regards to Mrs Moxon and your Sister, and with best wishes to yourself, believe me to remain, dear Mr M. sincerely yours

W. Wordsworth

The Pub^r of the Ch. of E. Mag: has an Agent (a bookseller) at Kendal by name Dawson, thro' him Mr Troughton of Ambleside receives copies, and the one intended for me might be sent thro' Mr D. in Mr Troughton's parcel. The parcel containing the 2 Vols: prepared for me may be sent to Messrs Whitaker, Ave Maria Lane—to be enclosed in Mr Troughton's parcel—to Ambleside.

MS. **1197. *W. W. to Edward Moxon***

Rydal Mount Jan^ry 14th 1837.

My dear Sir,

If you can procure for me a Copy of Dr Wordsworth's late Publication entitled 'Christian Institutes'[1] and at Rivingtons at the Trade Price I will thank you to procure it for a friend of mine.—It may be forwarded as I before directed—packages for me to be sent through the Kendal Month's Parcel from Whitaker's for Mr Troughton, Ambleside.—But it seems that there is some delay by this channel, for we have not *yet* received the 2^d Vol: of the new Edition. Pray mention what Rivington charges the Copy of Christian Institutes.

[1] *Christian Institutes*; a series of Discourses and Tracts selected from the writings of the most eminent Divines of the English Church. 4 vols., 1836.

[827]

They are getting rapidly through the 4th Vol:—but Mr Evans has not attended to my wish, by forwarding clean sheets *as quickly after they are struck off as convenient*—that I might collect the errata in time to make the stereotype plates as correct as we can. Let us have a line to say how you, Mrs M. and the Little ones stand this severe season—and with our united kind regards believe me sincerely yours

W. Wordsworth

MS.   ***1198. W. W. to Joshua Watson***

Rydal Mount Jan^{ry} 14th [1837]

My dear Friend

I enclose you a letter which I have received from Mr Stanger to which I shall reply by this day's post, and tell him of Lord Lonsdale's offer, and which, if I have any thing to do with the business, decides where the Patronage must rest. If, dear Sir, you have no objection to meet Mr S., and think there is the least probability of any good being done by your taking this trouble, a note from you, to the address he gives, would be answered I doubt not, by a call from him at any time you might propose, within the next 10 days.

I have not heard from Mr Wood since I sent him your dispatches.

With our united kindest regards to Miss W. believe me faithfully and aff^{ly} yours

Wm Wordsworth

MS.   ***1199. W. W. to S. C. Hall*** [1]

Rydal Mount Jan^{ry} 15th 1837

My dear Sir

Accept my thanks for your elegant present of the two volumes of the Book of Gems, which I received two days ago, and also for the very friendly letter that accompanied them. You speak

---

[1] Samuel Carter Hall (1800–89), editor of the *Art Journal*. In 1836 he brought out the first two vols. of *The Book of Gems; the poets and artists of Great Britain*. A third vol. followed in 1846.

feelingly of the pleasure which you and Mrs Hall had in seeing me some years ago—be assured that it was reciprocal, and nothing but overwhelming engagements, more than at my years I ought to have exposed myself to, could have prevented me seeking you out when I was in Town last Spring.

Being much engaged in a monthly race with the Press—in which a new Edition of my Poems has involved me, I have not had time for more than a glance at your part of the Volumes— but I must say how much I was pleased with your notice of our Westmorland Poet,[1] Langhorne—the Critique is very judicious, both as to his merits and his faults—I do not wonder that you are struck with his Poem of the Country Justice—You praise it, and with discrimination—but you might have said still more in its favour. As far as I know, it is the first Poem, unless perhaps Shenstone's Schoolmistress[2] be excepted, that fairly brought the Muse into the Company of common life, to which it comes nearer than Goldsmith, and upon which it looks with a tender and enlightened humanity—and with a charitable, (and being so) philosophical and poetical construction that is too rarely found in the works of Crabbe. It is not without many faults in style from which Crabbe's more austere judgment preserved him— but these are to me trifles in a work so original and touching.

You ask me to furnish you with a few notices of my life—an application to the same effect was lately made to me by a french Gentleman who had been engaged upon what he calls a 'long labor upon my works'—a translation I believe of many parts of them, accompanied with a commentary. My answer was, that my course of life had been altogether private, and that nothing could be more bare of entertainment or interest than a bio- graphical notice of me must prove if true. I referred him to Gagliani's [sic] Ed: which, as to the date and place of my birth, and the places of my education is correct—the date of my publications is easily procured—and beyond these I really see nothing that the world has to do with, in my life which has been

---

[1] John Langhorne, 1735–79. His *Country Justice* appeared in 1774–7. W. has elsewhere expressed his admiration for Langhorne.

[2] William Shenstone, 1714–63. His *Schoolmistress* was first published in 1737 (revised 1742).

so retired and uniform. Since the beginning of the year 1800 I have had a home either at my present residence or within two miles of it—tho', as appears from my writings, I have made excursions both on the Continent and on our own Island—and also that I have sometimes sojourned in Leicestershire.

With my cordial regards to Mrs Hall and every good wish to both of you whom I have often thought of with sincere esteem believe me to be truly yours Wm Wordsworth.

Address: S. C. Hall Esq re, Elm Grove, Kensington Gravel Pits.

K.   *1200. W. W. to R. Shelton Mackenzie* [1]

Rydal Mount, Jan. 24, 1837.

. . . If there be in America such a demand for English literature as your information respecting the recent edition of my poems implies, is it not reasonable that English authors should have some compensations in the way of copyright in that country, particularly as American authors have that privilege in England? . . . In a day or two the printing of the last volume of the edition of my poems now going through the press will be commenced. . . .

MS.   *1201. W. W. to Edward Moxon*
K(—)
Rydal Mount Jan y 28 th [1837]
My dear Mr Moxon,

I have rec d your letter this morning along with 2 Proofs bringing the 4 th Vol to page 336. These two, with *one* on Monday, are all I have had this week—Something less than 2 sheets more will, I expect, conclude the volume. I regret that the Memoir (making part of the Notes to this Volume) as it has been very much read, was not printed in larger type, the same as the Essay on

---

[1] Robert Shelton Mackenzie (1809–80), author and journalist; in 1833 editor of the *Liverpool Journal*, from 1834 to 1851 correspondent of the *New York Evening Star*. In 1843 he published *Titian*, a 3 vol. novel, in 1854 edited the 5 vol. ed. of *Noctes Ambrosianae*, in 1870 and 1871 wrote the lives of Dickens and Scott.

Epitaphs, at the close of the Excursion. But Mr Evans is in no fault, as I forgot to give directions to that effect. The Printer has already been furnished with nearly two thirds of the Copy for the 5th Volume, so that he can have no excuse, if he is not punctual.

I will tell you at once about the new pieces which this Vol: will contain; they are inaccurately stated in the 1st Vol:. One of the Political Sonnets is now *first printed* viz. 'What if our numbers barely could defy.'[1] In the Miscellaneous Sonnets is the one you have noticed, and in Eccl. Sonnets is one upon the Norman Conquest, beginning 'Coldly we spake the Saxons overpowered'.[2] In the same Volume is a short Poem beginning 'O life without the chequered scene'[3] of which the second Stanza is new, the first being taken from one in the same class, so that together they make an add¹ piece. A new Stanza, or rather additions to the amount of a new Stanza in the 3 Cottage Girls,[4] in the 5th Volume, I have added from my MS, 2 Poems to the class of the Evening Voluntaries,[5] one 72 lines the other 50 odd, and also an additional Epitaph, from Chiabrera,[6] which with Lines to the memory of dear Charles Lamb,[7] and those upon the death of Hogg[8] make a considerable increase of new matter in this last volume—But after all, the value of this Ed. in the eyes of the judicious, as hereafter will be universally admitted, lies in the pains which has been taken in the revisal of so many of the old Poems, to the re-modelling, and often re-writing whole Paragraphs which you know have cost me great labour and I do not repent of it. In the Poems lately written I have had comparatively little trouble.

We are sorry to hear that you have been plagued with the Influenza in your house—thus far we have escaped it, for which we are thankful. My Sister is better rather than worse, and I rejoice to say that my Daughter's health is greatly improved (cannot you tell us something about Miss Lamb, we are always anxious to hear of her). We talk confidently of moving south-

¹ Oxf. W., p. 309.
² Ibid., p. 426.
³ Ibid., p. 337.
⁴ Ibid., p. 344.
⁵ Ibid., pp. 459–60.
⁶ Ibid., p. 573.
⁷ Ibid., p. 584.
⁸ Ibid., p. 586.

ward, if all be well, in the course of the latter half of next month. God bless you and yours and believe me faithfully and aff^tly.

your Friend
W. Wordsworth

How is dear Mr Rogers?, and his Sister?

I hope the Books have been regularly sent to the Printers, and especially to Mr Stephen,[1] to whom we have given so much trouble. Our parcel with the 2nd Vols. have not reached us. The whole parcel directed to my daughter rec^d through Mr Stephen to-day was intended to be sent by your next parcel—we did not mean to trouble Mr S. to frank it. Many thanks for your kindness in procuring for me the new Books at Trade price. The proofs concluding the 4 books have reached us *this* morning and will be returned by this night's Post. Jan 28

Address: Edward Moxon Esqre, 44 Dover Street.

MS.

1202. *W. W. to Joshua Watson*

Rydal Mt Feb 1st [1837][2]

My dear Sir

I thank you cordially for your last letter—I have not seen Mr Stanger yet but enclose an extract of a letter from him— also one from a letter from Mr Wood received this morning—for which I have been waiting, and also a rough draft of my own letter addressed to Lord Lonsdale this morning, which will put you in possession of my present notions.

I must however repeat to yourself directly, that it is the *hostility* of the people of C and their perverse notions of Church matters and not the withdrawal of the subscriptions which would deter me if Ld L. continued to support us—from proceeding in the matter, encouraged as I am by y^r last letter respecting what might be looked for from the Societies.

I hope you and Miss W. keep clear of the Influenza, as I am thankful to say we have hitherto done. Pray let me hear from you at your convenience.

With affec regards from all, ever faithfully yours

Wm Wordsworth

[1] *v.* Letter, Oct. 24, 1836, *supra.*
[2] For W. W. to H. C. R. Jan. 28, *v. C.R.*, p. 354.

MS.   *1203. W. W. to Lord Lonsdale*

Rydal Mount Feb^{ry} 1st 1837

My Lord

It is mortifying to me after having given your Lordship so much trouble upon the matter of the intended Church at Cockermouth, to be obliged to send you the enclosed. Mr Stanger's letter and the ext^t from Mr Watson's would have been forwarded earlier, but I thought it better to wait for Mr Wood's reply to mine, written immediately after your Lordship empowered me to make known, where I thought it would be serviceable, your very munificent offer. Mr Wood's letter came this m^g and notwithstanding the encouraging expectations of support from the Societies held out by Mr Watson probably you will be of opinion, when you have read Mr Wood's letter, that the project must be suspended or given up as far as yourself and your friends are concerned: for my own part, *my* present feeling is, that unless you differ from me, we should leave the people of Cockermouth to take their own course; and this opinion I entertain, not so much in consequence of what Mr Wood says of the withdrawal of such and such subscriptions from Persons on the spot—as from what he says of the decided hostility of the people, and their present temper upon Church matters.

I expect Mr Stanger to call in a day or two, when I shall strongly express my regret that your Lordship's proposal has been so unwort[hily] received ; and shall state that I await your final answer and also the opinion of Mr Watson, before I can give my own, but if he presses for my *present* opinion I shall say that neither my feelings nor my judgment will allow me to apply to my friends in any quarter ;—on the contrary, I shall return what sums I have rec^d upon personal application, and what has been offered me by Strangers—and shall take no active part in what his Party may be disposed to do : but that if they build and endow, and the patronage be lodged in the *Bishop of the Diocese* (tho' not holding a favorable opinion of such Bps as we are likely to have in future) I would give my own mite, so convinced am I of the spiritual destitution of the place.

I cannot conclude, my Lord, without expressing what a pleasing and deep sense I have both from general and personal considerations, of

(cetera desunt)

MS.   **1204. W. W. to Joshua Watson**

[p.m. 14 Feb. 1837][1]

My dear Sir

I enclose a Copy of Lord L's letter just received—Your own, for which I feel *very greatly* obliged to you, has come by the same post—

Lord L's letter is so express upon the point of the business being suspended, that I must have submit[t]ed to his judgment even if it had not been in concurrence with my own. Nevertheless I cannot but regret that his Lordship did not before mention to me his disinterested dispositions—as you will find them expressed in his letter. To day I shall write to Ld L. to let him know that I shall not proceed with the affair—but hope however that he will permit me to make known in certain quarters the manner in which he intended in all probability to have acted.

I am indeed much mortified—My Neighbours Lady Fleming and Mr Bolton have both promised subscriptions—and Mr Benson Harrison of Ambleside had increased his sub^n to £50— so that I had every prospect of effecting a good deal, thro' my own applications—and with your inestimable assistance the thing might have been done notwithstanding the withdrawal of the Cockermouth subscriptions. But neither on acc^t of my respect for L^d L, yourself, and the societies, which are so much indebted to your labours, nor above all, of my veneration and love for the genuine Ch: of England, can I attempt to force upon the Inh^{ts} of C. a Church of which the present generation at least, appears so unworthy.

Mr Stanger being disappointed in not finding his own Carriage at Ambleside, proceeded to Keswick by the Coach—so that I have not seen him—and must write to him to-day.

I hope to have a peep at you in passing thro' London—before

[1] For W. W. to H. C. R. Feb. 11, *v. C.R.*, p. 337.

three weeks are over. I should have thrown myself upon your hospitality, but not having seen my good Friend Miss Fenwick when in town last Spring—I have been many months pre-engaged to sleep under her roof. My intention is to accompany Dora to Leamington—and if all goes well with her, she will probably proceed to Hampstead in April or May—when I trust she may renew her acquaintance with yourself and Miss Watson —to whom and to you we all beg our united affectionate remembrances. My Sister is no worse, and we have all thus far kept clear of Influenza—except my Son Wm. who is now with us pining for a sphere of action more suitable to his age, than his scanty employment at Carlisle

Ever most faithfully

Your obliged friend

Wm Wordsworth

Address: Joshua Watson Esqre, 6 Park Street, Westminster.

MS.　*1205.　W. W. to R. Shelton Mackenzie*

My dear Sir　　　　　　　　Feb^{ry} 23^d [1837][1]

　Your newspaper and obliging Letter were duly received and would have been earlier acknowledged, but for reasons which I am sure you will deem sufficient, viz incessant occupation preparatory to my leaving home for some time, hurry in carrying through the Press the Edition of my Poems of which the last Volume is now done, and finally the influenza which, though it has not yet touched me, has sadly disabled most of my family—

　Your verses written under such affecting circumstances do great honour both to your heart and head, especially the former copy, which is indeed very touching. I thank you for sending them to me.—The American Editor has misled you in respect to the Elegiac poem of mine which you have republished. It is not a new thing, but has been several times reprinted among my collected works, and you will find it in the 4th Volume of the one now in course of publication, which shall be forwarded to you according to the received address as soon as I reach London, which I hope will be in ten days time at the latest.

　[1] For W. W. to H. C. R. Feb. 20, *v. C.R.*, p. 339.

Many thanks for your interesting information about american piracies. At Keswick the other day I saw at Mr Southey's the newspaper you mentioned in your Letter as containing the whole of the Souvenir. It is a curiosity. If I can contrive to see the Chancellor of the Exchequer for a few minutes at this busy time, I will mention the particular to him. I think I told you before, that he is interested in the general subject of international law upon this question. Connected with copyright is a point, to me of much more importance, viz the lengthening the term. When I was in Town last spring I took much pain in drawing the attention of leading Members of the House of Commons of all parties, to this portion of the question. Sergeant Talfourd means to make a motion upon the subject, which I hope will be entertained by the House as it ought to be. I am not without hope of proceeding this Spring to the Continent, and soon after I reach London, but as this is very uncertain, I don't like to talk about it, because these things get into the Newspapers. Believe me dear Sir, with much respect

sincerely yours

Wm. Wordsworth.

The Newspaper containing your first copy of verses was laid aside with the intention of having the lines transcribed into a book; unfortunately it has been torn up (I have this moment discovered) by one of the servants, and that part of it wh. contains your verses—To the line

'Wilt thou not hover round that home of wh. thou art the light' is preserved. Might I trouble you to have transcribed for us the remaining portion, it can be enclosed in the parcel along with the books—this accident has annoyed us much.

Address: R. Shelton Mackenzie Esqre, Liverpool.

MS.   **1206. *W. W. to D. W.***

Friday afternoon March 17 [1837][1]

My dear and very dear Sister,

Here I am waiting on the Dentist and have snatched a moment to tell you, that I am worn out with hurry.—You will

[1] *For* W. W. to H. C. R. March 2, *v. C.R.*, p. 343.

be surprized but I hope not grieved to hear that I am starting for a trip upon the Continent with Mr Robinson. Our passports are procured, our carriage bought and we shall embark at the Tower Stairs on Sunday morning for Calais. How I wish you could have gone with us; but I shall think of you everywhere, and often shall we talk of you. I have seen the Marshalls, who made a thousand enquiries after you,—Mrs and Sara Coleridge who did the same. It is a week today since I arrived here and I long to be gone for I am fairly worn off my feet with flying from one part of the town to the other, and so many things to do. We shall write from abroad at length, and I hope you will be amused. Tell dear Joanna that I have just got her letter to Mary giving an account of her proceedings.

I should have written to you before, but I had not a moment's time when I forwarded Mary's and Dora's Letter, which told you about every thing.

Farewell my dearest Sister and farewell my dear Joanna, and kindest remembrances to all the household James, Anne, Jane and Dorothy ; and mind that you all take care of yourselves and of each other.

Your most affectionate Brother
W. Wordsworth

1207. W. W. to Robert Southey

K.   Portugal Street, London, Saturday Morning,
[March 18, 1837.]

My dear Southey,

To-morrow morning Mr Robinson and I depart by the steam-boat for Calais. I cannot leave England without saying farewell to you, and the expression of good wishes and prayers for yourself, your dear daughters, their afflicted mother, your son, and all your family.

I have just been a week under the roof of our excellent friend,[1] and enjoying the company of Henry Taylor.

I will now transcribe a few words from a letter of Mr Quillinan

---

[1] Miss Fenwick.

addressed to Dora, upon which for Landor's sake I shall make
no comment. I received the letter this morning, and never heard
a word on the subject the passage treats of.

'What has Mr Wordsworth done to that Welsh furioso, that
Landor the Savage, to excite his madness to such ludicrous
malignity and grandiloquent vituperation? Madmen are sometimes very subtle in malice. What of his trying to blow up a
flame of discord between your father and Mr Southey! as if two
such long-tried friends could quarrel at this time of day about
the opinion that one or the other might or might not entertain
as to the value of the other's poetry. Byron or Landor might
give up an old friend for such a cause, but Southey is too loyal-
minded to believe that W. ever seriously disparaged his talents,
or to be very irate if he really had had the bad taste to do so.
I am sorry for Mr S., for Landor is also a very old and prized
friend of his. It is remarkable with respect to L. himself, that
he is the man of all the literary men of the day, Southey perhaps
excepted [he forgets Coleridge or speaks perhaps only of the
living,] to whose ability and classical attainments I have most
frequently heard your father bear testimony, and that in the
most decided manner. His wrath at Mr Wordsworth for having
plagiarized his lines about the shell[1] is capital fun.'

Thus far Mr Quillinan, and not a word of all this did I ever
see or hear of before. Farewell again, and again.

Ever yours,

W. W.

MS.   *1208. W. W. to Isabella Fenwick*

Paris. Friday March 24th [1837]

My dear Miss Fenwick

To spare your eyes and to save time I shall write journal-wise.
Arrived at Calais between nine and ten, after a passage sufficiently trying for those who are subject to sea-sickness. Poor
Mrs Moxon suffered greatly, I not at all; for I went to bed at
three o'clock and as advised by Mr Rogers closed my eyes. The

---

[1] *Excursion*, iv. 1132–47; cf. *Gebir*, i. 170–7.

next morning snow and chill blasts. Detained at [?] by the Customs House, pass-ports 'till half-past one. Snow fell so heavily that we could not get further than Samer and saw little of the country. Tuesday—Snow heavy on the ground which obliged us to take, in one place, an additional horse. The day and road improved and we passed frequently through a pleasing Country of hill and vale; Montreuil strikingly placed upon a moderate eminence, Abbeville with its Cathedral still more agreeably in a valley, but all this every body knows. The landscapes though often agreeable to look upon are almost every where disfigured more or less by long lines of threadpaper trees placed so near each other that they cannot but spindle as they do: Multitudes of *lopped* trees in lines by the way side and the *pollards* where ever seen *all* so close together as to have no tops worth looking at. The Peasantry appeared everywhere taller and stouter than those of England are in a great number of counties; say Cambridgeshire, Herefordshire all Wales and many other parts. At the close of the long war they had become a dwindled race, the Conscription having swept away the flower of the Youth. They seem now greatly improved in strength and stature. Slept at Grandevilliers. Wednesday—Severe frost, not a sign of Spring upon the trees; nevertheless small birds chirping among the bushes here and there, and one Lark heard warbling aloft and soaring as if he wished to get out of the frosty region through which we were travelling. We were much struck with the appearance of Beauvais and went into the Cathedral, many persons at Mass, ten women for one man, but men of all ages and a few, a *very* few boys. The day was bright and by walking up the hills often we contrived to keep ourselves warm and were much pleased. Went into the Cathedral of St Denis, which has been undergoing extensive repairs. I am no critic in Architecture of any Age or Country but I was much gratified with what I saw there. In a recess of one of the side Aisles some priests were engaged in some sort of service, one boy chanting but none of the people present—Candles were arranged thus $\therefore$ and one might almost have thought that they were objects of worship, and a book, a large one was turned to and fro incessantly with the stand upon which it was placed, all this is no doubt well understood by Roman Catholics, but to an ignorant spectator, it has an air of mummery, form without spirit,—walked on before the Carriage and almost reached Paris before it overtook me. The variety of voitures on the road, their shapes and the pompous names of some of the public vehicles amused me much, while the rays of the setting sun made the clouds of dust glitter around those that took either side of the pavement. The pace of some was furious. I observed several horses slip on the pavement and then rear, but neither driver nor passengers seemed to care a jot about the matter! I have nothing to say about Inns, etc., which would be useful to you, only don't embark at the Tower stairs in a *low-priced steam-boat*. We had no choice, being so anxious to get on; but 5 shillings is a price so low as to tempt many persons of coarse habits and mean condition. You or any other Lady would have been annoyed, though a great part of our fellow voyagers were very respectable. We paid 3£ for the freight of the carriage. It seems likely to answer our purpose well. Observe also not to bring with you any clothes which have the appearance of being *new*. The man who rummaged my portmanteau observed a plaid jacket, he turned it over to another, a tall person who would have been handsome if he had not taken so much snuff; he turned it over to a third, named the Inspector who decided that I must pay ten francs for the entry of this precious piece of raiment into the Kingdom of France. I was *horrified* and assured the Inspector in the best French I could command that the habit was made 10 months ago and that I had worn it several times, for half a day or so,— 'Monsieur votre parole est infiniment respectable cependant l'habit est neuf', and he pointed to the collar in proof that he had a right to contradict me though as politely as possible. Take care therefore that you dont get into the same sort of scrape and have your veracity put to the same sort of test. Best way perhaps is to write one's name if it be possible on some part of the garment. I got off however without paying the fine.—What shall I say of Paris? Many splendid edifices and some fine streets have been added since I first saw it at the close of the year —91. But I have had little feeling to spare for novelties, my heart and mind having been awakened everywhere to sad and strange recollections of what was then passing and of subsequent events which have either occurred in this vast city or which have flowed from it as their source. Sat. Morning—Yesterday, Friday, spent 7 hours nearly in rambling on foot up and down. The frost severe, the poor Swans in basins of water in the Thuilleries garden hiding their bills and as much of their necks as they could among the pure white feathers of their wings, one pair were standing upon the ice, another couched upon the wooden platform in front of their little huts or kennels —the lions of the Fountains spouted out vigourously their glittering waters in striking contrast with their long beards of icicles. Went to the Louvre. The old Pictures removed to make room for the annual exhibition of French art. We were sorry for this as the new things gave us but little pleasure, though not uninteresting as shewing the present state of French art which really does not seem to have much to boast of—The most impressive picture we noticed has for its subject Lord Strafford kneeling down on his way to his place of execution to receive the benediction of Archbishop Laud. This is said to be purchased by the Duke of Sutherland; he has done well—for the artist deserves encouragement. Here we met Lord Lyndhurst. Mr Robinson reintroduced me. I had once been two or three days with him at Lowther but he seemed neither to remember my name nor person making a cold formal bow as to a perfect stranger. Is it that when raised in the world we have eyes and minds only for those above us? or that his Lordship did not catch my name and had forgot my person? We then went to the Luxemburg, a number of French artists copying there pictures which had better be buried. Here remembrances pressed upon me, some tragical, and some my dear Mary and dear Sister (for this letter is intended also for you) of very different character. Do you recollect how pleased we were in the gardens of this palace to see the Boys rolling and sporting and hiding themselves among the heaps of withered leaves, as they do with us among haycocks? From the Luxemburg we went through a part of Paris that is very interesting to me, the fauxbourg, St Germains to the Elysian fields. In the fauxbourg observed two splendid new houses rising up among the forlorn Hotels of the extinct nobility. We were told these belonged to rich individuals. One would have thought these parvenus might have pleased themselves by purchasing some of the old Hotels of the nobility. But there are qualities enough in human nature to account for the preference of new to old, independent of modern comforts—Went on to the Longchamp to see the parade of equipages in which the French indulge themselves there on Good Friday. There were a few splendid ones. One of them with four horses belonging to the Duke of Orleans. We were told he was in the carriage, and if there, fearless I hope of assassins. What pleased me most was to see the number of shabby vehicles, hackney coaches, cabriolets, &c., several of them crowded with children who seemed to enjoy themselves in spite of the severe cold—The triumphal arch which terminates the alley of the Longchamp is a grand structure worthy of being the entrance of this city or rather of announcing your approach to it. But why does not modern art dress her France and her victories with their wrongs? Dined at a Restaurateur's after a walk of six hours without resting and should have spent the Evening in writing letters but was afraid of hurting my eyes.—2 o'clock Saturday—Have been calling with Mr Robinson upon a friend of his. He will be of great use in furnishing us with the signatures of all the Ambassadors for our pass-ports. This gentleman is high in the foreign office. He resides in rather a fashionable street and after mounting 92 steps we came into what proved a suite of commodious apartments elegantly furnished. He is a great collector and fashioner of illustrations for scarce and beautiful books, goes to the expense of 3£ sometimes in binding a single vol:. He showed us Rogers's Italy embellished with 100 additional engravings, is illustrating my Poems, and has sent some of the Volumes (the present Edition) already to the Binder; one would be anxious to see what sort of embellishments he rakes together. Rogers's Italy is a much easier affair. But far more than with all his books was I pleased with his two Children, one a little fairy of a girl with dark hair curling about her temple and forehead, and the other a fine Boy of about twelve years. Allow me to say also, dear Mary, that the mother of these children had as sweet a countenance as one could wish

to look upon, with features as handsome as any woman of sense
need desire. Her Husband was a handsome man about forty
years of age, and spoke of French literature and particularly of
Molière, La Fontaine, and Bossuet with much animation. More
of this when I see you all. Now dont you think, this is a pleasing
specimen of French life; humility and elegant luxury happily
combined—humility in living 92 steps above the street door,
and elegance in these pursuits of taste, which no one, I think,
would be cynic enough severely to condemn. From this gentleman's house Mr Moxon and I went to Montmartre, for the sake
of viewing the City. There was the gigantic triumphal arch far
to the right, the columns of the beautiful church of the Madeleine
below us, the dome of the Invalides, the house of one of the
assemblies formerly the Hotel de Bourbon, the column in the
place Vendôme with Napoleon in his bronze greatcoat and
cocked hat on the top of it, and we saw nearly one half of the
vast City in clear prospect; bridges river and all, the other half
glimmered through smoke much thinner and lighter of course
than ours, with a kind of ghostly indistinctness. We descended
from the windmill, on which we stood, and looked back; there
was the miller looking out of a square open window with his
brown face, and cap as white as snow, not apparently at us, but
upon the City, with the nonchalance of the Philosopher in
Lucretius, who from the eminence of his wisdom regards the
world and all its wanderers as something far beneath his
anxieties.—Met soon afterwards, among the quiet houses upon
Montmartre, a Man and Woman decently dressed followed by a
little rabble of 40 or 50 boys and girls between 5 and 6 years of
age, all singing or making strange cries. Behind the pair of
adults came a female with an infant in her arms; they had been
baptizing it at a neighbouring church; and the small children
were begging, or giving thanks for, small pieces of money
liberally scattered among them; soon after passed a sweet little
girl tripping down the hill and singing to herself. I wished to
know whether a Hymn or a chanson, but she was afraid of being
asked, and stepped aside into a door. Entered an omnibus which
was empty, and filled gradually: Women of rather the upper
class came in smirking, but a peasant girl sat down by my side

with her embrowned face, and stiff and fixed features, as if they were not free to smile, at least in the dignified company of an Omnibus.—

I have written till my fingers are frozen, so good bye and God bless you all; if we can get our passports we shall set off to-morrow for Fontainebleau. I forgot to say that an Englishman, foreman of Gagliani, only confesses to the printing of 3,000 copies of my Poems, a very different story from what I had heard. These Printers however are destroying each other's trade by underselling, and Gagliani would be glad, he says, to have copyright extended to Foreigners.—Farewell once more.—Yours W. Wordsworth.

Dear Miss Fenwick, remember me most kindly to Mr Taylor, and beg him to forward this scrawl to Mrs Wordsworth. She will send it to Dora; pray supply all words that are missing, and turn what I have endeavoured to write into sense if you can. If you are so kind as to favor me with a Letter, address à Rome, poste restante—dearest Mary do you the same. I have written by Mr Moxon to the Master of Harrow. I have attempted to read over this whole writing by candlelight, but in vain, so turn into sense if you can and think it worth while. God bless you, my dear Friends.

P.S. Dear Miss F. I am ashamed of this scrawl, send it to Mrs W. as soon as you are stopped by the vile penmanship.

MS.   *1209. W. W. to D. W.*

Saturday Paris 25ᵗʰ March [1837]

My dearest Sister,

It is now near twelve at night and my eyes are worn out. I have only to say I have written at length to Miss Fenwick, to be forwarded to Mary and then to you, or perhaps first to Dora as nearest. We set off tomorrow for Fontainbleau on our way to Italy; how I wish your strength had been equal to the journey. I have seen the Baudouins all well, a thousand kind enquiries after you. We reached Paris on Wednesday evening, and I have rambled about everywhere. God bless you and dear

Joanna and kind remembrances to all the servants. And pray tell Mr Carter that I shall be greatly obliged to him if he will correct the misprints of the Stereotype of the Yarrow and send the corrections up to Mr Moxon, who is desirous to strike off from the Stereotype thus corrected a new edition with the additional Poems of the last, for the purpose of accommodating the purchasers of the Edition of 1832.

farewell again farewell my dear Friends.

Address: Miss Wordsworth, Rydal, Kendal.

MS.   *1210. W. W. to Catherine Clarkson*

Paris, Easter Sunday [p.m. March 28, 1837]

My dear Mrs Clarkson

I could not bring my mind to break in upon your grief after the sudden loss of your Son; nor can I now quit Paris where Mr Robinson and I crossed last Wednesday, without a word of sincere and affectionate condolence, which in deep sympathy I offer to yourself and your afflicted Husband. The sad tidings were told me by our common friend Mr Robinson at his chambers. May almighty God support you and your husband through this and all trials that await the remnant of your days; and may he give his blessing to the widow now bereft of her support, and to their poor child!

Mr Moxon who has kindly accompanied us thus far, will be the bearer of this to London. We are going, God willing, as far as Naples. Farewell my dear friend,

Yours most faithfully

Wm Wordsworth.

MS.   *1211. W. W. to his Family*
K(—)

Toulon 8ᵗʰ April [1837]

My dearest Friends,

I will ask a few questions first. How are you dearest Mary in health—the pain in your cheek and the dropsical swellings.

Tell me about these things whatever you write. And write again à la Poste Restante à Rome. I should have written particulars at Lyons but for a horrid cold in my head and nose and eyes which I caught on crossing the mountain Tarare 3000 feet high between the country of the Loire and the Rhone. This cold quite blinded me with streaming eyes, and took away the strength of which I was so proud. I am now recovering, but I have not yet learned the art of managing myself as to eating and drink. The diet varies so much and the strength of the wine differs so much in different places, that I have suffered from the headach; my wish would be to confine myself to milk with coffee or chocolate but milk I find binds the body; but too much of this, if anything serious happens to the health of either of my eyes I shall [?]. Upon the whole in despite of the coldness of the season such as has not been known for a century, we have had a great deal of enjoyment; but the annoyance has been great also. I will just mention what pleased me most. The day at Vaucluse, where I was enchanted with the power and beauty of the stream, and the wildness and grandeur of the rocks, and several minor beauties which Mr R. has not noticed, and which I should have particularised but for this blinding cold. I was much pleased with Nismes, with Marseilles, but most of all with the drive between Marseilles and Toulon, which is singularly romantic and varied. From a height above Toulon, as we approached, we had a noble view of the purple waters of the Mediterranean, purple no doubt from the state of the atmosphere; for at Marseilles, where we first saw it, the colour was not different from the sea of our own island. At Nismes the evening was calm, the atmosphere unusually clear, and the air warm, not from its own temperature, but from the effect of the sun. I there first observed the stars, as appearing brighter and at a greater variety of depths, i.e. advancing one before the other more than they do with us. I could mention a hundred little things that have interested me, and all of which would have been recorded, but for the bitter cold in my fingers, and streaming eyes. One of the few promises of summer which we have had is the peach-blossom abundantly scattered over some parts of the country, and very beautiful, especially when neighboured by the cypress, a tree that is plentiful in this part of the south of France. We cannot thus far have been said to be unlucky except in being obliged to *post* from Lyons to Avignon instead of floating down the Rhone which would have been delightfully done except for the bad weather on one day and at less expense a good deal whereas it took better than two days. Our carriage has stood the journey capitally; Mr Courtenay gave us a calculation of expenses thus, 180 days at 1 pound 1 £200 living expenses (they don't amount to so much as we find); carriage duty etc 35—2500 miles travelling at 1 shilling per mile 125, but we shall probably have to go much farther perhaps 700 miles; extras 10 shillings per day 90 pounds, for unforeseen contingencies 50 pounds, in all 500—but for the one great mistake as to distance, and barring serious accident to the carriage, or illness, this calculating would somewhat exceed the requisite sum.

We have escaped the gripe by which 6000 people in Marseilles alone have suffered, of the cholera we hear nothing. It is rather fortunate that yesterday my 67th birthday was decidedly the most impressive and agreeable since we left Paris though no part of it equal to the two hours [?   ] and one hour at Nismes. Vaucluse was to me worth 50 perusals.

The rest illegible

Address: Mrs Wordsworth, Brinsop Court, Near Hereford, Angleterre.

MS.   *1212. W. W. to D. W.*
K(—)

April 10th [1837]

My dearest Sister

I sit down to write to you at the City of Nice where we arrived two hours ago. You know that the place is celebrated for the softness and purity of its air but thus far we have rather seemed to be flying from the spring than approaching it. Yesterday we came from a place called Luc to Cannes. It snowed, it hailed, it rained, it blew, and lucky it is for you, notwithstanding the beauty of the country, that you were not with us. For in our half-open carriage you would have perished with cold; our fingers were frozen so as to be almost useless. We passed by Frejus founded by Julius Caesar, and much enlarged by Augustus. It stands near the Mediterranean and abounds with ruins and fragments of Roman antiquities; in particular, the remains of an amphitheatre and an aqueduct. The road from Frejus towards Cannes is of an Alpine or rather Appennine character, mountainous and richly wooded with pines, which though none of them very large trees refreshed our sight much by a vast expanse of verdure (for the green was light-coloured), after being detained so long among the arid and bare hills and mountains which appeared to be almost everywhere spread over the south of France at least as far as we have seen it. The first fine spreading and climbing wood we saw was on the road between Marseilles and Toulon. It was of pines. I will not fatigue you with descriptions of scenery and towns which would give you no distinct impressions but will simply say that from Avignon by Nismes, Aix, Toulon, Marseilles and to this place the face of the Country has much surpassed my expectations. The olive groves, when they first made their appearance, looked no better than pollard willows of bushy size; but they are now become trees, oftener a good deal larger than our largest hollies, though I have seen none so large as our best birch-trees. But they suffice to give a sylvan character to the whole Country, which was long wanting. Orange-trees also now occur frequently, in plots; and on entering this Town we first saw them with the fruit on, which on account of the severity of the winter is not good this year, being very sour. You can buy 12 in the street for three halfpence. At Cannes we saw the villa which, with a taste sufficiently odd, the owner of Brougham Hall is building there. Beautiful and splendid as the situation is, I should much prefer Brougham Hall, with its Lowther woods and two flowing streams, clear and never dry. Imagine to yourself a deeply indented bay like that, ᴗ ; on the right hand lofty mountains, and on the left hand, the ground sinking down into a low point of land, so as almost to meet an island upon which stands a fortress, famous as being the place where the Man of the *Masque*

[848]

de fer[1] was confined. Such is the general description of the bay
of Cannes. The Town lies behind the projection, under which
I have placed a cross; that projection is of rock, and adorned
with the ruins of a castle, with a church still in use, and also with
some decayed buildings of a religious kind. Lord B.'s villa
stands upon olive and orange groves that slope down to the
Mediterranean, distant about a quarter of a mile or less, a
narrow beach of yellow and smooth sand being interposed.
Broken ground runs behind the house, scattered over with olive
and other fruit-trees, also some pines; but the frost had sadly
nipped the oranges, and their leaves were scattered pretty thick
under the trees. If the dry channels of the ravines worn by the
occasional floods were constantly filled with pure foaming water,
and the rocks were of less crumbling material—they are a sort
of sandstone—this situation would be enviable, and yet still it
would want our oaks and birches, etc., as it does actually want
the chestnut and walnut trees that adorn, as you know well,
many parts of the north of Italy and Switzerland. Do not think
I say too much of Cannes when I tell you that beyond the left
or eastern horn of this bay, and near the road leading to
Antibes, which, as the map will shew, is the next town on the
road leading from Cannes to Nice, Bonaparte disembarked from
the island of Elba. The postilion pointed out the spot. Antibes
is the frontier town of France; like all the Towns of which I have
lately spoken except Aix, beautifully situated, Mountains in the
distance, and the blue waters of the Mediterranean in front, and
on one side. I am now writing on the 11th after a pleasant
[walk] yesterday evening and another this morning before breakfast in the environs of Nice. My dear Sister and all my dear
Friends how I wish you could see it, it is so charming a neighbourhood. The Town like all these Towns almost stands in a deep bay
and near the centre, where a river (large at some times if one may
judge of its power from the width of its channel now almost dry)
flows into the sea. As in the bay of Cannes ⤳ there is a rocky

---

[1] Count Ercolo Antonio Mattioli, Senator of Mantua, and private agent
of the Duke Ferdinand Charles, imprisoned twenty-four years for deceiving
Louis XIV in a secret treaty for the purchase of the fortress of Casale, the
key of Italy.—K.

projection such as I have marked crowned with forts etc that hides the Town of Nice from the harbour. The Town is richly decorated with Malls or public walks and built, in all that the stranger passing through it without stopping, is likely to see, in a stately not to say splendid style; but there are in it many streets and some half a mile in length almost that are not more than 4 yards wide. These are shady and cool; filled with the noise of artisans and the bustle of shops. This morning after having had my eyes dazzled with the sunshine and the glare of white streets and houses I was much refreshed by walking nearly half an hour in their long and cool vistas, for so I will call them. I said I would not tire you with descriptions and yet you have had nothing else. Tomorrow we shall take the road to Genoa, whence I hope to despatch this letter, so I will say no more than that I am getting rid of the ugly cold in my head and also of something worse, a lameness in my right hip, as I once feared, dearest Mary, something like your sciatica; for I could not stoop or lean forward without sharp pain. It was brought on by sitting so many days in a *constrained* position in the carriage to make room for a Nightbag and a Carpet-bag, which I ought to have placed under my knees, where now I have put them, and find them to be no annoyance. The pain was brought on in this way and then it [?] till it became much worse by rash and hasty climbing among steep and slippery rocks for the sake of commanding points of view: this injury however is almost entirely passed away, so also I hope is one that Mr R. caught somewhat in the same way—a violent sprain in the ancle by slipping on a steep rocky descent—his ancle swelled instantly to the size of a hen's egg, but the sprain is doing well so no more of mishaps or infirmities. So farewell, all dear friends, till we have been a day or two at Genoa.

God bless you all! It is now two o'clock at noon, my eyes as this letter shews are much recovered from the effects of the cold in my head; but be you all assured, that in such a month as this, this cannot but be one of the most unhealthy spots in Europe, exclusive of those where malaria prevails. It is so hot and so cold, just as you happen to be in the sunshine or shade. Again Farewell.

MS. 1213. W. W. to D. W., M. W., and Dora W.
K(—)

Rome Saturday 27ᵗʰ or 28ᵗʰ April [1837]

My dearest Sister, I begin with you because I wrote to you two sides and a half of close-penned lines from Nice on the 10ᵗʰ of this month, meaning to finish when I had been a day or two at Genoa; but I was prevented by a hundred causes. On Thursday afternoon we arrived at Rome, a Letter posted at Toulon will have told you of my proceedings to that place. The other, which I shall not send gave particulars of our journey to Nice Alps and over part of them to Genoa, so on to Massa then to Lucca and Pisa and by Volterra and Siena to Rome; where I confidently expected at least one Letter but found none. Today is a post day and if I do not hear from Mary I shall be certain there has been some mistake and I shall pass the next month nearly without the hope of tidings from any of you. From Paris I sent by Mr Moxon a double letter to Miss Fenwick to be forwarded through Mr Stephen to Mary and then to Dora and you; where and how Mary and Dora are I cannot guess. Unluckily I said to Mary that, as Mr Stephen had requested, her letter might be forwarded to him to save the English postage, whereas if this had not been [?] and she had paid the postage to Rome, which must be done, surely I should have heard of you. Now I know not where to address this for a speedy answer, pray dearest Mary write the moment you receive this addressing to Rome. Hoping the best of you all here let me say that we have both been quite well since I threw off my cold; only as I fully expected my bowels, owing to mistiming, to heat of travelling, over-exertion sometimes or a want of choice in diet, have been rather too torpid but without the slightest inconvenience, only one does not like this to continue, and now that we shall be comparatively at rest for a fortnight or three weeks things will I trust be soon as I could wish.

We are most agreeably lodged in the Piazza d'Espagna, and while we stay here shall live at little expense, nothing at all indeed compared with that of travelling. I have been delighted with a hundred things since we left Toulon but I should be lost if I went into details. Mr Robinson does not return from the office so I have given up all hope of hearing from you. This is

[851]

a most grievous disappointment, and I fear will sadly interfere with my enjoyment but I must bear it as well as I can. Dearest Dora where and how are you—I know nothing and tomorrow it will be six weeks since we left London. Of all things that I have seen at Rome the inside of St Peter's has most moved me. I have not yet been in the Vatican and have thus far contented myself with rambling under Mr R.'s guidance through the streets of Rome looking at few interiors except the four principal Churches, St Peter's of course being one of them. On Monday we shall go to the Vatican, and there examine the principal pictures, then make little excursions in the neighbourhood to Tivoli, Frascati, Albano, in short to see whatever is thought most worth seeing, and in the 4th week from this time at the latest we shall proceed either to Naples or turn our faces north-ward to Florence. I speak thus doubtfully because five or six cases of Cholera having appeared lately at Naples the Papal Government which is unusually strict has revived the Quarantine so that though people are free to go from Rome to Naples, they are not free to return. Nevertheless Mr Collins[1] the Painter and his family are going there on Monday having time at their [   ] and no fear of the disease. Neither have we but depend upon it if the quarantine be not taken off or mitigated, we shall, though to my infinite regret, give up Naples, and do as I have said. How much do I wish that you were all healthy strong and at liberty to pass the ensuing months with us here; nothing can exceed the interest of Rome but though I have seen the Coliseum the Pantheon and all the other boasted things nothing has in the least approached the impressions I received from the inside of St Peter's. Mr Francis Hare[2] has just called. We have seen Mr and Mrs Ticknor and Sismondi[3] the Historian, his Wife and her two Sisters old acquaintances of mine, and dearest Sister one of them of yours when we were at Coat-How House, Mr John Wedgwood's near Bristol. They were rejoiced to see me. Miss Mackenzie whose sister the Mr

---

[1] William Collins, R.A. (1788–1847), a popular landscape and figure painter, and the father of Wilkie Collins.

[2] Elder brother of Augustus and Julius Hare.

[3] Sismondi (1773–1842), author of the *History of the Italian Republics*, married Jessie Allen, sister-in-law of Sir James Mackintosh.

Mackenzie who was at Ambleside last summer married and took her name, has been very kind to us. She is an old friend of Mr Robinson and is a great admirer of dear Chris but I will not trouble you about persons and were I to begin with things there would be no end. Notwithstanding a season of unprecedented severity, so severe that not a green leaf is to be seen scarcely or the promise of one, on any deciduous tree till we came near Rome, I have been enchanted with the beauty of the scenery in innumerable places, though almost in full as many there is a deplorable want of beauty in the surface, where the forms are fine. Speaking of the Apennines in contradistinction to the maritime Alps, for one scarcely can say where one begins and the other ends, I should say that, as far as I have seen, they are both in beauty and grandeur immeasurably inferior, often lumpish in their forms, and oftener still harsh, arid, and ugly on their surface. Besides these mountains have an ill habit of sending down torrents so rapidly that the rivers are perpetually changing their beds ; and in consequence the vallies, which ought to be green and fertile, are overspread with sand and gravel. But why find fault when much that I have seen is so enchanting. We had scarcely been two hours in Rome when we walked up to the Pincian hill, near our hotel. The sun was just set, but the western sky glowed most beautiful. A great part of the City of modern Rome lay below us, and St Peter's rose on the opposite side ; and for dear Sir George Beaumont's sake I will mention that at no great distance from the dome of the church on the line of the glowing horizon was seen one of those broad-topped pines, looking like a little cloud in the sky, with a slender stalk to connect it with its native earth. I mention this because a friend of Mr Robinson's whom we had just accidentally met told us that this very tree which I admired so much had been paid for by our dear Friend, that it might stand as long as Nature would allow. Mr Robinson not yet returned so no letters! God grant that you may all be well. I do not send love and remembrances having so little space but give them to all friends or relatives at Brinsop, at London, at Rydal, at Keswick, at Ambleside, at Brigham and do not forget Dear Wm. at Carlisle nor Miss Fenwick wherever she may be, nor the Arnolds, but what does all this avail? Give me credit for thinking and feeling as I ought being so far from you all. Dearest Joanna how are you? and my dearest Sister I trust you do not stick so close to your fire; and Dora are you improving and Mary are you strengthening and how are the Invalids of Brinsop? The other side of the sheet shall be left for Mr R. It is now three o'clock and I am going to Dinner. We walked from 8 till eleven and I shall walk from half-past four to half-past seven. I feel quite strong except that sometimes I have an aching between the shoulders at the back of the neck such dearest Mary as I have heard you complain of. My eyes for them are wonderfully well as this letter written at a sitting will shew, and written after an hour's reading. Write instantly paying postage to Rome and not troubling yourself dearest Mary to send through Mr Stephen. God bless you all ever your affectionate Husband Brother and Father

Address: Mrs Wordsworth, Mr Hutchinson's, Brinsop Court, N^r Hereford, Inghilterra.

MS.   *1214. W. W. to M. W. and Dora W.*
K(—)

Saturday [? May 9; p.m. May 20]

My dearest Mary, Yesterday put an end to my anxieties and depression of mind by bringing me your most welcome Letter of the 17th April with a postscript from Dora of the 19th. Mr Stephen had kindly sent it to the English ambassador which perhaps occasioned delay of a day or two but I believe I had been unreasonable in calculating so confidently upon an answer to my Toulon letter upon my arrival at Rome. I have therefore to beg your pardon for writing in such bad spirits as I did. Dearest Dora your mother speaks of a letter from yourself to me but I have not received it. How glad I was to have so good an account of your health, and most thankful to Drs Holland and Brodie and to all your kind friends for their goodness to you. I rejoice that you are in Town, thank Mrs Harrison in my name with my best love and give the same to one and all of the family with whom you are. I cannot feel sufficiently grateful to God for the good account of you all except your poor dear Cousin at Brinsop, for whom there appears to be no hope. Of Sister and

Joanna also the accounts are good to my heart's delight.—Your Letter took off such a weight from me as I cannot describe, for I feared I should have no news till your answer came to mine from Rome, which would have had to follow us to Florence, for there is not the least chance of our being able to include Naples in our tour, on account of the Quarantine. In the course of next week we shall go to Tivoli etc etc and 3 or 4 days after our return will suffice for Rome. You will naturally wish for details, but what can I select out of such a wilderness of sights antient and modern, though I have not seen a 100th part of the indoor attractions, not yet even the Vatican, to which we go on Monday under the guidance of Mr Gibson the Sculptor. Several times however I have been at St Peter's, have heard Mass before the Pope in the Sistine Chapel, and after that seen him pronounce the benediction upon the people from a balcony in front of St Peter's and seen his Holiness scatter bits of paper from aloft upon the multitude, indulgences I suppose. Of the outside of Rome, and the ruins and the modern town, antient walls etc I have seen a great [? deal] both on foot and in a carriage, for which latter accommodation we are indebted to the kindness of Miss Mackenzie an old friend of Mr R. and sister-in-law to the Mr Mackenzie who with his son was at Rydal last summer. She is an amiable person and nothing can exceed her attentions. Mr Collins also, an acquaintance of Lord Lowther, has accompanied me on two excursions in the neighbourhood, one to the Monte Mario which commands the most magnificent view of modern Rome the Tiber and the surrounding country. Upon this elevation I stood under the pine redeemed by Sir G. Beaumont, of which I spoke in my former Letter. I touched the bark of the magnificent tree and could almost have kissed it out of love for his memory. One of the most agreeable excursions we have made was with Miss Mackenzie and Mr Collins to the tomb of Cecilia Metella and the other antiquities in its neighbourhood. This was on the first of May. The air was clear and bright, and the distant hills were beautifully clothed in air and the meadows sparkling with rich wild flowers. In our ramble after alighting from the carriage we came to the spot which bears the name of the fountain of Egeria; but this is all a fiction, nevertheless the grotto and its trickling water and pendent ivy and vivid moss, have enough of Poetry and painting about them to make the spot very interesting independent of all adjuncts whether of fact or fiction. Dearest Dora say to the Miss Marshalls that I hope they will one day see most of what I have seen, particularly the Cornice Road and Rome and its neighbourhood; as to yourself, notwithstanding your own and your Doctor's good report I fear you will never feel strong enough to adventure so far. I do not think dearest Dora that you could stand it, and after all it is very trying at this season of the year, and through all the summer and in winter the weather appears to be often very rainy and what may be called bad. This morning we have been with Mr Severn the Painter a friend of Keats the Poet. He has excellent health in Rome summer and winter; but his House stands clear of [? that area] and how does he live in Summer? why he is out in the open air at five in the morning with his Wife and children when she is well enough, returns at 7, paints all day and does not stir out again till an hour or so after sunset. But this sort of life you see ill suits anyone but a person with occupations like his. Upon the whole the weather since we came, or rather the state of the atmosphere, has not except upon the first evening of our arrival been favorable to landscape beauty. We have several times been out as early as six in the morning, but then the sun has too much power for beauty, and the evenings have all, since that one, been without fine nights. Of villas and their gardens I have seen I can scarce tell you how many, some from the views they command of the city, old and new, very impressive. But of churches and pictures and statues in them I am fairly tired—in fact I am too old in head, limbs and eyesight for such hard work, such toiling and such straining and so many disappointments either in finding the most celebrated picture covered up with curtains, a service going on so that one cannot ask to have a sight, or the church closed when one arrives at the door. All this will however be forgotten long before I get back to dear England, nothing but the pleasure, I hope, survive. The only very celebrated object which has fairly disappointed me on account of my ignorance I suppose is the Pantheon. But after all it is not particular objects with the exception perhaps of the inside of

St Peter's that make the glory of this City, but it is the boun[d]-less variety of combinations of old and new caught in ever varying connection with the surrounding country, when you look down from some one or other of the seven hills, or from neighbouring eminences not included in the famous seven. Tomorrow we are going into the Campagna to see a sheep-shearing upon the farm of a wealthy Peasant who lives in that *sad* and *solemn district*, as I believe it is around his abode, which lies about four miles along the Appian Way. And there this hospitable Man dwells among his herds and flocks with a vast household, like one of the Patriarchs of old.

I write with watering eyes; caused I think by the glare of the sun, but some tell me it is a slight touch of influenza. I wish it may and then it will go off. The influenza has been travelling with me or rather I with it since I left Rydal. I found it in London in Paris every where in the south of France and even greatly prevalent in Rome though abating. I should not have mentioned my eyes, but to account for this penmanship even more wretched than usual—nor should I have written today but to beg you to direct to Florence and remove your regret at my not having heard from you before. Your letter dearest Dora may be forwarded instantly through Mr Stephen to the Minister at Florence, so I should suppose, but that you can ascertain through Mr Taylor or himself and if there be any doubt of the elegibility of that mode of conveyance, notwithstanding the postage, pray write instantly by post, à la Poste Restante or as you may learn to do best, for I believe in some parts of the continent the post off: will not charge itself with letters so directed. This however is not the case at Rome. If you can send through the Minister so much the better, pray write instantly without waiting for Mother's reply to this and even if you cannot send through her write by the post. Say if the Master of Harrow undertook the off: and tell me all the news you can of our friends. I fear the legacy story is too good to be true. [   ] Here comes Mr Robinson to whom I resign the pen.

Love and blessings to all. W. W.

Address: Miss Wordsworth, John Marshall Esq, Upper Grosvenor St, London, Inghilterra.

MS.
K(—)

1215. W. W. to his Family

Albano May 19th [1837]

My dearest Friends,

It is just three weeks and two days since we reached Rome,
and on Tuesday next we shall leave it to take the road for
Florence. Since my last I have worked hard to see the most
remarkable things in Rome and its immediate neighbourhood—
Churches, Palaces, Villas, Ruins, Eminences—not Cardinals,
though I have seen numbers of these, but commanding points
of view, and all these with very great pleasure, and only one
drawback—the never-wanting proof that I am rather too old
for such *excessive* exertions, and that my bodily strength is
diminished within the latter part of these labours. But my
health thank God continues very good so I have every reason
to be thankful. We have passed a day at Tivoli with much
enjoyment and another at the Shepherd's hut in the Campagna.
On Wednesday we came to this place, went the same evening to
see the neighbouring Lake of Albano and yesterday made a
Tour round its sister lake or rather volcanic pool of Nemi. The
day was charming for our purpose, though every body here
cries out against the weather as worse than ever was known, for
200 years, at this season. That excellent Creature Miss Mackenzie brought us hither in her carriage, we are lodgers in the
same Hotel. Our intention is to return to Rome on Sunday, and
as I have said leave it on Tuesday morning. Today we shall
ascend Monte Cavo if the weather which is but lowering will
permit, and on our journey back to Rome we mean to visit
Frascati, Grotto Ferrata etc.—I would gladly single out from
what we have seen something the description of which might
interest you, but I seem to have little talent for dealing with
objects so new to me and with impressions in every respect so
different from what others receive. Of adventures we have had
none; of persons we have seen not many, and these chiefly
English Artists who by the by seem to live at Rome on very
good terms with each other. One of them Mr Severn, the Friend
of Keats the Poet, has taken my portrait, which I mean to
present to Isabella. I fear you will not, nor will she, be satisfied

with it, it is thought however to be a pretty good likeness as to features, only following the fact, he has made me look at least four years older than I did when I walked 7 hours in Paris without resting and yet without fatigue. Mr Severn this Monday had one of his children christened in one of the villas near Rome, Miss Mackenzie was Godmother, I attended and after dinner an Italian Gentleman, who had sung several charming airs, Roman, Neapolitan, Milanese and Venetian, recited a Poem which he had composed in Italian to my honor—I shall bring a copy of it to England. At Miss Mackenzie's where most of our evenings have been past, I saw a young Italian Lady, who was so struck with my resemblance to her deceased Father that, as she told Miss Mackenzie afterwards, she had been unable to suppress her feelings and had retired and burst into tears.

We are told that the cholera if existing at all at Naples need not be regarded; but the quarantine we both dislike so much that we keep, as I have said, to our resolution, and to tell you the truth I am not sorry to be so near the time of turning my face homewards; for the tour of Italy is too much to be taken in less than 8 months unless a person be young and very strong. The country is inexhaustible for those who are well read in antient story and classical Poetry and its natural beauty tempts you to exertion in every direction. Of the character of the people I can scarcely speak but by hearsay; for one's own transient observations often only serve to mislead one, at least it very often happens so—for instance, yesterday, in passing through the romantic little Town of Nemi, that crests with its picturesque towers and roofs a steep and lofty [? hill] on the shores of the lake of Nemi, I was grieved to see not less than 20 stout men lounging together in a small square about two o'clock. What a sad state thought I must these people be in, either without work or if they have it, too idle to turn to it. In the evening I learned from an intelligent Italian Physician who called on Miss M. that from about the middle of May to the middle of July the peasants of these little Towns and Villages rise at one or two o'clock in the morning, sometimes at midnight, and work in their vineyards till 8, and pass the middle of the day in chatting together or amusing themselves at some game or other.

They go to work so early because when the Sun becomes powerful as the morning advances young shoots and buds of the vine
would be injured by rubbing their clothes against them or touching them I suppose in any way. The spot from which I write is
surrounded with romantic beauty and every part of it renowned
in history or fable. The lake of Nemi is the celebrated Speculum
Dianae, and that of Albano is still more famous as you may read
in Livy the Historian. The window of the room from which I
am writing has a fine view of the Mediterranean in front. The
house was formerly a palace of the King of Spain, in the court
below is a fountain, water spouting from the mouths of two lions
into a basin, and a jet d'eau throwing up more that falls back
into the same basin. Thence descends a flight of steps 80 in
number, into a large Italian garden; below that the ground falls
in a slope thickly set with olives limes and fruit trees, then comes
a plain or what looks like one with plots of green corn, that look
like rich meadows, spreading and winding far and wide, then
succeeds a dusky marsh, and lastly the Mediterranean Sea. All
this is part of the antient Latium the supposed kingdom of
Æneas which he wrested, along with the fair Lavinia, from
Turnus. On the right, a little below the Hotel, is a stately grove
of Ilex belonging to the Palace or Villa Doria. This neighbourhood did till lately abound in magnificent trees oaks and elms and
others; some of these survive but a laurel, about a mile hence,
the [?] felled, to meet the gaming propensities of a Duchess, I
believe the wife of their [?]. I must now think of concluding.
At Florence no doubt I shall have a letter; *immediately* on
receiving this do you dearest Dora, if in London, write to me
at Milan by Post; and you dearest Mary write within a week
after you receive this to me at Venice (Poste Restante both
places). I shall write again as soon as I get your expected letter
at Florence. Dearest Sister and Joanna I hope you are going
on well, this letter is for you if you can read it. Give my love
to everyone, I name no one for I have no room; but I think of
you all a thousand times a day and often wish I were back again
at dear Rydal.—From Milan we shall go to Como and, for the
sake of old times, take the steamboat up to the head of the Lake,
returning by it the same day. But farewell and God bless you

all; when you write to Miss Fenwick say with my love that sometimes I am tempted to wish I had put off my journey to winter quietly with her at home. But this seems ungrateful, as I have had so much pleasure.

Address: Miss Wordsworth, J. Marshall's Esq., Upper Grosvenor St, London, Inghilterra.

MS. **1216. W. W. to Dora W.**

Wednesday 30th May [1837] Florence

'Vallombrosa I longed in thy shadiest wood
To linger reclined on the moss-covered floor!'[1]
This longing was fulfilled yesterday. We left Rome Tuesday last, as my letter from Albano posted there on the Saturday before said we should do, and after three diversions to each of the three great Tuscan Sanctuaries as they are called, viz Laverna, Camaldoli, and Vallombrosa we reached Florence at six yesterday evening having given a week to the journey. This is the 30th of May and this morning I have been at the post-off: where to my infinite mortification I find no Letter from anyone. I then went to the English Minister but was told that I could not see his secretary till half-past 12. Thither I shall go again, but with the faintest or rather no hope as my direction to you was that Letters forwarded through Mr Stephen should be Poste Restante. Ten weeks have I been from England (we left London on the 19th March) and only have received one Letter. You cannot conceive how this disturbs my mind and darkens my spirits; and not the less so because I believe it to be in a great degree my own fault. On leaving England I ought to have said, write me every 12 days so and so, in succession, naming the places, according to my best conjecture as to where we should reach, and how long we should remain in them. Well let me hope the best, and keep my thoughts as quiet as I can. Here we shall stay six days, we thought ten, but visits to the three monasteries were included in that calculation and these we have already taken in our way. Now to resume from the point of my

---

[1] Oxf. W., p. 345.

Albano Letter. We were there 4 days but during two the weather was so bad that we could do nothing, and accordingly left Frascati and Tusculum etc unseen. We however saw the best things, namely, went to the top of Monte Cavo, the antient Mons Albanus, and thoroughly explored the immediate neighbourhood of the two lakes Albano and Nemi. The journey from Rome hither has been a succession of delights. The Country beautiful and the weather favorable. Of the things which charmed me most I will mention Nervi, the fall of Terni, much the most impressive waterfall I ever saw, Spoleto and its neighbourhood, Perugia, the drive up the Arno to Beviena on our way to the Convent of Laverna, and along the banks of the same river towards Camaldoli, Laverna itself, Camaldoli and Vallombrosa, all of which retreats are deserving of their high reputation, and lastly Florence itself, the external appearance of which has been praised as much as it deserves. I should like to enter into the details of many of these things but it would be endless and I reserve particulars till my return; only I will tell you that I spare no pains, for example, yesterday I was on *Horseback* at five in the morning! to go to Vallombrosa, with a man on foot as my Guide. Mr R. judiciously declined going as he had visited the place at leisure six years ago. The distance from my starting place Ponte Sieve[1] is nine miles, 4 or more of steep ascent up a lofty mountain. As we ascended I looked back on the long winding vale of Arno, in several reaches of which the river and its banks were hidden by the vapours that had risen from it, and we proceeded first through vine and olive yards then through groves of oak and chestnut up and down for several miles. My Guide unfortunately was fond of short cuts, and took one of these against my wish, and pursued the path contrary to my advice, till it was lost in the thick wood and wholly ceased. Here I was obliged to dismount and we foundered about for a considerable time, at last by aid of a man who was attending one of the Charcoal pits, we regained the road; and after three hours of pretty hard labour for man and horse reached the Convent; where I was conducted by a Monk about the Church and the library, and shown a specimen of the chambers of the

[1] Pontassieve.

Monks and everything deemed interesting in the Convent. I was then furnished with a guide, and explored for two hours the holy places in the surrounding woods. Vallombrosa is somewhat improperly named, for in fact it is no valley at all, the place where the Convent stands, but rather what we should call a cove, or small level place on the side of a steep and lofty mountain, by the side of a torrent not very large which immediately behind the convent throws itself down a precipitous rock; and hurries on down what we should call a Ghyll into a deep yet rapidly declining mountain valley richly clothed in chestnut woods. Immediately surrounding the convent pine trees grow in abundance, with a few beeches and chestnuts, but right above these pine trees grow woods of beech and spread along a region in which snow is lying. It is remarkable that both at Camaldoli and Laverna also beech trees grow upon the loftiest ground, as if they were hardier here than pine trees, which does not seem to be the case among the Alps. About half past three I returned to Ponte Sieve having had a good dinner at the Convent where I left according to custom a small sum for the *poor*. The hot weather has at last set in; and the deciduous trees are looking green but not the oaks in the lofty situations where we have been nor the chestnuts in the loftiest. In ascending to Laverna, among the sternest solitudes of the Appennines I first heard the cuckoo; Mr R. had heard it the day before. Then also I saw primroses and daisies blooming side by side, and the same at Camaldoli, in which spot primroses will be found I should suppose a week hence. One of the great pleasures of our tour has been that passing through so many elevations of Country we have had the spring renewed upon us repeatedly. The white thorn and the broom have greeted us in full blow over and over again during the last eight weeks. And now I must quit my pen to go again to the English Minister—oh that I may have a Letter. This morning I read Talfourd's admirable speech upon copyright in which he makes honorable mention of me. Adieu my dearest Friends!

1 o'clock—I am just returned from the Minister Mr Abercrombie to whom I sent in a slip of paper with these words 'Mr Wordsworth will be greatly obliged to Mr Abercrombie if he will

let him know whether any letters for Mr W. have lately arrived under cover to Mr Abercrombie'. The answer by an Italian servant was none—and now I must go by appointment to feast upon one of the Galleries with what appetite I may—I have only to add, that spite of all my gratifications I shall be heartily glad to be in England as speedily as I can, having seen what is proper to see—Venice will be the last spot in Italy thank God where we shall be detained. I never was good at sightseeing, yet it must be done. Dearest Sister how I wish I knew how you are and you Dora are you improving and you Mary and how is Joanna and the fireside of Brinsop and how are John and Isabella and their little ones and Wm?—I have brought away from Rome a small portrait of myself for Isabella.

Thursday morning June 1st—I have been again at the post-off: but no Letter and I am quite at a loss how to direct this; whether to you dearest Dora at Mr Marshall's to all of whom present my love, or to your mother at Brinsop. If you be, Dora, with Mrs Hoare give my love to her and Miss Hoare and to the Master of Harrow of whom I often hear. For example yesterday Mr Ingram you may tell him inquired very cordially after him. Everybody seems glad of the fine weather as they call it and so it is but I have been better pleased with the unseasonable cold and wet, on account of my eyes which till yesterday have been for some time in their very best way. But yesterday dazzling sun and two unlucky hours of lamp and candle light at Mr Hare's, who is on his way to Munich, have put one of them into an irritated state. The health of both of us is good. Much as I am pleased with this place, for I have had a walk this morning as I had one of two hours on the banks of the Arno yester evening, I long to be on the move to bring me nearer to you all. Let your next be written instantly to Venice Poste Restante, paying what is required and ten days after at the latest write to me again directing to Salzburg Germany; if this Letter should be long in reaching any of you still write to Venice, for both there and at Milan directions will be left at the post-off: for forwarding the Letter. As we shall remain here 5 or 6 days I shall hope to hear from you—then please tell her on Tuesday next at the latest a day will take us hence to Bologna then we go by Modina, Reggio,

Piacenza, Pavia, Milan where a day by steam up the Lake, Lecco, Bergamo, then we shall see the lakes of Isea, and Garda, Brescia, Verona, Padua, Venice where we mean to stop a week or so then for Trieste, Innsbruck, Salzburg, the Austrian lakes near it, then Munich, and so to Heidelberg and London. How I long to hear from you—farewell one and all, dearest Mary I hope you have taken every possible care of your health and that you Dora are going on well and Sister and Joanna but all this I said before. Mr Robinson sends his love, again and again farewell.

Address: Miss Wordsworth, Mrs Gee, Hendon.

MS. *1217. W. W. to Dora W.*

Florence Sunday 4ᵗʰ June [1837]

A thousand thanks dearest Dora for your most welcome [letter], which I received two or three hours ago. My anxiety to hear from England had depressed my spirits so that I scarcely enjoyed anything; and now your long Letter has made me quite easy and comfortable. I delight to hear that you are gaining strength, and that Mother has got back to Rydal, where she found Sister and Joanna so well. Poor dear Mary H.[1] though you do not say so, is I conclude no more. God bless her innocent spirit—I loved her much. Mother's health you do not mention but I hope she strengthened—I shall be grateful to hear that she had taken the Baths at Leamington; my anxious thoughts about her symptoms have haunted me sadly since I left home. And now dearest Dora let me talk about meeting and the thought I have that we may return together to Rydal. Your visit to [?], and afterwards to the Coleridges, will detain you till we shall be so far on our way home that I trust it will suit you to wait for me; and I often think with delight of our visiting Lord Bacon's tomb at St Albans together on our way home; we taking our places by the Manchester Telegraph and being taken up at St Albans at 7 next morning as Mr Graves and I were when dear Mr Rogers was so kind as to accompany me so far on the way.

---

[1] Daughter of Thos. and Mary Hutchinson, born 1817.

I wrote on my arrival at this place last Wednesday—but was quite uncertain how to direct—I think in my eagerness to hear from you I did wrong to beg of you in my letter from Albano to write to Milan—There will I fear not be time but your letter will follow us to Venice where labour and pleasure, which have both been great (the labour for me, though nothing for my companion whose strength is wonderful). Since my last on Wednesday or Thursday I have been incessantly employed in visiting Churches, Galleries and spots in the neighbourhood that command views of Val d'Arno and the city which I find to be a most charming place, and one that for a residence is preferable to one [?   ], unless one's purse were so full as to make money no object. Everything here is within comparatively easy reach, Libraries, Galleries and the country. Yesterday I walked to a point called Bello Sguardo, as the name implies it commands a splendid prospect. Our Companion was a Gentleman Mr Spence who has married a lady of Florence and he took a villa upon this point. It is roomy and elegant quite private, with a garden coachhouse etc and he pays only 12 pounds a year for it, using it only in the summer months. I ought to add that he had it at [?] ready furnished though he says not very well. His fuel during the whole winter cost him 50 shillings, so that with 300 a year a Man at Florence might live quite in style! and with 800 like a prince. The evening before we were at a hill on the opposite side of the vale—Fiesole mentioned in the first book of the Paradise Lost, and this evening though I have been out 4 or 5 hours I shall go to the Cascina, the public evening walk and drive of the Inhabitants; where I suppose I shall be in the midst of a few acquaintance I have either met or made at Florence. Yesterday at Mr Hare's I met Lady Susan Percy, her brother Charles, both Coleorton acquaintance, and two days before Lord Charles Hervey whom I have known in London. He is an intimate Friend of the Master of Harrow. By the by I have not yet learned whether dear Miss Fenwick's [*erasure in MS.*] do not fail dearest Mary to write to her and give her my love saying how often I wished that we had been together at Rome. Of this be assured that I never shall go from home for any time again, without a female companion. My evenings would have been

very dull at Rome, if it had not been for dear Miss Mackenzie
to whom I became quite affectionately attached as I believe she
did to me. You know I cannot read by candle-light, so that
without her house to go to I must have gone to bed every night
at nine.

Monday morn. So I did last night and have got up before
five this morning to finish my Letter. I was much grieved
dearest Dora to hear so unpromising an account of your Uncle
Thomas's future recovery[1] and poor Mrs Lockhart! I had read
her death in the Newspaper for which I had been in part prepared,
as Dr Ferguson her physician told me in London that her constitution which had always been a bad one was dreadfully impaired. Her poor Father would have deplored her loss bitterly.
I have spent my time very pleasantly at Florence; it is so much
less fatiguing a place than Rome; but even here one has to *waste*
a great deal of labour in sight-seeing on account of Churches and
Galleries being closed when you expect them to be open. Yesterday I had no less than three pretty long walks which turned to
no account—the places being shut up, though I was under the
guidance of an Italian who lives in Florence. In the afternoon
we had an awful thunderstorm and heavy rain; it cleared up
and I went to the Public Drive where I saw most of the fashion-
ables of Florence; more than one half of them I thought English.
The ride is under trees and the ground is very damp. This place
I am told is very injurious to health and often avoided by the
Florentines, at times when the English crowd thither to the
great benefit of the purses of their physicians. Florence you
know lies low in a valley which widens a good deal below the
City, but the bases of the hill immediately opposite are not more
than a mile and a half apart. This makes the air sometimes
intensely hot, and no doubt it must often be very cold on account
of sweeping winds. Everybody complains of a great change in
climate in Italy within the late few years. Mrs Landor who was
visited yesterday at Fiesole by Mr Robinson and called in her
carriage to give us an airing or rather as it proved a damping in
the Cascina says they have had eight months winter here, a

---

[1] Thomas Hutchinson's horse had fallen upon him while he was riding
on the high road near Brinsop. He was a cripple for the rest of his life.

strong expression but really though we have had very hot *hours* to encounter while we have been in Italy, some parts of the day, particularly the evenings, have been so chill that a fire (by the way the Italians are quite afraid of fires) would have been almost always agreeable. I do not suppose I shall have time to fill the remainder of the sheet, as I have to go to the great Gallery for the last time and to several other places, and shall have much to do in preparation for our departure before five tomorrow morning, as we mean to go through to Bologna in one day—a long journey.

I am not surprised at the effect of Sergeant Talfourd's speech which I had read at length in the Times. It is judiciously and eloquently done, and I trust it will produce its effect, and that you all, my dear Children, may derive some little benefit from the measure it will lead to, after I am gone. The notice the Sergeant kindly took of me may excite some envy and spite, but upon the whole it will tend to swell the stream of my reputation and so widen the circulation of my works; for the good of readers I hope and also for Mr Moxon's sake, for I shall be delighted when he gets his money back. Do not my dearest Dora be hurt at your Uncle's coldness—I called him the bad Brother, he gave me so little of his time, not more I think than twenty minutes at the very utmost when I saw him in town. It is their way, and we must make allowance, taking people as they are. My dearest Mary how I long for a line from you, and a few words from my poor Sister, how is she about her fire and does she complain of her 'struggles' as formerly? Pray remember me to everyone in our household in particular and to the neighbours, to Mr Carr, the Dowlings, Mr Robinson, Mrs Robinson, Mrs Luff, the Cooksons one and all, in short say I forget nobody. Travelling would agree well with me if I had not quite so much to do at the places I come to and could keep free of constipation of the bowels which is impossible without using more medicine than I like. This is owing to change in diet and being mistimed as to meals. Now at Florence I am beginning to do well as I was at Rome when I came away, but tomorrow's long journey, and the irregularities, unavoidable ones, before us will mistime me again. My eyes keep marvellously well which is a great blessing, owing I believe in no small degree to the *faintly* blue spectacles I brought with me. These take away entirely the glow of the sun and I trust that with them on I shall be able to face it when it grows still more powerful. Blue spectacles or green, but nothing like so good as these, they are far too blue, are used by thousands in these places. For myself I have been most lucky in the forethought with which I have provided and clothed myself. Tell Mr Carter my long blue coat the same as his has been of inestimable use to me; I am now writing in it, I have worn it much and shall do in the carriage, it has served me over and over again as an additional blanket, and when I suspected damp sheets I slept upon it. The shoes which Sprott made me proved most excellent. I have worn them constantly, the soles keep out cold, for the floors indoors are often very cold and in the Churches in particular; it keeps out also the heat of the pavement in the streets which is often burning, and of course the damp. I got also in London an excellent pair of black wire spectacles which will guard my eyes from dust in the carriage, so that I hope to return in tolerable plight. Mr Robinson is naturally not so anxious to be at home as I am; who trust now that in the first week of September we shall be in England; except in Venice I think we shall not be detained more than two or three days anywhere, and this only at the Austrian or Bavarian Lakes near Salzburg and at Munich. To this last place write to me as soon as you receive this. I have already directed you I think to write to Salzburg; if not address me there instead of Munich. I would gladly beg for an answer to this at Venice but it would be imprudent, as I trust we shall have left that place before one could reach me, so write rather to Munich that I may not be disappointed. And now my dearest friends I must conclude with a God bless you all from the bottom of my heart. Love to John and Isabella and their little ones and to dear William and to London John of whose prize I was glad to hear. Give my love to Edith and her Husband and to all the Southeys and to the Coleridges, but there is no end to this. I shall write again from Venice certainly and if I find a letter at Milan perhaps from that place. Mr Robinson sends his love as usual—I have not time to read over this so make it out as well as you can. Again farewell W. W.

I am quite undecided whether to address this, Mary, to you or to Dora. Were I sure it would find her at Hendon it should be there.

Address: Miss Wordsworth, Hendon.

MS.   *1218. W. W. to James Stephen*[1]

Florence, June 5ᵗʰ —37

My dear Sir,

I had the pleasure of receiving by the ordinary Post yesterday, a letter of the 24ᵗʰ ult; which was most welcome. I feel somewhat fatigued by great, over great exertions in sight-seeing but am quite well in health, as is my Fellow traveller. We both promise ourselves great pleasure in telling you some thing of our adventures in Autumn. I trust we shall reach London by the beginning of Septʳ. To-morrow morning we start for Bologna. I have been much gratified by our six days stay in Florence.

With kind regards to Messʳˢ Taylor and Spedding, I remain my dear Sir,

Ever faithfully your
much obliged
Wm Wordsworth.

MS.   *1219. W. W. to Dora W. and M. W.*

Padua June 21ˢᵗ Wednesday [1837]

My dearest Dora, I begin with you to thank you for your Milan letter which I had the happiness of receiving the day we left that place. My last was from Florence. It has taken us 16 days to reach this place; our journey having lain through Bologna where we slept two nights, Reggio, Modena, Piacenza, Parma, Milan, Bergamo, Brescia, Verona and Vicenza which we left this morning. The mere posting might have been performed in a very few days but out of the 4 when we slept at Milan we gave one to Como, and one to the celebrated Carthusian Monastery called

---

[1] There is no indication on the MS. of the identity of the addressee of this letter, but the reference to Taylor and Spedding points to Stephen, and, moreover, Stephen had undertaken the franking of M. W.'s letters to W. W.

the Certosa near Pavia, two days we gave to the lake of Iseo and three to that of Garda: fortunate diversion for otherwise the long journey first to Parma from Bologna along the dead flat plain of Lombardy coasting the Appennines and from Milan along the same sort of country precisely coasting the Alps, would notwithstanding the attractions of the several towns, have proved at this season very tedious. But helped out by our incursions into the Alps among those magnificent lakes the whole thing has answered very well. Tomorrow will take us to Venice with the wonders of which City I shall consider our Italian tour as concluding. Then we shall set our faces fairly towards England; not to arrive there as soon as I could wish, for some sacrifices must be made for my fellow-traveller who has done so much to meet my wishes. But my dearest Friends you see that his situation and mine are in important respects very different. He has no home to turn to and I am anxious to be again at mine. He feels that we have incurred a good deal of expense and therefore when at a pleasant place is more disposed to linger longer than I have any inclination to do, so that to my great regret he talks of giving a fortnight to the Austrian and Bavarian lakes in the neighbourhood of Salzburg: this my dear Dora will tend to prevent my reaching London in what I feel to be what you call *decent* time. Yet still we will return together; whether by Brinsop or no must depend upon our convenience. After so long a ramble, I should certainly have put off that visit till another year, had it not been for Uncle Thomas's illness— this weighs much with me and I will strain a point to see them at Brinsop along with you if we are both tolerably well. But I assure you as the trembling of my hand shews this hot weather is playing the deuce with my nerves. My wrists are deplorably unstrung and my muscular strength much diminished. We have had no spring properly speaking, about three weeks since the Summer burst out at once into a profuse heat, and ever since we have been perspiring and drinking cold water from morning to night. Commend me to an English climate in preference a thousand times to what I have known of an Italian one. What I have seen both of Nature and Art in Italy have delighted me much, but I am convinced that none but young people, and

strong ones too, should attempt to explore Italy with less than
twelve months time at their command, and abundance of money
also to spare them bodily fatigue whenever money can do it.
We have been generous to ourselves in this way, but not as far
as moving about goes (especially in Towns) to the extent of what
would have been for me expedient; for as I said before nothing
is so exhausting as seeing sights in hot weather in large towns.
My dearest Mary and Sister, no words can describe my delight
in seeing the first objects in Milan which I recollected we had
seen together—though there were several things visited by us
in company that I was obliged to leave unseen, in particular the
Ambrosian Library and Leonardo da Vinci's Last Supper, but
I went to the Brera and to the Cathedral several times, not
omitting to mount among the Statues as high as the circle of
metallic stars; higher I did not venture, my head was too giddy
and my dearest Mary I wanted the support which your firmness
gave me when we ascended together. At three o'clock in the
morning we took the diligence for [? Cernobbio] got there by eight
embarked on the steamboat and I went to the head of the Lake;
Mr R. stopped to visit a friend at Menaggio where you recollect
he and dear Mr Monkhouse passed such a terrible night among
thousands of fleas. It would be idle to attempt to express my
feelings upon that expedition, whether I thought of my walk
with dear Jones, or of our enjoyment at so much later a period
of life upon the same ground. Though Mr and Mrs Ticknor and
their son and daughter went in the same boat as far as Bellaggio,
for we fell in with them at Como, I kept much to myself, and
very often could I, for my heart's relief, have burst into tears.
I wish Dora that you had been with me, that I might have
pointed out to you all the spots that your Mother your Aunt
and I had been delighted with. This would make the happiest
day of all my tour. In passing Cadenabbia things came upon
me as fresh as if they had happened the day before, and delighted
I was to find how little the forms and colours [of] objects had
faded from my memory. At six we were again in the Diligence
an omnibus chokefull and everybody gasping with heat. Between eleven and twelve we got back to Milan. The lakes of
Iseo and Garda were well worth the time we bestowed upon

them; at the head of the latter we stopped a whole day, of which I employed 8 hours in rambling among the Alpine heights. The scenery is magnificent and I was well repaid for my labour. When we meet I will tell you some of my little adventures, and endeavour to describe what we saw and did there as well as at Iseo—At Venice we shall see the Ticknors again and though I expect much pleasure there, and shall I trust carry away much that will remain in my memory for future delight, I frankly tell you, that my gladdest moment, after receiving your Letter if it bring no bad news, will be the one when I am in motion again for Dear England. I could tell you a hundred things of what I have seen, if I had space or were fonder of writing, or could write legibly, but I feel disposed to give utterance rather of thanks to God in which I am sure you will join who has enabled us to make so long and in some respects hazardous a journey without one ill accident or moment's illness to either of us; except if it deserves to be named the cold I caught in France. We have both escaped the influenza and all attacks of fever which, I assure you, is not a little to be dreaded from sudden checks of perspiration and other causes incident to this climate so different from our own. Yesterday we had a vitious horse put into the carriage, who backed dangerously at the first bridge we came to on leaving the post Town. I insisted upon another being brought, and not without difficulty prevailed. Such a horse in many places where we have been might have caused our destruction. When I think of Thomas's sad situation I am deeply thankful that all has gone well with us. Dearest Dora be assured that I will curtail our stay among the Austrian lakes as much as I can, with due regard to Mr Robinson's wishes, in order that I may reach London in as good time as possible. At Munich we shall be detained at least 4 days, and at least two at Heidelberg but not half a day anywhere else. If anyone would take a fancy to our carriage when I shall consider our *touring* is fairly over, we should most gladly sell it; and make our way direct by steam to Rotterdam and London. That would spare both time and fatigue but it is not likely because we cannot sell it without being repaid the deposit of duty we were obliged to make at Calais, so to that place I suppose we shall be compelled to go! I leave the rest of the space to say a word from Venice to acknowledge I hope the receipt of your letter.

Venice Friday 23 We reached this place yester evening after stopping 5 hours in the heat of the day at Mestro. We are well lodged where John W. recommended us to go. We are close by the place of St Mark, a splendid spot! What I have seen of Venice has fully equalled my expectations. No letter from you; yet surely I directed you to address me hither. I must bear my disappointment as well as I can. Dearest Dora, I am truly sorry for your tooth-ache, and Mary tell me about you all and dearest Sister how is she. Love to you all and kindest regards to the servants one and all and to Mr Carter and to all friends. The day you receive this dearest Mary write to me directly to Munich. How I long to be through all the sights of this place. The weather is insufferably hot; every now and then as I am writing such a cramp comes into my right hand, the hand with the little lump in the palm, that I am obliged to lay down my pen. Dora I am sorry about the leaves. I ought to have had a little Box for that purpose as [?] the flowers I plucked in different places have all crumbled away. Give my love to Edith and her husband, to the Watsons if you be with them and to all friends. We left Mr Augustus Hare seriously ill at Florence. I find a letter in the post-off: today from Mrs Hare telling me he is a good deal recovered. I think him however a man old for his years— Dearest Mary and Sister, Venice in situation very much resembles Amsterdam as Lombardy does Holland in general very much, but the architecture of Venice is wonderfully more splendid than Amsterdam. It is quite unique, inferior only to Rome and scarcely that. Again and again farewell. If I have no letter at Venice I shall scarcely write again till we get to Salzburg.

W. W.

Address: Mrs Wordsworth, Rydal Mount, Kendal, Inghilterra.

MS. *1220. W. W. to his Family at Rydal*
K(—)

[Salzburg July 5 1837]

My dearest Friends, here we are at Salzburg having arrived this morning, and found, dearest Dora, your welcome letter.

But I must go back; and speak about your letters. Mary, yours reached me at Venice, the day after I had written; one from Dora as I must have told you most fortunately the day I left Milan, so that in all I have received four; and shall confidently expect another when we reach Munich, where we shall not be for some little time, for Mr R. much to my regret talks of taking not less than a fortnight among what are called the Austrian Lakes not far from this place. I hope he will change his mind, as he has made so many sacrifices for me, I must make some for him. How thankful I am dear Dora that you are relieved from your suffering. Most earnestly do I pray that this may be the last of the kind you will have to suffer. Thank you again and again for your entertaining letter; and you dear Mary for yours, which brightened my stay at Venice. Our abode of six days would have been most delightful, but for two unlucky circumstances, the extreme heat of the weather and the smallness and aspect of my bedroom which during four nights (the two last I was able to procure a better) made me very uncomfortable indeed, endeavouring to sleep while I was actually in an oven. Our journey of six days or seven (Mr Robinson is out and he keeps the dates) from Venice through an Alpine country to this place has been charming; the weather though very hot sometimes for a few hours in the day mightily improved and my *perspirations* at an end. But I expect to have enough of them, when we get again into the plain country. But for your letters, I have received five, one from Mary at Rome date Brinsop April 17th one from Dora, Florence, another Milan, one from Mary, Venice, and lastly this of to day Salzburg. I began and wrote half of a letter at Venice but I thought it better not to finish it, and as it is now out of date I shall not send it. My health has been good, but certainly my Frame is weakened by the journey as I feel in many ways, as for instance the bodily exertion of rummaging in my trunk for something I wanted since I began this Letter, has brought a kind of cramp of pain to my stomach such as I have often felt upon like occasions but never used to have. This stomach weakness may be in part accounted for by the quantity of liquid which from extreme thirst I have been tempted to take, and it has been increased I will confess by the less excusable fault, the labour I have lately undergone in correcting a little Poem of 76 lines which I was tempted to write. This work disturbed or rather broke my rest for two or three nights when I might have had the benefit of the cool air of the Alpine country with sound sleep to recruit me. As these verses have cost me in this way more than they ought to have done I shall be much mortified if you do not like them and think them pretty good. I promise you solemnly that I shall attempt nothing of the kind again during this journey. The mistiming of meals, which is often unavoidable, and employment that would rob me of rest in the night are too much. As to over-hurrying, or rather mine, you are a good deal mistaken on this point. Six days apiece were quite enough for both Florence and Venice unless one had meant to make a study of the works of art there; so was the time we gave to all the other Italian cities unless we had had the same object. And as to posting, that, as our journey from Venice will shew, we have taken at leisure. Indeed I never wish to do otherwise except when the face of the Country is wholly uninteresting. I could write to you Volumes in the way of letters were I [to] touch upon all that I have seen felt and thought.

I have, however, to regret that this journey was not made some years ago,—to regret it, I mean, as a Poet; for though we have had a great disappointment in not seeing Naples, etc., and more of the country among the Apennines not far from Rome, Horace's country for instance, and Cicero's Tusculum, my mind has been enriched by innumerable images, which I could have turned to account in verse, and vivified by feelings which earlier in my life would have answered noble purposes, in a way they now are little likely to do. But I do not repine; on the contrary, I am very happy, wishing only to see all your dear faces again, and to make amends for my frequent bad behaviour to you all. Absence in a foreign country, and at a great distance, is a condition, for many minds, at least for mine, often pregnant with remorse. Dearest Mary, when I have felt how harshly I often demeaned myself to you, my inestimable fellow-labourer, while correcting the last Edition of my poems, I often pray to God that He would grant us both life, that I may make some amends to you for that, and all my unworthiness. But you know into what an irritable state this timed and overstrained labour often put my nerves. My impatience was ungovernable as I thought *then*, but I now feel that it ought to have been governed. You have forgiven me I know, as you did then, and perhaps that somehow troubles me the more. I say nothing of this to you, dear Dora, though you also have had some reason to complain. —But too much of this—I hope I shall be able to write the rest of this sheet more legibly as I have just been watering the ink which had got unmanageably thick as these few great blots shew. How sorry, dear Dora, I am for poor Mr Hallam; he had just been touring in the beautiful country where now we are before he lost his son so suddenly. Beautiful indeed this Country is; in a picturesque and even poetic point of view more interesting than most of what we have seen. It is something between the finest part of Alpine Switzerland and the finest parts of Great Britain; I mean in North Wales, Scotland, and our own region. In many particulars it excels Italy, I mean of course what I have seen of it; and also, greatly indeed, the south of France. The mountains are finely formed, and the Vales not choked up, nor the hillsides disfigured by the sort of cultivation which the sunshine of Italy puts thereupon—vines, olives, citrons, lemons and all kinds of fruit-trees. Yesterday we passed through a country of mountain, meadow, lawn, and the richest wood spread about with all the magnificence of an everlasting Park, such a character as we often find in England, but these things here are on so vast a scale compared with our landscapes. But I must not run on in this strain, but leave the rest of this sheet as you would wish Mary to Mr Robinson. How glad was I to have your account of my beloved Sister; oh my dear Sister do try to renew your love of Nature. How I wish I had you here for a few minutes, notwithstanding your love of your own Chair and your fire! Write to me at Heidelberg and that may be your last letter. Dora you shall hear of the time when I hope to be in town, as soon as I can come at all near a determination. You have never told me anything about the last Edition, how it has sold, how it is liked, and what John Carter thought of the printing of the latter part. But farewell and God bless you all and love to all the family every where and to all friends again farewell—I shall certainly write from Munich; and perhaps begin my letter before.   W. W.

Address: Mrs Wordsworth, Rydal Mount, N^r Kendal, England.

MS.   *1221. W. W. to M. W.*
K(—)

Munich Monday July 17 [1837]

My dearest Mary, twelve or thirteen days ago I wrote to you from Salzburg acknowledging the receipt of your most welcome letter. This morning we came hither, and I had the pleasure of finding another from you. I grieve much to learn that Dora's jaws still torment her. Poor Creature what is to become of her? How happy am I on the other hand to learn that you are so well, and my dear Sister is better. Thank her affectionately for the few words she wrote me. Since my last we have had a delightful ramble amongst the Austrian lakes which we have seen completely as we should have done also those of the valley but that the weather broke 4 days ago, and cut short our expedition though we did see three of these latter. At present I consider our *Tour* finished; and all my thoughts are fixed upon home, where I am most impatient to be; and conscientiously so, for I have hurried over nothing, notwithstanding your frequent hints to the contrary; which have rather hurt me, particularly as there are (as must be the case with all companions in travel) so many things in habit and inclination in which Mr R. and I differ. Upon these I shall not dwell at present, as the only one I care about is this; he has no home to go to but chambers, and wishes to stay abroad, at least to linger abroad, which I, having the blessing of a home, do not. Again, he takes delight in loitering about towns, gossiping, and attending reading-rooms, and going to coffee-houses; and at *table d'hôtes*, etc., gabbling German, or any other tongue, all which places and practices are my abomination. In the evenings I cannot read, as the candlelight hurts my eyes, and I have therefore no resource but to go to bed, while I should like exceedingly, when upon our travels, if it were agreeable to him to rise early; but though he will do this, he dislikes it much, so that I don't press it. He sleeps so much at odd times in the day that he does not like going to bed till midnight; and in this, and a hundred other things, our tastes and habits are quite at variance; though nobody can be more obliging in giving up his own; but you must be aware it is very unpleasant in me to require this. In fact, I have very strong reasons for wishing this tour, which I have found so beneficial to my mind, at an end for the sake of my body; for certainly either the diet or some other cause has very much shaken my nerves as this trembling of my hand writing, and the frequent cramps I have had in my hand since I began this page, sufficiently shew. My bowels have latterly been in better order and I have no pain anywhere, but my head is often cloudy and my nerves as I have said are much deranged. I sometimes think that the coffee and beer I take, for I have nearly left off wine, are too much for my nerves. If I dared do so I would leave off beer and wine altogether and coffee also, but milk I know is binding. Excuse all this; not a word of which would have been said had not both you and Dora blamed me so much for hurrying. In fact I have not hurried, but been very patient, considering the tiresome way in which when in towns I have been obliged to spend so many hours. If the state of my nerves and stomach would allow me to write verse I should never want employment, or if my muscular powers were as great as they have been so that I could walk all day long it would be the same, but that time is passed away, and I want the sight of your faces and the sound of your voices, when I can do neither the one nor the other, nor read to beguile the time. Therefore find no more fault, I undertook this journey as a *duty*, I have gone through with it as such, and except that as far as concerns my health having had a most unsuitable companion in Mr Robinson I have in consequence made many sacrifices of which he was not aware, I have kept duty constantly in my eyes, and have greatly enriched my mind; and I hope when I get home that I shall find my health not at all worse. So let us all be glad that I have made this upon the whole so delightful journey. I shall have a thousand things to tell you; and if I had ten years before me of such strength as I have had, you would see my future verses animated in a way that would please you all. Now for other and more agreeable things; but I find my handwriting shockingly unsteady.—Yet how can I say agreeable for to tell you the truth I fear that public affairs will now take a wretched course and that the young Queen under unwise guidance will abandon herself to the foolish and selfish Whigs. The elections about to be will I fear run much against the conservatives, indeed on these points all my thoughts are gloomy—so no more about them—

How long Mr Robinson will be loitering here I know not. The exterior of the place has for me no interest; but I believe it contains a large collection of works of Art some of which must no doubt be interesting, and tomorrow I shall begin with them —and I hope on the fourth day at the latest, I wish the third, we shall start for Heidelberg where we shall stay I suppose two days at least—All the rest will be straightforward travelling, so that I hope by the end of the third week from this time we shall be in London or perhaps a few days later. I wrote thus far before dinner at 2. From 3 to 5 I tired myself in walking about the place under the guidance of a friend of Mr Robinson, I have since been in my room alone. It is now $\frac{1}{4}$ past 7 and before 9 I shall be in bed, for sheer want of something to do, unless I tire myself with composition which I am resolved not to meddle with. I wish I could single out any part of our tour to give an account of, but we have no adventures, and since we left Venice, have had nothing to see but the fine country we have passed through and the employments of the people and their appearance. Yesterday was Sunday, we passed the greatest part of the day near one of the Bavarian lakes where the Queen Dowager my Co-Sponsor has a palace. The scenery compared with most we have seen since we entered the Alps is of a mild character more like our own but very agreeable. The People were all assembled in the little town for Church and I was much amused with their appearance. The women are the most gigantic race I ever saw and they wear a dress which makes them appear very high-shouldered and short-necked (like our Barlow jug). The men are a fine race, most of them wear bonnets shaped exactly like, and in height the same, as those of our old puritans. Some had a feather, like Hofer's,[1] stuck on one side sometimes with a

[1] For Hofer *v*. Oxf. W. p. 314.

flower but most only a flower in this hat or bonnet, and the flower never in front but almost always directly behind, which has a singular appearance. They pride themselves much upon the quality and workmanship of their stockings; one man's were so elabourately figured that I could not but ask him the price, he told me as much as 7 or 8 shillings, rather six or seven, I expressed my wonder, and he told me he had had those stockings and regularly worn them, I suppose on Sundays and feast days, for twenty years. I employed myself for more than 3 hours in walking about this beautiful valley, and conversing as well as I could with its interesting Inhabitants who have however one great fault, they are extremely fond of beer and drink immense quantities. But if we were to judge from the size and neatness and apparent comfort of their habitations, which however are built almost entirely of wood, from their dress, and the fertility and beauty of their country they are in an enviable condition.

I shall not send off this Letter till we have left or are on the point of leaving this place. At Heidelberg I shall inquire after Willy's lodgings, but this will be my last letter as I shall be in London I trust within not much more than a week of the time of your receiving this. Write to me by all means at Mr Moxon's through Mr Stephen. How I long to see you dearest Mary and all of you again. As to going to Bath or Brinsop I will do whatever is thought best; I feel that dear Thomas and Mary have strong claims upon me, and if both Dora and I are [we]ll, I hope I shall have courage to go and see them; b[ut I] do long to [be at] rest under our own roof! The verses may wait till I send them from London. Mr R. has had today a letter from a Money-friend in London who has a great deal to do with our joint-stock bank. He says many unpleasant things have come out respecting concerns of this kind; but none at all affecting the character of ours; so that if it continues to stand the test of examination and it is under excellent management I doubt not it will not only survive the storm but thrive upon the ruin of others. As you do not mention James I hope his health is restored; pray remember me most kindly to all the servants; Mr Carter also and to all friends. You little know how I love you all.

A man must travel alone, I mean without one of his family, to feel what his family is to him! How often have I wished for James to assist me about the carriage, greasing the wheels, etc a most tedious employment, fastening the baggage, etc., for nothing can exceed the stupidity of these foreigners. Tell him how I wish I had been rich enough to bring him along with me! But I must leave a scrap of paper for another day.—I have no cramp in my fingers since I began to write this afternoon and my hand is steadier, though the writing is execrable. God bless you all. Thursday morning 20th. It is fixed that we leave this place tomorrow noon. I think we should be four or five days getting to Heidelberg as the German postilions are so slow, and we shall stop at least half a day at Stuttgart at Ulm and Augsburg. So as you know the distance from Heidelberg to Calais you will be able to calculate within 2 or 3 days the time of our arrival in London. I am quite tired of this place, the weather has been very bad, and after the galleries close which is at 12 o'clock and one, I have nothing to do, and as I cannot speak German my time moves very heavily. The Ticknors are here and I have passed a couple of hours every evening with them. God bless you again.

Address: Mrs Wordsworth, Rydal Mount, Kendal, Angleterre.

MS.   *1222. W. W. to Edward Moxon*

Brussels 2nd August [1837]
My dear Mr Moxon,

Here we are after a most pleasant Tour, in good health and spirits. I write now to tell you that I hope to be in London, on Monday evening next, and I shall make my way directly to your hospitable door.—

Pray inquire after my Daughter at Mr Henry Coleridge's, or if it suits to write to Hampstead Heath at Mrs Hoare's, at one or other house you will be sure to hear of her, and let her know my intention. Remember me most kindly to Mrs Moxon and your Sister and Brother,—and believe me faithfully and affectionately yours

Wm Wordsworth.

MS.   *1223. W. W. to Dora W.*

Tuesday 8th [August 1837] Dover St. 44

My dearest Dora, Here I am; arrived at the Custom house yesterday at half-past 2, and got to this House between 7 and 8 where I found Mr Moxon and one of his Sisters. He had kindly come up from Ramsgate to welcome me. Why did not you mention your mouth, about which I am so anxious, in your kind note. Here I found also a short Letter from your Mother. As I have much to do, I shall not stir out till after three today; if Mrs Hoare to whom and Miss Hoare give my kind love, could come with you, or send you over in her carriage that I might have a few minutes talk with you, I should be greatly obliged. At all events let me have an answer by the Bearer. Ever your affectionate Father

W. W.

Address: Miss Wordsworth, Mrs Hoare's, Hampstead Heath.

MS.   *1224. W. W. to his Family at Rydal*

Wednesday morning [Aug: 9 1837]

My dearest Friends, On Monday at half-past 2 reached the Custom house—was detained several hours till our baggage could be examined and did not reach Mr Moxon's till near eight. Kind creature he had come up from Broadstairs, where his wife sister and children are for sea-air, on purpose to meet me. I received, dear Mary, your 2nd Letter at Munich—the one for Heidelberg did not reach that place till we had left it though 26 days had passed between my Salzburg Letter and the day we left Heidelberg—it followed me however to Brussels where I got it after much trouble, particulars of which I defer till we meet. Mr Moxon was so kind as to send his Boy over to Hampstead yesterday morning, and the consequence was Mrs Hoare brought Dora over to see me. I did not myself think her improved in looks, but that might be owing to the flurry of seeing me. I questioned her pointedly as could be about her health, and she answered frankly 'I certainly am better, except for my face I have little pain, and my appetite is good, but I do not gather strength as I expected. In short I can do little, that is a little exertion is too much for me.' But Mr Rogers is so kind as to take me over today to Hampstead where I shall see her again and I will write to you either tomorrow or next day. Her respect for Mr Carr's opinion, as being best acquainted with her constitution, has I think quite reconciled her to pass this winter in the South, which I rejoice in. Our plan is, as probably she has told you I am obliged to write this before I have seen her letter, is to go together to Chatham in the earlier part of next week; I will try also to manage for her going to Broadstairs for a week's sea-air and bathing, and I will remain with her there. The Rogers have a spare bed in their lodgings and I can easily get one in the place; we will then go to Brinsop together, if all goes on well, so that alas, alas! our meeting and the sight of my dear Sister and all Rydal friends must be deferred for some time. Thanks for your Letter which I found here—The memorandum will be attended to. I rejoice to hear that you are all well and that my dear Sister can walk by aid of a stick; we shall do great things together when we meet again.

From Munich we came through Augsburg, Ulm, Stuttgart to Heidelberg, where we slept three nights, and I went everywhere especially to the places where we had been together; the weather very fine. From Heidelberg through Mannheim Mainz Coblenz Cologne etc to Brussels, from Brussels to Antwerp by railway, and returned to Brussels the same day—this was to me a delightful day of recollections of you and Dora, from Brussels through Tournay and Lille to Cassel a charming place and St Omer with which I was much pleased, to Calais where we arrived about two in the afternoon and embarked about two in the morning; for the first three hours, the sea being rough, I was tremendously sick, and feel the inconvenience in my throat to this hour.—Dear Miss Fenwick is in town, she arrived yesterday. I called at her Lodgings, and saw her looking well for a few minutes. Today I shall see her again before I go to Hampstead. I also called on Mr and Mrs Johnson yesterday. Rogers called on me here, and I dined with him, but only stopped an hour and a half, having passed almost the whole day within always waiting for Dora and with her all the evening. I have sixty pounds left of the 200 I took with me, there is also the Carriage that cost us 70 pounds, but by that I fear we shall lose greatly, it is now at the Coach Makers. Pray give my affectionate regards to Mrs Bolton, I mean to write to her as soon as I can find a moment's leisure.

What a sad thing this Workington affair[1] is; but tell dear Isabella with my best love that I trust in God's goodness and that it will ultimately tend to the good of the whole, and every branch of the family. Congratulate John and Isabella also on the birth of their Son, with a thousand good wishes that he may prove a blessing to his Parents; say also all that is kind to Mr and Mrs Curwen from me. I would write to them, but they can easily understand how overwhelmed I must be with answering Letters that have accumulated for me here. I am glad to hear that James is recovered and hope that Anne Jane and Dorothy are all well. Tell Lady Farquhar I had the pleasure of meeting her sister Lady Conway and Amelia with another sister and I believe a third but I am not sure; she was of the family at Louvain on their way to Baden-Baden. They were well.

[unsigned]

MS.   *1225. W. W. to his Family at Rydal*

[? Thursday Aug. 10 1837]

My dearest Friends, I was obliged to send off yesterday a scrawl unfinished. I went with Mr and Miss Rogers to Hampstead—they to Miss B— I remained at Mrs Hoare's from half past two till six when they took me up, and Mr R. brought me to Miss Fenwick's 19 Lower Grosvenor Street where I remained till ten. Dora is in excellent spirits and I cannot but think a good deal improved in health. Everybody seems delighted with her. I have looked over her letters and find she has mentioned my toe. I must therefore add that in the great toe of my right foot I have had a slight aggravation of a redness and heat that I have had a little of for some years—I trust it will not prove anything but it attracted my attention in rather a disagreeable way which it

---

[1] *v.* Letter to Hamilton, Jan. 4, 1838, p. 912.

never did before. I think this was owing in great measure to fatigue and heat and to broken sleep caused partly by the Poem I now send you getting into my thoughts in the night-time. But far too much of this I hope insignificant affair.—This morning I am going to the Colonial Off:, Stamp Off:, Strickland Cookson, the Dentist, I have lost my last tooth but one, and Courtenay's if possible, so that I shall have enough to do. It is now eleven o'clock. Rogers, Moore, and Kenyon have been break-fasting here.—I enclose a note from Mrs Hook whom I have not yet seen. I shall be obliged to conclude this letter as the last probably without a signature. Have you packed up my Mr Moxon's two additional volumes of Cowper which have been waiting for some time to be called for by someone as you told him they would be; what is to be done with them. How to proceed about pupils for John I know not. I will do my best.— Mrs Howley begged me when I was last in Town to let her know of my return and she would come up to Town to fetch [me] to visit them. I fear I shall not have time to do this, I long so to be at home. But something might come of such a visit. Pray write by return of post if you can to this place.

I have this moment read your last letter to Dora to which I find nothing to answer—I am delighted you have got Henry with you and [? charmed] that you like him so much. Love to all friends whom I have not time to mention, W. W. Tell me whether you get into the Poem at once and how you like it.

Address: Mrs Wordsworth, Rydal, Kendal.

MS.   *1226. W. W. to his Family at Rydal*

Monday morning Mrs Hoare's, Hampstead

[Aug. 14 1837]

My dear friends, I have been very busy since my last; but I have mislaid your paper of Memorandums which I hope however is at Moxon's, so that I cannot at present say what I have left undone. On Saturday I walked hither, calling by the way upon Miss Fenwick, Mr Spring Rice, I saw the ladies but not him, he was at Downing Street, Mrs Hook and Miss Rogers. Yesterday evening I was at Sir Benjamin Brodie's and he has kindly allowed me to take Dora to him which cannot be before Friday next, on which day or Saturday I hope we shall go to Chatham when also she will see Dr Davy, so that she will have the best medical [advice]. I mentioned incidentally our poor Brother Thomas's case; his answer was very encouraging, he says he has lately had two cases under his care of two gentlemen who by accidents had lost the use of arms and legs; they are both recovering the use of them, though of course slowly, one of them is 70 years of age. He does not rely upon medicine, he says Time and care must do the work, the patient using as much exercise as he can bear. I said Thomas had been at Bath, he did not think much good likely to come of that; but that whatever strength[ens] the general health, such as good air exercise and cheerful spirits and a tranquil [?]; to these the sufferer must chiefly look for restoration, and he did not seem to doubt that in time it would come. I have seen much more of Dora; she certainly is not strong, I observe from time to time she puts her hand to her side as formerly, and shrinks a little in her posture. But then surely she must be upon the whole much better. Yester morning she was at Church which I think however a little too much for her, and thence she and I drove in a car to Hendon, of course she was a little tired on our return and lay down on the sofa, but I trust she will do well. She seems reconciled to staying for the winter in the south as we all desire it so much. Miss Fenwick means to pass the winter somewhere on the southern coast, and will be most happy to have Dora with her as long as she can, and will bring her down into Westmorland, in spring or early in the summer. Is not that a nice plan; dear good Creature Miss Fenwick is! She comes this morning to fetch me and she will talk over the matter with Dora, and I dine with her today to meet Mr Stephen and Mr Taylor. Tomorrow I breakfast with Miss Rogers to meet the American Minister and his lady. I have seen Courtenay twice, and shall see him again. He has just received rather more than 200, due on the annuities, with which he will purchase India bonds as a present investment adding them to the

[cetera desunt]

[887]

MS.   *1227. W. W. to M. W.*

August 15th Tuesday [1837]

My dearest Mary, Your pacquet reached me yesterday. The frank I was to have sent off on Monday, proved of a wrong date; and most unfortunately a pretty long letter I had written for you must have been left at Hampstead yesterday, now I have inflammation in my right eye and cannot write at length. I know not what to say to Wm's proposal, but that he must examine carefully before he mixes with anything of the kind. I had from Mr Courtenay papers of the annuities, dark and unpromising account, we erred in not accepting his proposal which would have put 500 into our pockets. I have such a hot skin and such feverish nights, that I am anxious to be gone from London. Yesterday I dined at Miss Fenwick's, dinner not till eight as Mr Stephen could not come before, remained till 12, I have not been up so late for 5 months and consequently a disturbed night and the inflammation in my eye—on Friday Dora will see Sir Benjamin Brodie with me and on Saturday I hope we shall be at Chatham. Sir B. says he has lately had two patients like Brother Thomas both recovering though slowly. Time, exercise, cheerful spirits, and hope must do the work, and not medicine. [?   ] I can write no more on account of the anger in my eye. Love to dearest Sister, farewell my dearest Mary I wish I were quietly at Rydal.

W. W.

MS.   *1228. W. W. to Dora W.*

[p.m. Aug. 15. 1837]

My dear Dora,

These came yesterday. How unlucky I am, the Letter I wrote to your mother under a wrong frank must have been left at Hampstead where you made the objection to its being crumpled up. I do not find it in my pocket-book neither can I find any where a letter for the Isle of Man from your Mother which I was to have got franked. I must also have left at Hampstead a pair of mottled half-stockings. I have got an inflammation in my right eye in consequence of a dinner deferred at Miss Fenwick's last night till 8 and not coming away till 12. I am anxious to be out of London and to be living somewhere in quiet—I feel I am living too fast—I had a very feverish and hot skin last night. God bless you—you will be expected at Mrs Hook's on Thursday. I found Sara Coleridge looking very ill—God bless you my dearest Dora, kindest remembrances to all.

W. W.

p.s. Upon opening your Letter to Mother, I find my own enclosed

pray be so good as to look for my stockings

Address: Miss Wordsworth, Mrs Hoare's, Hampstead Heath.

MS.   *1229. W. W. to M. W. and D. W.*

Broadstairs, Wednesday 23 August [1837]

My dearest Friends

I arrived here this morning. But I will take things in order. On Thursday last I dined with Mrs Hook in Regents Park, whither Dora had come in the afternoon. On that night as on the night before I slept at the Rogers's, where on Friday morning Dora joined me in a Fly and we went to Sir Benjamin B. What passed between them I do not exactly know, but on [?] he told me that nothing serious ailed her and that she only wanted strength. He approved of her remaining the winter in the South, which he said it would be well to try. From Sir B.'s we went back to Rogers, and then in a Coach to London Bridge wharf, where after waiting half an hour we embarked for Gravesend. We had a pleasant passage, a fine breeze, which she much enjoyed. At Gravesend we got into an Omnibus and reached Chatham Docks, just as they were at dinner, between five and six. She bore the fatigue of the day very well, but next day she was very *yawnative*, and more exhausted than I was prepared for. Mrs Smith took us in a carriage to call on the Nicholsons and upon Mrs Fletcher at whose house we met Dr and Mrs Davies[1] and their children. Miss Fletcher quite well and strong. On Sunday morning Dora did not go to Church, but the Nicholsons after offered to lend their carriage to take us to the Cathedral, Mrs Smith, she and I went. On Saturday I called on

---

[1] i.e. Dr. John Davy.

Colonel Pasley who has been ill, but is getting better, in an
inflammation of the trachea. On Monday Dora remained at
home. I called on Dr Davey and he took me to Cobham House,
4 miles from Rochester, a seat of Lord Dursley's. On that
day (viz. Monday) Dr D and Mrs Fletcher and Miss dined at
Mrs Smith's; and Tuesday noon I left Mrs Smith's with a hope
of getting on to Canterbury in time to be brought hither by Mr
and Miss Rogers, but the 2 first Coaches were full, so I arrived
too late, and was obliged to sleep at Canterbury which with the
expense of travelling from Canterbury cost me 12 shillings, but
I missed their company also. Dora thought it better on every
account she should remain at Chatham, in which she was quite
right as the journey hither would have fatigued her much;
besides her stay at Chatham would otherwise have been too
short. Having now seen a good deal of her, I can say, that I am
rather disappointed as to the state of her strength; in other
respects not so.—Therefore my dearest Friends let us live in hope
that she will be restored in time. At Chatham she received your
2nd Letter; your first with Isabella's enclosed I found here and
shall forward to her through Mr Stephen. I cannot say anything
fixed yet about our movements; but I shall not stay here more
than a week. Rogers and his Sister are both here; Moxon and I
dine there today. If possible I will go for two nights to the Archbishop's and then for Herefordshire. Dora wrote to Charles
Wordsworth to receive her for a night or two, and Mr Smith will
convey her up to Town. Tell Mr Carter I will call at Bell's. As
to her Chair for Thomas, I talked to Dr Davey about it, but
he seemed to be without distinct ideas on the subject, and
thought nothing so likely to answer as a Sedan Chair; so that
until I shall have seen Thomas I fear I can do nothing in the
matter. I have not been able to make out much of Isabella's
Letter, so that I know not if it may require any comments from
my pen. I hope John, our John, will be very careful what he
says, or writes, of the Curwen affairs—his words misled me a
good deal about the supposed amount of the loss. This must be
a very meagre Letter. I think I told you if I had had the
prospect of Dora's being at the seaside with Miss Fenwick or any
other friend I should never have thought of coming here, but

gone straight into Herefordshire, but having entangled myself in engagements with Mr Rogers and Mr Moxon I could not break through.—Your account of little Henry[1] delights me much. I hope you will be allowed to keep him till my return, pray do. I was up this morning at four, and had a dull ride hither. Yesterday I went in to Canterbury Cathedral and if it had been only 2 miles instead of 4 to Lee Priory I should have walked thither. Dora was much mortified when she learned I had directed my Letters through Mr Stephen to be forwarded hither, and I am myself sorry that I did so. This is Wednesday, by next Wednesday or Thursday at the latest I hope to be in London. So that a Letter in answer to this may be directed to Mr Moxon's. I had a violent [? Lax] for 2 days in London but it is gone off and I am well except the heat in the toe and something of numbness in my hands which I think is always worst after drinking a little, however little, more than usual. I feel strongly persuaded that I should do best to leave off fermented liquors altogether. How I long dearest Mary to see you again and you my dearest Sister, and all of you. Farewell W. W.

Thursday. My dearest M. I could not send this letter off yesterday as I intended. I am afraid you will be impatient for news. I am sorry to learn from the enclosed which I took the liberty of opening that Dora says her heart beats more lately. She never mentioned this to me, and I do not like to teaze her with questions about her health. Neither do you mention your own health, pray do, how is your chest? This must say I have contrived to read Isabella's[2] Letter which does her great credit.

Address: Mrs Wordsworth, Rydal, Kendal.

MS.

1230. W. W. to Dora W.

Broadstairs Thursday morning
[p.m. Aug. 25 1837]

My dearest Dora

Mr and Miss Rogers were gone when I reached Canterbury, it was not till near six; so I had to sleep there which with

---

[1] W.'s eldest grandson, born 1834.
[2] Presumably about her father's financial losses.

expenses of coaches before I got here cost me 12 shillings. I was called at 4 in the morning, hired a fly at Ramsgate, reached this door between 7 and 8. I wished much to write to you yesterday as I did to Mother, but I was engaged in various ways till it was too late: I found much difficulty in reading the enclosed Letter as I fear you will also. Yesterday was shocking bad weather, today is bright and pleasant, which I am especially glad of for your sakes, as you will I trust enjoy your trip to Sheerness. This is a very pleasant, though not a particularly amusing place; but the drives are agreeable; yesterday I went with Rogers to Margate and Kingsgate but it rained so we could not get out of the Carriage. We shall go again. Next Wednesday, I trust, I shall be in London. Probably today I shall write to Mrs Howley and if convenient I will go for two days to visit them, perhaps it would be as well you should stay at Chatham till my return, but all this may be fixed in time. The air is very bracing here today, and I think would agree well with Miss Fenwick and yourself. But Ramsgate may be as good and is no doubt much more amusing on account of the size of the harbour, the fine quays or piers, and the multitude of vessels.—I am quite sorry this Letter was not sent off yesterday but really my dear Child it was no fault of mine. Love to Mr and Mrs Smith and your cousin Mary and kind remembrances to Mr [?]

affectionately

W. W.

Address: Miss Wordsworth, W. Smith Esq, Chatham Docks, Chatham.

MS.   *1231. W. W. to M. W.*

Broadstairs Monday Augst 28 [1837]

My dearest Mary,

I have heard from Mrs Howley. The Moxons dont leave this place till Friday; I had meant to go on Wednesday, but they have prevailed on me to stay to go along with them. On Saturday I shall go to the Arch B^{p's} and return with him to Town on Tuesday morning, and on the Saturday following at the latest I trust that dear Dora and I will have reached Brinsop.—I have not heard of her since I came here but I shall write to her today with an account of my movements. Her intention was to go to Charles Wordsworth's if they could receive her. She cannot go to Mr Moxon's on account of the house being newly painted, nor shall I.—In the Letter I mean to write to Dora today I shall beg of her to let me know by post where she goes. She will of course remain at Chatham till I quit this place.

Lord Holland has begged through Mr Rogers that I would give them one day which perhaps I may do, but this will depend entirely upon Dora and [her] convenience. I wish she could have been with me here, for this is a very pleasant place with delight-ful air at this season of the year, though it must be very cold in winter, as indeed it is now, being full as nipping an air as in October with us. But Dora would have enjoyed it, and both Mr and Miss Rogers have their carriages here, so that she could have had an airing every day along the high grounds. We have been three times at Margate, and once at Ramsgate, and probably may go as far as Dover. I should have written more at length but my right eye is rather inflamed having been struck by the coldness yesterday in the R's carriage, and I was so imprudent as to read a good deal after dinner, when I felt it affected. Love to dearest Sister, ever most affectionately yours

W. W.

Address: Mrs Wordsworth, Rydal, Kendal.

MS.   *1232. W. W. to Dora W.*

No. 5 Prospect Place, Broadstairs

Monday, 28th. [1837]

My dearest Dora,

The Moxons leave this place Friday next, and have prevailed upon me to put off my departure, which I intended for Wednesday at the latest, to go along with them, by steam, embarking at Margate by ten on that morning.

On that day I hope to call at Bell's on account of the annuities, and on Saturday having heard from Mrs Howley, I shall go to Lambeth, probably to return with the Archbp who comes every Tuesday to Lambeth; if not with him, at all events I

shall return on that day at the latest.—Pray write to me by Post
and tell me where you will be in London. The best place for us
both would have been Mr Moxon's, but you must not be trusted
there on account of the newly painted House. I mean to sleep
on Friday at Mr Rogers, and the same on Tuesday when I return
from Addington Park. Lord and Lady Holland have warmly
requested me through Mr Rogers to give them one day; but in
this I should be entirely guided, my dear Child, by your convenience; being determined, if it suit you, to be at Hereford on
Friday night, at all events on Saturday at the very latest.

I have again mislaid the paper of Mother's commissions, if
you have it not; but I do not recollect anything in it which we
could effect, except to apply to Macrone, the Publisher, for Sir
E. Brydges Edit: of Milton, which Mr Moxon has undertaken
to do.

You would have enjoyed yourself here much, we have a comfortable Lodging with plenty of room for you, and both Mr and
Miss Rogers have their carriages here, with their horses, so that
you might have had an airing every day. This is a quiet pleasant
place with agreeable drives; we have been thrice at Margate, and
once at Ramsgate. I hope you saw from Chatham Docks the
glorious sunset we had on Saturday evening.

We shall embark on Friday at Margate for London at ten in the
morning, but probably you will not be inclined to leave Chatham
till my return from Addington Park, otherwise I might have had
the pleasure of seeing you on Friday, which would be much to me,
for I find it is a little mortifying to be so near you, and not be
with you, especially when we shall have to part so soon and for
so long a time.

Write to me by all means here if you can so that [the] Letter
may be here by Thursday morning, on Friday it would be too
late, as the Letters are not delivered till nine, when we may be at
Margate—if you have not fixed anything pray write to me at
Dover Street as soon as you have, but at all events let me hear
from you as soon as you can. Love to all kind friends about you,
your affectionate father.   W. W.

Address: Miss Wordsworth, W. Smith's Esq., Chatham Docks,
    Chatham.

_MS._   _1233. W. W. to M. W. and D. W._

My dearest Friends,   Dover Street 2nd Sep^{br} [1837]

The Enclosed Paper is for Mr Carter's custody. I called yesterday at Mr Bell's and expect to receive today his account of the monies paid to Mr Courtenay which I will either send or bring.

Dont send the portrait[1] to Isabella till I come. I will get it framed if she thinks it worth it, which I fear she will not, nor you either. The little drawing of Dora is charming, very like her; you would prize it highly.—Dont let any volumes of the Poems which you will find in the box be sold separate.—They sell very slowly at present, indeed no books at all sell. Today we shall see about the remaining Volumes of Sir Egerton's Milton—at 4 I leave this place for the Archbishop's, he sends a servant and a carriage for me, and shall remain till Tuesday, and on Friday we shall start for Hereford.

On Thursday I had a delightful excursion with Mr Rogers to Dover; the place is mightily improved as to new buildings since we were there, and I think it would suit admirably Miss Fenwick and Dora.

As Mr Rogers will not be in London to go with me to Holland House, I shall content myself with breakfasting there, on Wednesday, and that day I shall dine with Dora at Henry Coleridge's, and we both sleep that night and the next at Mr Rogers', and depart thence on Friday morning. So you are now aware of our movements.—As I find that Dora and I are writing the same things I shall give over, with my best love to Sister and a kiss to Henry. How I long to see you all—most tenderly and affectionately yours   W. W.

I think Dora is stronger.

_MS._   _1234. W. W. to Edward Moxon_[2]

        Brinsop Court n^{r} Hereford

Dear Mr Moxon,   Sept 13th [1837]

We had a beautiful day and reached Hereford in good time, Dora not being very much fatigued—The weather is at present

---

[1] i.e. by Severn, done in Rome, _v._ p. 858.

[2] For W. W. to Professor Reed, Aug. 19, _v._ Reed, p. 4. For W. W. to H. C. R. Sept. (early), _v. C.R._, p. 347.

so broken that we are unable to fix a day for setting off on our excursion for Tintern. Mr R.[1] is with Mr Monkhouse, *14* miles from this place up the Wye, but he will dine here to-day; he enjoyed himself as usual. I have contrived to get an inflammation in one of my eyelids in wh. the eye of course participates but I sh^d be ashamed of being dejected by such, I hope, passing privation when I see Mr Monkhouse on the verge of blindness as cheerful as the brightest day of Spring, he is indeed a noble example for every afflicted person.—

I find that I have brought away only one Vol: of Cowper which is more than enough, for neither are wanted here—Dora will therefore bring back with her to London this one and you will be so kind as to take the other out of my portmanteau.

I have nothing more to add than kind wishes in which Dora joins and a hope that you all continue well

Ever faithfully yours

Wm Wordsworth

I shall remain at this place till about Tuesday 26th when I start for the north and on Thursday ev.^g hope to be at home.

MS.　　　*1235. W. W. to Edward Quillinan*
M(—) G(—) K(—)

Brinsop Court, Wednesday Sept. 20th [1837]

My dear Mr Quillinan,

(I hold the pen for Father)

We are heartily glad to learn from your letter just received that in all probability by this time you must have left the unhappy country in wh. you have been so long residing. I should not have been sorry if you had entered a little more into Peninsular politics, for what is going on there is shocking to humanity, and one would be glad to see anything like an opening for the termination of these unnatural troubles—the position of the Miguelites relatively to the confliction of so-called liberal parties is just what I apprehended and expressed very lately to Mr

---

[1] i.e. H. C. R.

Robinson, who would not hear of it; very inconsiderately, I think, setting down that body as all but extinguished. He came down with us to Hereford with a view to a short tour on the banks of the Wye wh. has been prevented by an unexpected attack of my old complaint of inflammation in the eye; and in consequence of this Dora will accompany me home with a promise on her part of returning to London before the month of Oct^{br} is out. Our places are taken in to-morrow's coach for Liverpool, so that since we must be disappointed at not seeing you and Jemima here, we trust that you will come to Rydal from Leeds. This very day Dora had read to me your Poem again; it convinces me along with your other writings that it is in your power to attain a permanent place among the poets of England, your thoughts, feelings, knowledge, and judgement in style, and skill in metre entitle you to it; if you have not yet succeeded in gaining it the cause appears to me mainly to lie in the subjects wh. you have chosen. It is worthy of note how much of Gray's popularity is owing to the happiness with which his subject is selected in three pieces—his Hymn to Adversity, his ode on the distant prospect of Eton College, and his Elegy. I ought however in justice to add that one cause of your failure appears to have been thinking too humbly of yourself, so that you have not reckoned it worth while to look sufficiently round you for the best subjects or to employ as much time in reflecting, condensing bringing out and placing your thoughts and feelings in the best point of view, as is necessary. I will conclude this matter of poetry, my part of the letter, with requesting that as an act of friendship at your convenience you would take the trouble, a considerable one I own, of comparing the corrections in my last edition with the text in the preceding one. You know my principles of style better I think than any one else, and I should be glad to learn if anything strikes you as being altered for the worse. You will find the principal changes in The White Doe, in wh. I had too little of the benefit of your help and judgement: there are several also in the sonnets both miscellaneous and political—in the other poems they are nothing like so numerous, but here also I should be glad if you w^d take the like trouble. Jemima, I am sure, will be pleased to assist you in the comparison by reading new or old as you may think fit. With love to her I remain my dear Mr Quillinan, faithfully yours,

Wm Wordsworth.

Address: Edward Quillinan Esqre, Post Office, Falmouth.

MS.   *1236. D. W. to Mrs. Hoare*

[Sept. 1837]

My dear Friend

I know not when I last wrote to you—and now I have a hard task to write at all among the many thoughts which press upon me—I have had a long long struggle; but through God's mercy here I sit on my chair—with a clear head—and a thankful heart. I will give you some of the many verses which have slipped from me I know not how—since I cannot now so well express my thoughts and feelings to you.

To my kind Friend and medical Attendant T. Carr composed a year ago—or more.

Five years of sickness and of pain
This weary frame has travelled o'er
But God is good—and once again
I rest upon a tranquil shore.

I rest in quietness of mind,
Oh! may I thank my God
With heart that never shall forget
The perilous path I've trod!

They tell me of one fearful night
When thou, my faithful Friend,
Didst part from me in holy trust
That soon my earthly cares must end.

On that night Mr Carr left me because he could do no more for me, and my poor Brother went to lie down on his bed thinking he could not bear to see me die.

I hope I may recover the use of my legs, though at present I cannot walk without props to bear my whole weight.

It grieves me that poor Dora is not likely to come home this autumn or winter. God grant my dear Brother may soon arrive in safety! Pray give my best Love to Miss Hoare. I venture to hope that I may see you both again—

God bless you—

ever your affect^e

D. Wordsworth

When you see Charles or any of my nephews give my kindest love to them.

Monday—the day of Month I know not.

Do you ever see Sir Benjamin Brodie? If you do tell him I often and often think of him—and pray give him my kindest regards.

Address: To Mrs Hoare, Hampstead Heath, near London.

M.
K.
    1237. W. W. to Lord Lonsdale

Sept. 27 [1837.]

... After having had excellent health during my long ramble, it is unfortunate that I should thus be disabled at the conclusion. The mischief came to me in Herefordshire, whither I had gone on my way home to see my brother-in-law, who, by his horse falling on him some time ago, was left without the use of his limbs.

I was lately a few days with Mr Rogers, at Broadstairs, and also with the Archbishop of Canterbury, at Addington Park; they were both well, and I was happy to see the Archbishop much stronger than his slender and almost feeble appearance would lead one to expect. We walked up and down in the park for three hours one day, and nearly four the next, without his seeming to be the least fatigued. I mention this, as we must all feel the value of his life in this state of public affairs.

The cholera prevented us getting as far as Naples, which was the only disappointment we met with. As a man of letters I have to regret that this most interesting tour was not made by me earlier in life, as I might then have turned the notices[1] it has

---

[1] notices] So M. and K., but W. probably wrote 'notions'.

supplied me with to more account than I now expect to do. With respectful remembrances to Lady Lonsdale, and to your Lordship, in which Mrs W. unites, I remain, my dear Lord, faithfully,

your much obliged servant,

Wm. Wordsworth.

MS.[1] *1238. D. W. to Edward Ferguson[2]*
K(—)

Rydal Mount, Sunday, October 8th, 1837.

My dear Cousin Edward,

A madman might as well attempt to relate the history of his own doings, and those of his fellows in confinement, as I to tell you one hundredth part of what I have felt, suffered, and done.

Through God's mercy I am now calm and easy, and I trust my dear Brother's eyes are in a fair way of perfect recovery. They all feared he would lose his sight; but now he is very much better.

Your last letter has interested me exceedingly. Our poor good old Aunt and her patient nurse, how I feel for them! but God is merciful.

I am glad to hear of Eliz[th] Ferguson's happy prospects. Pray with my love to tell her that I wish her and her Husband all the happiness this world can give. I do not mean the wealth of the wealthy, for that can do little for us. My Brother C. is, as you say, in delicate health. His sons are quite well—one at Winchester, another at Harrow and the third (but oldest and therefore ought to have been first mentioned) a lecturer at Cambridge. My Niece looks charmingly, and is now, I trust quite well. My Nephew John is here with his oldest son, a charming little Boy, whose prattle amuses me (old Aunty as he calls me) very much. My dear Sister is well. Happy for all the house her health has been, on the whole, very good.

I have not seen dear Charles Lamb's book.[3] His Sister still

---

[1] From a copy of the letter found in W.'s passport-book, 1837.

[2] One of the family brought up by 'Aunt' Threlkeld, with whom D. W. lived at Halifax as a child, *v. E.L.*, p. 41.

[3] *The Letters of Charles Lamb with a Sketch of his Life* by Thomas Noon Talfourd. 2 vols., 1837.

survives —a solitary twig—patiently enduring the storm of life.
In losing her Brother she lost her all—all but the remembrance
of him, which chears her the day through. Give my best love
to your Sister, and Aunt if she can understand it.

May God bless you.

Yours ever truly,

Dorothy Wordsworth.

[P.S.] I must [send] you some of my verses. Observe the
lines were composed a year ago—*To Thos. Carr*, my Medical
Att^{dt} [*verses as supra*, p. 898].

MS.   *1239. W. W. to R. S. Mackenzie*

Rydal Mount Novr 25th [1837]

My dear Sir

Your parcel reached us on the 19th. The state of my eyes
obliges me to employ Mrs W's pen to thank you for it, and for
the enclosed letter. As it is not prudent for me to write with my
own hand, I cannot of course have yet become acquainted with
much of the contents of the books and papers which you have so
kindly sent—The Herbarium is a truly valuable one and will be
much prized by my daughter who is fond of such collections—
meanwhile, her Mother begs you to accept their joint thanks for
it, and the Forget-me-not, you so kindly have presented to them.
We have turned to the Poems in the Annual you have directed
us to, they are remarkable both for tenderness and poetical
spirit; the one upon your departed Child, is not unworthy of
ranking with the Mother's lays of Miss Browne[1] which we have
read, and been much pleased with; as also, the animated piece
in which the course of a river is traced from its fountain to the
sea: this was not less interesting to me on account of its reminding me, of Mr. Coleridge's *intention* of writing a poem to be called
'the Brook'[2] and of my own Duddon. These two pieces are all
that we have yet found time to read of Miss B's little book—for

---

[1] Phoebe Hindal Brown (1783–1861), American hymn-writer. Her chief
works were *Apology for my Twilight Rambles*, and *The Mother's Hymn-Book*
(1834).

[2] *v.* The Fenwick note to W.'s *Duddon Sonnets*.

in truth, we have had three other volumes sent us (within the last 10 days) to look over—besides arrears of other accumulations. If I could with prudence put my eyes to this work, it would not require a 4th part of the time occupied by things being read aloud. And now, not to speak of other demands, and parliament being sitting, the Newspapers cannot be neglected. I therefore need give no further explanation of my inability to report impressions—or give opinions with respect to the american publications—as soon as I am able, I shall glance my eye over them. In the mean while let me repeat my thanks for the copious specimens you have sent me, and in particular for Mrs. Sigourney's[1] volume—which, judging from the 'Mother's Sacrifice', and 'the American Indians', especially the former, I cannot but expect much pleasure from. I see there is a prose tale of yours—but you will not be hurt when I frankly say, I have not read it—for it is not once in a hundred times, that for many years past, I have been able to find time for reading prose fictions in periodicals—and too seldom indeed for the most celebrated novels.

What a pity a Man so wealthy did not provide in his will for the poor orphan Mourner—the story, as you have given it, is truly affecting; and the Sonnet gives the essence of the incident in a manner that does you much credit, and it is much to be regretted that you have not more time to give to the Muses, whom you serve so willingly and well. Are you aware that Cowper has been beforehand with you in the Ice-palace?[2]

Bryant's[3] poems we have not yet looked into, but if you are in communication with the Gentleman who sent the vol: to me, pray be so good as to thank him in my name—several of Mr. B's pieces have fallen in my way from time to time, some of which had merit of a very superior kind.

I must not conclude witho(ut) thanking you for your Portrait, it is a spirited and a very good likeness.

[1] Lydia Sigourney (1791–1865), a prolific American magazine writer in prose and verse, known as the American 'Hemans'. She came to Europe in 1840, and visited W. W. and Southey. She was specially famous for her obituary poems which, it was said, added a new terror to death.

[2] *The Task*, Bk. v, 127–176.

[3] *v.* Letter 1576 and *note.*

Excuse my writing so briefly in answer to your interesting communications—yet I feel I needed not to have made this apology, after what has been said above—and believe me to remain

faithfully, your much obliged

Wm. Wordsworth.

Our little County has just been disgraced by a horrible Murder[1] to which cupidity appears to have been the sole motive —thus placing us if possible below the most savage Irish.

Address: R. S. Mackenzie Esqre, Liverpool.

Hamilton.
G. **1240. W. W. to W. Rowan Hamilton[2]**
K(—)

Rydal Mount, December 21, 1837.

My dear Sir William,

The papers had informed me of the honour lately conferred upon you, and I was intending to congratulate you on the occasion, when your letter arrived. The electors have done great credit to themselves by appointing you, and not a little by rejecting the ultra-liberal Archbishop,[3] and that by so decided a majority. We are much pleased that your sister, who, we conclude, is well, has sent her poems to press, and wish they may obtain the attention we are sure they will merit. Your own two sonnets, for which I thank you, we read, that is Mrs Wordsworth and myself (Dora is in the South), with interest.

But to the main purport of your letter. You pay me an un-

---

[1] The *Westmorland Gazette* of Nov. 25 reports the perpetration of 'a most foul and horrible murder' near Orton, between Kendal and Killuth, on the night of the previous Saturday. One Thomas Hunter, a carrier, had been waylaid and shot, and his pocket book and the bag in which he carried his silver taken. The man suspected of the murder was brought up for trial before Mr. Justice Coleridge at the Assizes in February, but was discharged from lack of sufficient evidence.

[2] For W. W. to H. C. R. Dec. 15, *v. C.R.*, p. 349.

[3] Richard Whately (1787–1863), Fellow of Oriel College, Oxford, 1811, intimate friend of Edward Copleston and Thomas Arnold, a broad Churchman, and in politics an independent Liberal. Professor of Political Economy at Oxford from 1829 to 1831, when he became Archbishop of Dublin. Author of *Logic* (1826) and *Rhetoric* (1828), books which won a great reputation in their day.

deserved compliment in requesting my opinion, how you could best promote some of the benefits which the Society, at whose head you are placed, aims at. As to patronage, you are right in supposing that I hold it in little esteem for helping genius forward in the fine arts, especially those whose medium is words. Sculpture and painting *may* be helped by it, but even in these departments there is much to be dreaded. The French have established an Academy at Rome upon an extensive scale, and so far from doing good, I was told by every one that it had done much harm. The plan is this: they select the most distinguished students from the school or academy at Paris and send them to Rome, with handsome stipends, by which they are tempted into idleness and of course into vice. So that it looks like a contrivance for preventing the French nation and the world at large profiting by the genius which nature may have bestowed, and which left to itself would in some cases, perhaps, have prospered. The principal, I was indeed told the *only*, condition imposed upon these students is, that each of them send annually some work of his hands to Paris. When at Rome, I saw a good deal of English artists. They seemed to be living happily and doing well, tho', as you are aware, the public patronage any of them receive is trifling.

Genius in poetry, or any department of what is called the Belles-Lettres, is much more likely to be cramped than fostered by public support; better wait to reward those who have done their work, tho' even here national rewards are not necessary, unless the labourers be, if not in poverty, at least in narrow circumstances. Let the laws be but just to them, and they will be sure of attaining a competence, if they have not misjudged their own talents, or misapplied them.

The cases of Chatterton, Burns, and others might, it would seem, be urged against the conclusion that help beforehand is not required; but I do think that in the temperament of the two I have mentioned there was something which, however favourable had been their circumstances, however much they had been encouraged and supported, would have brought on their ruin. As to what patronage can do in Science, discoveries in Physics, mechanic arts, etc., you know far better than I can pretend to do.

[904]

As to 'better canons of criticism, and general improvement
of scholars', I really, speaking without affectation, am so little of
a Critic or Scholar that it would be presumptuous in me to write
upon the subject to you. If we were together, and you should
honour me by asking my opinion upon particular points, that
would be a very different thing, and I might have something to
say not wholly without value. But where could I begin with so
comprehensive an argument, and how could I put into the compass of a letter my thoughts, such as they may be, with anything
like order? It is somewhat mortifying to me to disappoint you.
You must upon reflection I trust perceive, that in attempting
to comply with your wish I should only lose myself in a wilderness. I have been applied to to give lectures upon Poetry in a
public institution in London, but I was conscious that I was
neither competent to the office, nor the public prepared to
receive what I should have felt it my duty to say, however
[? inadequately].

I have [had] a very pleasant and not profitless tour on the
Continent, tho' with one great drawback, the being obliged on
account of the cholera to return without seeing Naples and its
neighbourhood. Had it not been for the state of my eyes, which
became inflamed after I got back to England, I should have been
able to take Liverpool in my way home, at the time you were
there. The attack continued for a long time, and has left a
weakness in the organ which does not yet allow me either to read
or write; but with care I hope to come about.

My sister continues in the same enfeebled state of mind and
body. Mrs W. is well; but your godson, we hear, is suffering
from derangement of the stomach, so that at present he is not
a thriving child, but his elder brother is now remarkably so, and
he about the same age was subject to the same trials. We trust
that your little family are all flourishing, and with our united
affectionate regards believe me, faithfully,

Dear Sir W., yours,

Wm. Wordsworth.

I am sorry that I cannot send this thro' Lord Northampton,
because he tells me he is coming northward.

MS. **1241. W. W. to Alexander Dyce**
M(—) *G*(—) *K*(—)

Dec. 23, 1837

My dear Sir,

I have just rec^d your valuable Present of Bentley's Works[1]—for which accept my cordial thanks, as also for the elegant little Vol: dedicated by you to the Author, and for the leaf to be added to Akenside[2]—the one to Mr Southey shall be delivered to him, with your best respects, as you desire.

Is it recorded in your Memoir of A,—for I have not leisure nor eyesight at present to look,—that he was fond of sitting in St James's Park with his eyes upon Westminster Abbey? this, I am sure, I have either read or *heard* of him; and I imagine that it was from Mr Rogers. I am not unfrequently a visitor on Hampstead Heath, and seldom pass by the entrance of Mr Dyson's[3] villa on Goulder's Hill, close by, without thinking of the pleasure which Akenside often had there.

I cannot call to mind a reason why you should not think some passages in 'The Power of Sound' equal to anything I have produced;[4] when first printed in 'Yarrow Revisited', I placed it at the end of the Volume, and in the last edition of my poems, at the close of the Poems of Imagination, indicating thereby my *own* opinion of it.

How much do I regret that I have neither learning nor eyesight thoroughly to enjoy Bentley's masterly *Dissertation on the Epistles of Phalaris*;[5] many years ago I read the work with infinite pleasure. As far as I know, or rather am able to judge, it is without a rival in that department of literature; a work of which the

---

[1] *The Works of Richard Bentley*, edited with notes by A. D. 3 vols., 1836 and 1838.

[2] The leaf added to A. contained the saying of Henderson the actor, that 'A., when he walked in the streets, looked for all the world like one of his own Alexandrines, set upright'. This story W. W. had reported to A. D. on the authority of Rogers.

[3] Jeremiah Dyson (d. 1776), Akenside's patron, intimate friend, and 'good genius', and the editor, in 1772, of his poems.

[4] A. D., writing to W. on Dec. 7, had said 'Perhaps I am wrong in thinking that the *Ode on the Power of Sound* contains some passages as magnificent as any you have ever written'.

[5] Richard Bentley (1662–1742). His *Dissertation on the Epistles of Phalaris, and the Fables of Æsop* was published in 1697.

English nation may be proud as long as acute intellect, and vigorous powers, and profound scholarship shall be esteemed in the world.

Let me again repeat my regret that in passing to and from Scotland you have never found it convenient to visit this part of the Country. I would be delighted to see you, and I am sure Mr Southey would be the same: in his house you would find an inexhaustible collection of books, many of them curious no doubt; but his classical Library is much the least valuable part of it. The death of his excellent Wife was a deliverance for herself and the whole family—so great had been her sufferings of mind and body.

You don't say a word about Skelton, and I regret much your disappointment in respect to Middleton.[1]

I remain, my dear Sir,
faithfully, your much obliged
Wm. Wordsworth.

MS.   *1242. W. W. to S. C. Hall*

Decr. 23rd [1837]

My dear Sir

I have been anxious for the arrival of your volume, both on its own account, and that I might be at liberty to answer your last obliging note. The Book only reached me yesterday, it having been delayed at Mr Moxon's until he could send it in the same parcel with the new Ed: of Disraeli's 'Curiosities of Literature'.

Absurdly unreasonable would it be in me, if I were not satisfied with your notice of my writings and character—All I can say further is that I have *wished* both to be what you indulgently affirm they are. In the few facts of your Memoir, there is only one mistake or rather ina[c]curacy. You say he was educated *with* his almost [equally][2] distinguished Brother—My Br. Dr

---

[1] Dyce's edition of Skelton appeared in 1843; his Middleton in 1840. In his letter to W. W. of Dec. 7 he says that two volumes are already printed, but withheld by the publisher who was 'frightened at the state of the trade'.

[2] So the *Book of Gems*, but W. omits the 'equally'. The Memoir of W. W. opens the third volume, 1838.

W— he it is true was brought up at the same school—but being upwards of 4 years younger than myself—we could scarcely be said to be educated together—and I had left College before he came there. In Mr Chorley's[1] account of me in his 'living Authors' just published, there are several gross errors—among others he says my appointment as Distributor of stamps took place no less than 11 years after the date he assigns it.[2]

You will be sorry that the Copy of the Gem sent to me is imperfect—the pages from 128 to 137 being wanting—I shall therefore take the liberty of sending it back, thro' my Kendal Bookseller to Whittaker and Co, to be exchanged.

Not long after my arrival here I had the pleasure of seeing your Br. who came, as he may have told you, with Mrs Curwen, my daughter-in-law's Mother. We talked a good deal ab^t you and Mrs Hall, and I was much gratified with his intelligent conversation. I have not been able to do more than look into the Gem—my eyes being to(o) weak—tho' much amended. Pray accept my best wishes for Mrs Hall and yourself, and believe m(e) dear Sir to be faithfully y^r obliged

Wm. Wordsworth.

Address: S. C. Hall Esqre, care of Messrs. Whittaker and Co., Ave Maria Lane.

MS.   1243. *W. W. to Edward Moxon*

[Dec. 25 1837]

My dear Mr Moxon,

The parcel arrived safely yesterday and I thank you, both on my own part and that of my Son's for the handsome Vol. from you, which it contains. I forwarded Mr Southey's, as well as my Son's, by yesterday's Coach. Thank you also for your note, if Mr Quillinan had not told me that the Edition was reduced to

---

[1] *The Authors of England, a series of Medallion Portraits of Modern Literary Characters engraved by Achille Colas, with Illustrative Notices*, by Henry F. Chorley, 1838. (Preface dated Oct. 1837.)

[2] W. means that his appointment took place eleven years after the date to which Chorley assigns it. Chorley gives it as 1803.

700 Copies I should have been pleased to hear from yourself as he said he had done, some little time ago, that 900 only were on hand—as it was I was a little disappointed—more for your sake than my own. I will inform my daughter of Mrs Moxon's and your kind invitation to Dover Street, but I believe her engagements will not admit of her availing herself of your friendly proposal—She is now I trust at Cambridge and must return to Dover as soon as she has paid a long-promised, and often-interrupted visit, at Hampstead.

I *had* hoped that my carrying my Sister's journal through the press might prove a salutary interest to her—but as I no longer can cherish that hope, I must defer the publication—we find that the work perhaps would not interest her at all, or if it did, like everything that excites her, it would do her harm.

Mr Hall's Gem being imperfect, wanting no less than 9 pages, we shall be obliged to return it to be exchanged for a perfect Copy, and will take that opportunity of *safely* sending the Autographs for the two Copies of my Poems. My F^d Mr Powell[1] tells me that Mr Marshall (of the firm of Simkins and Marshall) had mentioned to him that the Sale of my 6 Vols was steadily increasing, and that he was persuaded an edition in one vol. would sell. It would be still for us to consider, however, [and] for me especially on acc^t of the stereotype, whether such an Ed. might not put a stop to the sale in 6 vols: and therefore be unadvisable if the 900 now on hand were reduced even to 200 (tho' you recollect we talked of entering upon such an Ed. when it should be reduced to 500)—Is the Colloquies on Religion[2] sent from you or the Author? if from you accept my thanks—if from him pray present my acknowledgements.

My eyes are nearly well, but do not allow me to read much. Kindest love to Miss Lamb. We rejoice to hear she is so well.

faithfully yours

W. W.

Address: Edward Moxon Esqre, 44 Dover Street.

---

[1] *v.* Letter 1270.

[2] *Colloquies on Religion and Religious Education*, by F. W. Faber, M.A., 1837.

1244. *W. W. to William Rowan Hamilton*

Hamilton
G.
K(—)

Rydal Mount, Jan. 4, 1838.

My dear Sir William,

From a hope of something starting up in my mind which might prevent my letter from being an utter disappointment I have not answered yours, as I wished to do, by return of post. But I am really still as much at a loss how to make my letter worth reading as if I had replied immediately. Allow me, however, to thank you for your last, which has completely done away with the vagueness of the former. I now distinctly understand you; and as to one of your leading points, viz. availing myself of publication through your Society, I may say that, if there had been among my papers anything of the kind you wish for, I should have gladly forwarded it to you. But it is not so, nor dare I undertake to promise anything of the kind for the future.

Though prevailed upon by Mr Coleridge to write the first Preface to my Poems—which tempted, or rather forced, me to add a supplement to it—and induced by my friendship for him to write the Essay upon Epitaphs, now appended to The Excursion, but first composed for The Friend, I have never felt inclined to write criticism, though I have talked, and am daily talking, a great deal.

If I were several years younger I would, out of friendship to you mainly, sit down to the task of giving a body to my notions upon the essentials of Poetry, a subject which could not be properly treated without adverting to the other branches of fine art. But at present, with so much before me that I could wish to do in verse, and the melancholy fact brought daily more and more home to my conviction that intellectual labour, by its action on the brain and nervous system, is injurious to the bodily powers (and especially to my eyesight), I should only be deceiving myself and misleading you, were I to encourage a hope that much as I could wish to be your fellow-labourer, however humbly, I shall ever become one.

Having disposed of this rather painful part of the subject of your letter let me say—that though it is principally matters of science in which publication through your Society would be serviceable, and indeed in that department eminently so, I concur with you in thinking that the same vehicle would be useful for bringing under the notice of the thinking part of the community critical essays of too abstract a character to be fit for popularity. There are obviously, even in criticism, two ways of affecting the minds of men: the one by treating the matter so as to carry it immediately to the sympathies of the many, and the other by aiming at a few select and superior minds, that might each become a centre for illustrating it in a popular way. Mr Coleridge, whom you allude to, acted upon the world to a great extent through the latter of these processes; and there cannot be a doubt that your Society might serve the cause of just thinking and pure taste should you, as President of it, hold up to view the desirableness of first conveying to a few, through that channel, reflections upon Literature and Art which, if well meditated, would be sure of winning their way directly, or in their indirect results, to a gradually widening circle.

May I not encourage a hope that during the ensuing summer, or at the worst at no distant period, you and I might meet, when a few hours' conversation would effect more than could come out of a dozen letters dictated hastily, as I am obliged to dictate this, because of an unexpected interruption when Mrs W. and I were sitting down, with the pen in her hand?

You are right in your recollection that I named to you the subject of foreign piracy as injurious to English authors, and I may add now that, if it could be put a stop to, I believe that it would rarely happen that successful writers, in works of imagination and feeling at least, would stand in need of pensions from Government, or would feel themselves justified in accepting them. Upon this subject I have spoken a great deal to M.P.s of all parties, and with several distinguished Americans. I have also been in correspondence with the present Chancellor of the Exchequer[1] upon it, and dwelt upon the same topic in a letter which I had occasion to write to Sir Robert Peel. Mr Lytton

[1] Spring Rice.

Bulwer, as perhaps you know, drew the attention of Parliament to it during the last session. Lord Palmerston said, in answer to him, that the attention of Government had already been directed to the measure, and that it would not be lost sight of, or something to that purpose. I may claim some credit for my exertions in this business, and full as much, or more, for the pains which I have taken for many years, to interest men in the H of C in the extension of the term of copyright,—a measure which I trust is about to be brought to a successful close by the exertions of my admirable friend Serjeant Talfourd. To him I have written upon the argument more than once. When this is effected, I trust the other part of the subject will be taken up with spirit; and if the Foreign Secretary,[1] in whose department the matter lies, should be remiss, I trust he will be stimulated thro' Parliament, to which desirable end the services of distinguished societies like yours, and the notice of the question by men of letters, in reviews or otherwise, would greatly contribute. Good authors (if justice were done to them by their own and foreign countries) would very few of them be in need, except through their own fault, now that reading is spread and is spreading so widely.

When I was in town last August, the American minister, Mr Stephenson, spoke to me with much indignation of the law and practice by which copyright was secured in England for American authors, while there was no reciprocity for English writers in America. But I must conclude, or I shall miss the post. The father of your godson is here, and begs to be remembered to you.

Did I ever mention to you that owing to the sea having swallowed up his father-in-law's coal-pits, John's income is much reduced, and he therefore feels it necessary to endeavour to procure a couple of pupils who could afford to pay rather handsomely for the advantages they would have under his roof? By this time he would have succeeded, but parents in the South have an unaccountable objection to sending their sons so far North. As the same might not be felt in Ireland, I take the liberty of mentioning his wish to you, being persuaded that if you can you will assist him in his aims. If your address to your

[1] Lord Palmerston.

Society should be published, could you send it me, and acquaint
me with what you have done?

Affectionately yours,

Wm. Wordsworth.

MS.   *1245. W. W. to Dionysius Lardner*[1]

Rydal Mount, Kendal 12th Jany 1838[2]

Sir,

I should have written to you immediately on my return from
the Continent, but I was obliged to hurry through London, and
since that time I have been without your address—

The subject which I had thought of is much more limited than
you suppose—being nothing more than an Account of the
Deceased Poetesses of Great Britain—with an Estimate of their
Works—but upon more mature Reflection I cannot persuade
myself that it is sufficiently interesting for a separate subject,
were I able to do it justice. The Dramatic and other imaginative
female Writers might be added—the interest would thereby be
encreased, but unity of subject would be sacrificed.—It remains
therefore for me to regret that I should have held out the least
hope that I might undertake any thing of the Kind—for which
I have no excuse but what you I hope will be satisfied with, that
I was taken by surprize.

I still am of opinion that something is wanted upon the subject—neither Dr Johnson, nor Dr Anderson, nor Chalmers, nor
the Editor I believe of any other Corpus of English Poetry takes
the least notice of female Writers—this, to say nothing harsher,
is very ungallant. The best way of giving a comprehensive
interest to the subject would be to begin with Sappho and
proceed downwards through Italy antient and Modern, Spain,

[1] Dionysius Lardner (1793–1859) of Trin. Coll. Dublin; Prof. of Nat.
Phil. at Univ. Coll. London. In 1829 he initiated *The Cabinet Cyclopædia
of Eminent Literary and Scientific Men*, which was completed in 1849 in 133
vols. 8vo. Volumes on the *English Poets* by Robert Bell appeared in 1839—it
was probably in connexion with these that W. made the suggestion referred
to in this letter.

[2] The date on the MS. looks more like 1828 than 1838, but on Jan. 12,
1828 W. was not at Rydal, nor had he been abroad since 1820.

Germany France and England—but, for myself, I could not venture to undertake the employment, two requisites being wanting—Books (I mean access to Libraries) and industry to use them.

Wishing you success in your [ver]y promising underta[king]

I remain Sir—

sincerely yours

Wm. Wordsworth.

P.S. The consequences of a severe fall have prevented me giving an earlier answer to your Letter—

Address: The Revd D. Lardner, etc. etc., Percy St., London.

MS.   *1246. W. W. to Edward Moxon*
K(—)

[p.m. Feb. 5, 1838]

My dear Mr Moxon

About a Month ago having occasion to forward (thro' Hudson and Nicholson Kendal) an imperfect Copy of the Gem (which was sent me by Mr Hall) to be corrected at Whitaker's, I enclosed the fly leaves which were intended for Mrs M.'s and Emma's copies of my Poems—not having had any report of the arrival of this book in Ave Maria Lane, and as your letter does not notice your having rec^d the said leaves, I think it proper to apprize you thereof, that you may enquire after them—they were simply returned in the stiff paper in which I received them, and directed to you.

I am rather pleased that you approve of the Sonnets in a separate Volume, not that I care much about it myself, except for the money that it would bring (and that mainly on account of an unfavorable change in the circumstances of my Son) but because requests that I would print such a Volume have reached me from many quarters. Mr Powell tells me that one of the City Publishers (Smith Elder & Co) to whom he had mentioned the subject said he was sure such a Publication would sell. You somewhat surprise me in purposing to print *one* Son: on a page, the whole number being I believe 415. Your plan and consequent price would make it a book of luxury, and tho' I have no objection to that, yet still my wish is, to be read as widely as is consistent with reasonable pecuniary return. A day or two ago Dr Arnold shewed me a letter from a Clergyman, an accomplished Scholar besides, entreating of me to publish my works in 'brown paper', that was the word, meaning I suppose the cheapest form, for the benefit of readers in the humblest condition of life—being convinced from his own experience, that my works were fitted to touch their hearts, and purify and exalt their minds. These were not his words exactly, but they were to this effect. Miss Martineau,[1] I am told, has said that my poems are in the hearts of the American People. That is the place I would fain occupy among the People of these Islands. And I am not at all sure that the abstract character of no small portion of my own poetry will at all stand in the way of that result. Though it would not in *itself* recommend them to the mass of the people.

These observations are merely thrown out as springing up naturally on this occasion. I leave the mode of publication entirely to your superior judgement, being persuaded that whatever there may be in these or any other works, fitted for general sympathy, *that* will find its way as education spreads to the spirits of many. I ought to add, as a personal motive for preferring a Vol. printed as you recommend, that it will gratify my daughter, whom I am always happy and proud to please— and before you decide, as to type and shape of page, would you take the trouble to communicate with her, and send a specimen to No. 3 Clarence Lawn, Dover.

I will write to you in reply to your query about the arrangement in a day or two—

Mrs W. joins me in thanks to you and Mrs M. for your kind

---

[1] Harriet Martineau (1802–76), novelist and miscellaneous writer on current social questions, a Unitarian and advanced Liberal. Her chief works were *Illustrations of Political Economy* (1832–4), *Deerbrook* (1832), *The Playfellow*, a series of Tales for the Young, including *Feats on the Fiord*, and *The Settlers at Home* (1841). She visited America in 1837. In 1841 she came to Windermere and a year later built 'The Knoll' at Ambleside where she settled, and saw a good deal of the W.s.

invitation which we will remember should we leave home—but I do not at present feel inclined to encounter the excitement of a Spring in London. With our joint affec. regards believe me sincerely my d^r M.

Yours

Wm. Wordsworth

P.S. I see an advertisement of a pamphlet written against the extension of Copy-right, but have met with no notice of it, either in Newspaper or review. Have you any reason for believing that Sergeant Talfourd's motion will meet with any opposition in the house—at all formidable? After all, about the Sonnets, may not there be some risk—*this* I should not like to encounter, much less should I chuse to throw it upon you. What say you of this important point which unaccountably I had overlooked?

1247. *W. W. to Dora W.*

K.

[? Feb.–March 1838.]

My dear Dora,

Read the following remodelling of the sonnet I addressed to S.[1] The personalities are omitted, a few lines only retained:

Oh, what a wreck! How changed in mien and speech!
Yet, though dread Powers that work in mystery, spin
Entanglings for her brain; though shadows stretch
O'er the chilled heart—reflect! far, far within
Hers is a holy Being, freed from sin:
She is not what she seems, a forlorn wretch;
But delegated Spirits comfort fetch
To her from heights that Reason may not win.

. . . . . .

Inly illumined by Heaven's pitying love,
Love pitying innocence, not long to last,
In them, in Her, our sins and sorrows past.[2]

The sonnet, as first sent to you and S., may be kept, if thought worthy, as a private record. The meaning in the passage you

------

[1] Southey.   [2] Oxf. W. p. 280.

object to is certainly not happily brought out; if you think it
better thus, alter it:

> Over the sacred heart compassion's twin,
> The heart that once could feel for every wretch.

The thought in the sonnet as it now stands has ever been a
consolation to me, almost as far back as I can remember, and
hope that, thus expressed, it may prove so to others makes one
wish to print it; but your mother seems to think it would be
applied at once to your dear aunt. I own I do not see the force
of this objection; but if you and Miss Fenwick and others should
be of the same mind, it shall be suppressed. It is already sent
to the press, but not as it now stands; if you think it may be
printed without impropriety, pray be so good as to superintend
the revise which I shall order the printer to send you: this would
save time, for I could not entrust the revise to the printer only.

The following is sent for your amusement; it will go by Mr
Fleming to Cambridge for your cousin John, to be printed without my name, if he thinks it worth while, in the—

[*Here follows Sonnet* 'Said Secrecy to Cowardice', *etc., as* Oxf.
W., p. 513, *but in l.* 14 Grote *for* —]

(unsigned)

K(—)   *1248. W. W. to John W.*[1]

Saturday, Mar. 10th, [1838.]

My dear John,

... In compliance with your wish, and that of other friends,
I am carrying through the press an edition of *all* my sonnets
in a separate volume. ... I was myself for making the edition
not expensive by publishing two sonnets on a page; but Dora
disliked this, and Mr Moxon thought that we should have a
better prospect of selling seven hundred and fifty at nine
shillings than fifteen hundred at a considerably lower price, two
sonnets on a page. ... Four new sonnets will be added, which I
have composed since the resolution of printing them in this
shape was taken. The whole number will scarcely be less than
four hundred and twenty.

---

[1] His nephew, son of C. W.

. . . People compliment me upon my looks, but I feel myself a good deal older within the last two years. I think my Continental exertions, and perhaps the heat of the climate, were something too much for me; but what agrees with me worst of all is residence in London, late hours of dining, and talking from morning to night.

This morning brought me a letter from Lady Frederick Bentinck, containing the sad news of the death of my excellent friend, Lady Lonsdale. She was in her seventy-seventh year, but when I saw her last November she had little or no appearance of infirmity. I loved her with sincere affection. . . . She has been as kind to me as an elder sister. . . .

I have sent you a sonnet which I shall not print in my collection,[1] because my poems are wholly as I wish them to continue, without *personalities* of a vituperative character. If you think it worth being printed, pray have it copied and sent to the *Cantabridge Chronicle*, without a name. . . .

And now farewell.

Your affectionate uncle,

Wm. Wordsworth.

MS.   *1249. W. W. to Edward Moxon*

13th March [1838]

Dear Mr Moxon,

When I see Mr Southey's Madoc containing 478 pages including title dedication prefaces with embellishments I shrink at the idea of one volume being charged according to your calculation 9/- as it cannot amount with notes and five new Sonnets and a short preface, to more than 440 pages at the utmost—but of course I submit to your superior knowledge and experience if you continue in the same mind.

May I trouble you to settle the enclosed bill for me at Longmans—Have you rec[d] the flyleaves yet? I found on enquiring of my bookseller on receiving your letter, that the parcel which contained them was still lying at Kendal, he not having had an

---

[1] *v.* last letter.

opportunity of sending it to Whitaker—as he receives parcels weekly from that house, we foolishly overlooked that he did not also send thither frequently, or we might have found other means of conveyance [for] this.

I have had this morning rather a melancholy note from dear Southey who has just lost his Brother, the Capt.—who died on his voyage from Denmark, and I grieve to say speaks of himself as being in depressed spirits and deranged health. Pray tell Mr Robinson when you see him that we had been looking for a letter from him for some time—My son John recovers very slowly from the Typhus fever—he is strong, but has scarcely slept at all for several weeks—it is seven since he was first seized.—My daughter is now at No 10 Chester Place Regents Park at Mr H. N. Coleridge's, where I am sure she would be glad to see you— as they do not keep a carriage it will not be in her power to make many calls during her short stay in Town.—With kind regards to Mrs M and your Sister in which Mrs W. joins believe me ever yours

W. Wordsworth

Address: Edward Moxon Esq, 44 Dover Street.

MS. **1250.** *W. W. to William Ewart Gladstone*[1]
K.

Rydal, Kendal, March 23ᵈ, 38.

My dear Mr Gladstone,

Most probably I am putting you to unnecessary trouble by this Letter, which is written solely to remind you that the 2nd Reading of Serjeant Talfourd's Bill stands for Wednesday, April 11ᵗʰ. In a Letter received this morning Serjeant Talfourd tells me that the Booksellers (rapacious Creatures as they are) are getting up a very strong opposition to his motion, and will be supported by the Doctrinaires (who are they? Warburton and Grote,[2] and id genus omne, I suppose). Upon the general merits

---

[1] W. had been introduced to Gladstone by Henry Taylor. In reply to this note G. asserted that he was 'staunch and firm in support' of the bill.

[2] Henry Warburton (1784–1858) and George Grote (1794–1871) the historian of Greece, were philosophical radicals and co-workers in many liberal causes. W. had already fallen foul of Grote over the ballot (*v.* p. 917).

of this question it would be presumptuous in me to enter in a Letter to you. But as to my own interest in it, it may not be superfluous to say that within the last three years or so my poetical writings have produced for me nearly 1,500 pounds, and that much the greatest part of them either would be public property to-morrow, if I should die, or would become so in a very few years. Is this just, or can a state of law which allows the possibility of such injustice be favorable to the production of solid literature, in any department of what is usually called Belles-Lettres?

> ever faithfully yours,
> Wm. Wordsworth.

I need not say how much I would rejoice to see you at Rydal Mount.

MS. *1251. W. W. to Sir William Gomm*

My dear Sir William, Rydal, Kendal, 24th March 38.

Knowing your attachment to literature, I venture to solicit your support by application to your parliamentary Friends in favour of Sergeant Talfourd's Copyright Bill; the second reading of which, stands for the 11th of april, *Wednesday.* The success of this measure is to me as a Man of letters not a little interesting though far less so than to many of my Contemporaries. I have however exerted myself for many years past to have it brought before the House, and am now taking much trouble to promote its success by application to my friends, among whom I could not but enumerate yourself. Of the Justice of the proposed law, I need not speak to one so enlightened as you are, nor need I insist upon its tendency to promote sound literature, without cheapning in the least degree its circulation, for the vast encrease of Readers will make it the interest of authors to publish in a cheap form.

With respectful Compl^s to Lady Gomm

> I remain
> dear Sir William
> faithfully yours
> Wm Wordsworth

Address: Col: Sir William Gomm, Upper Grosvenor St.

MS.   *1252. W. W. to Mrs J. M. Müleen*

Rydal Mount 28ᵗʰ Febʳʸ [1838].[1]

—'I cannot doubt that they whom you deplore
Are glorified; or, if they sleep, shall wake
From sleep, and dwell with God in endless love.'[2]

Wm. Wordsworth

You tell me that my writings have been your comfort and
solace in sickness and affliction; it was kind in you to do so; for
I meet with no reward comparable to such assurances.

(Autograph cut off.)

Address: Mrs J. M. Müleen, 21 Heriot Row, Edinburgh.

MS.   *1253. W. W. to Dora W.*

[Early April 1838]

My dear Daughter,

Thanks for your letter. Your Mother left Rydal on Tuesday
noon for Penrith that day, next for Carlisle, and will not return
till Saturday. Mr H. thought the journey too long for one
day.—

Poor Mr Wilkinson of Sedbergh died a few days ago, of inflammation in the chest, we believe, brought on by cold while
he was overlooking his workmen.—I hope you will be able to see
Tintern Abbey on your way to Brinsop, following up the Wye
as far as Monmouth and Ross, in which case you would pass
close by Mrs Elliot's near Goodrich Castle. Could not you write
to Thomas Hutchinson to meet you either at Monmouth, or
Mr Elliot's, in his Father's Carriage, at all events if you can see
Tintern and Piercefield without injurious fatigue, do so.—I am
sorry for the formidable opposition to the Copyright Bill; if
other Persons to whom it would be far more beneficial than to
me had done half as much as I have, it would be carried to a
certainty. I grieve much for Miss Fenwick's distress—but am
not in the least surprised at the turn the affair has taken. When

---

[1] As the postmark is March 29, 1838, it seems probable that the Feb. 28
is W.'s error for March 28.   [2] *Excursion*, IV. 188–90.

Mr T[1] began to pay attention to the Lady she must have been a mere child, and relative to his age which I presume is between 35 and 40, what is she now? If Men or Women will form engagements so little in accordance with nature and reason, they have no *right* to expect better treatment; better *may* come, but the probabilities are much against it. Observe I do not mean that rejection such as Mr T. has met with is a thing in regular course, and to be feared as such, but evils far worse to bear, evils without remedy occurring after marriage, or then first displaying themselves.—

We have not heard again from John, so I trust that neither he nor Isabella are worse—If you don't take care, one of these severe inflammatory colds will be carrying you out of this world, as poor Mr Wilkinson has been carried. You did well, very well, in not going to St Pauls.—To-day I have received three sheets of Sonnets; not having had one for nearly a month. I hope you will be able to take Mr Trench's Vol. of Poems with you, and read them, as I am sure from his letter to me, and his former productions, they must be of no common merit. Don't on any account send your Box by coach; the last containing the Bonnet and gown cost half a guinea carriage. I bought a Brussels Carpet at Pritt's sale—it fits the hall exactly, it is very little worse for wear, and cost 4. 11/- Owen's things were sold yesterday; I did not attend.—Your account of dear Southey rejoices me greatly.—As it will probably be long before we see the last Vol. of Sir Walter's life, tell us how you like it. The newspapers are, as they did in Sheridan's case, extolling his genius, that is his poetical genius, most ridiculously—these follies pass away and truth only remains.—I take no notice of the conclusion of your Letter; indeed part of it I could not make out. It turns upon a subject which I shall never touch more either by pen or voice. Whether I look back or forward it is depressing and distressing to me, and will for the remainder of my life, continue to be so.

[1] Sir Henry Taylor first saw Theodosia Alice Spring Rice in 1834, and proposed to her in 1836, when she was 17. No immediate answer was given, and in June 1837 he was definitely refused on religious grounds. However, the marriage took place in Oct. 1839 (*Autobiog. H. T.* (1800–75), i, pp. 213 and 286).

You appear to take delight in catching at anything derogatory to my judgment or discernment—I never said or thought anything more of the young Rice, than that she was very pretty, and [as] far as general appearance went, an engaging Girl or rather Child, for being small of stature she looked younger than she is; but I never exchanged three words with her in my life; so that of her heart or head, as fitting her for a wife, I neither did, nor cared to form any judgment. With Miss Rice I have conversed frequently, and deem myself competent to draw an inference, worthy of some regard, as to her character.

I can only add remember me most kindly to the Marshalls, Mrs M. in particular if you see her again. Sir Wm Gomm I wrote to upon the Copyright Bill and received a kind and flattering answer. He told me Lady Gomm was exerting herself much in support of it; and that he himself would do his best. I enter my 69th year the day you will receive this. Aunty is going on as usual. Love to dear Miss Fenwick.

Ever faithfully your affectionate Father,

W. W.

K.   *1254. W. W. to Sir Robert Peel*

Rydal Mount, Kendal, April 18th, 1838.

Dear Sir,

The consideration of your eminence as a statesman may, to a man of letters, be a sufficient apology for writing to you upon the subject of Serjeant Talfourd's copyright bill; and I am further encouraged to take this step by remembrance of the interest you kindly expressed (some time ago) in a concern of mine, by letter to Lord Lonsdale; and also in what you did me the honour of writing to myself upon the same occasion.

Allow me then to state the fact that if the bill do not pass, or a comprehensive one grounded upon its principle, I shall be aggrieved in the most tender points; and in respect to almost every individual eminent in Literature whom I have intimately known, I can of themselves or their heirs affirm the same.

The *justice* of the principle of the bill must be too obvious to so comprehensive a mind as yours to allow of my saying a word upon the subject; but there can be no presumption in declaring my opinion that, as a remedial measure, it is urgently called for. The literary talent of the country is in a great measure wasted upon productions of light character and transitory interest, and upon periodicals. Surely the extension of copyright, as contemplated in this bill, could not but avail greatly in putting authors upon exertions of a nobler kind, and in justifying and encouraging them to proceed.

I have the honour to be, with the highest respect,

Faithfully, your obedient servant,

Wm. Wordsworth.

1255. *W. W. to Serjeant Talfourd, M.P.*

Morning Post[1]
April 23, 1838. Rydal Mount, April 18th 1838.
My dear Sir,

A strong opposition, which has manifested itself by public meetings and petitions to the House of Commons, having started up among printers, publishers, and others to your Bill for amending the law of copyrights, and no other like countermovement being made by authors on their part, it has been suggested to me, from quarters entitled to great respect, that it might be of service if, along with a most distinguished literary friend, I should present a petition to Parliament, praying that the Bill may pass, or at least one in favour of its principle. This compliment has no doubt been paid me as one among the oldest of living writers, and of one therefore whose heirs must, in course of nature, be injured sooner than those of younger men, if the proposed measure be rejected. You will not be surprised if I feel some scruple in taking a step, though so well recommended, on account of an aversion to appear prominently in any public question, and because I am loth to think so unfavourably of Parliament as to deem that it requires petitions from authors as a ground for granting them a privilege, the justice of which is so obvious. I cannot bring myself to suppose that

---

[1] Privately reprinted by T. H. Wise in 1916.

the mere shadows of argument advanced by printers and publishers against the claims of a class to whom they owe the
respectability of their condition, if not their very existence,
should avail with any intelligent and disinterested assembly.
Yet further am I averse thus to petition Parliament, because I
would not ask as an individual suppliant, or with a single
associate, what in equity I consider to be the *right* of a class, and
for a much longer period than that defined in your Bill—for
ever. Such right, as you have stated in your admirable speech,
was acknowledged by the common law of England; and let them
who have cried out so loudly against the extension of the term
as is now proposed show cause why that original right should
not be restored. The onus clearly rests with them to do so; but
they have not attempted it, and are glad to take shelter under
the statute law as it now stands, which is a composition or compromise between two opinions; the extreme point of one being,
that, by giving his thoughts to the world, an author abandons
all right to consider the vehicle as private property; and of the
other, that he has the right in perpetuity, that descends to his
heirs, and is transferable to those to whom he or they may
assign it.

This right I hold to be more deeply inherent in that species of
property than in any other, though I am aware that many
persons, perceiving wherein it differs from acquisitions made in
trade and commerce, etc, have contended that the law in
respect to literature ought to remain upon the same footing as
that which regards the profits of mechanical inventions and
chemical discoveries; but that this is an utter fallacy might
easily be proved.

From the considerations above stated I decline to petition, as
suggested, and content myself, in the silence of others better
entitled to speak, with this public declaration of my judgment,
so that at least, my dear Sir, you may not be liable to be treated
as a volunteer intruding without wish or sanction openly expressed by any one of the class whose rights and interests you
have so much to your honour stepped forward to maintain.
Here this letter shall close, its purpose being answered, for no
general arguments from me, and no statements of fact belonging

[925]

to my own case, and which have come to my knowledge with respect to my illustrious friends Coleridge, Scott, Southey, and others, would avail to produce conviction where that has not been effected by your unrivalled speech made upon your first introduction of the Bill into the House of Commons, and by reasonings which have lately been set forth with great ability by writers in the public journals, who were more at liberty to enter into details than you could be while treating the subject before Parliament.

Should your Bill be overborne, which I cannot allow myself to fear, by the interested opposition now at work, justice, nevertheless, sooner or later, must triumph; and at all events the respect and gratitude which authors feel towards you and your coadjutors upon this occasion will be cherished by them to the last hour of their lives.

> I have the honour to be,
> My dear Sir,
> Faithfully yours,
> William Wordsworth.

MS.   *1256. W. W. to John Gibson Lockhart*

Rydal Mount Ap. 27 [1838]

My dear Mr Lockhart,

The time is come to which I thought it right to defer thanking you for your valuable present of the Life of Sir Walter Scott, as I have just received the last volume. I congratulate you sincerely upon having brought to a conclusion so arduous an undertaking: three of the volumes fell at different times into my hands while I was travelling abroad last summer. I need not say that I read them with lively interest—the other four I have since perused, as they reached me, and with still deeper concern. A day or two before our Friend's last departure to the South, he told me that upon reviewing his life, he could not but reckon it a favored, and upon the whole, a very happy one; nor do I think that your Narrative, melancholy as in many respects it is, proves the contrary: the most painful part of his trials, and that which in my mind causes the strongest regret, is the burthen of Secrecy, for a burthen it must have been to one of his open and genial nature, under which so great a portion of it was spent. If, as I suspect, his admirable Works would not, at least many of them, have been produced, but for the spur of worldly ambition, the world at large will, for the sake of those Works, be little disposed to blame what you yourself must have reckoned weaknesses, as is evident from the mode in which you account for, and with no inconsiderable success, palliate them. Again, in the misfortunes of the latter part of his life there is to be found much consolation both for those who loved him, and for Persons comparatively indifferent to his fate. How nobly does his character rise under his calamities, what integrity, what fortitude, what perseverance under pain both of body and mind —qualities which he himself would not have known he possessed to that degree, but for the very infirmities that were the origin and leading cause of his reverses of fortune—so that balancing one thing with another, and above all looking at his immortal Works, I feel at liberty after perusing your Memoir to accede to his own view that his was a favored and a happy life. For yourself, my dear Sir, and your friends it must be matter of sincere pleasure to have your name thus associated with that of your Father-in-law. So much of Sir Walter's affairs having become objects of public investigation, nothing remained for you but to act as openly and sincerely as you have done in writing his Life. Whatever complaints may have been made upon this point will pass away, and ere long your mode of treating the delicate and difficult subject will meet with universal approbation. In your P.S. you allude to the length of the work as having been objected to, and I hope you will not be hurt when I say, that I have been somewhat of the same opinion. The Diary of his northern voyage ought, I think, to have been printed apart from the life; and some of the letters also would have been more in their place, if separated from the narrative. But all this is of little consequence.

You notice some incorrect statements and express a wish that others may be pointed out for amendment in a future Edition.

There are a few trifling inaccuracies relating to Mr Southey and myself. Mr Southey was not at Storrs when Sir W. S. and you were entertained there along with Mr Canning, Prof. Wilson, and myself; nor did I accompany your Party to Lowther as you state—but only to Mr Marshall's at Hallsteads. The anecdote of Crabbe and the candle smoke[1] was often *told me* by Sir George Beaumont, and in the conclusion drawn from it by *him* I concurred, not so much as set down by Sir Walter that it was a proof of the Poet's *want of imagination* as of a sense of *beauty*, but I was not present when the thing occurred—whether at Murray's or elsewhere I do not recollect. 'And can you see any beauty in that?' was the exclamation of Crabbe when Sir G. having in vain attempted to stop his hand, gave vent to his regret for what had been done. Sir George's perception of beauty and grace in Art, and still more in Nature, was most exquisite— and broke forth from him perpetually, both when speaking of his remembrances, and when any thing met his eyes in which those qualities were apparent—and frequently where scarcely any one but himself would have been conscious of their existence. One word more on the story of the Bust. I have a crow to pick with 'honest Allan',[2] he has misled Sir W. by misrepresenting me. I had not a single wrinkle on my *forehead* at the time when this bust was executed, and therefore none could be represented by the Artist (a fact I should have barely been able to speak to, but that it was noticed by a Painter while drawing a Portrait of me a little while before) but deep wrinkles I had in my cheeks and the side of my mouth even from my boyhood—and my Wife, who was present while the Bust was in progress, and remembered them, from the days of her youth, was naturally wishful to have those peculiarities preserved for the sake of likeness, in

---

[1] *v.* Lockhart's *Scott*, ch. lxxiii, under date Jan. 1827.

[2] i.e. Allan Cunningham, Chantrey's Clerk of the Works. In a letter to A. C., quoted *Lockhart*, ch. xlix, Scott had written 'I am happy my effigy is to go with that of W.' [to the Royal Acad. Exhib.] 'for (differing from him in very many points of taste) I do not know a man more to be venerated for uprightness of heart and loftiness of genius. Why he will sometimes choose to crawl upon all fours when God has given him so noble a countenance to lift to heaven I am as little able to account for as for his quarrelling (as you tell me) with the wrinkles which time and meditation have stamped his brow withal.'

all their force. Chauntrey objected, saying those lines if given with shut mouth, would sacrifice the spirit to the letter, and by attracting undue attention, would greatly injure instead of strengthen the resemblances to the living Man. My own knowledge of Art led me to the same conclusion. I supported the Sculptor's judgment in opposition to my Wife's desire: this is the plain story, and it is told merely that I may not pass down to posterity as a Man, whose personal vanity urged him to importune a first-rate Artist to tell a lie in marble, without good reason; but in reality the sacrifice of truth would have been much greater, if the principles of legitimate art had been departed from. Excuse so many words upon what may be thought, but I hope not by yourself, an insignificant subject.—

And now, my dear Sir, let me condole with you on your sad bereavement; the tidings reached me in Italy—they cast a gloom over my mind, amid the splendours of that Country, for I knew the virtues of the departed and was an early admirer of the many attractions with which she was graced. Never shall I forget her light figure, her bounding step, her bright eyes, her animated tones when with a confiding simplicity that was quite enchanting she led my wife and her deceased Sister (our fellow traveller) and myself round the precincts of Abbotsford, then a small Cottage, to every object in which for antiquarian or other reasons, her Father who was then absent took an interest. This was in 1814 when he was on his voyage to the Shetlands. The last time I saw Mrs Lockhart was on a day when she took us in her carriage to the recitations at Harrow. She sate by me at the collation given at the Master, my nephew's house: these little particulars will not be without interest to you, as affording proof of my sympathy with your sorrow from the loss of one who was beloved wherever she was known.

I cannot conclude without expressing a hope that your Children are well—Mrs W. joins me in kind remembrances to yourself and begs me to say that she sincerely sympathizes in all I have said concerning your heavy loss.

With the best of good wishes I am faithfully yours

Wm Wordsworth

MS.   **1257. *D. W. to Dora W.***

[Spring 1838][1]

My dearest Dora

They say I must write a letter—and what shall it be? News—news I must seek for news. My own thoughts are a wilderness —'not pierceable by power of any star'[2]—News then is my resting-place—News! news!

Poor Peggy Benson lies in Grasmere Church-yard beside her once beautiful Mother. Fanny Haigh is gone to a better world. My Friend Mrs Rawson has ended her ninety and two years pilgrimage—and *I* have fought and fretted and striven—and am here beside the fire. The Doves behind me at the small window—the laburnum with its naked seed-pods shivers before my window and the pine-trees rock from their base.—More I cannot write so farewell! and may God bless you and your kind good Friend Miss Fenwick, to whom I send love and all the best of wishes. Yours evermore

Dorothy Wordsworth

P.S. by M. W.

The Doves have lived by day in Aunt's room ever since we went to Brigham when no fire was in the sitting-rooms—at night they are in the office and James likes their company.—Miss Belle is a wretched object to all but Anne.

MS.   **1258. *W. W. to Robert Southey***

Monday Morn^g [April 30 1838]

My dear Southey,

Thank you for clearing away my apprehensions—You will have [s]een from my letter to Sergeant T. that petitioning was not to my taste and why. But I think that the frequent recurrence of your name[3] in the debate is no excuse why you should

---

[1] The letter may be dated by the fact that Mrs Rawson died in 1837, and Peggy Benson in Feb. 1838, and that Dora was staying with Miss Fenwick in the early months of 1838.   [2] Spenser, *F. Q.*, I. i. 7.

[3] Serjeant Talfourd obtained leave to bring in his Copyright Bill on May 12, 1837: he moved the second reading on April 25, 1838. In the course of the debate Southey's name was often mentioned in conjunction with those of W. W., Scott, and others.

not write and send [th]e letter as approved of by Sir J. G.[1]—not being mentioned at y[r] own request.

[Y]ou perhaps have seen that a Mr Walker[2] has given notice —'that upon the motion being made for the Copy-right bill going into Committee, he should move, for its being considered in Committee that day six months'. Which in other words is putting an extinguisher upon it. This Mr W.—whoever he may be, is a new enemy, for his name does not appear in the division. I have no doubt that stupidity and cupidity will cause more Mr Walkers to rise up and therefore it is incumbent upon us all to do the utmost we can—*speedily*—consistent with our other duties and engagements. As far as *we* are personally concerned, and *I* especially, it is little comfort to say the thing *will* be carried some day or other—My Excursion was printed in the same year as your Roderic and 4/5[ths] or more of my writings would therefore fall a prey to Mr Tegg[3] like your own, instantly on my death, or 4 years after were I to die tomorrow.

But to return to your letter—it would be read I am very sure with great effect on the day when Mr Walker means to make his hostile motion.—You question its prudence—I cannot see how a statement of facts from your self can do aught but good—as to the question as[4] one of natural right, or as a right in perpetuity established by common law, the less those points are dwelt upon at this crisis, the better, but I can see no harm in barely stating y[r] opinion as I have done in my letter to Sergeant T. By the bye that letter before publication was sent by me to him to determine whether or not it s[d] be publ[d], and he thanked me for it warmly—as being sure that it would be of service.

The facts you thought of stating, and any others bearing upon the subject would I repeat be of great weight. Nor perhaps

[1] Mr McIntyre suggests that Sir J. G. is Sir James Graham (1792–1861), a native of Cumberland, first a member of the Whig party under Lord Grey but later a Tory under Peel.

[2] His name was not Walker but Wakley. He moved his motion on May 9 after Serjeant T. had moved the Committee Stage of the Bill. As a result Talfourd did not move the second reading again till Feb. 27, 1839.

[3] Thomas Tegg (1776–1845), a bookseller, famous for his popular reprints of English Classics, and a stout opponent of Talfourd's Bill. He had written in 1837, *Remarks on the Speech of Serjeant Talfourd on the Laws relating to Copyright*, and in 1840 he followed it up with a pamphlet *Extension of Copyright proposed by S[jt] T*. (*v.* p. 1010).   [4] as] of MS.

would it be amiss to glance at the injury which to y^r knowledge would accrue, to the Heirs of Coleridge and to y^r other friends, myself included. Coleridge['s] earlier poems including the Ancient Mariner *have* been published as you foresee our own would be, exactly as they first appeared, but in all probability much deteriorat[ed] by reckless printing.

As to the Att^y Gen's proposal[1] I could not relish it—I should both dislike and dread such a tribunal.—Besides, such a distinction would put those Authors on whom it was conferred in an invidious position. Let the remuneration come from [the] public who would chearfully bestow it—We[2] want no pensions and reversions for our heirs, and no monuments by public or private subscription—We shall have a monument in our works if they survive, if they do not we should not deserve it. So with regard to a lease from the dictum of the Privy Council, if our works cease to be called for, the privilege would be but a mockery and an occasion of malignant sarcasm from the evil disposed.

I have found applications to Ladies of use in spurring Members to do their duty—Your old friend Mrs Hughes[3] is a person of wide acquaintance and indefatigable zeal—You recollect how she stirred in getting Kenyon into the Atheneum—a word to her from you—might keep many a man from his claret or his evening Party, and the battle be won by an attendance so gained.

Ever aff^{ly} yours

Wm Wordsworth

I wish you had mentioned y^r health.

MS.   *1259. W. W. to Thomas Noon Talfourd*

[p.m. Kendal May 3, 1838]

My dear Mr Talfourd

Don't let your hopes down, or relax—True it is, we have cause to fear about Sir R. Peel. He declined voting, because he

---

[1] The Attorney-General had suggested, in the debate on April 25, that the extension of copyright might be vested in the discretion of the Judicial Committee of the Privy Council.

[2] This passage, from 'We' to end of paragraph, is printed by K among the letters of 1814.

[3] The wife of Thos. Hughes, D.D., Canon of St. Paul's, and an intimate friend of Scott, who refers to her in a letter to Southey, July 8, 1824, as 'my clever, active, bustling friend'.

had not made up his mind. I will give you his difficulties in his own words, in a letter I have just had from him—

'I confess to you that I do not see my way clearly. If the right of the author to such extended protection be admitted, can we refuse it in the case of Patents? and of every discovery mainly owing to the ingenuity or skill of the discoverers. There are also the difficulties of determining what constitutes an original work, as distinguished from plagiarism, difficulties incident indeed to any degree of protection, but increasing with the protraction of it. And there are too the difficulties of effectually preventing piracy in Countries not subject to our jurisdiction.'—Sir R. concludes with obligingly [? apprising] me that he will consider maturely the arguments in favor of the Bill, and that his regret will on my account be increased if he should not be convinced by them—These are his last words and not very encouraging—

On the other hand Mr Horseman member for Cockermouth, who takes great interest in the success of the measure and is very sorry that though he endeavored to attend, he was not able, tells me that he has little or no doubt you will be successful, and that the more numerous the attendance the more sure you are to do so; for, says he, 'There is a general and strong feeling in all [?   ] and parties, in favor of the claims of Authors'— Mr H. must know a great deal about the mind of his Party at least; for is he not what is commonly called 'Whippet'?

I do not know Mr H. personally, but he has written me two long and interesting letters upon the subject, and you may depend upon his Cooperation.—Mr Attwood member for Whitehaven is also very zealous and will stir up the other Cumberland Members—

I shall write to Sir R. Peel today, and will cut out of the newspaper that part so eloquently expressed of your speech of the little analogy between Patents and copyright—I shall also touch briefly his other objections. Ever faithfully and gratefully yours W. Wordsworth. I am glad you are printing your speech.

P.S. This day I have heard from Mr Lockhart who tells me that unless your Bill be carried he considers the emancipation of Abbotsford all but hopeless. He then stated the particulars.

How beautifully you touched, or rather hinted, poor dear Sir Walter in his last struggles! Alas for the heart of the Solicitor-General! I shall write to Mr Johnson, and mention your wish to see him. I [?   ] and this above request, fearing I might not accomplish my purpose of writing the enclosed excuse the liberty I take, I pray you,   W. W.

Address: Mr Sergeant Talfourd, M.P., Russel Square, London.

K.   *1260. W. W. to Sir Robert Peel*

[May 3, 1838]

Dear Sir Robert,

I am unwilling to encroach so far upon the kind and flattering expressions of your letter and the assurance it gives me that you will maturely consider the important subject to which it relates; but pray allow me to do this, and yet something more.

As you may not have seen or heard what Serjeant Talfourd said upon Patents, and such cases of copyright as his bill mainly looked to, I have taken the liberty of annexing part of the passage from *The Times*, that it may be read with less trouble.

'It remains to be proved that the protection granted to patentees is sufficient; but supposing it to be so, although there are points of similarity between the cases, there are grounds of essential and obvious distinction. In cases of patent, the merits of the invention are palpable, the demand is usually immediate, and the recompense of the inventor, in proportion to the utility of his work, speedy and certain. In cases of patent, the subject is generally one to which many minds are at once applied; the invention is often not more than a step in a series of processes, the first of which being given, the consequence will almost certainly present itself sooner or later to some of these inquirers; and if it were not hit on this year by one, would probably be discovered the next by another; but who will suggest that if Shakespeare had not written *Lear*, or Richardson *Clarissa*, other poets or novelists would have invented them? In practical science every discovery is a step to something more perfect; and to give to the inventor of each a protracted monopoly would be to shut out all improvement by others. But who can improve or supersede (as is perpetually done in mechanical invention) these masterpieces of genius? They stand perfect, apart from all things else, self-sustained, the models for imitation, the source whence rules of art take their origin. And if we apply the analogy of mechanical invention to literature, we shall find that, in so far as it stands, there is really in the latter no monopoly at all, however brief. For example, historical or critical research bears a close analogy to the process of mechanical discovery, and how does the law of copyright apply to the treasures it may reveal? The fact discovered, the truth ascertained, become at once the property of mankind, to accept, to state, to reason on; and all that remains to the author is the style in which it is expressed.'

Of the broad distinctions I may not, perhaps, be an impartial judge, as I have had the honour of hearing them adopted from suggestions of my own, and they appear to have made an impression upon the public. The conclusion of the extract meets in fact the difficulty stated by you of determining what constitutes an original work, as distinguished from plagiarism. Dr Arnold is now engaged in writing a *History of Rome,* in which I know that he will be greatly indebted to Niebuhr, but I have no doubt of the subject being treated by him in such a manner that neither Niebuhr—had he been an Englishman, and written in English—would be found, were he alive, to complain, nor could any competent tribunal to which the case might be referred condemn the subsequent writer for having made an unfair or illegal use of his predecessor's labours. So would it always be with the successful labours of men of honour and great talent employed upon the same subjects; and it is only upon the productions of such authors that the proposed extension of term has any bearing. Mere drudges and dishonest writers are sometimes protected by the law as it now exists; but their works, if not cried down at once, soon die of themselves, and the plundered author seldom thinks it worth while to complain, or seek a remedy by law. For these reasons—though suspecting my judgment when it differs from yours—I cannot see a formidable difficulty here; nor can I agree with your opinion that the difficulty incident to any degree of protection increases with the protection of it. I incline to think that the contrary would be the fact.

As to piracy, much wrong is done by it; but imperfect as protection must be in this case, is not that rather a reason for prolonging it at home, in order that there may be, in its duration, something of an equivalent for what is lost by foreign injustice?

The feeling is strong, however, among leading men in America in favour of international copyright. So it is, I believe, in France; and last year I was told in Paris, at Galignani's, that their trade of this kind was destroying itself by competition and underselling. But, if we cannot altogether succeed in this point, *est quodam prodire tenus;* and let us hope and trust that justice, gratitude, and generous feelings will gain ground among nations, in spite of Utilitarians and Economists who would banish such qualities from our heads and hearts, as they have done from their own; and to the discomfiture of overgrown publishers, who—to my knowledge—have instigated their misled dependents to oppose the measure.

Permit me to state a fact as throwing light upon the reasonableness of lengthening the term of copyright. My own poems, and I may add Mr Coleridge's, have been in demand since their first publication, but till lately only to that degree which confined both publisher and author, in common prudence, to small editions, the profits of which were accordingly small to the publisher, and the residue to the author almost insignificant. I have gained much more from my long-published writings within the last five or six years than in the thirty preceding, and the copyright of much the greatest portion of them would die with me, or within the space of four years. And if from small things we may ascend to great, how slowly did the poetry of Milton make its way to public favour; nor till very lately were the works of Shakespeare himself justly appreciated even within his own country.

Pardon me for writing at such length, and believe me, gratefully, and with the highest respect,

Your faithful servant,

Wm. Wordsworth.

[936]

MS.   *1261. W. W. to Thomas Wyse*[1]

Rydal Mount, Kendal.

Sir,   May 3ᵈ, 1838.

On the suggestion of my friend and neighbour, Mrs Graves, I take the liberty of addressing a few lines to you on the subject of the Copyright Bill now before Parliament, and also of forwarding by her desire a short paper which, as you will see, I was indu[c]ed to write upon local considerations.

With the exception of a certain class of Theorists who by system think it at once expedient and right to get work as cheaply done as they can, tho' at whatever cost of health, comfort and life to the workmen, all disinterested Persons are of opinion that thoughtful genius and persevering industry do not derive sufficient reward and encouragement from the protection afforded by the law, as it now exists. Nor will it be denied, by men of comprehensive mind, that the character of our literature would be raised by the proposed extension; Gibbon could not have written his history with the law even as it now is, had he not been a man of fortune. The question as lying between Publishers and Authors is as easily disposed of, so that all that remains, is the objection, stated by you, 'that prolonged protection to Authors would kill all cheap Editions'. Conscientiously speaking, I do not believe anything of the kind, and for reasons glanced at in the paper I take the liberty to send you, and your perusal of which, as it is not long, I venture to request. You are no doubt aware that there has been and still continues a conventional arrangement among Publishers who have purchased Copy-rights, not to interfere with each other's exclusive claims, after their rights by law have expired. This convention is breaking down under the force of the rapidly increasing demand for books, the consequence of extending education and an increase in the wealth of the community. Booksellers, while they enjoy exclusive right by law, are every year finding it more and more their interest to sell an increased number of Copies at a low price rather than a few at a high one. The same considerations would operate in the same way upon the heirs and descendants of Authors—as it is already doing among themselves—with a

[1] M.P. for Tipperary.

further motive in both cases of increased honour and distinction to the name and family. Besides, it would be of greater consequence to *them*, than to Publishers who have each the works of *many* to profit by, and they would naturally take more care to give to the public correct Editions. Nothing can be more detestable and injurious to knowledge and taste than the inaccuracies in the low priced Editions, that are thrown out upon the world by Tegg, and others of his stamp. After all, for the great body of the people *dirt-cheap* literature, excuse the term, is rather a disadvantage than a benefit; in America whole volumes of works produced in England are often as they come out to meet the appetite of novelty each sold in a newspaper form for three-halfpence or twopence a piece—but what good is done by them? They are as carelessly treated and as recklessly destroyed, as they were unthinkingly bought—and if you take a higher point in the scale, the effect is much the same. Libraries, even very small ones, are almost unknown in America, except among the upper ranks of their society. The books which really improve the human mind are those that tempt to repeated perusal, and are read till they sink into it—and are even treasured up in the very shape they bore, when the reader first felt grateful to the Author for the good he had done him. This observation applies in its degree to the poorest mechanic, or rural labourer. Do but look at the fate of tracts and books that are distributed gratis! or cast your eye upon the way in which education works, that is purely eleemosynary, and compare the results with those, where a sacrifice has been made, or more difficulty encountered. But I am tiring you, and must beg your excuse. Concluding with a hope that the examination you intend to give to the subject will lead you to support the Bill, both by your vote and influence among your friends, and also by speaking in its favour (which could not but have great weight) when the motion is made for its going into Committee,

I have the honour to be, Your obed^t Servant,

Wm. Wordsworth.

The latter part of this letter is mainly a transcript from what I had prepared to send to some journal or other, in which perhaps it may appear.

MS.   *1262. W. W. to John Gibson Lockhart*

Rydal Mount May 4th [1838]

My dear Mr Lockhart,

I am much gratified by your having taken in good part all that sincerity urged me to say upon the subject of your Book; and rejoice to hear that the sale has been so large. What you add concerning Abbotsford grieves me much, and will strengthen my desire to do more than I have done, and that I assure you is not a little, in support of Serg^{nt} Talfourd's Bill. If we should be defeated this Session, there ought to be a combined effort among Authors for the purpose of overcoming the opposition. The indifference among Members of the H. C. for the most part, to any but party measures, is after all the great difficulty in our way. If we all bestirred ourselves among our several Friends, to induce them to consider the measure, and if convinced of its justice and expediency give it their support, they would take the requests as a compliment and not a few would with pleasure range themselves on our side. This I write from *experience*, for I am pretty sure, that without my own endeavour in this way the Bill would not have proceeded so far. Among the intelligent who consider the principle of the Bill (the Utilitarians do not deserve the name) dispassionately, and who, admitting the injustice done to Authors, are desirous of a remedy, the difficulties seem to be chiefly in giving extended protection to Authors, yet at the same time witholding it from those whose mechanical inventions give them claim to apply for Patents. There comes with this class the difficulty of determining what constitutes an original work, as contradistinguished from Plagiarism; and lastly the impossibility of preventing publication in countries not subject to our jurisdiction; this is incidental to the law as it now stands. And the objection with these Reasoners strengthens as the privilege is protracted. Though there are difficulties undoubtedly in all these points, they will not, I think, be found insurmountable, by those who distinctly perceive the delusions so industriously spread in respect to other bearings of the measure.—Being sure that both from general and particular, not to say *personal* motives, you will do your utmost, I drop the subject. But what leads you to attribute the opposition to *small* Publishers? Longman presided at the public meeting and Murray countenanced it. Mrs Wordsworth rejoiced with me to hear that your children have got through a trying disease, that took one of our's, a fine Boy of six years and a half, away from us. Be assured that our best good wishes attend them, and we should like to know how your Brother, Mr Charles Scott, is, for we heard with much concern an ill report of the general state of his health. I have no objection to my notes upon the Diary being given in my own words but should like first to see the passages again, as the whole Letter was written without any such view. Therefore be so kind as to send it me at your leisure and I will return it. But it is time to subscribe myself, as I do sincerely, and with great respect, your obliged Friend

Wm Wordsworth.

I feel ashamed not to have noticed your wish to see me at your Brother's in Lanarkshire; my travelling engagements for next summer, if I leave home at all, lie unluckily in quite a different direction. But cannot we see you and yours in passing or re-passing? pray offer my best remembrances to your Brother.

Address: J. G. Lockhart Esqre, 24 Sussex Place, Regent's Park.

MS.   **1263. W. W. to Daniel Stuart**
G.
Rydal Mount Ambleside
May 9th,[1] [1838.]

My dear Mr Stuart,

I have just received your communication. I grieve much for the necessity of the disclosure, which does more, much more, than justify yourself.

There is a question before Parliament in which, as an Author both upon personal and higher motives, I am much interested. Among your friends and acquaintances is there no member of the H.C. whom you could interest in doing justice to men of Letters in this matter? Pray do your utmost; for the opposition is strong and persevering. I know not where to address you. Believe me to be, very faithfully yours,

Wm. Wordsworth.

[1] For W. W. to H. C. R. May 9, *v. C.R.*, p. 360.

MS.
G.
K(—)

1264. *W. W. to Daniel Stuart*

May 17, 1838.

Dear Mr Stuart,

In Mr Gillman's life of Coleridge just published, I find these words:—'The Proprietor of the Morng Post, who was also the Editor, engaged Coleridge to undertake the literary department. As Contributors to this paper, the editor had the assistance of Mr Wordsworth, Mr Southey, and Mr Lamb. Mr S., from his extreme activity, and with a rapidity and punctuality which made him invaluable to the Proprietor, etc. The others were not of the same value to the Proprietor.'

In the extracts from the Gent's. Mag. you sent me the other day, speaking, I imagine, of the Morng Post, *you* say, 'At this time, I do not think Wordsworth sent anything.' You have here been speaking of a Salary being given to Mr C. and Mr L., as contributors to the Morng Post, and the passage, coupled with that of Mr G.s, would lead any one to infer that I was a *paid Writer* of that Paper. Now, for my own part, I am quite certain that nothing of mine ever appeared in the Morng Post, except a very, very, few sonnets upon political subjects, and one Poem called the 'Farmer of Tillsbury Vale,'[1] but whether this appeared in the Morng Post or the Courier, I do not remember. In the Courier were printed 2 articles in continuation, amounting together to 25 pages, of the Pamphlet I afterwards published on the Convention of Cintra. The Sonnets and the Pamphlet were written by me without the slightest view to any emolument whatever; nor have I, nor my Wife or Sister, any recollection of any money being received for them, either directly from yourself (as E. and P. of those Papers), or mediately through C.; and I wish to know from you, if you have any remembrance or evidence to the contrary. But certain I am, that the last thing that could have found its way into my thoughts would have been to enter into an engagement to write for any newspaper— and that I never did so. In short, with the exception of the

---

[1] 'The Farmer of Tillsbury Vale' had appeared in the *Morning Post* of July 21, 1800. W. had apparently forgotten that 'The Convict' (Oxf. W., p. 620) had also appeared in the same paper (on Dec. 14, 1797).

things already mentioned, a very few articles sent to a West^d
Journal, during the first West^d contest, one article which I was
induced to publish in a London newspaper, when Southey and
Byron were at war, and a letter, the other week, to the Kendal
Mercury upon the Copyright question, and a letter to Sergeant
Talfourd on the same subject, published in the Morng Post, not
a word of mine ever appeared, sent by myself at least, or as far
as I know, by any other Persons, in any Newspaper, Review,
Magazine, or Public Journal whatsoever. By the bye, I ought
to except two sonnets and a light Poem, not connected with my
works, which were printed in some Provincial Journal.

I will be obliged to you if you will answer at your early convenience the question put above; as I wish to write to Mr G.,
whose book, I am sorry to say, is full of all kinds of mistakes.
Coleridge is a subject which no Biographer ought to touch
beyond what he himself was eye witness of.

When you write pray tell me how Mrs Stuart, yourself, and
your family, are. Mrs W. unites with me in kind regards to
Mrs S. and yourself, and believe me to remain, faithfully yours,

Wm. Wordsworth.

Address: Daniel Stuart Esq., 9 Upper Harley Street, London.

MS.
K(—)

1265. *W. W. to Edward Moxon*

May 21 [1838]

My dear Mr Moxon,

A few days delay has been caused by a visit I have been paying to Lord Lonsdale at Lowther—but by this day's Post I send
all the Notes and a short Advertisement and table of Contents
—The volume will contain twelve New Sonnets. So that when
I get the proofs back from the Printer—with the remainder of
Clean Sheets in order to see that the notes are referred properly
to their respective pages—my part of the work will be over. I
cannot form a conjecture whether this Publication is a well
advised one or no—if it should at all interfere with the sale of
your Six Vols, I shall exceedingly regret our having been persuaded to undertake it. I should wish to have a few Vols of the

Sonnets sent down here—and at the same time a dozen copies of the six Vols. which you will charge me with, as heretofore. The Poems will be placed in the hands of the Bookseller at Ambleside who sells a Copy now and then—with no add[1] charge from me—by which means, she, being in a small way, and having no connection with London, gets a better profit than were she to procure them from a Country Bookseller, who has such connection.

The extension of term in Copy-right, whatsoever becomes of the principle during this Session, being both just and expedient is sure of being carried sooner or later. In the meanwhile, by being the single exception among Publishers who have united to oppose it, you have done yourself great honor—and acted to your advantage also—depend upon it. Many thanks for your parcel rec[d] thro' the hands of Mr Graves.

If you have remaining on hand some copies of Serg[t] Talfourd's 9th Speech, pray send me at least three, when you send the books—I have already mentioned this wish to the Sergeant—

What success has attended his Tragedy[1]—he is an interesting man—for talents, Genius, and energy of mind. Mention Miss Lamb to us when you write—and with our Love to her, and give our kindest regards to your household. We expect our daughter home in about 10 days.

Ever faithfully y[r] much obliged
Wm Wordsworth

Address: Edward Moxon Esq., 44 Dover Street.

MS.
K(—)

1266. *W. W. to ?*

Rydal Mount June 9th [1838]

My dear Sir

Never had a book, a reprint especially, such a tedious and long journey through the Press as my Vol. of Sonnets. It is however on the point of being finished, and pray when you hear of its being advertized go or send to Moxon's where I have directed a Copy to be laid aside for you, as a small return for your many attentions to me and mine.

---

[1] *Ion*, published 1836.

Mr Gillman's Book is not better than I feared I should find it. It is full of mistakes as to facts, and misrepresentations concerning facts. Poor dear Coleridge from a hundred causes many of them unhappy ones was not to be trusted in his account either of particular occurrences, or the general tenor of his engagements and occupations. Mr G. may be more fortunate when he shall come to what he himself had an opportunity of observing, but there again I have my fears. Of idolatrous Biography I think very lightly: we have had too many examples of it lately; take Mr Wilberforce's life by his Sons as a specimen; and Coleridge I am afraid will not be dealt more wisely with. Observe in what I have said above I do not mean to impeach poor C.'s veraciousness, far from it, but his credibility. He deceived himself in a hundred ways; relating things according to the humor of the moment, as his spirits were up or down, or as they furnished employment for his fancy, or for his theories.

As you do not mention your health I hope it is quite restored. The Copyright Bill goes on but unpromisingly.

Ever my dear Sir

most faithfully yours

Wm Wordsworth

MS. *1267. W. W. to Benjamin Robert Haydon*[1]

Rydal Mount, 25th June, 1838.

My dear Haydon,

I lose no time in replying to your letter. It gives me much pleasure to see you writing in such high spirits, as I conclude that you are prospering. It would ill become me not to say that I must deem the dedication to me of your Lectures an honorable distinction, and the more gratifying as it comes from the feelings to which you have given utterance in your letter.

I have not seen any extracts from your Lectures, but I have somewhere heard that you speak of Michel Angelo in terms of disparagement to which I cannot accede, and therefore I should

---

[1] For W. W. to H. C. R. June 18–24, *v. C.R.*, p. 364.

like that, in the terms of your dedication, you would contrive as briefly as you can to give it to be understood that I am not pledged to the whole of your opinions in reference to an Art in which you are so distinguished.

Pray present my kind regards to Mrs Haydon, and

Believe me to be faithfully yours,

William Wordsworth

Address: B. R. Haydon Esq., 4 Barwood Place, Edgware Road, London.

MS.   *1268.   W. W. to W. Strickland Cookson* [1]

Rydal Mount 25th June [1838]

My dear Mr Cookson,

Many thanks for your Letter and all the trouble you take about my little affairs.

I feel much obliged by your undertaking to place the 400£ as you did on the 12th of May last.—

The proposal of your Letter of yesterday is not so satisfactory. I will state my objections and doubts.

The proposed security is so and so; but the party will not be in *possession* till after the death of another person.—Am I to understand that in the case the borrower should die before the present owner of the property, I should have a lien upon it; and if so, how could that be turned to the benefit of my estate? not at all I suppose during the life of the Lady, so that the security would resolve itself into the sufficiency and integrity of the two Persons who are to be Sureties for the regular payment of the interest.—Am I right in this view of the case? if so, with due submission to your superior Knowledge and experience, I should deem the transaction wholly inadviseable.—

Even if such security could be given as would attach to the Estate, in case of the Borrower dying before the Lady, I submit whether there might not be difficulties in ultimately recovering

---

[1] W. Strickland Cookson, son of the Cooksons of Kendal, acted as W.'s solicitor, and was one of his executors.

the principal after her death; But of this you must be a much better judge than I am—

I have as usual consulted with Mr Carter.[1] He is no Lawyer any more than my self—and is more decidedly against the thing even than I am, adding another consideration, that he is afraid of our little property being so much scattered as it is. And he is quite against selling the India Bonds for what appears to him so questionable an investment.—

Could you find a moment to answer these questions—

Would there be a lien upon the Estate in case the Borrower should die before the Lady who is now in possession?—I suppose so.

Have you the means of being satisfied of the respectability of the Sureties who might be offered?

The lender with a power of sale to be exercised in case the interest be not punctually paid, is proposed. Could this be of any avail during the life of the Lady?—

—I have nearly 400£ lying in the Kendal Bank at 2 and a half per cent which is tangible for this, or any other investment that should be quite satisfactory, and the requisite sum could be made up by money in Mr Courtenay's hands.

After all I have so much confidence in your caution and judgement, and am so sensible of my own inexperience, that I have not been quite at ease in writing the above; which is too indec[is]ive for my own taste and feeling.—You say the *only* objection is, the party not being in possession. Briefly, in what way and to what degree does this, with your experience in business, strike you as an objection.—If I had confined myself to putting at first this simple question I might have spared you the trouble of reading this long and perhaps confused Letter, and myself that of writing it.—Pray let me hear from you once more, and I will then decide absolutely.

We are glad to hear that you and Mrs C. mean shortly to visit West[nd].

ever my dear Sir
faithfully your much obliged
Wm Wordsworth

[1] So MS., *but* W. *means* Carr, *v.* next Letter.

The family at Nook End are all well. Dora came home two or three days ago. She does not complain, but looks much thinner than when she left us in the Autumn.—

MS.   *1269. W. W. to W. Strickland Cookson*

Tuesday 26th June [1838]

My dear Mr Cookson,

I am so much dissatisfied with the confused, wordy, and indecisive Letter I wrote you yesterday, that you must excuse my returning to the subject.

I have carefully reperused your Letter, and reconsidered the subject.

The only objection, you say, is that the Party will not be in possession, till after the death of a Lady 77 years of age.—

I ask is there in this fact any further objection than[1] what is involved in the contingency of the Lady surviving the person who wishes to borrow the money, and the contingency of the insufficiency of the proposed sureties?—For I presume *now* with confidence, that the Lady has only a life's interest in the Estate, and that the Borrower has power at present to mortgage the Estate, in other words, make it responsible for the money, independent altogether of his outliving the Lady or not.—If this view be correct, and you have satisfactory means of ascertaining the sufficiency of the two proposed Sureties, I now think that I am justified in closing with the proposal, the lender being armed, as is proposed, with a power of sale.—

I am of the same mind as to not disturbing the India Bonds. What is wanting to complete the £600 beyond the sum which may be in Mr Courtenay's hands, shall instantly be supplied through Wakefield's Bank,—

I have talked the matter over with Mr Carr, and he confirms me in my resolution to place the money as you propose.

On Mr Carr's suggestion also I mention that he has 3,500 £ now in his hands, which he is desirous of placing upon un[e]xceptionable security at as good a rate of interest as could be procured.—If he could effect this he would go abroad immediately,

---

[1] than: that MS.

and he would be very glad if you could assist him, through your professional aid, in carrying his wish into effect.—

> I remain
> My dear Sir
>> faithfully your much obliged
>>> Wm Wordsworth

Address: W. S. Cookson Esqre, 6 Lincoln's Inn, London.

MS. **1270. *W. W. to Thomas Powell*[1]**

[28 June 1838][2]

My dear Sir,

As you will see by your own Book which I return I have misunderstood your wishes; I must now request you to accept on the part of your Son a copy of my Poems from myself. The Parcel will go to Kendal today to be forwarded by the Mail.

Your Volume would have returned immediately, but I was hoping for some opportunity to return it, free of expense.

Be so kind as to present my sincere acknowledgements to Dr Smith for his valuable Work, Divine Government,[3] both for its own sake and the Compliment paid in sending it to me as a Stranger.—The subject has been in part and shall be, maturely, considered by me when more at leisure than this present season allows me to be. Thanks for your lines. They are pleasing; but is there not an error in the word 'lay' for 'lie'?

Your Godchild is still more interesting to me as being the Daughter of a distinguished Person who was so infamously traduced for having done his duty to his Country, and to mankind, by his bearing towards one of the worst Enemies of the

---

[1] Thomas Powell (1809–87), dramatist and miscellaneous writer in verse and prose, published *Poems* in 1836, '42, '46, and '47, a romantic play, *The Blind Wife*, in 1843, which ran through six editions, and collaborated with R. H. Horne in *A New Spirit of the Age*, 1844. In 1839–40 he projected a volume of *Chaucer Modernized*, to which W. W., Horne, and Leigh Hunt contributed, *v.* later Letters. In 1849 he took up his residence in America.

[2] Dated by the last words of the Letter.

[3] Thomas Southwood Smith, M.D. (1788–1861), preacher, doctor, and great sanitary reformer, the friend of Jeremy Bentham, who left him his body for dissection. His *Illustrations of Divine Government* (1816) had a wide circulation, and reached its sixth edition in 1866.

human race that ever existed; one who had the noblest opportunities of doing good that ever fell to the lot of Man, and who
to selfishness and vulgar ambition sacrificed every thing—

Your Parcel came as you wished free of expense—

The Copyright Bill, at least the principle of it is, I think, sure
of being carried next Session, it must be so if justice have any
weight with the Legislature.

Pray excuse this Letter written in great hurry on the morning
of the coronation

[signature cut away]

I have just received the amended Bill; be so good as to thank
Mr Chapman.

MS. K. 1271. *W. W. to William Ewart Gladstone*

June [1838]

My dear Mr Gladstone,

Your decision was most judicious, and I thank you sincerely
and cordially both for your exertions on this occasion and
through the whole business, and for your kind letter.

The cause is at once so just, and the measure so expedient,
that I have not a doubt of the principle being carried, provided
those who understand the question (which they cannot do,
without being sensible of its importance) support it with due
zeal, in, and out of Parliament. If you can point out any way
in which I can be useful, I should be happy to do my best. You
are perhaps aware of the reasons why Sir R. Peel withholds his
support; he was so obliging as to state them in a letter to me.
Perhaps it would be as well, however, if I should briefly give
them. His difficulties are three.

First, if we grant extension of right to authors, says he, how
can it be withheld from applicants for Patents? secondly, how
can the originality of a work be defined so as to discriminate it
from a Plagiarism? and lastly, how can we prevent works being
reprinted in countries over which we have no jurisdiction?

I answered these several objections as well as I could, and
satisfactorily as I thought; but not, I fear, to Sir R.'s conviction.
All these hesitations arise out of that want of due confidence

in the principles of justice, which is the bane of all practical politicians.

Thanks for your animated stanzas from Manzoni.[1] I have often heard of the Ode, but it never fell in my way. You have puzzled me about a new sonnet of mine in the Quarterly,[2] I presume the last number; what could it be, and how could it get there? I have lately written 13 new ones, which will appear in the edition of the whole of my sonnets in *one* volume which Moxon is about to publish; but none of these were ever given by me to any writer in that review or any other.

I hope that your attendance in Parliament is not too much for your health. Many urgent applications are made to me to sign the Petition that went from Kendal and the neighbourhood, in favour of immediate abolition of negro apprenticeship—I refused to do so, and am sure I shall never regret that resolution. Your own speech was masterly. Ever yours with high respect and faithfully,

W. Wordsworth.

MS.   **1272. W. W. to John Kenyon**

[June 1838][3]

I understand that you, Mr Robinson, and Southey and his Son purpose taking a trip on the Continent, this summer. It is a promising scheme, and I am heartily glad of it for all your sakes, especially for Southey and Robinson, who is getting too old for the lonely and distant ramble that he talked of in Norway and Sweden. I took too much out of myself in my Italian tour; the diet did not agree with me, and the exertion in the heat was too much for a man of 67. Nothing however

---

[1] Alessandro Manzoni (1785–1873), author of *I Promessi Sposi* and *Gli Inni sacri*. To which of the *Inni* reference is made here is uncertain.

[2] An article in *The Quarterly* for June 1838, on 'Arts and Artists in England' has this note: 'The following Sonnet on Napoleon at St. Helena in Sir R. Peel's Collection is not in our copy of W.'s poems, and may be new to many of our readers: "Haydon! let worthier judges" (&c. as Oxf. W., p. 277).' The Sonnet was written in 1831, and published in 1832.

[3] The first pages of the letter are missing but it can be dated by references to the receipt of K.'s poems and to H. C. R.'s projected 'ramble' in Norway (*v. C.R.*, pp. 362, 366).

should I like better than going again, (with my wife and family) and two years of leisure; then I could accomodate myself to all the novelties of climate, diet, exercise etc. By the bye, Mrs W. begs me to say that some passages of your Vol.,[1] the moon-light especially, remind her of parts of my own Work (still in MS) upon my early life. This is not the first instance where our wits have *jumped*, as great wits are apt to do. Ever with Mrs W's best remembrances faithfully your obliged

Wm Wordsworth

Address: John Kenyon Esqre, 4 Harley Place.

MS.   *1273. W. W. to Edward Moxon*

[June–July 1838]

My dear Mr Moxon,

Cast your eye at your leisure over the two enclosed Letters. They in a great measure explain themselves. I have only to add that Southey discouraged any hope of the poems spoken of being published by you, or indeed any one else, and simply told Mr Shand how sorry I was that he had been thrown on so un-promising a way of gaining his bread. I was a good deal pleased with the modesty and humility of his manner, when I exhorted him to discard all notion of distinction, for the present at least, to controul his inclinations, and write or labour merely for his bread, till he should put himself at ease; and that *then* it would be time enough for his thinking about indulging his Genius—I added that I was well aware of your kindness of disposition, and thought it possible, but barely so, that you might be able to point out to him some line of exertion among publishers, by which he might earn something towards his frugal maintenance. This was all the hope I held out to him, adding that with that view I would write to you and enclose his letter if he had no objection. On the contrary, said he, I should be thankful. It seemed to me possible that something might be procured for his translations from the German, from some Editor of a magazine.

---

[1] *Poems, for the most part occasional*, 1838. The first poem was entitled *Moonlight*—its *argument* reads: Moon—suggestive of poetic feeling, as observed in Childhood, in Boyhood, in Manhood, &c. Cf. *Prelude, passim*.

There is also merit in his Poems, they are free from false ornaments, but not striking enough to attract attention in their
presentation, where poetry finds so little favor with the Publick;
Mr Kenyon's and Mr Milnes'[1] and Mr Trench's[2] poems have all
great merit and not a little originality. They have pleased us much.
I will write my acknowledgments to their respective authors.

Pray send a Copy of my Sonnets to Sergeant Talfourd; and
one to Mr Dyce, from whom I have received so many of his own
Books and whom I can only repay in this way; and give one to
Thomas Powell from me when he calls for it.—The rest of my
Friends must patronize the Book, which is a Book of Luxury,
that I would not have taken the trouble of carrying through the
Press but on their account. There will be thirteen new Sonnets,
one however of the number has been published in some of the
provincial newspapers—

Ever most faithfully yours

W. W.

As the Vol will amount, with notes, Contents etc to above
480 pages I am inclined to think that your suggestion or Mr
Robinson's, of having a portion of the Copies with a 2nd title
page (so as that they who preferred it in 2 volumes might have
their wish) ought to be acted upon; but do in this matter as you
may think best.

MS. *1274. W. W. to Edward Moxon*

July 4th [1838]

My dear Sir,

Thanks for your last Letter announcing the despatch of the
parcel, and telling me that you would endeavour to serve Mr
Shand. It gives me some pain to have to let you know, that
yesterday, when I was passing through Keswick, Mr Southey
shewed me a Letter from the Landlord of the Head Inn Carlisle,
the Best, in which he stated that Mr Shand after staying some
days in his House went off leaving a bill of £7 6s. 0d. or thereabouts unpaid. I hasten to tell this to you, in order that if
he should call you may be prepared to act as you think proper.

[1] *Poems of Many Years*, 1838.
[2] *Sabbation, Honor Neale*, and other Poems, 1838.

I feel much obliged by your meeting my wish by an assurance that you will make an attempt to serve him, but dismiss that promise entirely from your thoughts. The worst part of the transaction, bad enough in all respects, is that being poor and needy, as he probably is, he should have gone to the most expensive Inn in the Place. This admits neither of excuse nor apology; had he been pennyless or nearly so and gone to a public house suitable to his condition, and even left his bill unpaid, from sheer necessity, that would have been an action much to be blamed, but still pity and compassion might have qualified one's censure, and would have done so. But in this case I cannot find an excuse. To save you the disagreeableness of any explanation, or even interview with him, unless you think proper to see him, I have enclosed a note which may be given to him. How long he may have continued such practices cannot be learned, and could one be sure this is his first performance one might still with *caution* try to serve him.

I shall be absent three weeks upon a Tour in the Counties of Northumberland and Durham. I write from a Lady's house three miles from Carlisle. I am accompanying Miss Fenwick tomorrow, we start by the railway from Carlisle to Newcastle, we have most beautiful weather.

I am afraid what with the Coronation and the Long Vacation, our Vol: of Sonnets will have a poor chance of attracting the least notice.

With kind regards to Mrs Moxon and your Sister and remembrance also to your Brother believe me faithfully yours

Wm Wordsworth

MS.
K(—)

1275. *W. W. to Edward Moxon*[1]

Rydal Mount July 28th [1838]

My dear Mr Moxon,

I have been wandering for more than a month in the counties of Durham and Northumberland, and am now fixed at home, I trust for a long time.

The parcel of Books arrived during my absence, and I have

---

[1] For W. W. to H. C. R. July 28, *v. C.R.*, p. 367.

not yet had time to do more than glance at it. Mrs W. began to thank you, which I do also, on my own part, for your kindness to my Son, who, we are most happy to hear, is shaking off the sad effect of his Fever. He tells me you say the Sonnets and poems are doing well. I have not heard a word about them from any other quarter. It was well that a few new Sonnets were added, as I find them serve well as an advertisement in the provincial papers, which extract some one or other of these or more as may suit the Editor's fancy. The Examiner drolly enough says that a Sonnet on the Ballot, his favorite Hobby, damns the Volume. By the Bye pray procure from Mr Bradbury the clean sheets that succeed page 432; otherwise those we have up to that Page will be useless; and I should be sorry to lose the Copy. They can be sent with any Parcel which you may have to forward in future, only let them be procured and kept for that Purpose. Is it true that you are going as far as Italy? Mr Robinson will give you all the directions you can possibly want.

With kindest regards to Mrs Moxon, yourself, and Sister and Brother, I remain dear Mr Moxon,

faithfully yours

Wm Wordsworth

(*Mrs W. writes*)

Pray fill up the address to Haydon and send it to the 2ᵈ P. Office. This shocking paper Mr W. always lay[s] hold of when left to himself [and it] does not at all suit his penmanship. Many many thanks for your Kindness to my Son. Be so good as send a copy of the sonnets to 'Master Herbert Coleridge from Dora Wordsworth' and put another copy inside for Mr Quillinan when he calls for it. Kind regards to Mrs M. and loving hopes and wishes to your children. Your copies of the poems will be returned properly inscribed by the first safe opportunity.

MS.   **1276. W. W. to Benjamin Robert Haydon**
Haydon[1](—)

My dear Haydon,   Rydal Mount July 28 [1838]

I received your 2ⁿᵈ Letter more than a month ago when I was

---

[1] But in *Haydon* misdated Feb. 28, 1839.

upon the point of setting off for Northumberland and Durham where I have been detained till yesterday. In the course of this tour I wrote to you at some length; but upon consulting your Letter when I had written my own I find no date but the general one of London and though you are a distinguished Person I thought that the Post office might nevertheless be ignorant of your habitat. I therefore did not send my Letter. Since it was written I have had an opportunity of reading your Essay in the Encyclopaedia, and neither in that, nor in your Letter, do I find any thing said concerning Michael Angelo, to which I object. I acknowle[d]ged him to be liable to all the charges you bring against him; it would only be a question between us of the *degree* in which he is so. Therefore do not take the trouble of sending your essay for my inspection before hand. I need only add, that through Messrs Whitaker Booksellers Ave Mary Lane, I can receive any parcel addressed to me under cover to Messrs Hudson & Nicholson, Booksellers, Kendal, to be forwarded by Mr W. in his first Parcel to Messrs Hudson & Nicholson, with an under cover for me—

There are some opinions in your essay about which I should like to talk with you; as for example when you say that Raphael learned *nothing* from Perugino but what he had to unlearn. Surely this is far from the truth; undoubtedly there is in him, as in all the elder Masters, a hardness and a stiffness, and a want of skill in composition, but in simplicity, and in depth of expression he deserved to be looked up to by Raphael to the last of [his] days. The transfiguration would have been a much finer picture than it is if Raphael had not at that period of his life lost sight of Perugino and others of his predecessors more than he ought to have done.—Whoever goes into Italy, if Pictures be much of an object with him, ought to begin where I ended, at Venice. Not as I did, with the pure and admirable productions of Fra Bartolomeo at Lucca and with Raphael at Rome, so on to Florence, Bologna and Parma and Milan: and Venice by way of conclusion. Italian Pictures ought to be taken in the following order or as nearly as may be so, Milan, Padua, Venice, Bologna, Parma, Florence, Rome.— Your essay does you *great credit*; and your practise, I trust still more. I had a sad account of the French Academy at Rome; the students appear to be doing little or nothing and spend their time in dissipation.—Believe me with kind regards to Mrs Haydon

ever faithfully yours

W Wordsworth

Address: B. R. Haydon Esq., 4 Burwood Place, Connaught Terrace.

MS.   *1277. W. W. to Edward Moxon*
K(—)

[July 29 1838]

My dear Mr Moxon,

In my Letter of yesterday I omitted to request you would send a Copy of the Sonnets to Mr Stephen, and this happened exactly because his claim on my remembrance in this way was so much stronger than any other. Pray let the Book be sent before publication. What a queer Creature Lord John Russell is! Only think of his coming out against the Copyright Bill at this late hour. It is like all his other proceedings. Pray tell Mr Rogers with my kindest remembrance (how is he by the bye?) that I wish he could put a little sense into the head of his noble Friend upon this subject. Ever with kindest regards to you and yours   most faithfully

Wm Wordsworth

How are your Children? I have now with [? me] a grandson two years and a half old, who is the delight of his Grandmother and myself and indeed the whole House. Our Daughter will return in ten days at the latest.—

It won't be long till we have a railway as far as Preston from London; when that is done I shall insist upon a whole party of you coming down to see us; and be assured that if I retain life health and strength every successive spring I will pass not less than one fortnight in London.

MS.   *1278. W. W. to Sir Henry Bunbury*[1]

Rydal Mount Kendal July 30th [1838][2]

Sir

On returning home after a month's absence I have had the pleasure of receiving the Correspondence, and Memoir, of Sir Thomas Hanmer, for which you will accept my sincere thanks. My acknowledgements also are due to you for a Letter which reached me some time before I left home; but I deferred making them till the Book you announced, should arrive.

In respect to the Letter which I took the great liberty of addressing to Mr Fox[3] long ago and which you have given to the world I own that I feel some difficulty in expressing myself, in writing, as I could wish, though I should find none in doing so viva voce. It is, no doubt, gratifying to me to be told that the sentiments and opinions there expressed are so much in accordance with your own, and that in your judgement they are of sufficient importance to interest the world at large. Nor am I aware upon reperusing the Letter of which I had but a vague recollection that any reason exists why I should particularly regret that it has seen the light—But I will not conceal from you that I never set any value upon my Letters; and that it has ever been my wish that they should be destroyed as soon as read, and that I have frequently requested this should be done. Allow me further to say that publishing the Letters of a living Person without his consent previously obtained furnishes a precedent the effect of which, as far as it acts, cannot but be to check the free communication of thought between Man and Man. This is surely an evil; nor can I at all approve for this same and many other reasons the practice, now so prevalent, of publishing the

---

[1] Sir Henry Bunbury (1778–1860) entered the Coldstream Guards and was later M.P. for Suffolk. He was the emissary chosen in 1815 to communicate to Napoleon the Cabinet's decision that he was to be exiled to St. Helena. A staunch Whig, he voted for the Reform Bill when it was carried by one vote. He was a good judge of art and letters, and had a fine library and collection of pictures. In 1838 he published the *Correspondence of Sir Thomas Hanmer, Bart., Speaker of the H. of C., and other relicks of a Gentleman's* [i.e. Bunbury's] *Family.*

[2] For W. W. to H. C. R. July–Aug., *v. C.R.,* p. 368.

[3] *v. E.L.,* p. 259.

Letters of distinguished persons, recently dead, without the consent of their representatives.—

As the openness and sincerity which pervade my Letter to Mr Fox are qualities by which no doubt it was recommended to you, I have had less scruple in speaking upon the present occasion without reserve. I have only to add that promising myself much pleasure from the Contents of your Volume

I have the honor to be

with thanks

sincerely yours

Wm Wordsworth

Address: Sir Henry Bunbury, Bart., London. Try Warrens Hotel.

K.   *1279. W. and M. W. to John Kenyon*

Rydal, 17th Aug., 1838.

My dear Friend,

I have been so much pleased with the power and knowledge displayed in Miss Barrett's volume of poems[1] which you were so kind as to send Mr W. some time ago that I am desirous of seeing her translation of Æschylus. Would you send me a copy through Mr Moxon, and tell me also where it is to be bought, as two of my acquaintances wish to purchase it?

We hear of you through that kindest of creatures, H. Robinson, but not a word about your coming down, as you had given us leave to hope you might have done, but on the contrary that you are going off with your brother. A thousand good wishes attend you both, and pray remember us to him most kindly.

Ever affectionately yours,

William and Mary Wordsworth.

MS.   *1280. W. W. to James Marshall*

Rydal Mount Thursday [p.m. Oct. 11, 1838]

My dear Sir,

I am sorry I cannot have the pleasure of seeing you at Coniston to morrow, as I had hoped. My old Horse I find on

[1] *The Seraphim*, published 1838: her translation of *Prometheus Bound* had appeared in 1833.

my return has to go to Patterdale on Saturday, if a pair of broken knees will permit him, and he is quite unequal to two successive days travelling. Besides, the fine weather seems quite gone. I am truly, sorrow [*sic*] for this disappointment—My eyes are far from well but no worse, I think, for my late excursion.
ever faithfully you(rs)

Wm Wordsworth

Address: James Marshall Esq., Coniston Water-head.

K(—)   *1281. W. W. to Mrs Thelwall*

November 16, 1838.

Madam,

Circumstances were not favourable to much intercourse between your late husband[1] and myself. I became acquainted with him during a visit which he made to Mr Coleridge, who was then residing at Nether-Stowey. . . . Your impression is correct that I, in company with my sister and Mr Coleridge, visited him at his pleasant abode on the banks of the Wye. Mr Southey was not of the party, as you suppose.

After the year 1798 I do not recollect having had any intercourse with Mr Thelwall till he called upon me at Grasmere on his way to Edinburgh, whither he was going to give lectures upon elocution. This must have been some time between 1801 and 1807, and I once called upon him in London. After that time I think I never saw him. . . .

Whether Mr Thelwall wrote much poetry, or not, I am ignorant; but I possess a small printed volume of his, containing specimens of an epic poem and several miscellaneous pieces. . . . Mr Coleridge and I were of opinion that the modulations of his blank verse were superior to those of most writers in that metre. . . .

With best wishes I remain, madam,

Sincerely yours,

Wm. Wordsworth.

[1] John Thelwall (1764–1834), reformer and lecturer on education, arrested and tried for sedition with Hardy and Horne Tooke in 1794, but acquitted. He settled in 1798 at Liswyn Farm, Brecon. In 1800 he resumed his work as a lecturer.

MS.
M(—)
K(—)

1282. *W. W. to Edward Moxon*

Rydal Mount, Decr 11th [1838.]

Dear Mr Moxon,

Very many thanks for your valuable present of Shakespeare and Jonson, they are handsome books and I hope will repay you. You must have had a very pleasant tour, all the cities and places you speak of as having seen in the North of Italy, were included in my late tour with Mr Robinson. You mention Lago de Garda; I hope you went to the head of it—if not, you missed some of the most striking scenery to be found anywhere among the Alps. I wish you may be able to realize your plan of going to Rome next summer, I will talk to you about it when I come to town in spring—as Mrs W. and I mean to do, if all be well with us, and around us.

As to the Ed: in one Volume, I wait for your proposals. In the meanwhile I have to observe of the specimen sent me of the type etc, I think so little is gained by having the lines wider apart that I would chuse the 36 sheets in preference to the 40, but on account of the overflowing lines I could myself have no pleasure in looking at either the one page or the other. In the American ed:, which you saw, not a single 10-syllable verse overflows, whereas in the pages sent me as specimens there are 9 in one, and 11 in the other; which both disfigures the book very much and occupies so much space. The enclosed paper gives the length and width of the American page, within the marginal line, being within a hair's breadth *short*. Could not the book be printed on paper sufficiently wide to allow of a ten-syllable verse being uniformly included in one line, as something very considerable would be saved in space. This would lessen the cost which wider paper would require. I repeat that I have an insurmountable aversion to overflowing lines, except when they cannot be avoided. On this subject, however, as a mere suggestion for Printers, I would ask, whether the overflowing word would not be better placed, as formerly, near the end of the verse it belongs to than so near the beginning of that line and of the next.

I am in hopes that my nephew, John Wordsworth of Cambridge, will correct the proofs for me,—he promised to do so when he was here a few weeks ago, but I grieve to say he has been very unwell since, and may not be equal to the task; but I shall write to him on the subject—he is the most accurate Man I know, and if a revise of each sheet could be sent to him, the edition would be *immaculate*. Unless he can undertake this office, such has been the state of my eyes that I dare not venture upon it, and I should little like trusting to another, as I could scarcely call upon Mr Carter so soon again,—besides, if it came *here* it could not but take up time of mine which I can not spare.

If Sergeant Talfourd's bill should not pass I know not what will come of poor Authors and their Works. The American example will be followed here to the letter, as far as it can; and what do you as a Publisher say to an Ed: of *the whole* of my Poems being now sold in America for 1 fr., 25 cents, or something less than 13*d* of our money? This is a fact, as I learned the other day by a letter from that country, and in India, as I have just learned from a like authority, a Calcutta Ed: is sold for 6 rupees; so that we are cut off from the Indian market unless international copyright touches that quarter. The respectable Publishers there are anxious about a remedy for this evil.

Excuse this long letter, and believe me, with Mrs W. and Dora's kind regards to you, Mrs Moxon, and your Sister, to be very faithfully yours,

Wm Wordsworth.

Has Mrs Moxon received a couple of Hares forwarded some weeks ago?

MS.　　*1283. W. W. to John Gibson Lockhart*

Rydal Mount, Decr 24th [1838]

My dear Sir,

I am sorry that it did not suit you to give us a call on your return from Scotland, where I have no doubt you must have passed your time much more agreeably than one can well do in London, in the summer season at least. Your Brother was I hope well; my daughter and I remember with much pleasure the couple of days we passed under his roof.

The occasion of my writing to you at present will appear if you will be so kind as take the trouble to read the enclosed. I know nothing of the young Man, the Author of the Work, upon which the letter turns—and I have only to say that the letter was forwarded to me, by a near Relative of Mrs Wordsworth with a request that if I could take the liberty to mention the subject to you I would do so. My reply was, that I could certainly venture to send the letter, but I would not undertake anything more; feeling that I could not even guess how far it would suit you as Editor of the Qu^{rly} Review to notice the work either direct or indirect.

Mrs W. and my Daughter unite with me in kind regards and best wishes for yourself and your Children, who we earnestly hope are well—

believe me my dear Sir,

faithfully yours

Wm Wordsworth

Address: J. G. Lockhart Esq., Sussex Place, Regents Park.

MS.   *1284. M. W. to Jane Marshall*

Rydal Mount, Decr 26th [1838][1]

My dear Friend,

Our dear Sister talks of writing to you herself, but as her *intentions* are not to be depended upon, I must at once acknowledge the safe arrival of your friendly Birth-day offering—I wish you could have been present to see the exultation which sate upon the changed countenance when I was summoned to her room, and saw the contents of the basket spread at her feet—it having been opened in her presence by Dorothy; who, pulling out in triumph, one bird after another, and eagerly going on *still* searching for *more*—your old friend (in her *waggish* way) observed to her—'You're sure to find the eggs they have laid

---

[1] For W. W. to H. C. R. Dec. ? and Dec. 22, *v. C.R.*, pp. 372–5.

by the way.' This habit of bantering, which now is not un-
frequent with her—so different to her character in former days
—shews a great change, yet a wonderful acuteness and quick-
ness of mind. And indeed, we all think that in other respects
her mind is less feeble that it was, and certainly her memory is
improved—and for a much longer space we can keep her interested by conversation, tho' her uncomfortable *habits* are still
as bad as ever. Her bodily health has been remarkably good—
except that within the last two days—owing to her having eaten
some trifle, in which she is not generally allowed to indulge—
her stomach has been a little disordered—so that we find it is
quite necessary to be careful to confine her to such food as *we
know* to be suitable to her. The Turkey *at her request,* was not
dressed on Christmas day but reserved till tomorrow, that it
may honour the board upon our Grandson's birthday, when he
will be 3 years old—the family with his good Godmother, Miss
Fenwick, are to dine at 1 oc., his own, as well as 'Old Aunty's'
dinner hour—and in the midst of our festivity the chief Provider
for our Feast will not be forgotten—as I am sure your old friend
would be in your thoughts and heart, upon *her* own birthday—
at Headingly.

My *Brinsop* B^r keeps improving—but you will be sorry to hear
that neither my B^r nor Sister at Douglas are well—poor Joanna
confined by Lumbago, unable to visit Henry who is more
seriously afflicted—and I fear declining. God bless you and
yours—with a thousand thanks—my d^r Friend aff^{ly} y^{rs}

M W[ordswor]th.

Address: Mrs Marshall, Headingly, near Leeds.

1285. *W. W. to William Rowan Hamilton*
Hamilton
K(—)

Rydal Mount, January 20, 1839.

Your letters and the verses under Lord Northampton's covers
were received towards the end of September. In the few words
of prose annexed, you tell me you do not expect an answer 'till
it should be easy and pleasant to me to write'; you will not, I

trust, deem that I have abused this friendly privilege when I tell you that I have been prevented from writing by a succession of indispositions, one of which disabled me from either reading or writing, such was the state of my eyes, for upwards of two months. Although I am still suffering from the effects of a severe cold, I cannot let slip the opportunity of sending you, by my friend and neighbour Mr Graves, a few words to thank you for your poem on the *Elysian Fields*, and that in which you have done me so much honour by the affectionate manner in which you speak of me. Be assured, my dear Sir William, that without the help of these interesting lines I should retain a most lively remembrance of our first meeting, and of the hours so pleasantly and profitably spent in your Society, both in Ireland and at Rydal.

My daughter avails herself of the same opportunity to write to your sister Eliza, of whom we all think with a thousand good wishes and a sincere affection; we know not what favour her volume of poems[1] may have met with from the public, but we are convinced that they merit a degree of approbation far beyond what it is too probable they will receive, poetry being so little to the taste of these times. I am strongly persuaded that in my own case, should I have first appeared before the public at this late day, my endeavours would have attracted little attention; forty years have been required to give my name the station (such as it is) which it now occupies.

Alas for your unhappy country! I know not when I have been more affected by a public occurrence than when I read Lord Charleville's account of his interview with Lord Norbury,[2] within so few hours of that nobleman's horrible assassination, and then to see that event followed by such a speech as O'Connell made upon the mode in which it had been treated by the Lord Lieutenant and Lord Charleville. How long is the reign of this monster over the British Islands to endure?

[1] *Poems* by Eliz. M. Hamilton, Dublin, 1838.
[2] On Jan. 1 Lord Norbury was shot in broad daylight near his own house at Kilbeggan, and died on the 3rd. There was, apparently, no religious or political motive for the crime, and Lord N. was universally popular. O'Connell suggested that the murderer was one who was bound to him by the nearest of natural ties, and had a material interest in his removal.

Your godson is still with us, his father and mother being in London. Yesterday he asked where Dublin was, and what it was. I was surprised how the word came upon his lips, or the place into his thoughts; but he solved the difficulty by letting us know immediately that his 'godfather Hamilton lived there'. The day before he had seen his godfather Southey for the first time, who had come for a few days on a visit to your co-sponsor, Miss Fenwick, who has taken a house at Ambleside for a year. Southey, you will be sorry to hear, did not seem in good spirits. His depression was owing, we think, to the rather alarming state of health in which his youngest daughter has been for some time. I wish I could have written you a more interesting letter, but I am obliged to employ the pen of Mrs Wordsworth, who herself is not quite so well as I could wish. Little William is at this moment leaning upon the table on which his grandmother writes; upon being asked what we should say to you, his reply was—'A kiss!' which he gave to be transmitted. With a thousand kind wishes to you and yours, in which my amanuensis cordially joins, I remain your affectionate friend. . . .

_MS._   *1286. W. W. to Edward Quillinan*

[Late Jan. 1839]

My Dear Mr Quillinan

(I[1] hold the pen for Mr W. who, you will be sorry to hear, is very unwell)

You are quite right in supposing that you have not forfeited my friendship, and as Dora has fully explained to you the state of my feelings I certainly do not consider it any 'intrusion' your accepting Miss Fenwick's invitation—and shall be pleased to see you at Rydal Mount.[2]

I remain, dear Mr Q., faithfully and aff[ly] yours

Wm Wordsworth

[1] i.e. M. W.

[2] E. Q. had not visited Rydal since December 1837. In Jan. 1838 W. first learnt of the mutual affection of Q. and Dora, and had strongly opposed their marriage, chiefly on the grounds of Dora's ill health, and Q.'s lack of means to support a wife. In the summer of 1838 Miss Fenwick brought about a compromise 'your father reconciling himself to all objec-

MS.
K(—)

1287. *W. W. to Robert Southey*

Ambleside, Feb. 18 [1839]

My dear Southey,

I had yesterday a letter from Sergeant Talfourd, acknowledging the receipt of a Petition which at his desire I had prepared, and expressing his satisfaction with it. He tells me that
Sir Robt Inglis holds one from Dr Arnold, which he means to
present. But as he does not say that he has either received or
heard of one from you, I have some little fear that you may not
have made up your mind to take that step. I write to beg that
you will do so, from a *strong* conviction that if your name be not
found in the list of Petitioners the effect upon the measure will
be very injurious. Excuse the anxiety which has put me upon
troubling you in this way, which however I have had less scruple
in doing, as we have, I know, been so long in sympathy upon this
important subject—in which, as a public man, you yourself led
the way. You will have seen that the 2nd reading stands first
on the list for the 27th.

A severe cold in the head which seized me about 6 weeks ago
ended in an attack of Lumbago, by which I have been a good
deal annoyed—I am now (at Miss Fenwick's) in a steady course
of recovery and, barring a relapse, hope to be quite well in 3 or
4 days—Miss F. we think has not been quite so well—but seems
pretty well to day. Quillinan left this house at 6 oc this morning
—having been here since last Monday—on his way to Ireland.
I had no private conversation with him—but thro' Dora he
understands what my judgments and feelings are—and we all
seemed at ease with each other.

I rejoice that we are likely to have dear Bertha and her
Husband as our Neighbours—We hope earnestly that Kate continues to amend. Pray give our kind love and best wishes to
them both—they will be concerned to hear that Miss Althea

tions, and willing to consent when there could be any reasonable surety of
your being provided for, and there being no hindrance to your attachment
in the meantime.' But W. made no secret of his dislike of Dora's engagement, though he had consented to it: hence Q.'s reluctance in accepting
Miss F.'s invitation.

North is no more, she died at the house of her married Sister in
Dublin 3 days ago—She left home for the benefit of better
medical advice—but has sunk thro' weakness.

Ever affec^{ly} yours

Wm Wordsworth

MS.   *1288. W. W. to Professor Henry Reed*[1]

K(—)

Rydal Mount Feb 22^d—39

My dear Sir

Your letter of the 3^d of Jany accompanying your reviewal of my
Poems, reached me about 10 days ago. I sincerely thank you for
both, but I had received and read the article before—the ' New
York Review' having been sent me from London by a friend, to
whom I have been obliged in the same way, occasionally. In
respect to one particular both in your letter and critique, I can
speak without diffidence or hesitation; I mean the affectionate
tone in which you give vent to your feelings of admiration and
gratitude—'Grant me thy love, I crave no other fee' is the
concluding line of a valedictory sonnet at the close of a Volume
(lately published by Mr Moxon) consisting of my Sonnets only.
This sentiment is, I assure you predominant in my mind and
heart; and I know no test more to be relied upon than acknowledgments such as yours, provided the like have been received
from Persons of both sexes, of all ages and who have lived in
different latitudes, in widely different states of society, and in
conditions little resembling each other. Beyond what I have
now said, I feel scrupulous in expressing the gratification with
which I read your critique, being so highly encomiastic as it is
—all that I can say with confidence is, that I endeavoured to do,
what much and long reflection on your part justifies you to your
own mind, in saying, I *have* done. It may amuse you to hear
an odd proof that those Poems for whose fate you entertain no
doubt, are yet sub judice elsewhere, in the 'Delhi Gazette',—

---

[1] I owe the complete text of this letter to the kindness of Professor
Broughton, the editor of the *Wordsworth–Reed Correspondence* (1933).
The original did not come to light in time for reproduction in his volume.
For W. W. to H. C. R. Feb. 19, *v. C.R.*, p. 378.

mark the place—a vituperative article appeared not long ago upon the subject, which was answered by another writer with great zeal and ardour, to the entertainment no doubt of the Palankeen critics of that enervating climate.

This letter is I feel very unworthy of being sent so far, but I have at present so many engagements, that it would be inconvenient to me to write at greater length—besides I am far from sure that I could satisfy you or myself if I were to attempt it. Let me add however that if the recently created facilities for crossing the Atlantic should tempt you to visit this Country [? I shall be glad] to see you, and pay you all the attention in my power.

The state of my eyes obliges me to employ an amanuensis, which I hope you will excuse and believe me to remain (these words are in my own handwriting)

affectionately your's

Wm Wordsworth

K(—)   *1289. W. W. to John Kenyon*

Rydal Mount, February 26th, 1839.

My dear Mr Kenyon,

... Mrs Wordsworth begs me to thank you cordially for your lady-friend, Miss Barrett's[1] poems, which you sent her some time ago. Miss Barrett appears to be a very interesting person, both for genius and attainments. ...

Faithfully yours,

Wm. Wordsworth.

MS.   *1290. W. W. to Edward Moxon*

[Bath] April 8, [1839]

My dear Mr Moxon,

Will you be so good as to pay the amount of the enclosed to Messrs Longman & Co? We are here for a week, and about the end of the 5th week hence I hope for the pleasure of seeing you and yours. Will you be so kind as to fill up the enclosed address

---

[1] Probably the volume containing *Prometheus Bound* and miscellaneous poems, 1833; *v.* letter of Aug. 17, 1838.

for Mr Stone the artist?[1] Pray remember me kindly to all enquiring friends, especially Mr Rogers and Mr Kenyon. Mrs W. wrote to Mr Robinson yesterday

ever faithfully your much obliged friend

Wm Wordsworth

Affectionate remembrances to Mrs Moxon and your Sister, if writing, not forgetting little Emma.[2]

K(—) *1291. W. W. to Thomas Noon Talfourd*[3]

[p.m. Bath, April 11, 1839.]

My dear Serjeant Talfourd,

Your letter just received has mortified me, not a little, that you should have had so much trouble and made such a sacrifice, to meet so unworthy a House of Commons. The consideration of the heartlessness and injustice of that Assembly is what vexes me most in the whole business. I entirely approve of the publication you meditate. Only, by selecting two or three petitions you might offend some of those authors to whom the like distinction was not paid. I therefore submit whether it would be advisable to print any of them.

As a fact connected with my own case I will mention that, in the year 1805, I concluded a long poem upon the formation of my own mind, a small part of which you saw in manuscript, when I had the pleasure of a visit from you at Rydal. That book still exists in manuscript. Its publication has been prevented merely by the personal character of the subject. Had it been published as soon as it was finished, the copyright would long ago have expired in the case of my decease. Now I do honestly believe that that poem, if given to the world before twenty-eight years had elapsed after the composition, would scarcely have paid its own expenses. If published now, with the aid of such reputation as I have acquired, I have reason to believe that the profit from it would be respectable; and my heirs, even as

[1] Frank Stone (1800–59), a painter of 'pretty sentimentality', and the father of Marcus Stone. He was a member of the Watercolours Society and in 1851 elected A.R.A. He was a friend of Rogers.

[2] Moxon's daughter.

[3] For W. W. to H. C. R. April 10, *v. C.R.*, p. 382.

the law now is, would benefit by the delay; but in the other case neither they nor I would have got a farthing from it, if my life had not been prolonged; the profit, such as it might be, would all have gone to printers and publishers, and would, of course, continue to do so. What could be more——?[1]

I wish my arrangements would allow me to be in Town before the bill comes on again. With best wishes I ever am

Much obliged, and affectionately yours,

W. Wordsworth.

MS.   *1292. W. W. to Edward Quillinan*

Bath. 13th April [1839]

My dear Mr Quillinan,

By yesterday's post I rec^d a letter from Dora, containing a long extract from one of yours to her.[2] Upon the subject of this extract I cannot enter without premising, that calling upon her in so peremptory a manner to act on so important an occasion *during the absence of her parents,* is, to say the least of it, an ill-judged proceeding. And this I must, notwithstanding my present knowledge that the proposal you have made to her, and thro' her to me, was agitated between you when you were at Rydal; and notwithstanding any thing that appears in your letter, in justification of its being made now. As sincerity required this declaration from me, I make no apology for it, nor do I, dear Sir, think you will require one.—I will now come to the point at once. Your Letter contains these sentences, which are the only ones I shall touch upon.

'If hereafter I should have an opportunity of making a provision for you, I will certainly do so, and I could not ask you

---

[1] This —— is more likely to represent K.'s discretion than W.'s.

[2] Before his recent visit to Rydal Q. had written to Dora, urging her to risk marrying him at once, despite his financial insecurity. Dora had not replied, and Q. had not raised the question during his visit, but he had now repeated it in the letter above referred to, which reached Dora soon after her parents had left for Bath. W. thought, naturally but erroneously, that Q., while at Rydal, had discussed the matter with Dora, and that he was now trying, in her parents' absence, to induce her to break the compact they had previously accepted (*v.* p. 965, note). Q. was deeply offended by this letter of W.'s and sent to it a heated and ill-judged reply which even his advocate Miss Fenwick strongly condemned. W. did not answer it.

to run the risk if I thought it possible that my death would leave you destitute of resources from *my* side, I have not any fear as to that. The thing is will you *dare* to run the rough chance?'— Before I enter upon the former sentence, I must direct your attention to the fact, that you must have overlooked the state of health in which Dora has long been, or you cannot have been fully aware of it; or you could not have called upon her Parents, thro' her, circumstanced as they are, as to age, to give their Daughter up to '*a rough chance*'.

But from the former part of what I have copied, I must infer, that, tho' you can settle nothing upon her at present, you are not without hope of being able to do so etc etc. Now it is *my duty* to request of you, my dear Sir, to state as specifically as you can, upon what the hopes and expectations implied or expressed in the above Quotation from your Letter, rest. I mean in respect of a provision in case of your death.

There is no call for my saying more till I have received your answer upon this point, which I beg may be, on all our accounts, as definite and explicit as possible.

Wm is here and in a state of health that causes us much anxiety—the Bath waters do not seem to agree with him, and his stomach and bowels are much deranged. Miss F. owing, we hope, solely to the severity of the weather, is not quite so well as she was at Ambleside. We all unite in affectionate remembrances to yourself and Children, and believe me, my dear Mr Q., faithfully yours,

Wm Wordsworth.

MS.   *1293. W. W. to W. L. Bowles*[1]

Apr 23^d [1839]

My dear Mr Bowles

It is very mortifying that this Concert should happen on Friday, as I am engaged to be at Bristol on that very day. Mr Moore I may, I hope see in London, otherwise I should regret still more than I do this disappointment. It would have given much pleasure to see Mrs Moore, and her son. Mrs M. I well

[1] William Lisle Bowles (1762–1850), poet: his first published volume, *Sonnets* 1789, had been a great influence upon Coleridge in his youth.

remember, as she was when I had the pleasure of breakfasting with her in her own Garden Cottage at Paris; and it is most unlucky that I must miss this opportunity of renewing my acquaintance with her—I need not add how happy I should have been to see you again; and to talk with you and think in your presence, of old times, and departed Friends—I shall return to Bath on Friday Evening. On the Wednesday following I go to Salisbury returning next day to Bath, and on Friday the 2nd of May, depart for London.——

I am just going to write a Note to your Friend Mr Wiltshire proposing to call upon him to morrow, with Miss Fenwick and Mrs Wordsworth, to see his fine pictures—He has kindly called twice upon me.——

Mrs Wordsworth leaves Bath on friday first for Hereford— She unites with me in kindest regards to Mrs Bowles and your self, and believe me my dear Mr Bowles

      faithfully and affectionately yours

                Wm Wordsworth.

Address: The Revd W. L. Bowles, Bremhill, nr. Chippenham.

MS.   *1294. W. W. to Charles Henry Parry*[1]

             12 North Parade [Bath]

             Thursday evening [April 1839]

My dear Sir,

I should have been up with you this morning to breakfast but one of my eyes being a little affected yesterday, I was afraid of encountering the cold wind at so early an hour, being engaged tomorrow morning I can say no more at present than that I will do my best to be with you at ½ past 9 oC. on Saturday morning, to breakfast; we all regret much having been from home when you and the ladies called. On Saturday we will talk over your kind invitation for which in the mean while accept our united thanks.

        Believe me to be

          faithfully yours

              Wm. Wordsworth

---

[1] C. H. Parry, M.D. (1779–1860), a physician who practised in Bath.

MS.   ## 1295. W. W. to Joseph Cottle

Farfield House April 26th '39.

My dear Friend

I am truly sorry not to have found you here, as Mr Peace[1] and I expected. My allowance of time is so short, that I must take an early coach for Bath and can do no more than beg you to accept the best wishes of your old and true Friend.

Wm Wordsworth

Pray let your sister Mrs Hare know how much I regret missing her——

1296. W. W. to Dora W.

MS.
Cornhill, 1893. K.

[p.m. April 27, 1839]

My dear Daughter,

The Letter which you must have received from Wm[2] has placed before you my judgement and feelings; how far you are reconciled to them I am unable to divine; I have only to add, that I believe Mr Q. to be a most honorable and upright man, and further that he is most strongly and faithfully attached to you—this I must solemnly declare in justice to you both; and to this I add *my blessing upon you and him*; more I cannot do and if this does not content you with what your Br has said, we must all abide by God's decision upon our respective fates. Mr Q. is, I trust, aware how slender my means are; the state of W's health will undoubtedly entail upon us considerable expense, and how John is to get on without our aid I cannot

---

[1] The City Librarian of Bristol.

[2] William, a devoted son and brother, had written to both Dora and Q. to try and ease the situation, and to explain dispassionately his father's point of view. It will be seen from this letter that W. W. had already in a measure relented, but Q. still harboured his resentment and made no attempt to meet W.'s practical objections (*v.* Letter 1300), though in a letter to Dora of May 12 he admitted their justice. ('I do not pretend to think that our prospects are such as will not make many people call our marriage madness.') The *Cornhill* and *K.*, by attributing this Letter and No. 1303 to the year 1828, have been largely responsible for current errors as to W.'s conduct in relation to Dora's marriage.

foresee. No more at present, my time is out; I am going to join Miss Fenwick at Miss Pollard's.

ever your most tender hearted and affectionate Father
Wm Wordsworth.

In a beautiful churchyard near Bath I saw the other day this inscription:

Thomas Carrol Esqr
Barrister at Law
Born — so — died, so —
Rest in peace, dear Father —
There was not another word.

Thursday—Y^r letter to me just rec^d—thanks, I will write from Brinsop. M.W.[1]

MS. **1297. W. W. to Thomas Spring-Rice**

Private Bath April 28th [1839]

My dear Mr Spring Rice,

This morning I have received a Letter from my Son in which he speaks of himself as truly grateful for the manner in which you received him, and the interest you so kindly take in a matter that nearly concerns me, and which I would gladly hope may have a successful issue. That nothing may be wanting on my part, I have resolved to set off for London to morrow morning.

A note or message addressed to me at 44 Dover street will be sure to reach me, and I should be happy to wait upon you at any time you may appoint—. on second thoughts, however, it seems best that to save you the trouble of writing or sending,— I should call in Downing street on Tuesday morning, in the assured belief that if it be not *perfectly* convenient for you to give me a minute or two of your time, you will frankly let me know—

I grieve to hear so sad an account of Lady Theodosia's state,

Believe me to be
my dear Mr Spring Rice
faithfully your
much obliged
Wm Wordsworth

[1] A p.s. added by M. W. to the top of the letter.

MS.   *1298. W. W. to Dora W.*

56 Russell Square May 1ˢᵗ [1839]

My dearest Dora,

Private. Maugre this tender beginning this will be only a Letter of matter of fact and business.—I left Bath on Monday, on account of a Letter from Wm—Have you been told that the Chancellor of the Exchequer[1] addressed a Letter to me at Bath proposing to transfer my office to Wm? W. went up immediately to Town, and after a week I followed him to be upon the spot; and do what I could to place the matter upon an advantageous footing—We wait the result of Mr S. Rice's endeavours, but I fear the thing will prove impracticable. Dont say a word upon this subject to any one but Mr Carter.—

Now for business, pray read what follows to Mr C— first I should like to know what have been the net profits of my office to me for the last few years, after deducting his salary, and what he has annually had.

Next I should like to be instructed as to what I can do, while I am here, to have such statements made of our general money concerns, as may be intelligible and regular: next, I should like to know from him what we possess as far as he can make it out.—

By the bye, I saw Mr Courtenay last night, he gives a most flattering account of the Provincials, in which he has 18,000 pounds of his own money—he attends every day, so that nothing can go wrong without his knowledge.

Wm is in health better a good deal than at Bath, but far from well: when Miss Fenwick arrives I shall take him to Dr Ferguson.—

On Saturday your Mother and I shall meet at Miss Rogers to

---

[1] Thomas Spring-Rice (1790–1866), M.P. for Limerick, 1820–32, for Cambridge, 1832–9; a steady Whig. Chancellor of Exchequer, 1835–9: in Sept. '39 created Baron Monteagle; married (1) Theodosia, daughter of the first Earl of Limerick (d. 1839) and (2) in April 1841, Marianne, eldest daughter of John and Jane Marshall. He was a great admirer of W.'s poetry. Henry Taylor, his son-in-law, reports that he said that '*The Happy Warrior* was worth a thousand sermons'. W. had first met him in Ireland in 1829. (*v.* Letter 886.)

stay till Thursday, then we go to the Marshalls, afterwards to the Ricketts; then I hope to Cambridge and then home—I shall keep this Letter open till the afternoon—that you may know what becomes of the Copy-right.

Pray do not work hard, I cannot bear you should—at copying the Poem, nor let Eliz. Cookson do so—Give my love to her—and kind remembrances to the Servants, one and all; with a thousand loving regards and remembrances to my dear Sister—How is she, how are you yourself, and how is Dorothy—address under cover to Sergeant Talfourd, Temple.—

I say nothing of your affairs, as you have had all I can say; except that my best wishes and prayers for you are perpetually repeated.

My own health is good—except that my feet fail, especially about the ancles, which makes me afraid of walking much upon the flagged streets.

Tell me how many copies of the Poems 6 vols you have at the Mount.

[*unsigned.*]

MS.   *1299. W. W. to Thomas Spring-Rice*

41 Upper Grosvenor Street,

May 11th '39

My dear Mr Spring Rice,

I write merely to acknowledge with thanks the receipt of your Note and the accompanying document.

As soon as a more settled state of public affairs shall allow you to give attention to what I have to observe upon your kind communication, I shall be glad of an interview at any time or place which you may do me the honor to appoint.

Believe me
my dear Mr Spring Rice
faithfully
your much obliged
Wm Wordsworth

MS.   *1300. W. W. to Dora W.*

(*With Postscript to D. W.*)

[May 1839]

My dearest Dora,

I cannot let the frank go without a word or two from myself.
Your Mother has no doubt told you of all our movements, some
of which have been too fatiguing on account of our missing *Cabs*
where we wished to find them: and of Omnibuses we have yet
made no use.—

Our project as to the Transfer has been baffled—so that we
are, as we have been, among the unlucky—I mean baffled by
the resignation of Ministry:[1] what Sir R. Peel may think himself
able to do for us I know not.—By Saturday at the latest (indeed
it cannot be done earlier) I will call with Wm upon Dr Ferguson
whom I prepared for the visit yesterday, having accidentally
met him in Portland Place. Wm's case is a strange one, he was
very much better on coming to London. The excitement, I
suppose, did it and he had fallen off much when he left us on
Monday for Chatham; so that one knows not what to think of
it—I scarcely venture to hope that he will be improved in health
when he returns.

Now let me thank you and Elizabeth C. for the labours you
have gone through in transcribing that long Poem; pray, when
it is done, let it be sealed, and deposited with Mr Carter, to
provide against any unlucky accident befalling the other.

My eyes continue in almost their very best way, notwithstanding lamp light, candle light, late Dinners, late hours, for
the night I was at Miss Watts's Ball, going to oblige that good
and kind Lady, Mrs Ricketts, I was not in bed till half after one.

I cannot my dear child but wish that your mind were put at
rest by Mr Q. on this under all circumstances harassing and
trying affair. I wait for your report of his answer with anxiety;
so does your Mother, no doubt, though we do not talk about the
subject.

---

[1] Lord Melbourne had just resigned. Sir Robert Peel was invited to form
a ministry, but declined, and Melbourne took office again, but Spring-Rice
was not in the new Cabinet.

Your delightful description of the beauty that Spring has poured around you makes me wish to be present as Spectator and Listener—God Bless you, my dear Daughter, for ever and ever. Love to Elizabeth and kind regards to all the Household, and all enquiring Friends. Jane has seen little or nothing of London yet, but she *has seen* the *Queen.* To day she goes to the Zoological Gardens. Once more farewell, my dear Dora—ever your affectionate Father, W. Wordsworth.

I have purposely deferred sending love to you, my dear Sister, that I might address you in particular. I am glad to hear that you have been out among the Birds and Flowers, and in the sweet sunshine, and I expect to find you in all things marvellously improved when I return. A thousand remembrances and love to you: were you here, you would delight in the prospect we have from the windows of Regents park—and its trees so green and its bright flowers. Ever your W. W.

The world says Mr Rogers is going to be married to a girl of 20 named Jane Clerk—but I am sure it must be all nonsense.

MS.   *1301. W. W. to Walter Kerr Hamilton*[1]

May 30th [1839]

41 Upper Grosvenor Street

My dear Sir,

Thanks for your letter. My intention is to leave London for Oxford, Monday 10th June. Having received an invitation from the Master of University College to dine with him that day, I have written to him to say that I shall be happy to do so, and on that night I hope to be received as your Guest.

Believe me to be

truly your obliged

Wm Wordsworth.

Address: The Rev. Hamilton, Merton College, Oxford.

---

[1] W. K. Hamilton (1808–69), a pupil of Dr Arnold of Rugby, elected Fellow of Merton in 1832, and in 1854 consecrated Bishop of Salisbury.

MS.   *1302. W. W. to M. W.*

Sat. morn. June 8 [1839]

My dearest Mary

Having nothing particular to say I should not have written now but for the Frank. I long to know that you found Dora pretty well and that you both reached home in good plight. Pray tell dear Miss Fenwick that I met Mr and Mrs Villiers[1] at H. Taylor's breakfast—Mrs V. wonderfully better, and both looking well. Yesterday I was only able to go to Mr Taylor's breakfast, being disabled by the pain returning to my ancle so bad that I could not walk; and Determined last night to consult Sir B. Brodie but it is so much easier today that I shall hardly trouble him. But should the pain return I should not go to Coleorton but proceed from Oxford either on Friday or Saturday at the latest; if Saturday I shall stay over Sunday with the Arnolds. I do not mean to walk at all today for fear of bringing back the pain. This morning I went with Susan to breakfast at Mr Rogers, thence to make a farewell call at Lambeth; I did not see the Archbishop; called also on Mr Spring Rice but found him engaged—he will communicate with me this afternoon by letter. Today we dine at home and go to the Opera, tomorrow have breakfast at Mr Kenyon's to meet Mr Webster reckoned the first man in America and then a lunch and dinner with Mr Powell and in the morning start for Oxford. How I wish I were with you and long that the Oxford business was over. I shall have done all my calls, except Lady Coleridge, Mr Haydon and poor George Dyer; all of which would have been got over yesterday but for this plaguy lameness; whether a mere overworking of the tendons of the ancle or rheumatism or gout I know [not]; and if I can would like to consult Dr Ferguson tomorrow.

Yesterday I had a long interview with Mr Quillinan[2]; tell

[1] Thomas Hyde Villiers, a friend of Henry Taylor, and his colleague at the Colonial Office.

[2] Q. had at last put his injured pride in his pocket and called on W. This, it must be remembered, was the first occasion on which he had stated to W. his exact financial position. Their conversation was renewed, at W.'s request, two days later (*v.* next letter) with happier result, and on the 11th Q. wrote to Dora 'How delighted you will be . . . at what I have to tell you. . . . Your Father and I are right good real friends. On Sunday

dearest Dora.—I fear it was not satisfactory to either party. He seems wretched at the thought of the marriage being put off; and, as I told him, I could not look at [it] with that chearfulness and complacency and hopefulness which ought to accompany such a transaction. As the event is inevitable I told him I felt it my duty to try to make the best of it; but how I should succeed I could not tell. But said I blame no-one; I only do regret that the affair should have pressed on this way in my absence, this was [?] of all, only I must add that I felt easier for having seen him and that our interview was perfectly friendly.—Now my dearest Mary read as much of this to Dora as you like—unless I go to Coleorton I perhaps shall not write again; if I do I will however briefly—

Dearest Child how came you to say I never sent love to you— I love you incessantly, how could I have suffered what I have done were it not so. A thousand loves to you, and all tender thoughts for my dear sister. [?]

Farewell dearest Mary

W. W.

MS.   *1303. W. W. to Dora W.*
Cornhill. K.

Sunday morning, 9 o'clock [June 9 1839]

My dearest Dora,

I am looking for Mr Quillinan every moment. I hope to revive the conversation of yesterday.

The sum is: I make no opposition to this marriage. I have no resentment connected with it toward any one: you know how much friendship I have always felt towards Mr Q., and how much I respect him. I do not doubt the strength of his love and

morning I went again . . . and he read me that most kind letter he had written to you' (i.e. Letter 1303) 'From that moment all was right. I dismounted from my high horse, never more to get on its back by my fault at least, to him. . . . He spoke to me with all the affection of a friend and a father.' Though W. found it difficult for a time to live up to this, so that in the following Sept. Q. complained to Dora that he was trying to influence her against him, there is no evidence, after that Sept., of any but cordial relations between them. But later letters to Miss Fenwick show that he never wholly approved of Q. as a son-in-law.

affection towards you; this, as far as I am concerned, is the fair side of the case.

On the other hand, I cannot think of parting with you with that complacency, that satisfaction, that hopefulness which I could wish to feel; there is too much of necessity in the case for my wishes. But I must submit, and do submit; and God Almighty bless you, my dear child, and him who is the object of your long and long-tried preference and choice.

Ever your affectionate father,
Wm. Wordsworth.

_MS._   **1304. W. W. to Edward Moxon**[1]

Rydal Mount July 6th 1839

My dear Mr Moxon,

I sent you some days ago under cover to Mr St Talfourd a sheet of corrections being all that are required for the first Vol. of the stereotype Edition of my Poems. I now write by my nephew to say that in the parcel of books which you sent me was a vol. printed for the Camden Society entitled Plumpton Correspondence:[2] as the same parcel contained three vols printed by the same Society for which I am indebted to Mr Robinson, I think it not improbable that he in his kindness designed a copy of this book also for me. [? But the copy] which has reached me contains on a fly leaf the words 'To Sir N. H. Nicolas B^t with the Editor's regards', from which I fear that this Copy has been forwarded to me by mistake. Was I sure of this I would at once return the book by my nephew, but it would save trouble if the copy not improbably intended for me by Mr Robinson could be transferred to Sir N. H. Nicolas in lieu of the one which I retain—for the present at least. Should there be no copy of the Plumpton Correspondence intended for me by Mr Robinson, I will return the copy I have by the first opportunity: the objects of the Camden Society are

---

[1] For W. W. to H. C. R. June 22, _v. C.R._, p. 384.

[2] _Plumpton Correspondence—Letters, chiefly domestic, written in the reigns of Edward IV, Richard III, Henry VII, and Henry VIII_, ed. Thos. Stapleton, 1839, _v. C.R._, p. 389.

praiseworthy, and the specimens they have given not a little interesting.

Pray let me know when you go abroad if you do go, and take care to charge the printer to be careful in executing the alterations in the stereotype and as I said before I should like to have the [?] upon those already sent. With kindest reg^{ds} to Mrs Moxon and your Sister, and Brother

Believe me my dear Mr Moxon

faithfully yours

Wm Wordsworth.

MS.   *1305. W. W. to Benjamin Robert Haydon*[1]

Rydal Mt July 8th 39.

My dear Haydon

I wished to have called upon you again before I left London— but during the last few days of my residence there I was disabled by a sprain in my ancle—which put a stop to many attentions of the same kind, I had intended to pay to my friends. Since my return, I have received from you a letter of warm congratulation upon my reception at Oxford. The tribute of applause was far beyond any thing of which the Papers gave account—not excepting that of the Mng Post, which came nearest the truth.

Your Picture of the Duke of Wellington I thought very promising but excuse my saying—that as you had given that of Buonaparte with his back to the Spectator, I could not help wishing that you had not repeated so much of the same position in that of his Conqueror. I do not know that I am right in this remark but such was my impression.

You are a much better judge of Exhibitions than I am, but I did think that in choice of subjects and the Manner of treating them, tho' that was far short of what one would wish, there was a good deal of promising Talent—The genius of our times in your art is ruined by painting to Commission that is

---

[1] For W. W. to H. C. R. July 7, *v. C.R.*, p. 389.

under the controul of those who order the Pictures.—Landseer[1] if he does not take care will be killed by this. In y^r Lectures, pray dwell upon this mischief—and point out as you may do, without giving just offence, instances of its deplorable effect— Take for example that picture in Ld Westminster's Gallery, a family piece—Is it possible a Man of his genius and skill could have painted such a thing except under the like baneful influence?

Ever faithfully y^{rs}

Wm Wordsworth

MS. **1306. W. W. to Edward Moxon**

Rydal Mount August 30th [1839]

My dear Moxon,

In respect to the Yarrow,[2] I only mentioned it for this reason, —we had just at the time when I saw it, prettily got up and charged 3/6 in the Shop, received from you at our request half a doz. copies charged to us 3/7, these copies being got up in the ordinary way. They were ordered to favour a worthy person in Ambleside, who sells books supplied to her by her son, a stationer in Kendal—Therefore she cannot sell them at this price, as so much nicer copies being to be had at the other shop at a lower rate. I thought proper to mention this to you, not with any view of objecting to your selling them so neatly got up at a lower price, or at any price you think proper, but to prevent the unpleasantness which I have mentioned in future. To conclude the subject if I may judge from the demand in this neighbourhood for this Vol. of Yarrow, so got up—the sale of it may be expected to be considerable.

I grieve exceedingly to hear of your situation in respect to the editions of Fletcher and Massinger. Hartley keeps out of our way, I would have called on him this very morn^g but it is

---

[1] Sir Edwin Henry Landseer (1802–73), the famous animal painter, elected R.A. 1831, knighted 1850—probably the most popular artist of the day. In 1815 he had received valuable hints from Haydon, who gave him dissections of a lion, and bade him study anatomy, Raphael's cartoons, and the Elgin Marbles.

[2] *Yarrow Revisited and other poems*, 1839. This was the third edition of *Yarrow Revisited*.

stormy weather, and I dare not go out.—no exertions here shall
be spared to spur him on to bring the work to a conclusion. As
to poor dear Mr S.'s[1] case I am certain that whatever he can do
he will do to fulfil his engagement, and that your loss will meet
with every just consideration on his part, for a more conscientious and upright Man nowhere breathes.

The two remaining Vols. of corrections will be sent in the
course of a fortnight or three weeks. I must make them without
the assistance of Mr Carter, as he is going to Liverpool for that
time. I am pleased you liked the slight corrections in your
Sonnets. Now for your trip to Florence—would not you contrive to make a little circuit in going from Lyons down the
Rhone by steam as far as you can go towards Marseilles, and
thence by Toulon and Nice, and along the Cornice road to Genoa
and so on to Massa and turn off to Lucca and Pisa, and so to
Florence. Or if straitened by time, go by steam from Marseilles
to Genoa at once. But nothing can be more beautiful than the
whole land road from Nice by Genoa to M. Farewell with best
wishes from all to yourself and your family. I remain my dear
Mr M.

faithfully yours

Wm Wordsworth

M.
G.
K.
1307. *W. W. to John Peace*

Rydal Mount, Aug. 30, 1839.

My dear Sir,

. . . It was not a little provoking that I had not the pleasure
of shaking you by the hand at Oxford when you did me the
honour of coming so far to 'join in the shout'. I was told by a
Fellow of University College that he never witnessed such an
outburst of enthusiasm in that place, except upon the occasions
of the visits of the Duke of Wellington,—one unexpected. My
nephew, Fellow of Trinity College, Cambridge, was present, as
well as my son William, who, I am happy to say, is much better
in health than when you saw him in Oxford. He is here, and
desires to be kindly remembered to you. . . .

[1] i.e. Southey.

MS.   *1308. W. W. to Lord Monteagle*

Rydal Mount Septr 6th 1839

My dear Lord

'It is only a congratulatory letter'—such I was once told was the observation of the private Secretary of a certain eminent Lawyer who had just been raised to a high office and a Peerage —upon which the new Peer had the letter thrown into the fire, as had been the fate of a score or two others received upon the same occasion, the Signatures, most of them perhaps, not looked at.

Fearing that the like might be the doom of the few words, which when I first heard of your elevation to the Peerage, I felt prompted to write to you, I have been induced to defer the expression of my own friendly interest in this event till the press of congratulations was over, and I now trust that a favorable acceptance will be given to my best wishes that you may have health and happiness long to enjoy the honor and privileges which have been conferred upon you, as the reward of severe and anxious Service.

We have lately had a very pleasant visit from Cordelia Marshall, and from her, as from other quarters, we have heard with much pleasure, that Lady Monteagle's health was greatly improved; the state of comparative repose in which you now are placed will allow you to see much more of each other, and that no relapse may occur to disturb or sadden your domestic Circle, is the sincere prayer, my dear Lord, of your faithful and much obliged

Wm Wordsworth

MS.   *1309. W. W. to Sir William Gomm*[1]

Rydal Mount Ambleside Octb 29th [1839]

I deem myself fortunate, dear Sir William, in being at home when your Letter arrived, as I can thank you for it as I do most

---

[1] By a curious error of W's, impossible to account for, this and all succeeding letters to Sir W. G. are addressed to *Gordon* instead of Gomm. There is no question as to the identity of the addressee, e.g., on one of them he is addressed as 'Lieut.-Gen. Sir W. Gordon, Governor of Mauritius'.

sincerely by return of Post, and with good hopes that my Letter will reach you before you leave Spithead. You have obliged me greatly by the service you have render[ed] my Nephew,[1] and I feel happy in the opportunity of offering my very best good wishes for Lady Gomm and yourself upon leaving your own Country. May health prosperity and happiness attend you both, and may you return to England without any cause whatsoever to regret the sacrifices which cannot but be made upon yielding to the calls of duty upon such occasions.—

Sir James MacGregor[2] has been very kind in offering my Nephew so agreeable a Station and I thank you for enclosing his Letter. The Young Man is in high spirits, though just recovering from the Small Pox, which he caught in the Hospital of Fort Pitt. As he had had the Cow-pox before, the Disease was nothing like so severe as it would probably otherwise have been, so that I trust he is already fit for his departure.—

The Papers speak of the probability of Sergeant Talfourd being raised to the Bench. I wish he may be so, notwithstanding the loss the Copyright Bill would suffer by the event; for I am sure he would be much happier and I trust still more useful in that calm and dignified station, than as a Representative obliged to fashion his proceedings, and to a certain degree his opinions to the standard of a popular assembly.—

I will take care that his publication upon the Copy Right Bill shall be duly sent you.

Repeating my good wishes for yourself and Lady Gomm, in which Mrs Wordsworth were she here, would most cordially join I remain my Dear Sir Wm

faithfully your much

obliged Wm Wordsworth

Address: Lieutenant General Sir William Gomm etc etc etc
Ryde, Isle of Wight

Readdressed to: No. 6 Grosvenor St. London

[1] i.e. John, son of R. W.
[2] Sir James McGrigor (1771–1858), spelled MacGregor in the army lists, army surgeon; in 1809 Inspector-General of Hospitals; served under Wellesley in the Peninsula 1811; Director-General of Army Medical Board 1815–51; F.R.S. 1816; baronet 1830.

MS.   *1310. W. W. to Edward Moxon*

Rydal Mount Nov^{br} 1st [1839]

My dear Mr Moxon,

I have sent the corrections of the Excursion which though appearing formidable relate to little more than the punctuation.

I have now done with the six Vols: which may be put into circulation as soon as they are complete, only I think it right to add the 12 Sonnets which are already published in the Vol: of sonnets, and which were written since the 6 Vols: were published, and these must take their place as an appendix at the end of the 5th Vol:, with a small notice that shall be sent in about *10* days at the latest; in the meanwhile the Excursion may be corrected and struck off.

I have not ceased to stimulate Hartley Coleridge in every possible way to finish his notice and I have done all that was possible in the still more difficult case of Mr Southey, but I am most happy to say that I heard two days ago that things looked brighter in that quarter. Mr S. has resumed the labour of selecting and transcribing, tho' I have not learnt yet that he has ventured upon original composition; before I was aware of this improve-ment in his health I recommended in consequence of the melancholy account his son gave of it that you should be written to—this was last Monday m[ornin]g and perhaps you may have received a letter on the subject.

My daughter thanks you for the Vols: of Shelley[1] which she values much. I am not aware that I have anything more to add —I leave home on Tuesday for a week but before I go I will endeavour to see H. C. again and if I do not succeed will set upon him one of his friends, a neighbour of mine, as I have done before, he having great influence over him. Miss Gillies an artist who paints in miniature of whom you may have heard has come down from London on purpose to take my portrait and it is thought she has succeeded admirably. She will carry the

---

[1] In 1839 Moxon published the first collected edition of Shelley's poetry, ed. by Mrs Shelley; in June 1841 proceedings were instituted against him for blasphemy. He was defended by Talfourd and the judge summed up in his favour, but the jury convicted. Moxon was ordered to come up for judgment when called for, but he received no punishment.

picture with her to London where you may see it if you think it worth while.

Ever faithfully yours

Wm Wordsworth

Might it not be well if it could be done without expense or disfiguring the Title Page to add 'second stereotype impression' or something to that effect on the Title Page, if the first Vol: be not already struck off? By the bye I have received this day from India a translation of one of my *Sonnets* into the Hindu tongue by Mane Chunda Milton. Have I spelt the word right?

Address: Edward Moxon Esq Dover Street, London.

MS.   *1311. M. W. to Mrs S. T. Coleridge*

Nov. 21st [1839]

My dear Mrs Coleridge,

Your letter was given to me on my return from a visit to my Durham Relations a week ago, but since that time I have been confined partly to my bed consequent upon a bad cold, taken in the course of our homeward journey; which was prolonged by paying visits by the way. Our friend Miss Fenwick was my fellow-traveller—indeed it was my *inducement* to leave home, that she was going to visit the Taylors who live in the same neighbourhood as my friends, and that I had an opportunity of travelling with her. We were absent three weeks, and took Keswick on our way home, for the purpose of seeing dear Southey, and paying my respects to his wife. We found S., I am happy to say, better than I expected from all the melancholy accounts I had had; but alas, alas there is a sad change; yet his being better than he had been tends to give hope that perfect rest, time, and mild weather (for he is very sensitive to cold) may restore him to something like his former self. The earnest prayer of all—especially of *us* who know of what important consequence his invaluable life is universally—as well as in his own family. It is truly an awful thing to think of such a mind being prematurely so weakened, but these decrees are from a Power who knows what is best—and our duty is to submit, but not without hope. Mrs Southey was very kind, and seemed much in her place, was exceedingly glad to see us (Miss F. and I met Wm there who had returned from a visit to Brigham) as was your Sister Lovell, who was looking as well, and as comfortable as I ever saw her, and the two ladies seemed to be very cordially united in their feelings, and care of the Invalid. Kate had left Keswick for Rydal a day or two before our arrival there, and Cuthbert was expected at home that day from Carlisle where he had been paying a visit of a week to my son William. You will be glad to hear that *dear Willy* reports himself as being less annoyed by his complaint of late. Poor fellow, I have had much anxiety about his health.

I have seen Kate several times since my return, and think her looks and spirits much improved—she drank tea with us last evening, and returned home with Miss Fenwick to Ambleside afterwards, where she means to spend a few days, with that dear good woman who is a treasure to us all. Bertha I have not seen, she is not quite well and did not come up, and I have not been able, as yet, to go to her. Nothing unusual to her situation is the matter with her, and she has been remarkably well; and I never saw any one's looks so much improved as hers, since she became a resident in Rydal. Dear Creature, I trust she may do well—she will make a nice Mother, and she need not be a more happy one, than she is a Wife. Herbert looks delicate, but I hear no complaints of his health.

I have not seen, nor heard *particularly* of Hartley since my return, but I hope Moxon's work, if not done, is nearly so, as he told Mr Quillinan (who arrived here on Tuesday) and who called upon him with a message from Moxon, that he should not dine out till he had finished. As soon as this is accomplished, I know we shall see him with his packet, to be sent off from this house.

I will enclose you his bills, which have been paid, and tell you the amount of monies remaining in his purse. But my head is not clear enough (indeed it is never clear *enough*, for nothing in the course of my life ever bothers me like accounts) to see whether I am right or wrong in my calculations,—only knowing my intentions are honest I am easy on that point, as I am sure, dear friend, you will be. I must however tell you—what you may have forgotten—that Moxon gave Hartley, when he was here, £3,—all he c^d spare out of the provision he had made for his journey, but promised to send him £7 in addition, to make up £10 which Hartley begged to have: the £7 was sent by Willy from M., we kept this whole sum back for some time, till poor H. asked for a part of it, and got £3, and at the same time he mentioned the Keswick Tailor's bill, which you will see, and we propose to pay it from the remaining sum—he willingly consented so that so much, at any rate, of his earnings has been turned to a good account—as you will find, a trifle of this fund still rests with me. We cannot say, poor fellow, that his expenses are great—but how well would it be for himself if his great talents were applied as they ought to be to his entire maintenance. We must however congratulate ourselves that he is going on as well as he now seems to be doing, and hope for the best for the future.

My Sister Joanna is now with us—she and I were among our friends in Durham. She was then looking well—but like myself has since had a bad cold from which she is still suffering, and she has lost her good looks. She begs her affec. remembrances to you and Sara, and was very glad, as we all are, to hear a tolerable account of you. She was very little upon the Island, where she has now two nieces, last summer, and I rather think did not see your Sisters; she means to pass the winter with us, and return in the spring to her favourite Island, to which she is as much attached as ever, notwithstanding the sorrow she has undergone. But her pure and happy spirit binds her to the point where she feels she can be of most use, and find most leisure to fit herself for the change which at no distant day awaits us all.

William, I am glad to say, is quite well, Dora tolerably so, and all the Brigham family flourishing. Grandfather is come home delighted with his youngest grandchild Charles, and with all the rest in degree. With love believe me d^r Mrs C. ever affect^{ly}

M. Wordsworth.

The purse contains £27. 10 and I hold balance of Moxon's £10, £1. 18. 4. So we are rich enough.

Address: Mrs S. T. Coleridge, 10 Chester Place, Regents Park.

1312. *W. W. to Lord Monteagle*

Rydal Mount 23^d Dec^{br} —39

My dear Lord

Let me hope that I am justified in offering you my condolence upon the grievous loss which you have sustained—

I should have scarcely ventured to break in upon your Sorrow, had I not heard, through Miss Fenwick, from Mr Taylor in what an admirable manner the affliction was borne by yourself and the children of the departed. Having thought much and often upon you all during this trial I trust that this expression of sympathy, in which Mrs Wordsworth sincerely joins, will carry with it some sense of comfort, as I am sure it will be kindly received. To Mr and Mrs Taylor, and to your Daughter Mary, more particularly, for of her I have seen more, I beg to be affectionately remembered upon this mournful occasion.

Pray accept my thanks for the Letter which I received from you some time ago. Nothing but the importance of the points upon which it turned prevented my replying to it at the time. I felt I could not by Letter treat them to my own satisfaction and far less to your's; and therefore I was silent in the hope that an opportunity would at some time or other be offered when the difficulties that stood in my way might be removed by conversation

I remain—

My dear Lord

faithfully your obliged

Wm Wordsworth

Address: Lord Monteagle, Mansfield St, London.

1313. *W. W. to Lord Monteagle*

Decr 30th, 39

My dear Lord

Your Letter, and the Enclosure, gave me, and let me add my family, great pleasure. I hope you will also excuse my having shewn both to Miss Fenwick. We were all made happy by this additional proof that your affliction was borne by yourself and those most dear to you, with christian resignation and with the best solace of Christian hope. We congratulate you upon having a Son on whose youthful mind piety has made so deep an impression, and in whom good principles have taken such firm root.

I was gratified by the touching allusion you make to a passage in the Excursion and I am accordingly encouraged to present to your notice a stanza in one of my minor Poems which you may not be acquainted with. As it often recurs to my memory, in the trials to which grief has subjected me, it will be taken by you, (by which I mean understood and felt,) in its true degree and meaning.

> Thou takest not away O Death!
> Thou strikest—absence perisheth
> Indifference is no more;
> The future brightens on our sight;
> For on the past hath fallen a light
> That tempts us to adore.[1]

Your notice of Mr and Mrs Taylor was delightful to us all.— His solid virtues have, through Mrs Southey and Miss Fenwick, been long known to me. To the happy pair, to yourself, and yours, we present our best wishes.

ever my dear Lord faithfully your's

W Wordsworth

MS.   *1314. W. W. to Thomas Powell*
Mod. Lang. Notes, 1930.

[late 1839][2]

My dear Mr Powell

Excuse my not writing earlier as I wished to do—From a letter of mine to Dr Smith, which I enclose you will learn every thing respecting the Sanatorium to which your last letter referred,—so that I need not here dwell upon the subject—I am glad that you enter so warmly into the Chaucerian project, and that Mr L. Hunt is disposed to give his valuable aid to it. For

---

[1] *v.* Oxf. W., p. 583.
[2] For W. W. to H. C. R. Dec. 7th, *v. C.R.*, p. 394; for W. W. to Henry Reed Dec. 23, *v.* Reed, p. 13.

myself I cannot do more than I offered, to place at your disposal the Prioresses Tale, already published, the Cuckoo and the Nightingale, the Manciples Tale, and I rather think, but I cannot just now find it, a small portion of the Troilus and Cressida—you ask my opinion about that Poem—speaking from a recollection only of many years past, I should say that it would be found too long—and probably tedious. The Knights Tale is also very long, but tho' Dryden has executed it, in his own way observe, with great spirit and harmony, he has suffered so much of the simplicity, and with that of the beauty, and occasional pathos of the original to escape, that I should be pleased to hear that a new version should be attempted upon my principle by some competent Person. It would delight me to read every part of Chaucer over again, for I reverence and admire him above measure, with a view to your work, but my eyes will not permit me to do so—who will undertake the Prologue to the C. Tales? For your publication that is indispensible, and I fear it will prove very difficult. It is written, as you know, in the couplet measure, and therefore I have nothing to say upon its metre— but in respect to the Poems in stanza, neither in the Prioresses Tale, nor in the Cuckoo and Nightingale have I kept to the rule of the original as to the form and number and position of the *rhymes*, thinking it enough if I kept the same number of lines in each stanza, and this I think is all that is necessary—and all that can be done without sacrificing the substance of sense, too often, to the mere form of sound—

I feel much obliged by yr offer of the 1st Ed: of the Paradise Lost, and I apprehend from what you say that you are already aware of my possessing a Copy—otherwise I should not have felt justified in accepting the one you so kindly intend for me— The copy I possess was given me by Mr Rogers—and your's shall take its place on my shelves by its side. Mr Moxon is about to send down a parcel of books in which your valuable present might be included, with a certainty that it would arrive safe.

It is thought by every one that Mrs W.'s Portrait (who appears, as now engaged writing for me) is an excellent likeness —The chalk drawing has yet a good deal to do at it. Dora has been *attempted*, but not yet, as we think, with much success. I think you will be delighted, with a profile Picture on ivory of me, with which Miss G. is at this moment engaged, Mrs W. seems to prefer it as a likeness to any thing she has yet done. We all rejoice as you and Mrs P. will in her general success in this neighbourhood. Thanks for your kind enquiries after Mrs W's health—she is I am glad to say quite well again, and joins with Miss G., my Daughter, and myself in affec regards to you and Mrs P.—and believe me

Ever faithfully and aff^{ly} yours

Wm Wordsworth

M.
K. **1315. W. W. to Lady Frederick Bentinck**

Rydal Mount, Ambleside, Jan. 3, [1840.]

My dear Lady Frederick,

Yesterday brought us melancholy news in a letter from my brother Dr Wordsworth, which announced the death of his eldest son.[1] He died last Tuesday in Trinity College, of which he was a fellow, having been tenderly nursed by his father during rather a long illness. He was a most amiable man, and I have reason to believe was one of the best scholars in Europe. We were all strongly attached to him; and, as his poor father writes, 'the loss is to me, and to my sorrowing sons, irreparable on this side of the grave. . . .'

W. W.

M.
K. **1316. W. W. to C. W.**

Friday, Jan. 3, [1840.]

My very dear Brother,

It is in times of trouble and affliction that one feels most deeply the strength of the ties of family and nature. We all most affectionately condole with you, and those who are around you, at this melancholy time. The departed was beloved in this house as he deserved to be; but our sorrow, great as it is for our own sakes, is still heavier for yours and his brothers'. He is a

---

[1] John W.

power gone out of our family, and they will be perpetually reminded of it. But the best of all consolations will be with you, with them, with us, and all his numerous friends, especially with Mrs Hoare, that his life had been as blameless as man's could well be, and that, through the goodness of God, he is gone to his reward. . . . I remain,

your loving Brother
Wm Wordsworth

MS. **1317. *W. W. to Mrs Gaskell*[1]**

Rydal Mount 9th Jan^{ry} 1840.

My dear Madam,

I must thank you for the pains you have taken, though unsuccessfully, for the Almery[2] which I cannot help still wishing might be turned over to me by the owner. The only means that seems open for procuring it under the circumstances, is the getting as good a piece of antient furniture which possibly might be accepted as a substitute. With this view I shall make enquiries among my Friends. It is true that there is an account of this Relique in Mr Harter's Book; wherein he mention its Relation to our Family. He gives a Copy of the Latin Inscription corresponding with what Mrs Beaumont reports. Nevertheless, as he confines himself to that without giving a sketch of it, were it not presuming too much upon your kindness I should be glad of a drawing of the thing, especially as it might enable

---

[1] Elizabeth Cleghorn Gaskell (1810–65), author of *Mary Barton* (1848), *Ruth* (1853), *Cranford* (1853), *Wives and Daughters* (1866), *Life of Charlotte Brontë* (1857), &c., &c.

[2] This Aumbry has on its front the inscription HOC OPus FIEBAT Ao DNI MoCCCCCoXXVo EX SUPTU WILLMI WORDESWORTH FILII W FIL IOH FIL W FIL NICH VIRI ELIZABETH FILIE ET HEREDS W PCTOR DE PENYSTO QoRN AIABUS PPICIETUR DEUS. (This work was made in the year of our Lord 1525 at the expense of William Wordsworth son of William son of John son of William son of Nicholas husband of Elizabeth daughter and heiress of William Proctor of Penyston on whose souls may God have mercy.) It remained in the possession of the W.s of Peniston, Yorkshire, till 1780–90, when it was sold to Sir Thomas Blackett; his daughter Diana who inherited it married Col. T. R. Beaumont (1758–1829), and their son Thomas Wentworth Beaumont (1792–1848) gave it to the poet, *v.* Letter of May 23, 1840; it has ever since been a treasured possession of the W. family, *v. The Wordsworths of Peniston*, by Gordon Graham W., privately printed, 1929.

me to judge what sort of a Work would be most likely to be taken in its place.

I feel truly obliged to Mr De Wint for the attention he is disposed to pay to Miss C. Marshall's and my request in favor of your young Friend. We are all pretty well under this roof. Hoping that Mr Gaskell and yourself are the same, I remain with the Kindest wishes of the Season in which Mrs W. and my daughter unite, faithfully

dear Madam
your obliged
Wm Wordsworth

MS.　　　**1318.　W. W. to Edward Moxon**

Rydal 10th Jan^y '40.

My dear Mr Moxon,

Having an opportunity of returning the three Volumes by the hand of Mr Westall,[1] who will be in town by the end of next week (this is Saturday), I prefer sending this by him, and charging the Binder, negligent as he has been, with the Carriage. —Mr W. has been a week with us taking a few sketches with a view to the illustration of my Poems. The Weather and a bad cold had been much against him, but he has done pretty well. In particular he has made one very good drawing in perspective of the interior of our chief sitting-room. It has a most picturesque appearance and I cannot but think would be acceptable to those who take an interest in my writings. He has done the outside of the House and the surrounding landscape.

I set my face entirely against the publication of Mr Field's MSS.[2] I ought to have written to him several weeks ago, but feeling as I did truly sensible of the interest he took in my character and writings and grateful to him for having bestowed so much of his valuable time, upon the subject, I could not bring myself to tell him what I have just with all frankness stated to you. I must

---

[1] William Westall (1781–1850), younger brother of the more famous Richard W., A.R.A., 1812. He had spent much time in the Lake Country between 1811 and 1820 and was intimate with W. W., Southey, and Sir George B. He was much employed in illustrating topographical works.

[2] The MS. of Barron Field's 'Memoirs of the Life and Poetry of W. W.', still unpublished, is in the British Museum (MS. Add. 41325–7).

however do so. Mr Field has been very little in England, I imagine, for above twenty years and consequently is not aware, that much the greatest part of his labour would only answer the purpose of reviving forgotten theories and exploded opinions. Besides, there are in his notions things that are personally *disagreeable* (not to use a harsher term) to myself and those about me. And if such an objection did not lie against the publication, it is enough that the thing is *superfluous*. In the present state of this Country in general, how could this kind natured Friend ever be deceived into the thought that criticism and particulars so minute could attract attention even from a few?

Hartley has positively affirmed to my Son and another Gentleman, that he considers his part of the Work at an end. 'True', said he, 'I could go on for ever, but 60 Pages—20 more than Jonson—are surely enough.' I write this in consequence of your saying in your last 'The introduction to Massinger is still unfinished'. Perhaps all is right by this time.

I have not sent the Spectacles by Mr Westall, hoping that some person in the neighbourhood may set them right.

Murray used to say that advertizing always paid. So it might with him—but with old books like mine I should imagine that adv.^{g} frequently repeated on the forthcoming of a new Ed: would never answer, and therefore I am myself against it rather—I leave the decision to your friendly judgment. If I have overlooked anything requiring notice, tell me in your reply. I enclose a slip of paper from my Clerk—the erratum noticed is important and I should there[?fore] like to have it inserted in such Copies as are not put into circulation. faithfully yours with remembrance etc

Wm Wordsworth

Please pay to Longman on our account the enclosed bill.
Address: Edward Moxon Esq, 46 Dover Street, London.

K(—)   *1319. W. W. to Barron Field*

Rydal Mount, January 16, 1840.
My dear Mr Field,

I have at last brought myself to write to you. After maturely considering the subject, however painful it may be to me, I must

[997]

regret that I am decidedly against the publication of your Critical Memoir; your wish is, I know, to serve me, and I am grateful for the strength of this feeling in your excellent heart. I am also truly proud of the pains of which you have thought my writings worthy; but I am sure that your intention to benefit me in this way would not be fulfilled. The hostility which you combat so ably is in a great measure passed away, but might in some degree be revived by your recurrence to it, so that in this respect your work would, if published, be either superfluous or injurious, so far as concerns the main portion of it. I shall endeavour, during the short remainder of my life, to profit by it, both as an author and a man, in a private way; but the notices of me by many others which you have thought it worth while to insert are full of gross mistakes, both as to facts and opinions, and the sooner they are forgotten the better. Old as I am, I live in the hope of seeing you, and should in that event have no difficulty in reconciling you to the suppression of a great part of this work entirely, and of the whole of it in its present shape. . . . One last word in matter of authorship: it is far better not to admit people so much behind the scenes, as it has been lately fashionable to do. . . . Believe me to be,

Most faithfully, your much obliged

Wm. Wordsworth.

MS.   *1320. W. W. to Thomas Powell*

Saturday, Noon—18th Jan^{ry} [p.m. 1840]

My dear Mr Powell,

Many thanks for your beautiful Milton, and your Stilton which arrived safely yesterday. I must now briefly advert to certain points in your last Letter. You seem in too great a hurry to be in the *press* with Chaucer. He is a mighty Genius as you well know, and not lightly to be dealt with. For my own part, I am not prepared to incur any responsibility on the account of this project, which I much approve of, beyond furnishing my own little Quota; which I almost fear now must be confined to permission to reprint the Prioress's Tale, if thought worth while; and the Cuckoo and Nightingale which is ready; but with great diligence have Mrs Wordsworth and I looked in vain among my papers for the MS which contains the Manciple's Tale, and if I am not mistaken a small portion of Troilus and Cressida—It contained also, by the bye, a Translation of two Books of Ariosto's Orlando, and this and other of its contents, I should be sorry to lose altogether.—

My *approbation* of the Endeavour to tempt people to read Chaucer by making a part of him intelligible to the unlettered, and tuneable to modern ears, will be sufficiently apparent by my own little Contributions to the intended Volume. But *beyond this* I do not wish to do any thing; or rather it could not be right that I should. Little matters in Composition hang about and teaze me awkwardly, and at improper times when I ought to be taking my meals or asleep. On this account, however reluctantly, I must *decline* even *looking over* the MSS either of yourself or your Friends. I am sure I should find some thing which I should attempt to change, and probably after a good deal of pains make the passage no better, perhaps worse—This is my infirmity, I have employed scores of hours during the course of my life in retouching favorite passages of favorite Authors, of which labour not a trace remains nor ought to remain—

As my connection with the intended little work originated with you, and probably the work altogether, why should not you, with the consent of Coadjutors [?] the management of it, both as to Editorship and the choice of a publisher. You could prefix an advertisement expressing how the Attempt came to be made, and upon what principles it was conducted.—I hope I have now made myself sufficiently intelligible, and that Mr Horne[1] &c will not be hurt that I decline, for the reasons above given, the pleas[ure] which it would otherwise be, of perusing his MSS.— I wish him and Mr Hunt,[2] to whom present my kind regards,

---

[1] Richard Hengist Horne (1803–84), poet and miscellaneous writer, and friend of Mrs Browning; his best known works are his long poem, *Orion*, which he published at a farthing (1843), and his essays, *A New Spirit of the Age* (1844). [2] Leigh Hunt.

success in their disinterested labours. My love and reverence for Chaucer are unbounded. Affectionately

Your much obliged

W. W.

Miss Gillies returns to us today or tomorrow. She has been absent since Wednesday.

MS.   *1321. W. W. to Edward Moxon*

Rydal Mount 27 Jan. '40.

My dear Mr Moxon,

I sit down to thank you for the Beaumont and Fletcher, which I see you have kindly dedicated to me. The others all except Hartley's and my Son's which is here, awaiting an opportunity, have been sent to their several destinations. I should have written sooner but I had nothing particular to say; nor have I at present.

You know the general state of my eyes to be such as that they allow me to read very very little. In consequence I am yet unacquainted with Mr Leigh Hunt's play,[1] and Mr Darley's Thomas a Beckett,[2] for which I am sorry, but it cannot be helped. Pray when you see either of these Gentlemen tell them this with many thanks for their obliging attentions.

I do not see much of poor Hartley C. but my opinion continues the same that though he writes much and very ably, he is not to be depended upon for unfinished work. I believe he is upon the whole more regular as to Drink than he used to be but the other day I was very much shocked to meet him quite tipsy in Ambleside Streets—poor Fellow.

The Sonnets upon Capital Punishment which I sent you, then no more I believe than 4, are now 11. I should not be sorry to put them into circulation on account of the importance of the

[1] *A Legend of Florence*, produced at Covent Garden on Feb. 7, 1840, gained a brilliant success. It was much praised by the Queen, who saw it several times.

[2] George Darley (1795–1846), poet, critic, and mathematician. His *Thomas à Becket* appeared in 1840, and also his Edition of Beaumont and Fletcher, which he had undertaken for Moxon in place of Southey.

subject if I knew how. I cannot print them in a Magazine for
reasons you are aware of. All here are pretty well, as I hope you
all are. My Son is with us and sends his kind regards, ever yours

W. Wordsworth.

MS.   *1322. W. W. to Thomas Powell*

[Early 1840]¹

. . . but you are quite welcome to the Prioress's Tale, Cuckoo
and Nightingale, and the passage from the Troilus and Cressida.
When you see Miss Gillies pray tell her that she is remembered
in this house with much pleasure and great affection, and a
hundred good wishes for her success. Her picture just arrived,
appears to be much approved ; but of course as to the degree of
likeness in each there is great diversity of opinion. How mortifying in this respect would be the Profession of a Portrait-Painter
if the Artist did not rise above the common region of inexperi-
enced judgement. Pray let me hear from you at your leisure.
With best remembrances to Mrs Powell and yourself and kind
regards to your Brother believe me faithfully yours

Wm Wordsworth

My eyes are in their better way, but alas they allow me to
read very little. The general health of us all is good, thank God.

The non-arrival of Miss Roughridge's portrait was a great
disappointment.

MS.   *1323. W. W. to Isabella Fenwick*

(*fragment*)

[1840]²

. . . But whatever may be the execution of the portions done
by Mr Powell and his Friends the attempt cannot but excite
some little attention to the subject, and in so far as it does will

¹ This fragment must have been written soon after the letter of Jan. 18,
when he had found the mislaid passage from *Troilus and Cressida*, and after
Miss Gillies had left Rydal.
² Undated, but probably written about this time.

tend to a good purpose. Chaucer was one of the greatest poets the world has ever seen. He is certainly, at times, in his comic tales indecent, but he is never, as far as I know, insidiously or openly voluptuous, much less would a stronger term, which would apply to some popular writers of our own day apply to him. He had towards the female sex as exquisite and pure feelings as ever the heart of man was blessed with, and has expressed them as beautifully in the language of his age, as ever man did. But it is time that I should stop. I have noticed but few points in your Letter; but be assured every word of it was interesting to me. God bless you, my dear, dear Friend.

Wm Wordsworth.

MS.   *1324. W. W. to Joshua Watson*

Rydal Mount Feb. 11th 1840

My dear Sir,

Yesterday I received the Enclosed; respecting which there must be some mistake.

On the 26th Febry last my Daughter called in Park Street; and, not finding you at home, She left with your *Housekeeper* the amount of the enclosed Demand, under cover directed to you. How it comes yet to be standing in my name on Mr Harrison's Books I do not see how, under this circumstance, I can explain, without troubling you which I very much *regret*. Would you be so kind as either to write to me upon the subject, or directly, yourself, satisfy the applicants.

This occasion has emboldened me, to do what I could not venture upon before, that is, to assure you of my own sympathy and that of Mrs Wordsworth and my Daughter upon your afflicting and desolating loss.[1] I do not presume to speak of consolation *that* your own mind, I know, has through prayer furnished you with, from the first feeling perhaps of the blow. But the assurance that Friends have in some degree our sorrow is always more or less grateful to the suffering mind, and that assurance I humbly offer from my heart; and we all join in this

---

[1] Watson's only daughter Mary Sikes W., who had been married two years before to the Rev. H. M. Wagner, had just died, leaving two sons.

tribute. God bless you my dear Sir, and believe me with fervent prayers that you may be supported from above under this and every other affliction.

Faithfully and affectionately yours,

Wm. Wordsworth

Pray present my respectful sympathy to Mr. Wagner, along with the expression of a hope and prayer that the little one may prove a blessing to you Both.

W. W.

MS.   *1325. W. W. to Cordelia Marshall*

Rydal Mount Feb^ry 19th 1840

My dear Cordelia,

If you had known how little my *promised* Letter was likely to contain[1] you would not have honoured it with a wish for its arrival—In fact when I told Mrs W. or Dora I should write to you myself, it was because I thought it became me to do so, in order to thank you for your Drawing from the far Terrace. I like it much, but sincerity compels me to say, not so well as the Sketch—The fault is in the management of the projecting fir-bough in its connection with the round Island. This you will easily correct when we have the pleasure of seeing you as I hope we shall, next summer.—

I shall be truly glad to receive the Drawing of the Cabinet from the pencil of Mrs Gaskell—

Dora has been a week gone from home; this day, she takes up her Abode at her Friend Sarah Coleridge's 10 Chester Place, near the Colyseum, Regent's Park. She chuses to be there at this time for quiet's sake, in order to avoid the bustle of a Wedding at Mrs Hoare's Hampstead, the Bride who has been long resident with Mrs H— is Louisa Lloyd. Dora describes herself as well, but we know her to be weak, and She was looking miserably thin when she left us. They had a most agreeable and unfatiguing journey by Railway from Preston.—Miss Fenwick is well and no doubt will contrive to see you as soon as you arrive in London. After this week she changes her Lodgings, so I cannot give you her address—

---

[1] *MS.* contained.

The Author of Ernest[1] is Mr Loft son of the late Capel Loft near Bury St Edmunds, so you need not trouble yourself with further inquiries, as I know a good deal about him. He was a distinguished Scholar when at Trin: Coll. Cambridge—

I hope you will all enjoy yourselves in London; there is no likelihood of our going thither this Spring, in fact every other year in London is quite enough for my strength. I find it too hard service, though Mr Rogers 7 years my Senior does not.

I have no news for you—this neighbourhood being quite barren of any thing so precious. Miss Gillies's pictures we learn are much liked, especially one of Mrs Wordsworth and my self in the same Piece. I shall be glad if you and all your family approve of them. Pray be so good as to let Mr Wyon know that we are anxious to have back the two Medallions improved, as he promised. Dora could bring them with her, if he could finish them immediately.—Poor dear Mr Southey is no better; with affectionate remembrances to yourself, Father and Mother and Sisters and all your friends in which Mrs W joins

          I [? remain] ever your

                    W. W.

MS.   *1326. W. W. to Edward Moxon*
K(—)

                              Feb. 21st 1840.

My dear Mr Moxon,

Not being able to meet with H. C. immediately on receipt of your Letter, I wrote him a note a couple of days after; I told him its Contents—I have since seen him and done all I could.— And now let me give you in respect to him a piece of advice once for all, viz. that you *never* engage with him for any *unperformed* Work, where either time or quantity is of importance. Poor Fellow he has no resolution—in fact nothing that can be called rational volition, or command of himself, as to what he will do, or not do. Of course I mean setting aside the *fundamental* obligations of morality. Yesterday I learnt that he had disappeared from his Lodgings, and that he had been seen at

---

[1] A poem privately and anonymously printed in 1839, said by Harriet Martineau in her *Autobiography* to be 'of prodigious power, but too seditious for publication'.

8 o'clock that morning entering the Town of Kendal. He was at Ambleside the night before till 11 o'clock, so he must have [been] out [a] great part of the night. I have lately begun to think that he has given himself up so to his own [? whims] fancies reveries, abstractions etc that he is scarcely in his right [mind] at all times. I admire his genius and talents far more than I could find words to express, especially for writing prose, which I am inclined to think, as far as I have seen, is more masterly than his Verse. The *work* manship of the latter seems to me not infrequently too hasty, has indeed too much the air of Italian improvizatore production.—

Mr Powell, my Friend, has some thought of preparing for Publication some portions of Chaucer modernized so far and no farther than is done in my treatment of the Prioress's Tale, that will in fact be his model. He will have Coadjutors, among whom I believe will be Mr Leigh Hunt, a man as capable of doing the work well as any living Author. I have placed at my Friend Mr Powell's disposal in addition to the Prioress's Tale, three other pieces which I did long ago, but revised the other day. They are the Manciple's Tale, The Cuckoo and the Nightingale and 24 Stanzas of Troilus and Cressida. This I have done mainly out of my love and reverence for Chaucer, in hopes that whatever may be the merit of Mr Powell's attempt, the attention of other Writers may be drawn to the subject; and a work hereafter be produced by different pens which will place the treasures of one of the greatest of Poets within the reach of multitudes, which now they are not. I mention all this to you, because though I have not given Mr Powell the least encouragement to do so he may sound you as to your disposition to undertake the Publication.— I have myself nothing further to do with it than I have stated. Had the thing been suggested to me by any number of competent Persons 20 years ago I would have undertaken the Editorship, done much more myself, and endeavoured to improve the several contributions where they seemed to require it. But that is now out of the question.—

I am glad to hear so favorable an account of the sale of the new Edition. The penny postage has let in an inundation of complimentary Letters upon me. Yesterday I had one that would amuse you by the language of awe, admiration, gratitude etc in which it abounds and two or three days ago I had one from a little boy eight years old! telling me how he had been charmed with the Idiot Boy etc etc. In several of these Letters there is one thing which gratifies, viz. the frequent mention of the consolation which my Poems have afforded the Writer under affliction and the calmness and elevation etc which they have produced in him.

My Paper is quite full. I hope you will see my dear daughter from time to time. Tomorrow she goes to Number 10 Chester Place, to her friends the Coleridges. Kind remembrances to Mrs Moxon and your Sister and Brother.

I am not inclined to go to London this Spring. Visiting, talking, late dinners etc are too hard work for me

(unsigned.)

M.
K(—)

1327. *W. W. to Henry Alford*[1]

[p.m. Ambleside, Feb 21, 1840]

My dear Sir,

Pray excuse my having been some little time in your debt. I could plead many things in extenuation, the chief, that old one of the state of my eyes, which never leaves me at liberty either to read or write a tenth part as much as I could wish, and as otherwise I ought to do. It cannot but be highly gratifying to me to learn that my writings are prized so highly by a poet and critic of your powers. The essay upon them which you have so kindly sent me seems well qualified to promote your views in writing it. I was particularly pleased with your distinction between religion in poetry and versified religion. For my own part, I have been averse to frequent mention of the mysteries of Christian faith; not from a want of a due sense of their momentous nature, but the contrary. I felt it far too deeply to venture on handling the subject as familiarly as many scruple not to do. I am far from blaming them, but let them not blame

---

[1] Henry Alford (1810–71), poet and hymn writer—author of the famous harvest hymn, 'Come, ye thankful people, come'. His *Poems* appeared in 1832 and 1835, *The Abbot of Muchelnaye* in 1841. He became Dean of Canterbury in 1857.

me, nor turn from my companionship on that account. Besides
general reasons for diffidence in treating subjects of Holy Writ,
I have some especial ones. I might err in points of faith, and
I should not deem my mistakes less to be deprecated because
they were expressed in metre. Even Milton, in my humble
judgment, has erred, and grievously ; and what poet could hope
to atone for misapprehensions in the way in which that mighty
mind has done ?

I am not at all desirous that any one should write an elaborate
critique on my poems. There is no call for it. If they be from
above, they will do their own work in course of time ; if not, they
will perish as they ought. But scarcely a week passes in which
I do not receive grateful acknowledgments of the good they have
done to the minds of the several writers. They speak of the
relief they have received from them under affliction and in grief,
and of the calmness and elevation of spirit which the poems
either give, or assist them in attaining. As these benefits are
not without a traceable bearing upon the good of the immortal
soul, the sooner, perhaps, they are pointed out and illustrated
in a work like yours the better.

Pray excuse my talking so much about myself; your letter
and critique called me to the subject. But I assure you it would
have been more grateful to me to acknowledge the debt we owe
you in this house, where we have read your poems with no
common pleasure. Your 'Abbot of Muchelnaye' also makes me
curious to hear more of him. But I must conclude. I was truly
sorry to have missed you when you and Mrs Alford called at
Rydal. Mrs W. unites with me in kind regards to you both ; and
believe me

My dear Sir
Faithfully yours
Wm Wordsworth

M(—)
K(—)   *1328. W. W. to Lord Morpeth*

March 2, 1840.

. . . I never did seek or accept a pension from the present or
any other administration, directly or indirectly. . . .

MS. *1329. W. W. to Dora W.*

Monday [? March] 9th [1840]

My very dear Child,

I have been much troubled at this severe illness of yours, especially bearing in mind the old *habit* of your Body. If I could but learn that any progress had been made in correcting *that* it would make me happy indeed. I am therefore very anxious that you should see Dr Ferguson, and not for once merely, but with such intervals of time as would allow him to ascertain the effects of anything he might prescribe. On this account, and in order that the time of dear Miss Fenwick's departure may be delayed thereby as little as may be, I wish your visit at Hampstead to be shortened. The Marshalls will be most happy to receive you. —Now for lighter matter! the weather here continues to be enchanting; sharp frost, I own, in the night, but in the day time the sun without a cloud is as warm as summer. Mr Carr exclaimed again the other day 'it is just as we had the air at Sorento last year at this time; I could almost think I was there again'.—We had Roby[1] here the other evening; he brought along with him young Mr Colman of Brathay. They drank tea and the youth in his modesty made an offer of moving, but Roby, to shew I suppose on what familiar terms he was here, said, 'no, no'. The attempt was repeated three times with the same result, and the poor youth was forced to remain till within a few minutes of nine. Your Mother in the course of the evening said, Miss Gillies' picture of Mrs Hopkinson is much admired in London. Yes, replied he, I always thought it her *chief dövr*, you know he has undertaken to teach his Daughter *French*! ! ! We talked about a new ministry, which was said to be in contemplation. Lord J. Russel to be Premier, Lord Brougham etc to have office. Pshaw! said I, or something like it; and Mr R. gravely, yet with a smile, observed 'These ephemeral administrations never last.' When I told this to dear Aunty, she was delighted above measure.

---

[1] i.e. Robinson, a Rydal neighbour, son of the W.s' friends the Robinsons of York. He was known in the W. family as 'Roby' to distinguish him from H. C. R., to whom he was not related.

I have had a friendly answer from Lord Morpeth. He tells me he *actually said* words to which I have no objection whatever, so moderate your wrath.—I was desirous that my Letter should as soon as possible be in Mr Powell's hands, otherwise I should have requested Miss F. to send it to you.—There was, and continues to be, an unpleasantness about John's having Plumbland in which good Mr Curwen had no part. It rises entirely out of Henry's *cupidity,* and John's good nature standing in the way of due reflection

[*cetera desunt*]

MS.
K(—)

1330. W. W. to Edward Quillinan

Rydal Mount March 9th '40

We have to thank you my dear Mr Quillinan for two long Letters both of which were very acceptable and interesting. I will first touch upon the points of business, by noticing the information you have procured about modelling which seems sufficient for fulfilment of my promise to the person at Keswick. —Upon consulting Mr Courtenay's Letter, I find he says: 'as the Bank is *chartered,* your risk would be less:' what do these words mean? is it that I should only be answerable to the amount I have subscribed or engaged for, or what else? I do not like the *principle* of these Banks; however well they be conducted for a time; you neither have nor can have security for like caution and judgement continuing: and therefore I intend, at present at least, to withdraw when the next statement of accounts is made (which will be shortly) if I can do so without material loss.—Mr Liddell spoke from personal kindness to me, and the value he sets upon my writings. But he judged ill and I am sorry that he mentioned my name. I have written to Lord Morpeth and had, as Dora will tell you, a friendly and satisfactory answer.

I do not acknowledge the force of the objections made to my publishing the specimens of Chaucer, nevertheless I have yielded to the judgments of others, and have not sent more than the Cuckoo and Nightingale. You noticed properly Talfourd's *blunder,* if it be not a misprint.

Tegg[1] is what you say. He has written two long and stupid Letters to the Times, in one of which the Blockhead says, 'look at the profits, the enormous ones of such and such people'— Now that is so far from being an objection to the Bill, that it is one of the strongest reasons in favor of it. The large and increasing instant demand for literature of a certain quality, holds out the strongest temptation to men, who could do better, writing below themselves, to suit the taste of the superficial Many. What we want is not books to catch purchasers, Readers not worth a moment's notice, not light but solid matter, not things treated in a broad and coarse, or at best a superficial way, but profound or refined works comprehensive of human interests through time as well as space. Kotzebue was acted and read at once from Cadiz to Moscow; what is become of him now? But Tegg has the impudence to affirm, that another Paradise Lost, or a poem as good, would at once produce £10,000 from Mr Murray and others. 'Credat Judaeus Apella.' Paradise Lost is indeed bought because people for their own credit must now have it. But how few, how very few, read it; when it is read by the multitude, it is almost exclusively not as a poem, but a religious Book.

But even were it true that substantial work would at once secure a wide circulation, justice would still be violated, by withholding from the Descendants or Heirs of a great Author the further advantage he is so strongly entitled to. The wretch Tegg says his 'line is to watch expiring Copyrights', and would be, no doubt, if he dared to murder the authors for the sake of getting sooner at his prey. But too much of this disgusting subject. We have here and have had for the last three weeks, through the whole day, celestial weather, and the stars by night brilliant almost as in the West Indies. For the two or three last days there has been a sort of steaming heat, as in summer, especially towards sunset, but it goes off and the nights are clear as I have described. I disturb myself with thinking that Dora *might* have escaped her terrible cold if she had remained here; but she has had what she deems a far more than sufficient set off, in her enjoyment of your company, and that of her other Friends.

[1] *v.* p. 931.

I cannot however altogether forgive dear Sara Coleridge being such a monopolist of your conversation in Dora's presence. It was to say the least indelicate; but blue-stockingism is sadly at enmity with true refinement of mind—John's new living has been overstated by Isabella; it is £420 per ann: I have written a long Letter to Dora this morning, and my back aches, with stooping in the way which I am so little accustomed to. Mary is engaged with company or she would [have] added a few words. She sends her love and thanks—and believe me with love to your Daughter, my dear Friend,

faithfully yours
W. Wordsworth

Address: Edward Quillinan Esq., 121 Crawford Street, London.

MS. **1331. *W. W. to Benjamin Robert Haydon***
K.
Rydal Mt Ambleside Mar. 12th—40

My dear Haydon,

Though I have nothing to say but merely words of congratulation,[1] hearty congratulation, I cannot forbear to thank you for your Letter. You write in high spirits, and I am glad of it; it is only fair, that having had so many difficulties to encounter, you should have a large share of triumph. Nevertheless, though I partake most cordially of your pleasure, I should have been still more delighted to learn, that your pencil, for that after all is the tool you were made for, met with the encouragement which it so well deserves.

I should have liked to be among your Auditors, particularly so, as I have seen, not long ago, so many first-rate pictures on the Continent; and to have heard you at Oxford would have added largely to my gratification. I love and honor that place

---

[1] This is a reply to a characteristically ecstatic letter from B. R. H. which begins 'My dearest W., At last I have accomplished one of the glorious daydreams of my youth, viz. Lecturing on Art at the University. I have been received with distinction by the Vice-Chancellor and heads of Colleges, granted the Ashmolean Museum, and gave my first lecture yesterday which was brilliantly attended and positively hailed.' He concludes 'I would thank God with my last breath for the great opportunity of doing my duty. Hurra! with all my soul. Your affec. old friend, B. R. H.'

for abundant reasons; nor can I ever forget the distinction bestowed upon myself last summer by that noble-minded University.

Allow me to mention one thing upon which, if I were qualified to lecture upon your Art, I should dwell with more attention than, as far as I know has been bestowed upon it; I mean perfection in each kind as far as it is attainable. This in widely different minds has been shewn, by the Italians by the Flemings and Dutch, the Spaniards, the Germans, and why should I exclude the English? Now as a masterly, or first rate Ode or Elegy, or piece of humour even, is better than a poorly or feebly executed epic Poem, so is the picture, tho' in point of subject the humblest that ever came from an easel better than a work after Michael Angelo or Raphael in choice of subject or aim of style if moderately performed. All styles down to the humblest are good, if there be thrown into the doing all that the subject is capable of, and this truth is a great honour, not only to painting, but in degree to every other fine art. Now it is well worth a Lecturer's while who[1] sees the matter in this light first to point out through the whole scale of Art what stands highest, and then to shew what constitutes its appropriate perfection of all down to the lowest. Ever my dear Haydon

faithfully your's

Wm Wordsworth

MS.   *1332. W. W. to Mrs Gaskell*

Rydal Mount March 25th '40[2]

Dear Madam,

Pray accept my sincere thanks both for your obliging Letter and [? also] the trouble you have taken towards putting me in possession of a drawing of that interesting relique of my ancestral Name-sake. May I beg also that you would make my acknowledgements to the Draughtsman who went without a dinner in the service of one unknown to him, and tell him I should be glad if he would give me an opportunity to straight[en]

---

[1] who: *written* whose
[2] For W. W. to H. C. R., March, *v. C.R.*, p. 400.

the account (if that were possible) at my own table. The view which Mr Brackenbridge takes of my pretensions to become, through Mr and Mrs Beaumont's kind consideration, the owner of this memorial of my family, is flattering, and I should like him to know that it was gratifying to me. I still cherish a hope that Mr and Mrs Beaumont may be induced to look at my wish, simple as it may be deemed, in the same light.

My Daughter is now staying at Mr Marshall's in Grosvenor Street, and if the drawing could be directed to her there she would bring it down safely and I should have it in the course of a month.

It gives me sincere pleasure to be told that I have been in any degree influential for the improvement of Miss Brandreth in the charming Art to which she has attached herself; and I am truly sensible of the honor Mr De Wint[1] has done me in this matter. Miss Brandreth with whom no doubt you are in communication, will oblige me by telling him so, with the expression of my regards to Himself and Mrs Dewint.

Pray present my respects to Mr Gaskell and believe me with kind regards, in which Mrs Wordsworth unites: faithfully your much obliged

Wm Wordsworth

MS.   *1333. W. W. to Isabella Fenwick*

[March 26, 1840]

After I had sent off my Cuckoo verses[2] I felt as if they wanted something of solidity, and am now tempted, my beloved Friend, to send you, in Joanna's writing, a copy slightly revised, with an additional stanza toiled at unsuccessfully yesterday evening, but thrown off in a few minutes this morning. We all like it and hope you and Dora will do the same. But it is too lately born for sound judgment, and I never sent to any one verses immediately after they were composed without some cause for regret I had been so hasty.

---

[1] Peter De Wint (1784–1849), landscape painter, one of the finest water-colourists of his time.

[2] 'The Cuckoo at Laverna', Oxf. W., p. 361.

I called again upon Mrs Pedder after the receipt of your Letter; all is settled though not exactly according to your wish. I found she could not *bind* herself to let you have the house any part of September; from what she said I felt myself not justified in pressing. She said however that though she could not ensure you the house for that month she would do all in her power to meet your wishes. She is desirous of new-painting two of the bedrooms. I was rather afraid of that, and only consented to it upon condition that the work was begun instantly. She said it should be so, by tomorrow at the latest. This is a good time, for the workmen have little to do. As we are yet five weeks from the first of May I trust the smell of the paint will be quite gone. Pray remember us most kindly to your dear Sister, and though I particularize no one else, all your connections at Bath are in our thoughts, most affectionately yours, W. W.

M
K. 1334. *W. W. to Dora W. and Isabella Fenwick*

7th April, 1840.

My dearest Dora,

Though my left eye has been rather troublesome these two or three last days, I cannot forbear writing to you, and let the letter serve for dear Miss Fenwick also, upon the morning of my seventieth birthday. I am, thank almighty God! in excellent health, and so is your dear Mother, and though some of my thoughts, upon this occasion, are naturally serious, even to sadness, I am, upon the whole, in a chearful state of mind. The day is bright as sunshine can make it, and the air fraught with as much stir and animating noise as the wind can put into it.

Your mother finds her ancles weak from the shock and sprain of her fall and consequent confinement, or I should have tempted her out with me to walk on the terrace, from which I have had an entertaining view of the merriment of the servants, with help from Arthur Jackson and his Brother, shaking the glittering dust out of the carpets.

Sister is very comfortable, and we are going on nicely, though wishing much for your return. Yesterday I dined with Mrs

Luff, after calling at the house high up Loughrigg side where dwells the good woman who lost her two children in the flood last winter. The wind was high when I knocked at her door, and I heard a voice from within that I knew not what to make of, though it sounded something like the lullaby of a Mother to her Baby. After entering I found it came from a little sister of those drowned Children, that was singing to a bundle of clouts, rudely put together to look like a Doll, which she held in her arms.

I tell you this little story in order that, if it be perfectly convenient, but on no account else, you may purchase what may answer the purpose with something more of pride and pleasure to this youngling of a nurse. Such is your mother's wish, I should not have had the wit to think of it. No matter, she says, how common a sort of thing the doll is, only let it be a good big one.

Dear Miss Fenwick,

Mrs Luff does not wish to part with her sofas, but they are quite at your service, and she would be pleased if you would use them till she has a house of her own. But that time is, she fears, distant, her American property is so unpromising that she has scruples about taking Old Brathay. Now, should she decline it, might it not, as the Owner is willing to make some improvement, accommodate you for a time? I don't much like the thought; but, as a 'pis aller', it might possibly do until Mr Hill may be tempted to give his Cottage up.

I find from a talk with Mrs Fleming that they are disposed to make improvements, could they let it for a term; and a term, with liberty of course to underlet, is what you want. But all this we long to talk over with you, among a thousand reasons for wishing you back again.

It had escaped my recollection when we heard about the woods and forests, and the Villiers' kindness, that I talked this matter over with Lord Lowther, when he was Surveyor of that department, and he told me there was scarcely a single office under him that was an object, at least *then* a come-at-able one.

Were he in England now I should be inclined to ask him if my recollection be correct. But I must leave, which I do, dearest

Friends, with love to you both; and wishes for many happy returns of your own Birthdays.

Ever most affectionately yours,

Wm Wordsworth.

P.S.—Mrs Pedder is putting up a new staircase in some part of the house for the convenience of her new Tenant. Dearest Dora, your mother tells me she shrinks from Copies being spread of those Sonnets;[1] she does not wish one, on any account, to be given to Miss Gillies, for that, without blame to Miss G., would be like advertising them. I assure you her modesty and humble-mindedness were so much shocked that I doubt if she had more pleasure than pain from these compositions, though I never poured out anything more truly from the heart.

MS.   *1335. W. W. to Edward Moxon*
(*With P.S. by W. W. Junior*)

Rydal Mount April 12th 1840.

Dear Mr Moxon,

I enclose an application just received and for an answer I have referred the Gentleman to you, stating that if *you* do not object I shall not withhold my consent.

My Son John and his Brother William are both at present staying under this roof. They are well, and were they present would send their kind remembrances.

Ever faithfully yours

Wm Wordsworth

Please send the Daily news here for ten days to come. I have given up all thoughts of going up to Town this Spring. yours most afft[ly]

W. W. Jun.

MS.   *1336. W. W. to Edward Moxon*

[p. m. April 14, 1840]

My dear Mr Moxon

I have been looking for a Letter from you as I wished to know how far you could meet my wishes in respect to the sum I have

---

[1] The two sonnets on Mrs Wordsworth's portrait, painted by Miss Gillies, *v.* Oxf. W., p. 279.

to advance for my Son John. If anything be due to me, but only due, remember, as I stated pray send it in a Bank post Bill, as soon as convenient, or at all events let me know what you can do—but do not I repeat put yourself out of your course, as I shall have some more money directly.—

I should like to have a sight of Mr Christie's Pamphlet upon perpetual Copyright of which the Morning Post, giving an unanswerable extract, speaks highly. I suppose it is not so large but that it might be sent through Post without much expense. Let it be *prepaid* and put down to me, if I am right as to the size of it—

I am truly anxious that Sergeant Talfourd's, and Christie's pamphlet also, should be sent to Lieutenant General Sir William Gomm, Jamaica; but of course not by Post. You will be able to learn through what Channel things of this kind go to Persons in his station. He is Commander in Chief of the forces in the West Indies. Dora is coming north about the 20th, or a day or two after. You might send anything by her. She will be found at Mrs Hoare's, Hampstead Heath.

ever faithfully yours

Wm Wordsworth.

MS. *1337. W. W. to Dora W.*

Wed. mor^g [Spring 1840]

I sit down, my beloved Child, to write to you without the least prospect of anything being contained in my Letter to entertain you. But the account you give of your susceptibility of Changes in place or weather so troubles me that I cannot help entreating with my own pen that you would put yourself, as to exposure, moving about etc, upon the invalid list. I am anxious exceedingly about this hoarseness which seems by your last to have recurred as bad as ever. Let me beg that you would not think of going to Church nor enter an open carriage; and in short that you would keep yourself in a temperature as equable as possible.

But for anxiety about your health I should be quite pleased with your prolonging your stay in London and the neighbourhood; though I cannot help often wishing you were here to enjoy this enchanting weather that we have had now nearly five weeks. Sun and moon have lately vied and are still vying with each other which can do most to beautify this beautiful country. James, you know, is not only a Painter, but a little of a Poet. While he was working in the garden the other evening and we were admiring together the things [?] he said—'And look at Wansfell what a *heat* that is', pointing to the deep copper reflection of the light from the western clouds, in which the mountain was steeped, 'each had his *glowing* Mountain',[1] as you remember in the Excursion. We rejoice in the prospect of dear William —the woods and forests are the very thing for him ; fresh air and horse-exercise just what he wants. I am most grateful to our Friends whether they succeed or no. But what a strange Creature is your Br John. Not a word in his letter to you upon the point of insuring his life, which I pressed upon him so earnestly. It was indeed only to enable him to do this that I encountered all the disagreeables of writing a long letter to Mr Curwen upon what I then understood to be *Henry's* proposal that 100£ of the £200 annuity should be transferred to him. And what stuff about his playing the dinner-Patron to the poor curates in Brigham Parish! Let the Lay-reader or any great Squire of the neighbourhood do this, if needful. *He* as Incumbent for Brigham was as much plundered by the Reformation and by monastic abuses preceding it as any of the poorest among the Curates. They are fellow-sufferers. In all this I see kindness of feeling more hasty than wise, too much of the little vanity of great-manism (a queer word coined for the occasion) and that sad want of circumspection that is shewn in almost all his proceedings. This, I assure you, troubles me, notwithstanding all his good and amiable qualities, whenever I think of him.

Tell Mr Quillinan, I think he has taken rather a *narrow* view of the spirit of the Manciple's Tale, especially as concerns its *morality*. The formal prosing at the end and the selfishness that pervades it flows from the genius of Chaucer, mainly as characteristic of the narrator whom he describes in the Prologue as eminent for shrewdness and clever worldly Prudence. The main

[1] *Excursion*, ix. 447.

lesson, and the most important one, is inculcated as a Poet ought chiefly to inculcate his lessons, not formally, but by implication; as when Phoebus in a transport of passion slays a wife whom he loved so dearly. How could the mischief of telling truth, merely because it *is* truth, be more feelingly exemplified. The Manciple himself is not, in his understanding, conscious of this; but his heart dictates what was natural to be felt and the moral, without being intended, forces itself more or less upon every Reader. Then how vividly is impressed the mischief of jealous vigilance and how truly and touchingly in contrast with the world's judgments are the transgressions of a woman in a low rank of life and one in high estate placed on the same level, treated. But enough; continue dear Dora to write as often as you can.

There is a probability of Miss Fenwick's getting for the Summer Mrs Froggatt's house.

Love to the Marshalls, Mrs Hoare, Mrs Gee etc etc.

Your most affectionate Father

MS.　　　*1338. W. W. to Isabella Fenwick*

[? Early 1840]

I sit down to write to you my very dear Friend with nothing to say in the way of *news*, and so much in the way of feeling to which I can do no justice, and which it would be superfluous to express if I could, that I am not a little at a loss what to touch upon.—One particular however I must express, namely, that your absence has convinced me I never can be at ease, if you were in this country and not within hourly walking reach of us. It is an odd thing to say, but it is true, that I enjoy the thought of your separation from us now where you are, and are likely to be, among Friends to whom you are so dear, and who are so dear to you. But I could not endure your being long, at such a distance as Calgarth even, where you would be so much parted from us, without any compensation from the company of your other Friends, and your kindred. Besides, looking at the matter selfishly, I feel that I should be perpetually on the fret, having you so near, and seeing what would appear to myself, and all of us so *little* of you as unavoidably we should see. A few years ago, as I have often said to you, it would have been otherwise; a walk of 6 or 7 miles would have then been nothing, and I could have done it without loss of time, as my mind might have been employed in composition all the way. So much therefore is settled that we must have you *near* us. When I think of this I borrow hope from yourself and from Mary and Dora, otherwise I should despond. Mr Hill is now fixed at Rydal, Mr Combe at Bellevue and we cannot expect a House to spring up out of the ground like a mushroom. Still I will try to hope, as I ought to do.—

I have been twice at Grasmere since you went away, all my other walks have been in the opposite direction, along the Rotha to the bridge, and several times round by Ambleside. Yesterday when I was crossing that Bridge, I saw to my great sorrow several of the trees that grow near it in the field by the waterside levelled with the ground. They were a great ornament, a few were still standing, Mr Cookson the Proprietor was there and I entreated him earnestly to spare them but all in vain—Money, money, is the God of the old in that rank of life, almost in every case, whatever it may be elsewhere. Your few words upon London talk and Society are very depressing. If hopelessness were not a sin I should be without hope. We appear as a nation, at least the prominent portion of us, to be sinking deeper and deeper every month, in dishonesty and dishonor. Good men and sincere Patriots, ought to look upon this as a trial of their resignation to the decrees of Providence, yet at the same time, as a call upon them to do their utmost in every way towards counteracting the mischief—

Pray tell Mr Villiers that I am deeply sensible of his kind feelings towards my Son. Be his destiny what it may, it never will be mended by any writing of mine, this I feel and in some degree lament. But as long as such iniquity as the heads of both Parties, Russel and Peel, are disposed to perpetrate in the matter of Copy-rights, how can it be expected that literary men will ever be dealt with as they ought to be. This injustice I shall never cease to resent; nor can I feel aught but contempt for the understanding of men who are unable to perceive that their opposition to this Bill is strictly *preposterous*; the worth of the article is upon their scheme sacrificed to presumed, and even falsely presumed, facilities for its circulation. Common sense points the other way; do what you can to assist in making books good in the first place,

(cetera desunt)

MS.   1339. W. W. to Sir William Gomm[1]

Rydal Mount Ambleside April 1840

My dear Sir Wm.

   Your Letter dated 25th Feb^{ry} I had the pleasure of receiving a fortnight ago; I feel much obliged by it and return you my sincere thanks. It was very kind on your part to think of introducing my Nephew to Sir Howard and Lady Douglas; and he has already been written to, to inform him of your intention to do so. We have heard from him twice since his arrival in the Ionian Islands, the climate of which agrees perfectly with his health, and he is much pleased with his situation. He says, nevertheless, he would prefer being attached to a regiment stationed in that quarter, to being on the staff; for two reasons principally; he would not be subject to such sudden changes of place, and he should have more to do in the way of his profession.

   It gives me much pleasure to learn that your present situation is so agreeable to yourself and Lady Gomm; and there seems to be no doubt of its continuing so if you do not suffer from the climate, which we who have never been in the Country have perhaps unreasonable dread of. Every one has heard of the glorious scenery and striking and beautiful exhibitions of nature and natural effects with which Jamaica, and those Islands in general, abound. And sure I am that you both have hearts and minds to enjoy them. Your exertions among the mountains will I hope not tempt you to forget the lameness under which you suffered not long ago. Mischiefs of that kind, and indeed all others affecting the Body have long memories. Last spring I was at Bath for a few weeks; and being so inconsiderate as to take very long walks (immediately after coming out of the warm bath) up and down those steep hillsides, I sprained, with that exertion and a slip of my foot, one of my ancles; and though by

---

[1] <i>v.</i> note to Letter 1309.

[1021]

pouring cold water upon it I effected apparently a complete cure, I find that I cannot walk on the mountains over rough ground, as I used to do, without recalling something of the injury.

You enquire about the Copyright Bill—It has been asleep some time, but comes on on the 28th Inst^nt. I am full of fears about the issue.—My Publisher, Mr Moxon has had orders to send you Sergeant Talfourd's pamphlet, and another in favor of the measure, by Mr Christie.—I have not lately been in communication with any one upon the subject so that I know nothing but what the Papers will tell you. Should there be any important publication upon it, I will take care it shall be forwarded to you.

Our Country is now in exquisite beauty, and we have had for the last ten weeks such a season as I cannot remember. No climate, all things considered, health and exercise included, could I think surpass ours as it has been for the time I have mentioned.

Mrs W— unites with me in kindest remembrances and a thousand good wishes to yourself and Lady Gomm, and believe me to be my dear Sir Wm

very faithfully your
much obliged
Wm Wordsworth

Address: Lieu. Gen. Sir Wm. Gomm Bt. etc. etc. etc., Kingston, Jamaica.

MS.   *1340. W. W. to W. F. Wilson*

Rydal Mount, Ambleside 20th April '40.

Sir,

My Friends are not satisfied with any Engraving of me, and therefore I cannot point out any in particular. The worst in my own judgement is that prefixed to the two last Editions of my poems[1]

I am, sir, your obed^nt Servant
Wm Wordsworth.

Address: W. F. Wilson Esqre, 52 Princes Street, Edinburgh.

[1] i.e. that engraved by W. H. Watt from the portrait by Pickersgill at St. John's Coll., Cambridge.

MS.   *1341. W. W. to John Gibson Lockhart*

Rydal Mount April 1840

[p.m. 28th]

My dear Mr Lockhart,

Having received some little time ago the last Volume of the Second Edition of your Memoir of Sir Walter, I sit down to thank you for the very valuable Present. The embellishments give a great additional Value to the Edit: they are judiciously selected and well executed. The former copy, which I received from your kindness also, I have presented to my younger Son who prizes it as it deserves.

The state of my eyes, though at present in their better way, does not allow me to read much, so that I should not be able to compare the two editions and to look at the corrections and additions with the care which I know they must deserve, and be assured I regret much this inability.

You will grieve to hear that poor dear Southey is gradually declining both in mind and body. I should apprehend from some disease of the brain, but his Keswick medical attendant cannot make this out, and calls it premature old age; in which conclusion he must, I think, be mistaken. The Patient was for all kinds of exercise quite a strong man two years ago; and his life has been most regular, and all his habits, those of study included, under his own command, and judiciously and temperately managed.

The Copyright Bill is to come on again on the 28th. Has your relation to Sir W. Scott prevented your noticing this important subject in the Quarterly? I cannot but think that an able Article upon it in that journal would do more towards putting the question in the way of being carried than any thing else.

I hope your dear Children are well. Believe me my dear Mr Lockhart

very faithfully

your much obliged

Wm Wordsworth

Address: J. G. Lockhart Esq., Sussex Place, Regent's Park, London.

MS.   *1342. W. W. to Thomas Powell*

Rydal Mount First of May /40

My dear Mr Powell,

Your kind present arrived in due time and your welcome Letter after it. It gives me much pleasure to learn that your Brothers health is going on so well; he and all about you have our best wishes. Mrs W— and I have both been in good health during the spring which for beauty of weather has exceeded all that I remember. We have been eleven weeks almost without rain; and the east winds are so broken by our mountains and tempered, that being softened also by the warmth of the sun we have scarcely felt any annoyance from them. One beautiful feature of the season has been most remarkable,—the profusion and size and splendor of the wild flowers; I do not remember having seen in England any thing like it. I have almost lived in the open air, with nothing to complain of but that my eyes will not stand reading. How sadly this has been the case you may judge by my not having yet ventured upon the perusal of Mr Leigh Hunt's play, though I received it several weeks ago. Pray tell him this with my thanks. I could get some one to read it to me, but this I don't like; it being my misfortune never to have an adequate perception, or right feeling of any thing read to me by others; I mean any thing that is not mere matter of fact or plain reasoning. Say to Mr Hunt further, that I wait in hope of this pleasure from his work, but if I continue to be disappointed I must submit to bear it—

Not long ago I made mention in a Letter to you of a certain Critic,[1] the only one whose strictures on my writings had ever given me concern worth speaking of. I was hurt and even wounded by his unworthy mode of proceeding. He has lately written to me a long Letter of penitential recantation to which I have replied as, I trust, it became me. I therefore wish that no traces of my displeasure should exist; and accordingly I *beg* of you that if that Letter be not destroyed which I should wish to be the case with all my others, to whomsoever addressed,

---

[1] Chauncey Hare Townshend, *v.* Letter 904, and *note*.

you would immediately put it into the fire and also give me assurance that you had done so—

Are you sure that it would answer to modernize the *whole* of Chaucer? I fear much would prove *tedious* and other parts to be objectionable upon the other grounds which I have formerly adverted to. You are welcome to my Cuckoo and Nightingale [and] to [the] small part of the Troilus and Cressida, and were my own judgment only to be consulted to the 'Manciples tale', but there is a delicacy in respect to this last among some of my Friends which though I cannot sympathize with it I am bound to respect. Therefore in regard to that piece you will consider my decision as at present suspended. I must now conclude, with kind remembrances to Mrs Powell and yourself in which Mrs W unites and ever[y] good wish for yourself and yours

ever faithfully your much
obliged Wm. Wordsworth.

MS.
M.
K.

1343. *W. W. to Charles Henry Parry*

Rydal Mount Ambleside May 21ˢᵗ 1840

My dear Sir

Pray impute to any thing but a want of due sympathy with you in your affliction my not having earlier given an answer to your Letter. In truth I was so much moved by it that I had not at first sufficient resolution to bring my thoughts so very close to your trouble as must have been done had I taken up the pen immediately. I have been myself distrest in the same way though my two children were taken from us at an earlier age, one in her fifth and the other in his seventh year[s], and within half a year of each other. I can therefore enter into your sorrow more feelingly than for others is possible who have not suffered like losses. Your departed Daughter struck me as having one of the most intelligent and impressive Countenances I ever looked upon, and I spoke of her as such to Mrs Wordsworth, my Friend Miss Fenwick and to others. The indications which I saw in her of a somewhat alarming state of health I could not but mention to you, when you accompanied me a little way from your own door; you spoke some thing encouraging, but they continued to haunt me, so that your kind communication was less of a shock than it would otherwise have been, though not less of a sorrow. How pathetic is your account of the piety with which the dear Creature supported herself under those severe trials of mind and body with which it pleased God to prepare her for a happier world. The consolation which Children and very young Persons who have been religiously brought up, draw from the holy Scripture ought to be habitually on the minds of adults of all ages for the benefit of their own souls, and requires to be treated in a loftier and more comprehensive train of thought and feeling than by writers has usually been bestowed upon it. It does not therefore surprize me that you hinted at my own pen being employed upon the subject as brought before the mind in your lamented Daughter's most touching case. I wish I were equal to any thing so holy, but I feel that I am not. It is remarkable however that within these last few days the subject has been presented to my mind by two several persons both unknown to me, which is something of a proof how widely its importance is felt, and also that there is a feeling of my not being wholly unworthy of treating it. Your Letter my dear Sir, I value exceedingly, and shall take the liberty, as I have done more than once with fit reverence, of reading it in quarters where it is likely to do good, or rather where I know it *must* do good.

Wishing and praying that the Almighty may bestow upon yourself, the Partner in your bereavement, and upon all the fellow sufferers of your Household that consolation and support which can proceed only from his grace, I remain My dear Dr Parry

Most faithfully your much obliged

Wm Wordsworth

MS.   *1344. W. W. to Mrs Gaskell*

Rydal Mount May 23rd 1840.

My dear Madam,

I have the pleasure of letting you know, though perhaps this may be no news to you, that Mr Beaumont has kindly presented me with the Crypt[1] in which you were so good as to interest yourself on my account. I owe you many thanks and pray accept them as cordially as they are offered. Without your friendly influence I never should have obtained this Relic of my good old Ancestor.

Yesterday I received the Letter from Mr Brakenbridge telling me that he had been directed to forward it to me; and as the conveyance is by water to Kendal, it will be easy and safe; and I shall direct our Carrier to call for it instantly so that in a few days it will be probably under my roof.

We are all in good health. You and Mr Gaskell are I hope the same. Finding two successive seasons in London rather too exhausting I do not mean to go thither this spring.

With a thousand good wishes in which Mrs W. and Dora unite I remain my dear Madam faithfully your much obliged

Wm Wordsworth

MS. ## 1345. W. W. to Mrs Gaskell

Rydal Mount Ambleside 18th June '40[2]

Dear Mrs Gaskell,

The Crypt is arrived and you must be thanked again for your effectual exertions to procure it for me. It is certainly one of the handsomest and most interesting Reliques of the kind I ever saw, and will be I trust duly valued[3] by my descendants after I am no more.

I have written to thank Mr and Mrs Beaumont this very day, and now let me add that it would give us all no common pleasure to shew it to you in the humble room in which it stands. To be sure it is not seen to such advantage as in its late station; however there is much in feeling to make up for that, and every Friend of ours who has seen it has looked upon the memorial of past times, and of my good old Ancestor (for such we must suppose him to have been) with due interest. Mrs W. and my

[1] W. means the Aumbry, v. Letter 1317.
[2] For W. W. to H. C. R., June 3 and June 8, v. C.R., pp. 408 and 411.
[3] valued *written* valuable.

Daughter unite with me in kind remembrances, and good wishes
for yourself, Mr Gaskell and your family, and believe me dear
Madam faithfully

your much obliged

Wm Wordsworth

MS.   *1346. W. W. to H. W. Pickersgill*

Rydal Mount 29th June, 1840

Dear Sir

I should have replied to your letter immediately but I wished
to make some enquiry about a house fit for your purpose. We
have one close by us, which I think may suit, as it has tall
windows with half shutters fronting every aspect: all that is
wanting at present is, the permission of the Gentleman to whom
it belongs—who is now absent—but will shortly be at home—
indeed I believe in a few days, when I have no doubt of his being
ready to accommodate us—and I can say for my own part, that
I am at liberty, and shall be glad to gratify Sir Robt Peel's wishes
by sitting to you when it suits your convenience to visit Rydal—
but I regret to add that we have in this house at present, and
shall have until the month of Sepr visitors, which will prevent
our accommodating you with a lodging under our own roof—
which, if you could defer your journey till that month, would
not be the case. Should it be more convenient to you to come
immediately—or during the month of August, if you will inform
me I shall be happy to secure a lodging for you as near to Rydal,
if not *in* the village, as I can—so that you may join us at meal
times—when we shall always be happy to see you—

Mrs W. and my daughter join me in Comp^{ts} and believe me
to be, dear Sir

faithfully yours

Wm Wordsworth

PS   Pray dont start without letting me know two or three
days before, that I may be sure to be at home.

W. W.

Address: H. W. Pickersgill Esqre, Soho Square, London.

[1028]

M.
K(—)
1347. *W. W. to Lady Frederick Bentinck*

July,[1] 1840.

I hope, dear Lady Frederick, that nothing will prevent my appearance at Lowther towards the end of next week. But I have for these last few years been visited always with a serious inflammation in my eyes about this season of the year, which causes me to have fears about the fulfilment of any engagement, however agreeable. Pray thank Lord Lonsdale, on my part, for his thinking of me upon this occasion.

On Monday morning, a little before nine, a beautiful and bright day, the Queen Dowager and her sister appeared at Rydal. I met them at the lower waterfall, with which her Majesty seemed much pleased. Upon hearing that it was not more than half a mile to the higher fall, she said, briskly, she would go; though Lord Denbigh and Lord Howe felt that they were pressed for time, having to go upon Keswick Lake, and thence to Paterdale. I walked by the Queen's side up to the higher waterfall, and she seemed to be struck much with the beauty of the scenery. Her step was exceedingly light; but I learned that her health is not good, or rather that she still suffers from the state of her constitution, which caused her to go abroad.

Upon quitting the park of Rydal, nearly opposite our own gate, the Queen was saluted with a pretty rural spectacle; nearly fifty children, drawn up in avenue, with bright garlands in their hands, three large flags flying, and a band of music. They had come from Ambleside, and the garlands were such as are annually prepared at this season for a ceremony called 'the Rush-bearing'; and the parish-clerk of Ambleside hit upon this way of showing at Rydal the same respect to the Queen which had been previously shown at Ambleside. I led the Queen to the principal points of view in our little domain, particularly to that, through the summer house, which shows the lake of Rydal to such advantage. The Queen talked more than once about having a cottage among the lakes, which of course was nothing more than a natural way of giving vent to the pleasure which she had in the country. You will think, I fear, that I have dwelt

[1] For W. W. to H. C. R., June 19 and 24 and July, *v. C.R.*, pp. 414 and 416.

already too long upon the subject; and I shall therefore only add, that all went off satisfactorily, and that every one was delighted with her Majesty's demeanour. Lord and Lady Sheffield were the only persons of her suite whom I had seen before. Lord Howe was pleased with the sight of the pictures from his friend Sir George Beaumont's pencil, and showed them to the Queen, who, having sat some little time in the house, took her leave, cordially shaking Mrs Wordsworth by the hand, as a friend of her own rank might have done. She had also inquired for Dora, who was introduced to her. I hope she will come again into the country, and visit Lowther.

Pray excuse the above long story, which I should not have ventured upon, but that you expressed a wish upon the subject.

What enchanting weather! I hope, and do not doubt, that you all enjoy it, my dear Lady Frederick, as we are doing.

I ought not to forget, that two days ago I went over to see Mr Southey, or rather Mrs Southey, for he is past taking pleasure in the presence of any of his friends. He did not recognise me till he was told. Then his eyes flashed for a moment with their former brightness, but he sank into the state in which I had found him, patting with both hands his books affectionately, like a child. Having attempted in vain to interest him by a few observations, I took my leave, after five minutes or so. It was, for me, a mournful visit, and for his poor wife also. His health is good, and he may live many years; though the body is much enfeebled.

Ever affectionately yours,
Wm. Wordsworth.

We hope your lameness will soon leave you, that you may ramble about as usual.

MS.   *1348. W. W. to C. W. (Jun.)*[1]

[July 1840]

My dear Christopher,

I forward this Letter sent to me by mistake; as there is no call for my answering it, you will probably think right to take the trouble—

---

[1] Written on pp. 3 and 4 of a letter intended for Christopher Wordsworth,

We were much shocked to hear of the death of Mrs Wagner,[1] it will be [a] sad blow for her Father, as for all his nearest friends, your Father in particular—

We hope that Susan and the Baby continue to do well, and that you are in good health. Is this about the time of your vacation; if so, where do you purpose spending it?

I had a Letter from Charles the other day with a sermon of his Composition, his first attempt he says—I am glad to see him so employed, and hope that his natural spirits are coming back. We are all pretty well here; rather overpowered just at this time with strangers. But pray understand that we shall always at all times, be happy most happy to see you and yours.

You are probably aware that a Niece of our Friend Miss Fenwick is about to become a cousin of Susan's.—

We have lately been a party of seven, on a Tour of seven days, Keswick, Buttermere, &c. Ennerdale, Calder Abbey, Wastdale, Eskdale, Duddon, Broughton, Furness Abbey, Coniston. We enjoyed ourselves much Mary, Dora, Miss Fenwick, a Niece of hers, Mr Quillinan and his elder Daughter, who are here on a Visit. At the end of next week I go to Lowther to meet the Judges and Lawyers.—The Queen Dowager paid us a visit for the sake, we must humbly suppose, of seeing the Waterfalls, and views from our ground, which I shewed her majesty. We were all pleased with her manner; she shook your Aunt cordially by the hand, and begged to be introduced to Dora. All went off well, and she seemed highly gratified with the beauty of the Country in general, and her reception in it. With Love to Susan, and kisses to the Baby, in which Mary and Dora unite, ever

Your affectionate Uncle

Wm. Wordsworth

from John von Horn, D.D. (12 York Street, Covent Garden, July 29, 1840) and sent to W. W. by mistake. Dr von Horn's letter begins:

Sir,—My attention having been directed to your excellent work on Greece [*Greece: pictorial, descriptive, and historical*, 1839], I beg to suggest that it would sell well also in Germany, if translated in the language of that country, which I should be ready to undertake.

[1] *v.* Letter to Joshua Watson of Feb. 11, 1840.

MS. ### *1349. W. W. to ?*

Rydal Mount 17th August 40

Sir

Having been from home I could not reply earlier to your Letter—I have no such Poem as you require in Mss, and therefore cannot meet your wishes and those of your Friend which I regret; and also that I could not give you this information earlier—

I remain

Sir

sincerely yours

Wm Wordsworth

MS. ### *1350. W. W. to E. R. Moran*

Ambleside Sep^t 2^d 1840

Dear Sir

I take your communication very kindly, and thank you for it—the thought that runs thro' the Sonnet gives it a great interest. I am writing where I have it not before me, or I should have taken the liberty of quoting one line towards the conclusion, in which the word *to* occurs twice causing an inelegance both of sound and construction which might be easily remedied.

Tho' not very anxious about making Proselites it is nevertheless natural that I should be pleased to hear of Converts, or *Convertites* as with the authority of Shakespear and others you give the word. I can claim no merit in being a Member of the Camden Society as you are, owing as I do the position of my name there, to the kindness of a friend—who unknown to me placed me on the list; the Papers and Works selected are many of them valuable—My Brother's and my nephew's names, I am happy to see, are among the subscribers

I remain dear Sir

yours respectfully

Wm Wordsworth

Address: E. R. Moran Esqre, Globe Newspaper Office, London.

MS.   **1351. W. W. to Benjamin Robert Haydon**
K(—)

Rydal Septr 2nd 1840

My dear Haydon

We are all charmed with your Etching; it is both poetically and pictorially conceived, and finely executed. I should have written immediately to thank you for it and for your Letter; and the enclosed one, which is interesting, but I wished to gratify you by writing a sonnet. I now send it, but with an earnest request that it may not be put into circulation for some little time, as it is warm from the brain, and may require, in consequence, some little retouching. It has this at least remarkable attached to it, which will add to its value in your eyes, that it was actually composed while I was climbing Helvellyn last Monday. My daughter and Mr Quillinan were with me; and She, which I believe had scarcely if ever been done before, *rode* every inch of the way to the summit, and a magnificent day we had.

Poor dear Mrs Haydon! I am very sorry that she is so ill as you describe. God grant that she may soon recover her Health. We congratulate you heartily upon your flattering prospects and reputation which this last work cannot but encrease. You call it an Etching; I pres[ume] hence and from the face, that the engraving is not quite finished. Am I right? The outline of the face we all think too faint—that is not sufficiently distinguished from the Paper. Ever faithfully

with best wishes, yours

Wm Wordsworth

[Here follows *Sonnet suggested by Haydon's picture of the Duke of Wellington upon the Field of Waterloo 20 yrs after the action*; ll. 1–8 and 13–14 as Oxf. W., p. 278, but ll. 9–12.

    In his calm presence. Since the mighty deed
    Him years have brought far nearer the grave's rest,
    As shows that face time-worn. But genuine seed
    Has sowed—that bears, we trust, the fruit of fame]

Composed while ascending Helvellyn Monday Aug 31st 1840

Wm Wordsworth

_MS._   *1352. W. W. to H. W. Pickersgill*

Rydal Mount Sep^t 3 [1840]

My dear Sir

Mr Rogers has arrived this evening, and unfortunately I cannot prevail upon him to stay longer than till Monday morn^g. When I wrote to you the other day, trusting that as I had not heard from him he would not be here so soon, or that if he did come it might have suited him to wait till you had finished with me, I wished you to come as soon as you could. Having been long engaged to accompany Mr R. to Lord Lonsdale's I am now under the necessity of requesting that your journey may be deferred for at least a fortnight. I am the less reluctant in making this request as your note does not speak positively of its being convenient to you to be here at this time, and you add that to suit my convenience you could defer your coming.

I much lament this clashing of engagements, but I cannot blame myself for it.

Pray let me hear from you by return of Post

very sincerely yours

W. Wordsworth

Address: H. W. Pickersgill Esqre, Soho Square, London.

_MS._   *1353. W. W. to Benjamin Robert Haydon*
_K._

Friday [Sept.] 4th, [1840.]

My dear Haydon

Correct thus the lines toward the close of the Sonnet:

As shows that time-worn face. But he such seed
Hath sown, as yields, we trust, the fruit of fame
In Heaven etc—

You will see the reason of this alteration—it applies now to his life in general and not that particular act as before—You may print the Son. where and when you like, if you think it will serve you—only it may be as well that I should hear from you first, as you may have something to suggest, either as to the title, or the lines.

Yours &c in haste,

Wm Wordsworth

1354. *W. W. to B. R. Haydon*

Rydal Mount, Monday Sep^t 7th, 1840.

I am quite ashamed to trouble you again, but after considering and reconsidering, changing and rechanging, it has been
resolved that the troublesome passage shall stand thus

> In his calm presence. Him the mighty deed
> Elates not brought far nearer the grave's rest
> As shows that time-worn face. But he such seed
> Hath sown as yields, we trust, etc.

faithfully yours

W. W.

1355. *W. W. to B. R. Haydon*

Rydal, Sept. 10th, [1840.]

By is certainly a better word than *through*, but I fear it cannot
be employed on account of the subsequent line, 'But, *by* the
Chieftain's look'.

To me the two 'bys' clash both to the ear and understanding,
and it was on that account I changed the word. I have also a
slight objection to the alliteration 'By bold' occurring so soon.
I am glad you like 'Elates not'; as the passage first stood, 'Since
the mighty deed'—there was a transfer of the thought from the
picture to the living Man, which divided the Sonnet into two
parts—the presence of the Portrait is now carried thro', till the
last line where the Man is taken up. To prevent the possibility
of a mistake I will repeat the passage as last sent, and in which
state I still consider it finished—and you will do what you like
with it,

> 'Him the mighty deed
> Elates not, brought far nearer the grave's rest,
> As shews that time-worn face. But He such seed
> Hath sown as yields,' etc.

I hope you are right in thinking this the best of the three. I
forget whether I thanked you for your sketch of the Slave-trade

picture.[1] Your friendship has misled you. I must on no account be introduced. I was not present at the meeting, as a matter of fact; and tho' from the first I took a lively interest in the Abolition of Slavery, except joining with those who petitioned Parliament, I was too little of a Man of business to have an active part in the Work—Besides, my place of Abode would have prevented it, had I been so inclined. The only public act of mine connected with the Event, was sending forth that Sonnet which I addressed to Mr. Clarkson,[2] upon the success of the undertaking.

Thank you for your last letter. I am this moment (while dictating this letter) sitting to Mr. Pickersgill, who has kindly come down to paint me at leisure, for Sir Rob[t] Peel, in whose gallery at Drayton the Portrait will probably be hung by that of my poor Friend Southey. I am, dear Haydon, faithfully yours

Wm. Wordsworth.

P.S.—Your suggestion about the Engraver is very candid, but the Verses taking so high a flight, and particularly in the line 'lies fixed for ages', it would be injurious to put forward the cold matter of fact, and the sense and spirit of the Sonnet both demand that it should be suggested at the sight of the *Picture*.

MS.   *1356. W. W. to B. R. Haydon*
K(—)

Rydal Mount, Sept. 11th, [1840.]

My dear Haydon

Your remarks are just and had passed thro' Mrs W's mind and my own—nevertheless I could not otherwise get rid of the prosaic declaration of the matter of fact that the Hero was so much older. You will recollect that it at first stood

'Since the mighty deed
Him years,' etc.

[1] The picture represents a meeting of the Anti-Slavery Society at the Freemasons' Hall, with Clarkson speaking. It is now in the National Portrait Gallery.
[1] Oxf. W., p. 312.

I know not what to do with the passage, if it be not well corrected as follows

> Him the mighty deed
> Elates not: neither doth a cloud find rest
> Upon that time-worn face; for he such seed
> Hath sown etc.

I sent the Sonnet as it was before corrected—to Mr Lowndes as you desired.

When you print it if it be in the course of next week, pray send a copy to this house and another to me at Lowther Castle—whither I am going to-morrow

> Very faithfully your's
> W Wordsworth

The space for alteration in this troublesome passage, you will observe, was very confined, as it was necessary to advert to the Duke being much older, which is yet done in the words time-worn face—but not so strongly as before

> W W

MS.   *1357. W. W. to B. R. Haydon*

Friday [Sept. 11, 1840]

Dear Haydon

I have just rec⁴ your letter and am glad you are so well pleased with the Sonnet. This morn⁸ I sent off an imperfect correction—and now have to beg you to read it thus.

> 'His life is brought far nearer the grave's rest,
> As shews that time-worn face. But he, such seed
> Hath sown, as yields &c—

Mr Rogers is arrived and speaks highly of your picture of Wellington and tells me you have done one of Buonaparte for him.—Ever yʳˢ &c.

> W Wordsworth

I said in a former Letter, you were quite at liberty to *print* the Sonnet, when and where you liked. But perhaps it would be better to hold it back a little, as that would afford an opportunity of paying a Compliment here and there by sending it in Mss as you design to do to the Queen Dowager—

I am much pleased as we all are with the idea of your coming down, and painting me on my own ground poetically. Do not impute this to vanity; I do think you would make of it a fine Picture. But there is one, I fear insurmountable objection, you cannot afford to work without pay, nor can *I* afford to pay you. And I see not how you can expect from any quarter a pecuniary remuneration. Do ponder this before you commit yourself.

I am sorry that your poor wife appears to be no better. I truly grieve for you and anxiously wish for her recovery. Let me hear from you again at your leisure.—

P.S. As the Sonnet first stood, there was a pleonasm in

Him Years have brought
and *time*-worn face.

By reading His Life—&c. that is avoided.

Address: B. R. Haydon Esq ʳᵉ, London.

MS.   1358. *W. W. to Dora W.*

Monday Morning [p.m. Penrith Sept. 14, 1840]
My dearest Dora

Thanks for your 2ⁿᵈ Letter. We must look out for another Horse—I never should be at ease with this.

I now write to express some little *selfish* regret that your return is likely to be put off. This is *solely* as that will deprive me of the gratification of seeing Wm under this roof. Mr Rogers and I leave for Drumlanrigg on Monday as I told you, and I had hoped that as you meant to quit Carlisle on Friday, Wm would have come hither on that day. But I do not desire (far from it) that you should change your last intention, as I am sure you would enjoy yourselves at Carlisle; and I like the notion of your going to take a peep at Newcastle. Lady Frederick has just said to me how glad they would be to see Wm on Friday to stay longer than Monday if convenient. But he can come at some time when I am not here, for example, when he returns from Rydal.

Take care, and let Ebba do the same, that you do not catch cold by alternations of heat and exposure—Love to you all, and believe me your most affectionate Father

W Wordsworth

Address: Miss Wordsworth, Stamp Office, Carlisle.

MS.   *1359. W. W. to Isabella Fenwick*

Lowther, Monday Morn. [p.m. Sept. 14, 1840]

A thousand thanks, my most dear Friend, for your letter, and the good news it contained. Pray God you may go on so well.

You know of my intended expedition with Mr Rogers to the Duke of Buccleugh's. The Duchess's Letter to Lady F. was in such a strain, and especially in the modest way in which she mentioned the Duke's wish to see me, that it would have been ungracious to refuse; but I cannot help grudging the time; particularly as dearest Mary will be so soon setting off for Herefordshire, and as it is not certain but that you may think yourself well enough to go into Durham; in which point you might be deceived, and I and Dora would lose your company for perhaps a month. You may think perhaps that I dwell too much on these separations from beloved friends, but the uncertainty of human life, particularly for people so far in years as Mary and I are, and accustomed to illness as you have been, is perpetually before me. You must therefore, my beloved Friend, excuse this infirmity, and so must Mary who I hope will read this.—Mr R. told me yesterday that a Friend of his went to Dr Bailey, and said to him 'I am come to consult you about several complaints or diseases I am troubled with.' 'What age are you?' 'I am seventy.' 'O' replied the Doctor, 'that is disease enough for any thing'. And, would you believe it? the poor Man took this rather inconsiderate expression so much to heart that it was supposed to have hastened his departure out of this world. It would not, I assure you, have done so with me, but when I think of any beloved Friend I cannot help having something of the

Doctor's view of the case. And, I repeat, this must be my excuse with those I love best.

I have little to write about from this place. You would hear under what circumstances we crossed Kirkstone and that I was above measure enchanted with the views from Mr Askew's walk. I could scarcely tear myself away to the pair who were waiting in the Carriage.

The poor Horse has come down again, so that we must part with him. This is very mortifying. Love to Isabella; as I perhaps may not write to Mary today she must content herself with this scrawl to you. Mr Haydon's note which she sent me has bothered me much, I mean about the alteration in the Sonnet, so that I know not how it will come out at last. Lady Frederick prefers

> Elates not; neither doth a cloud find rest

> Upon that time-worn face, For the etc, and so did Mary, and you, I believe. If it were [not] for the subject I should care nothing about it. And now, dearest Friend, and dearest Mary, and poor dear Sister, farewell. Take care of yourselves, most affectionately yours W. Wordsworth.

Address: Miss Fenwick, Ambleside.

MS.   *1360. W. W. to Isabella Fenwick*

Thursday Morning, 11 o'clock [p.m. Sept. 17, 1840]

Your Letter my beloved Friend has delighted me, though after giving an account so perfectly satisfactory of Tuesday, you are obliged to add on Wednesday morning 'a very tolerable night'. But if upon the whole you go on as well as you have done, what reason shall we all have to be thankful! Dont grieve about Mrs Pedder's resolve to return to her House; nor if you cannot get another to your mind—I shall not, nor will Mary, we shall be happy to have you under our roof—and for Dora, it will be the best medicine she can have!—Yesterday we had wretched weather, and to day it is little better, so Mr R. [and I] must content ourselves with a two hours' walk as we had yesterday in the cloister here which commands a very pleasing view of trees and a visto of lawn; the trees having already got some thing of the autumnal tinge. This is a very beautiful region for persons resident. Strangers who merely come and go are likely to be disappointed. But the windings of the River among woods and rocks for those who have leisure to pursue them are truly charming; and if you follow the paths when they lead from the level ground up to commanding points, you have fine distances over plains now bright with ripe cornfields, and at all times interesting in connection with the far-off blue mountains, and distant as they are, these mountains, from many points of the grounds, seem to touch the unbroken domes of wood above which they rise, and when seen thus, with the river rolling and murmuring below, the effect is enchanting. Nevertheless, (and were the attractions here ten times as great it would be the same) I cannot [help] wishing, half the day through, that I were back again amongst you. Mary writes me that you think of going together to Halsteads about the 30th, and hopes that I will accompany you. Certainly I will, and that most readily.

The verses that Mary has sent me are much above the common run, and I shall be sure to take care of them. I have not seen the unfortunate sonnet printed; only think of 'forever,' being given instead of 'for ages'—thus turning the passage into down right nonsense! The liability to these errors is a very strong reason why poetry composed with care should never be first published in Newspapers, unless the author has an opportunity of correcting the press.

I am sorry that the old Picture is so much inferior to the last. Mary says it has a lack-a-daysical look; and I can well believe it. How unlucky the Artist did not send it down by Mail—he might then have inspected it as he wished to do. If I go to London in the Spring, and my eyes should be in as good order as they are at present, the picture shall meet me there and I will get P. to retouch it. And now my dearest Friend with repeated thanks to dear Isabella, I must bid you goodbye, ever most affectionately your grateful

Wm Wordsworth

Address: Miss Fenwick, Ambleside.

MS.
Haydon.

1361. *W. W. to B. R. Haydon*

23rd September, 1840.

My dear Haydon,

I received your Letter the Evening before I left Lowther, and reply to it on my first leisure.

Believe me to be duly sensible of the respect you pay me by naming your last born after me. My name being conjoined with that of Wilkie, will, I hope be of use on some future day to your Son, by attaching an interest to my writing, which may induce him to become better acquainted there than otherwise he might have been. Nevertheless I cannot but feel a wish that you had selected a Sponsor far short of my age and one whose station in society might have enabled him to serve his Godchild in a way which I can have no means of doing. But the impulse of feeling to which you have yielded[1] will at least prove to the Boy that there are other things of value in human life, according to your estimation, besides world advancement and prosperity. Pray present him with my best good wishes, which I offer trusting that he will not fail in the important duties which his profession will lay upon him and that he will look up to the Father of us all for guidance and support upon every trying occasion of his life.—As you do not mention his Mother, I venture to hope that she is no worse, and if so improvement may be looked for which God grant—

I am glad your Lecture was so much applauded—

The unlucky Sonnet I have not yet seen in print—The reading—

> Elates not, brought far nearer the grave's rest
> As shows that time-worn face. But [? He]

is most liked by the best judges, especially by Mr Rogers who is now writing at the same table with me.—

Excuse more, as I find on my return home, many Letter[s] that require immediate Answer

ever my dear Haydon
truly yours

W Wordsworth

[1] yielded: *written* yielding.

Pickersgill was gone so that Mrs W— could not turn your recommendation [to] account. She thanks you for your interesting Letter—The Portrait by P— is liked by my friends, and I hope won't displease you—

_M._ **1362. W. W. to the Rev. T. Boyles Murray**

Rydal Mount, Ambleside, Sep. 24, 1840.

Dear Sir,

Upon returning home after an absence of ten days, I have the pleasure of finding your obliging letter, and the number of the 'Ecclesiastical Gazette' containing the 'Ecclesiastical Duties and Revenues Act': for both marks of attention I beg you to accept my sincere thanks. As soon as I can find leisure, I will carefully peruse the Act; at present I can only say that I look upon changes so extensive and searching with a degree of alarm proportionate to my love and affection for the Establishment with which they are connected.

As you have put me in possession of the 'Gazette,' I can scarcely feel justified in looking to the fulfilment of your promise to send me the Act, separately printed. Indeed, I feel that it would be giving yourself more trouble than there is occasion for.

It pleases me much to learn that Mrs Murray and you enjoyed your ramble among the lakes.

Believe me to be, dear Sir,

Faithfully,

Your obliged servant,

Wm. Wordsworth

_MS._ **1363. W. W. to H. W. Pickersgill**

Septr 24 [1840]

My dear Sir

The Bearer is Mr Blakesly of Trin. Coll. Camb. a friend of mine; pray let him see my picture, and if anything else in your Gallery so much the better—

ever faithfully yours

Wm Wordsworth

Address: H. W. Pickersgill Esqre, 18 Soho Square.

M.
K.
1364. W. W. to Lady Frederick Bentinck

Rydal Mount, Sept. 26, 1840.

Dear Lady Frederick,

Mr Rogers and I had a very pleasant journey to Rydal the day we left all our kind friends at Lowther. We alighted at Lyulph's Tower, and saw the waterfall in great power after the night's rain, the sun shining full into the chasm and making a splendid rainbow of the spray. Afterwards, walking through Mr Askew's grounds, we saw the lake to the greatest possible advantage. Mr R. left on Thursday, the morning most beautiful, though it rained afterwards. I know not how he could tear himself away from this lovely country at this charming season. I say charming, notwithstanding this is a dull day; but yesterday was most glorious. I hope our excellent friend does not mean to remain in London. . . . We have had no visits from strangers since my return, so that the press of the season seems to be over. The leaves are not changed here so much as at Lowther, and of course not yet so beautiful, nor are they ever quite so as with you, your trees being so much finer, and your woods so very much more extensive. We have a great deal of coppice, which makes but a poor show in autumn compared with timber trees.

Your son George knows what he has to expect in the few sheets which I enclose for him.

With many thanks for the endless kind attentions which I received from you and others under your father's hospitable roof, and with my grateful respects to him, and a thousand good wishes for all, I remain, my wife and daughter joining in these feelings, my dear Lady Frederick, affectionately yours,

Wm. Wordsworth.

MS.
1365. W. W. to Thomas Powell

Rydal Mount, Oct. 16th, 1840

My dear Mr. Powell,

I thought I *had* replied to your Letter, and I am the less surprized at my mistake because when I had read it, it did not strike me that I had any thing important to say upon the subject—

You asked me indeed to point out any thing in Chaucer which in my judgment was best worthy of attention or most likely to please—

Taking for granted that by every one indelicacy would be avoided; and also extreme lengthiness, to which Chaucer is sometimes prone, I felt that there was no call for my interference, and that it was best to leave every one to his own choice. On that letter therefore I have only to express my satisfaction that you are pleased with the contributions, especially with the Prologue which always appeared to me the most difficult thing to deal with.

Yesterday I received a letter from a Lady from which I transcribe the following. 'I have read in a Newspaper that you are about to publish Chaucer's Tales modernized'—and a friend also tells me that he has seen an advertizement of your Publication in which my name stands first in large letters.—Now dear Sir, you will remember that the condition upon which I placed these things at your disposal was, that for many reasons I should not be brought prominently forward in the Matter—but that my communications, given *solely* out of regard for you and reverence for Chaucer, should appear as unostentatiously as possible. I am therefore much concerned for what has been done, as it cannot be undone.

To return to the Lady above mentioned, and it would be best to let her speak in her own words 'I have for my amusement modernized Chaucer's beautiful Tale of Constance, and my friends (probably partial ones) have thought I had succeeded in preserving something of the spirit and tone of the original, and perhaps under the same delusion I fancy that with your corrections and improvements it might be worthy of appearing in the Work advertized, and if you are not provided with a modernized Constance, I would send my attempt to you. I am engaged with Griselda.'

This Lady I have seen once some years ago, but am altogether unable to judge of her competence.—Of course I declined to have any thing to do with corrections or improvements, but told her in my answer that if she had no objection to submit her production to your judgment I would introduce her by letter to you

—so that she might learn all particulars regarding the publication, both as to what was done and what was intended, and I told her that the Newspaper had misled her as to my part in the Concern, adding what it really was—as I have above stated to you.

One word more, I hope you have stated that my versions had been lying by me many years.

We were sorry to learn you h[ad been] ill—I am thank God! in good health and have just returned home from a 10 days absence with Mrs W. who is also well—and joins me in regards to yourself and Mrs P, your Son and Br included—and believe me to be

faithfully yours
W Wordsworth

Address: Thos Powell Esqre, 2 Leadenhall Street, London.

MS.   ## 1366. *W. W. to Basil Montagu*

Rydal Mount, Ambleside, Oct^{br} 17, 1840

My dear Montagu,

I have been shamefully long in acknowledging the receipt of your Tract upon Quaker funerals, and thanking you for it. My fault would have been greater but that I read it carefully upon its reaching me. It gives me pleasure to add that I approve of the spirit in which it is written. With kind regards to Mrs Montagu, and best wishes for her yourself and all yours, I remain dear Montagu, sincerely and faithfully your obliged Friend

Wm Wordsworth.

MS.   ## 1367. *W. W. to Isabella Fenwick*

Sunday morn. [Early Nov. 1840].

I wished my *dearest Friend* (observe I readily adopt your term) to write to you yesterday, but I could not bring myself to do so, without either holding back from you a fact which if told might cause you some uneasiness, or telling you the thing as it was, viz. that since Thursday I have been a good deal disordered in my body. I am now glad that I did not write, as I am decidedly better this day. Whether the diarhoea with which I have been affected has been caused by the atmosphere, or from something that I have eaten or drunk which has disagreed with [me] I cannot say. But the Medical Man whom I consulted yesterday says that such attacks are common at this season and that he has little doubt that I shall be well in a couple of days; and I am inclined to be of his opinion, I am so much easier to day; and if you do not hear from me again by next post be assured all is going on satisfactorily.

Your Letter, my beloved Friend, was most welcome; and especially as you say nothing but that you are well. How sad I was to part with you!—it seemed so easy to accompany you as far as Newcastle, and the weather was so inviting. But surely it would have been a little piece of extravagance, at least I thought so, for it would not have been treating Wm well to leave him behind. I should otherwise have indeed enjoyed seeing with you that beautiful Country over again which we travelled through together. Wm and I did not go into the Corby Grounds, for it was not a public day, but we walked under the Grand viaduct, and crossed the Ferry and visited the Church of Weatherall and strolled about the Village. Here survives one of those pleasant rural features, a village green. It was purchased by the Inhabitants when the Enclosure of Inglewood forest took place, and I was delighted to see the Children, Boys and Girls, playing upon it. Formerly there stood at a corner of the Green a Maypole, and the stone platform remains from which it rose, but there is no maypole—and why, think you? Some of the Inhabitants were for having it raised upon the same place, in the corner of the Green, and others contended that it should be in the middle, and so not being able to agree there is no Pole at all—Can we wonder at the disputes which vex the Great World, in politics and Religion etc—when these Rustics cannot agree about so indifferent a matter?

Our walk altogether was not less than eight miles—a little too much for Wm, I was not at all tired, and the day was indeed glorious, a *borrowed* day[1] as Mrs Carrick called it, but she might

---

[1] The phrase is still current in the district for a fine day in a rainy season.

have almost added borrowed from Heaven. As we were returning towards Carlisle we were passed by a Lady driving her grown-up Daughter in a Pony chaise. They were both gaily dressed and exactly alike. The Mother's appearance seemed to say (for she was a widow) that she was looking out for another Husband. Her former one married her in India and left her by will half his fortune, naming her in the Instrument his wife and *Niece*, as in fact she was. I should have thought this incredible, but W. vouches for the fact. The Husband was an Army Surgeon.—In the evening I walked down to the River, and had from the Bridge a glorious view of the western sky with its reflection in the water. Next morning was wet and dismal, a more uninteresting ride than that from Carlisle to Allonby cannot well be imagined. From Allonby to Workington the road passes along the seashore or very near it; and that is always more or less impressive. Before 4 o'clock the Sun broke out and the sky was driven over by stormy Clouds beautifully tinged with golden and amber light, and endlessly diversified in form. Next day came on my Indisposition, so that I have nothing to add but that we had on that evening a wondrous and for this place, a splendid Ball. How they mustered so many Gentlemen I cannot guess. Of the males all I remarked was that they were uncommonly tall. One *Lady* had exquisitely beautiful eyes, eye-lashes, and brows, quite for a Picture—and there was a Miss Atwood distinguished, though a girl, by a matronly or Minerva dignity and beauty which one does not often meet with. But though striking in appearance she is not a person to fall in love with.

And now my dearest Friend it is time that I should respond to the affectionate language in which you speak of our prospects. I could fill pages with the subject but I dare not trust myself with it. All that you have said has an echo in our hearts, and mine rings with it. God almighty bless you, and make us worthy of the love which you cherish for us, and give us grace to profit to the utmost by your presence and conversation! O that you were back again and dearest Mary, too, and that we were all under one roof. Wm departs tomorrow; and so do I for Brigham if the day prove fine. He has been there already and gives a most favourable Report of the Children, but says that Isabella is far from well. I will probably return to Rydal on Tuesday—if not on Wednesday at the latest—pray write again and above all mention your health.

Do present my very kind remembrances to Mr and Mrs Taylor, and if you meet Archdeacon [?] say how glad I should be to see him at Rydal. With kindest love to Isabella and best re-membrances in which Wm joins both to yourself and her, I remain my pretious Friend most gratefully and affectionately yours

Tuesday noon.   W. Wordsworth

MS.   *1368. W. W. to Isabella Fenwick*

Rydal Mount Saturday Evening.

14th [November, 1840]

I wished, my dearest Friend, to have written the day after I returned Home, but I was occupied all the morning, and have since been interrupted when I was sitting down for the purpose of writing. As I hoped my indisposition was going off I did not write from Whitehaven which I left on Monday noon, John having driven over to fetch me. I found the children *all* well and looking well; but their poor Mother much otherwise. She is suffering from a kind of intermittent fever which has weakened her much. On Tuesday we should have gone to Plumbland, John's new Living, but the morning was very unfavorable, so I was not sorry to keep in and about the House. Of dear Wm. I can say little more than that he seems scarcely altered; I could have judged something better of him if his person had not been so disguised in a kind of frock jacket. What progress he has made as to intelligence I could not tell, but his countenance is as attractive I think, perhaps, as ever. John, the next Boy, though backward in talking has also a very interesting countenance, is remarkably well grown, stout and lively, and the Baby is all that a mother could wish. With the exception of Jane, the eldest, they are all fresh complexioned—she is a little sallow or rather dark, but quick as lightning. Henry is slow, but affectionate in his looks and ways. Pray, my dear Friend, excuse this minute account, as I had little else to write about from that place, unless I had dwelt, which would have been tedious, upon the beauty of the prospect up and down the fine River and Vale, as seen from the Window.

On Wednesday we left Brigham, John driving the Gig. Nothing could be more striking than the view of Bassenthwaite Water as we proceeded under the woods of Wythop-brows with Skiddaw opposite, clad in sunbeams and vapory lights and solemn shadows. We did not call at Greta Hall, as we had learnt that Kate and Cuthbert were gone to Levens. Our drive continued most pleasant till we reached the bridge that stands, upon the Ambleside Road, three miles beyond Keswick. From this Bridge we spied the mail Coach, coming from Ambleside, on the top of the Hill which slopes rapidly towards the Bridge. Nothing could be done by John but to cross the Bridge and draw up close to the wall on our left: this he did: but the Coach came full speed towards us down the Hill, the Driver neither slackening his pace, nor taking the least care to keep clear of our wheels, though he had at least 70 paces to check his Horses in, and a yard of spare ground on his left, when his Wheels struck ours with extreme violence. And here let me tell you that through God's mercy we escaped personal injury; but the shock drove the horse and gig a few yards back, in the straight line of the road; a swerve was then made, and our carriage was driven through a small gap in a wall into a plantation that lay a yard perpendicular below the level of the road. The Horse was driven along with the Carriage and we in it, the stones of the wall tumbling about us. The Horse plunged furiously: we partly got and were partly thrown out; the shafts of the carriage were broken off, the traces snapped. The Horse got back into the road and away he flew, desperate with fear, and gallopped 7 miles to the Grasmere turnpike gate, the shafts and traces sticking to him to the last. Providentially he met no Carriage in a narrow part of the road, else great mischief might have been caused. We sent by the coach to Keswick for a chaise, and procured a Cart in a neighbouring Farm House to take the Gig to be repaired at Keswick. But enough of this ugly affair. I was a good deal shaken but I trust I am no worse—John was not at all hurt.

I thought of you, Isabella, and poor Hannah. What would have been the situation of either of them on the Dickey of your carriage had it met with such a shock? I wish you were safe at home again, and dearest Mary too. In the paper of today I have read of two railway accidents both causing loss of life. I ought to have mentioned that as the road narrows as you round the Hill John was compelled to draw up where he did, the road being there both level and broader than any where else. So that the Coachman cannot be too severely blamed for his recklessness. John is gone home today upon his poor Horse, which though somewhat stiff and sore, I hope will have escaped without lasting injury.

I found dear Sister very well for her, but Dora—voice gone with one of her worst colds: yesterday it was still worse, but today it seems loosening. Kate Southey and her Brother are returned from Levens and she sleeps here to night. She is now with her Sister. I wish I could add that my indisposition was quite removed. I never had any thing of the kind that lasted more than a day or two before, but I am certainly much better than for the first three days. Having been so much from home lately, and so much tossed about and unwell, I cannot muster courage to face the notion of going into Herefordshire, for in addition to, or rather the night previous to, the Gig accident, I had struck my head (while rising from stirring the fire at Brigham in the dark) violently against a projecting black mantelpiece, which I had forgotten, though I believe not a visitor or inmate was ever two days at the House without suffering from it; it projects so dangerously. But all is well with me, as far as I know. And now, though so late, let me say how happy I was to learn from your affectionate Letter to Dora that your own health is good. I know that you are not careless of it, and I believe that you are most judicious in managing yourself. How we long to see you again! My dear Mary will be sadly disappointed if I dont go to her—but unless I am quite well I could not possibly go, and I really do think that at this season it is a long journey to take for persons of her and my years, though I am truly pleased that she has seen her dear Brother. Kindest

Love to you, my excellent Friend, in which Dora unites. Love to Isabella and best remembrances to your Host and Hostess.

ever your W. W.

Address: Miss Fenwick, Wilton Hall, Bishop Auckland.

M.
K.
1369. *W. W. to Lady Frederick Bentinck*

Rydal Mount, Monday Evening [Nov. 16, 1840]

The accident after which you inquire, dear Lady Frederick, with so much feeling, might have been fatal, but through God's mercy we escaped without bodily injury, as far as I know, worth naming. These were the particulars: About three miles beyond Keswick, on the Ambleside road, is a small bridge, from the top of which we got sight of the mail-coach coming towards us, at about forty yards' distance, just before the road begins to descend a narrow, steep, and winding slope. Nothing was left for John,[1] who drove the gig in which we were, but to cross the bridge, and, as the road narrowed up the slope that was in our front, to draw up as close to the wall on our left (our side of the road) as possible. This he did, both of us hoping that the coach-man would slacken his pace down the hill, and pass us as far from our wheel as the road would allow. But he did neither. On the contrary, he drove furiously down the hill; and though, as we afterwards ascertained by the track of his wheels, he had a yard width of road to spare, he made no use of it. In consequence of this recklessness and his want of skill, the wheel of his coach struck our wheel most violently, drove back our horse and gig some yards, and then sent us all together through a small gap in the wall, with the stones of the wall tumbling about us, into a plantation that lay a yard perpendicular below the level of the road from which the horse and gig, with us in it, had been driven. The shafts were broken off close to the carriage, and we were partly thrown and partly leaped out. After breaking the traces, the horse leaped back into the road and galloped off, the shafts and traces sticking to him; nor did the poor creature stop

[1] John] K. reads 'James', which the previous letter shows to be incorrect. M. has J—.

till he reached the turnpike at Grasmere, seven miles from the spot where the mischief was done. We sent by the coach for a chaise to take us to Rydal, and hired a cart to take the broken gig to be mended at Keswick.

The mercy was that the violent shock from the coach did not tear off our wheel; for if this had been done, John,[1] and probably I also, must have fallen under the hind wheels of the coach, and in all likelihood been killed. We have since learned that the coachman had only just come upon the road, which is in a great many places very dangerous, and that he was wholly unpractised in driving four-in-hand. Pray excuse this long and minute account. I should have written to you next day, but I waited, hoping to be able to add that my indisposition was gone, as I now trust it is. With respectful remembrances to Lord Lonsdale, and kindest regards to yourself and Mrs Thompson I remain,

Dear Lady Frederick, affectionately yours,

Wm. Wordsworth.

MS.   *1370. W. W. to Isabella Fenwick*

[p.m. Nov. 24, 1840]

Little more than a week my dearest Friend will bring you to us, so that I almost feel as if this Letter were a welcome to you at our door. Thanks many and grateful for your last, which happily gave us no reason to believe that your health was suffering. The weather has here been windy almost beyond experience and I have sometimes feared that the passages of this old House would in like weather of severe winter prove too cold for you. But we will take every possible care to prevent this, and Dora and I have already given repeated lessons to the Servants upon the really important point of keeping our many Doors shut, one and all. Her cold is certainly much better, though not so well to day as yesterday. This morning was wet, and yesterday fine. But her voice is come back, and I trust that the hard barking cough will be gone before your return. Last night she was kept up till past midnight and this did her harm.

---

[1] John] K. reads 'James', *v. note* p. 1052.

She had numerous Letters to write and so had I, many of them occasioned by the accident. You will not be displeased that the Queen Adelaide has been so gracious as to give it a command to Earl Howe to express her 'sincere trust' that neither I nor my Son was injured, etc etc. Our answer to Royalty required some pains, though not quite so much as the Durham Presentation Copy which you will not easily forget. We hear pretty regularly from dearest Mary. She never mentions her health, therefore we hope it is at least as good as usual. Her last letter, of yesterday, was almost entirely about me; as in justification of my not going to Brinsop, which she seemed hurt at on account of our Friends' disappointment, I had told her that I felt too much shaken in body, by my last accident, and, I scarcely knew how, too much depressed in spirits to go so far for so short a time. Dear Creature, she speaks of being with us by the end of next week.

In compliance with the earnest request of Col. and Mrs Howard, and also of Lady Frederick Bentinck, I go on Wednesday to Levens to meet Lord Lonsdale, Lady F. etc. there. I shall make a point of returning on Friday, both because I have been far too much from home lately, and because I wish to be with dear Dora. Here enters Lady Cadogan, as she calls herself, my dear ruin of a Sister. She is for her wonderfully well, except for her malady of 'bizzing' which is much encreased upon her. I hope she will drop it ere long. 'Who are you writing to?' she says. 'To Miss Fenwick.' 'Give my love to her.' I hope she will stay with us an hour this evening.

Dora has told you that she supposed were Anne in Carlisle by one of the three o'clock Saturday Coaches that would do. Otherwise she must have gone to Carlisle on Friday. She left us on Friday. If Saturday three o'clock be not soon enough, or we heard in the meantime of different arrangements made by you, Dora will let Anne know. You will not I trust be likely to leave Keswick, as probably you will come that way, before the Mail Coach arrives. This I am most thankful for, as I cannot bear the thought of you meeting that dangerous vehicle. Kate Southey left us to day after a most melancholy visit, made so by Mrs Southey's conduct and the manner in which she was supported in it by her Uncle. Mrs S. is a strange Creature, putting herself upon the sternest abstractions of marriage rights and privileges, as established by Law, and this in a case where the Husband was incapable from failure of mind to fulfill the Contract in the sense which the Law requires. What a sad thing all this is. But there will be a way of mercy out of it for the poor Child, I trust, as for all sufferers.

And now my beloved Friend farewell, farewell and welcome in one breath. How rejoiced shall we be to see you, and what a happy week if God so pleases; for as I told you Mary will be with us also, before it ends. Dora sends her dear Love. Pray present the same from both of us to Isabella. Remember us also kindly to Mr and Mrs Thorp, and believe me ever faithfully and tenderly yours

Wm Wordsworth

Address: Miss Fenwick, Thos Thorp, Esqre, Alnwick.

MS.   *1371. W. W. to Isabella Fenwick*

Monday Noon. [Nov. 1840]

I cannot refrain my dearest Friend from welcoming you to Keswick; but I have another reason for writing. Pray let Anne point out to you the spot where we incurred our peril; I am sure it will be gratifying to you to give thanks to God for our escape as you pass it.—It is very good in you to stop for the purpose of comforting the afflicted; but let me caution you to bear in mind that poor dear K.[1] is too apt to put unwarrantably an unfavourable construction upon some of Mrs. S.'s proceedings. This is very pardonable considering K.'s position, nevertheless one should be upon one's guard lest compassion and sympathy so justly due from her Friend should countenance that infirmity of mind. May we not expect you about one, Wednesday at the latest. Should it not rain, so as to make me an improper Companion in your carriage, I will meet you. Dora's cold is better, in the chest and voice, much better, but the throat is a good deal disordered. She was the worse for a ride into Easedale which the beautiful weather tempted us to take—

I have seen Edward Wilson about his house.

ever yours W. W.

[1] i.e. Kate Southey.

MS.　　　　*1372. W. W. to B. R. Haydon*

[late Nov. 1840]

My dear Haydon

All is well thank God at least as far as we know. Though the account given in the newspapers was in the main very accurate the peril incurred was even greater than there spoken of; the two joints of the little finger of my left hand are both sprained but I am aware of nothing worse than this small hurt. God bless you with kind remembrances to Mrs Haydon, believe me ever faithfully yours

Wm Wordsworth

Mrs Wordsworth who is in Herefordshire first heard of the accident from ourselves, and my Daughter, who is at home, knew nothing of it thank Heaven till we told her ourselves. If the horse had not been stopped by a turnpike Gate he would have gallopped on to Rydal or Ambleside with the shafts hanging to his sides, as it was he ran a race of 8 miles.

K(—)　　　*1373. W. W. to John Taylor Coleridge*

Nov. 28th 1840

There are certain principles as to flower gardens upon which my mind is made up: for example, whenever a house fronts a grand or sublime scene of mountains, I would not admit beds of flowers and shrubs, with lawns interspersed, those diversities of shape which are so pleasing when we meet with them in wild Nature. I would either have no flowers, or an architectural garden with terraces and formal beds, after the manner of the French or Italians. But a scheme of this kind requires something of an antique air in the house to correspond with it. In such a site, or with such a building, the garden would at once be referred to the house, and would obviously depend upon it, without having other pretensions. Nevertheless, we often see, in such situations, a disposition of flowers and shrubs and lawns, which is neither Art nor Nature, and accordingly it is to me displeasing to look upon. . . . When the landscape has no grandeur, but is somewhat Arcadian, a little Cyclades of exotic shrubs and flowers may be introduced in front of a house with good effect. . . .

MS. **1374. W. W. to Mr Hook**

Rydal Mount Decr 7th –40

My dear Sir

Accept my thanks for your letter, and the enclosed verses, which were read in this House, by us all with pleasure; and I may say that as a composition they do the Author no little credit—I need scarcely add, that it cannot but be gratifying to me to learn that my endeavours have been felt in the way which you allude to, and especially among the class to which the person who has thus given vent to his feelings belongs.

You will be pleased to learn that I frequently receive testimonies from Individuals who live by the labour of their hands, that what I have written has not been a dead letter to them; and for this reason chiefly, I shall propose to my Publisher to print the Excursion in double column, so that it may circulate as cheaply as can be afforded.

The peril which my Son and I incurred was even more formidable than the account of the Newspapers represent.—thro' the mercy of God my Son escaped without injury, and I only slightly hurt.

With the united kind regards of Mrs W. and my Daughter to yourself and Mrs Hook

I remain, my dear Sir faithfully your obliged

Wm Wordsworth

MS. **1375. W. W. to Robert Bigsby** [1]

Dec. 15. 1840

Sir

Upon the point to which your obliging Letter refers me, I have really nothing to say. My Writings like those of any other Author who has given his to the World are open to the praise or censure of every one who thinks them of sufficient consequence to be noticed. Wishing your intended publication the success which I have no doubt it will merit, I remain Sir sincerely

Your obliged Ser^{nt}

Wm Wordsworth

Address: Robt Bigsby Esqre, Repton, N^r Derby.

[1] Robert Bigsby, antiquarian and minor poet (1806–73)—his *Miscellaneous Poems and Essays* appeared in 1842; a copy was in W.'s Library.

MS.
K(—)

1376. *W. W. to Edward Moxon*

Dec. 17th '40

Dear Mr Moxon,

Your parcel has arrived to-day containing however one book which must have been put in by mistake—viz. the 2nd vol. of Moore's Poems now in course of publication, and intended, by the direction, for Mrs Shelley.—Mr Robinson I am happy to say is coming down to us—and if no earlier opportunity than his return should occur, it may be sent back by him free of expence.

Thanks for the information you gave me, some time ago, about the expence of printing the Sonnets I wrote to you about —if I come to town in the Spring I may perhaps act upon it. You told me the Excursion was out of print. What do you say to reprinting it in double column, stereotyped, all but the pages —so that the same plates might serve hereafter, the paging being altered for the concluding part of the vol: when the whole shall be published in one? I have two motives for this, the one a desire to make the book acceptable to Mechanics and others who have little money to spare, and next to shew from so many instances, with which this would concur, that books are as likely to be sold as cheap as they can be afforded, should the term of copyright be extended, and that in fact, they could in that case be sold cheaper, as—there being no dread of competition—Editions might be larger—and would, of course, be sold at less price. Let me hear from you on this point at your earliest convenience.

You mentioned when you were here that you were in the habit of supplying Parish Libraries with books. My Son John is about establishing one—his is a very poor neighbourhood, and he is not likely to receive much assistance from it—so that if you could lend a helping hand, any books you could furnish him with would be most acceptable—as were those you kindly sent to the Library at Ambleside.

I am glad the Hares came safe. Mrs W. hopes Mrs M. may find them good—and with her good wishes united to my own and my daughter's believe me ever

sincerely yours

Wm Wordsworth.

[1058]

PRINTED IN
GREAT BRITAIN
AT THE
UNIVERSITY PRESS
OXFORD
BY
JOHN JOHNSON
PRINTER
TO THE
UNIVERSITY

MS. *1377. W. W. to ?*

[1840?]

My dear Sir,

We all thank you for the trouble you have taken in making inquiries about the State of Credit in Pensylvania. I am happy to assure you Miss Fenwick's money is lodged not in the Pensylvania Bank as you apprehended, but in a State Loan—so that other friends, as well as myself, think that under these circumstances[1] there is little ground for fear but that the interest will be paid—tho' no one can calculate as to the time. In this uncertainty she feels herself obliged to decline taking your house—and gives way, with satisfaction to our Neighbour Mr Hill, who stands in need of more accommodation than is afforded by the house which he at present occupies. He himself will in all probability write to you to-morrow upon the subject.

In the course of next week, for I am very much engaged at present, I trust I shall be able to bestow due consideration up[on] the sketch of the Epitaph of your excellent Parents, which you have done me the honor to submit to my revisal. If it should not suit you to wait so long as till towards the latter end of the week, pray let me know and I will do the best that I can.

Thank you for the interest you express about my family at Brigham—you will be glad to hear that the last account, which was 3 days ago, was an improved one—and as we have heard nothing since we understand the Sufferer to be going on favourably,—and think the rest of the family are doing well.

I remain dear Sir, with kind remembrances from Miss F. and Mrs Wordsworth, faithfully

Your's

Wm Wordsworth.

[1] *written* commonstancies.